COMMUNION OF SAINTS

THE UNITY OF DIVINE LOVE
IN THE MYSTICAL BODY OF CHRIST

Stephen Walford

COMMUNION OF SAINTS

The Unity of Divine Love
in the
Mystical Body of Christ

Foreword by
His Eminence
Cardinal Gérald Cyprien Lacroix
Archbishop of Quebec
Primate of Canada

First published in the USA
by Angelico Press
© Stephen Walford 2016
Foreword © Cardinal Gérald Cyprien Lacroix 2016

For information, address:
Angelico Press
4709 Briar Knoll Dr.
Kettering, OH 45429
angelicopress.com

ISBN 978-1-62138-216-4 (pb)
ISBN 978-1-62138-217-1 (cloth)
ISBN 978-1-62138-218-8 (ebook)

NIHIL OBSTAT: Rev. William Wilson
CENSOR DEPUTATIS
IMPRIMATUR: †Rt. Rev. Philip A. Egan, BA, STL, PhD
Bishop of Portsmouth, 3 August 2015

*(The Nihil Obstat and Imprimatur are official
declarations that a work or pamphlet is free of doctrinal
or moral error. No implication is contained therein that
those who have granted the Nihil Obstat and
Imprimatur agree with the contents, opinions,
or statements expressed.)*

Cover design: Michael Schrauzer
Cover image:
The Last Judgment
Leandro da Ponte, called Leandro Bassano
c. 1595–1596

CONTENTS

Dedication

I dedicate this book to my dear wife Paula, with love, gratitude and affection for her patience always, and especially these past months.

> In this age of revolt, no longer confined to Europe, but worldwide, when atheistic "Leagues of the Godless," the spawn of Russian Bolshevism, are multiplying throughout the nations and the way is being prepared for a terrible conflict between the spirit of Christ and the spirit of the Evil One, now more than ever must we live by this mystery of the communion of saints.... We must pray and pray with all earnestness that the Kingdom of God may come, placing our petitions in the hands of Mary Mediatrix to present to her Son.   Fr. Reginald Garrigou-Lagrange, O.P.[1]

1. Fr. Reginald Garrigou-Lagrange, *Providence* (Rockford: Tan Books, 1937), 366–367.

Note

All biblical citations that I have used in my own original text are taken from the Knox Bible, copyright, Baronius Press, London. All Scriptural passages contained within quotes are kept in their original form. Concerning the former, I have decided to use the translation of Monsignor Ronald Knox, which he completed in 1948, because alongside the Clementine Vulgate which had been the official Latin text of the Catholic Church for centuries, Mons. Knox studiously cross-checked his translation with Hebrew and Greek texts; consequently we get closer to the inner theological and spiritual heart of Sacred Scripture.

Abbreviations

CCSL: *Corpus Christianorum, Series Latina*, Turnhout, 1953–. A critical edition of all the Latin texts from the first eight centuries of the Christian era.

PL: *Patrologia Latina*, ed. Jacques-Paul Migne, 217 vols., Paris, 1844–1855. A collection of ancient Christian texts in Latin.

PG: *Patrologia Graeca*, ed. Jacques-Paul Migne, 161 vols., Paris, 1857–1866. A collection of ancient Christian texts in Greek.

Acknowledgments

I owe a debt of gratitude to many people for their considerable and varied contributions in bringing this work to fruition. I would like to thank His Eminence, Cardinal Gerald C. Lacroix for his most gracious contribution in writing the foreword, and to His Eminence Cardinal George Alencherry for his kind letter of endorsement; I thank them both also for their prayers, blessing, and encouragement. I also thank Rev. Professor Thomas Kollamparampil, Dr. Scott Hahn, Fr. Henry Wansborough, Bishop Philip Egan, and Fr. Bill Wilson for their time and contributions. Special thanks go to Rev. Professor Thomas Weinandy, who gave me much of his time to discuss various theological opinions. I am very grateful to him for allowing me the benefit of his expertise and knowledge.

I would also like to express my great appreciation to Lubna Walford, and the Sisters of the Carmelite convent of Lisieux for their precious help in translating various Latin and French texts. I am indebted to Kevin Knight, founder of the magnificent website newadvent.org, for his generosity in allowing me to utilize such a great resource. To Paula, Daniel, David, Sophie, Joseph, and Anna, I express my heartfelt thanks for their patience, particularly whenever I commandeered the computer.

Finally, I thank the Lord Jesus for granting me the precious opportunity to write about this beautiful subject, and for guiding me—especially in those moments when I struggled to make progress. May the Lord be praised forever in his communion of saints!

✿ Foreword ✿

A CATECHIST introduced a seven-year-old child to the magnificent icon of the Holy Trinity by Andrei Roublev and asked him: "What do you see?" The boy immediately responded: "Oh! It's open, we can enter!" This is the Good News that Jesus came to reveal: God's heart is open, there is a place for us at his Table, we can enter into his presence, we are invited and called to establish a loving relationship with him and to establish a Covenant.

When we meet parents who present their child for the sacrament of Baptism, we ask them why they want to have their child baptized. Often what we hear is: "So our child can enter and become a member of God's family." What a beautiful response! If only the parents could grasp the profound meaning of their response and the consequences of what they are about to celebrate. Baptism opens the life of a human being to nothing less than holiness and eternal life.

From the moment we are baptized, we become members of a new community—that of the Father, the Son and the Holy Spirit. We are incorporated in a communion that is eternal. We not only become sons and daughters of God, we also become members of the Mystical Body of Christ. We are the People of God, called to holiness. The Second Vatican Council elaborated a Trinitarian ecclesiology: People of God the Father, the Body of Christ, and the Temple of the Holy Spirit.

All of that is included when we say that we are Church. Pope Benedict XVI shared reflections on this topic during one of his encounters with the priests and clergy of the Diocese of Rome: "This 'we are Church' requires me to take my place within the great 'we' of believers of all times and places."[1]

What is "our" place in this community of believers? How do we relate to all the other believers who have preceded us? The following pages will certainly help you respond to these questions and help you discover the fullness of our Catholic doctrine. The author, Mr. Stephen Walford, takes us on a journey—a very interesting and well-planned journey—which is enlightened by the Word of God, nourished by the Fathers of the Church, and guided by the Magisterium of the Church. A journey that may well lead all who choose to take this road less traveled to discover an irresistible invitation to holiness.

When we become aware that the Church is the Communion of Saints, we can no longer live as isolated individuals, or feel that we are alone or forgotten. We belong to God, we are members of God's family. We are the People of God. In our Family, we are all sinners. Saint Paul reminds us very clearly: "For all have sinned and fall short of the glory of God, being justified as a gift by His grace through the redemption which is in Christ Jesus."[2]

If we dare humbly admit that we are sinners, we also confess that we are all loved by God in his infinite mercy and called to holiness. Through Baptism we have received the seed of eternal life and participate in the Communion of Saints. Together, from the place where we stand today—members of the Church Militant, of the Church Suffering, and of the Church Triumphant—we experience a communion that can only be divine because it is God who is at its

---

1. Pope Benedict XVI, *Meeting with the parish priests and the clergy of Rome,* February 14, 2013.
2. Romans 3:23–24.

origin. He is the Source, and it is because of His Divine Mercy that we can hope to enter into full Communion with the Father, the Son, and the Holy Spirit.

Little did that little boy know how profound and meaningful were his words: "Oh! It's open, we can enter!"

Many before us have entered into God's presence. A life of communion and unity begins here and now and continues to grow into eternity. Baptism is a one-way ticket to holiness in the Communion of Saints. May these inspiring pages help us continue our "Journey." I pray as Saint Paul did when he wrote to the Philippians: "May God who has begun this good work in you now bring it to fulfillment."[3]

Cardinal Gérald Cyprien Lacroix
Archbishop of Québec
Primate of Canada

3. Philippians 1:6.

↞ Preface ↠

ONE OF the greatest challenges facing the Catholic Church, and Christianity in general, at the dawn of the third millennium, is the journey towards full unity—a unity willed by the Lord Jesus Himself when he prayed to the Eternal Father: "That they may all be one" (Jn. 17:21). This desire for full communion, at the heart of the Gospel message, and central to the mission of Jesus, opens before us a magnificent vision of God the Father's plan for our salvation: "kept hidden from the beginning of time in the all-creating mind of God" (Eph. 3:9): essentially the unification and glorification of a transfigured humanity where sin and death are destroyed forever.

We have witnessed in the years since the Second Vatican Council a new openness to the promptings of the Holy Spirit in ecumenical relations, whereby the landscape has been transformed from one of outright hostility to patient dialogue and genuine fraternity. In essence, a new dimension to this pilgrim path has emerged at the very time when secularism and a post-Christian culture threaten to submerge the Gospel message through a variety of subtle and not-so-subtle persecutions. Saint John Paul II spoke of this aspect in his encyclical *Ut unum sint*:

> Thanks to ecumenism, our contemplation of "the mighty works of God" (*mirabilia Dei*) has been enriched by new horizons, for which the Triune God calls us to give thanks: the knowledge that the Spirit is at work in other Christian Communities, the discovery of examples of holiness, the experience of the immense riches present in the communion of saints, and contact with unexpected dimensions of Christian commitment.... The Church of God is called by Christ to manifest to a world ensnared by its sins and evil designs that, despite everything, God in his mercy can convert hearts to unity and enable them to enter into communion with him.[1]

---

1. John Paul II, Encyclical Letter, *Ut unum sint*, May 25, 1995, www.vatican.va.

It is difficult to see how Christians can bear witness to the love and mercy of Jesus Christ toward a world such as ours if they are divided, or if Christians of various denominations at times give a false impression of what it is to live an authentic, faith-filled way of life. This perhaps explains why Pope Francis appears so often to criticize Catholics who do not live the Gospel as they should; for if they do not live by the Beatitudes, how can others be convinced to do the same? The Church asks us constantly to seek an interior renewal by which Jesus can pass through the streets of our time and place and be seen by the spiritually wounded as the Divine Doctor—source of eternal life and hope. With the Lord as its head, the members of His Mystical Body are all called to participate in bringing to fruition the gathering of a redeemed humanity by dispelling the darkness of despair and setting the world on fire with a blaze of divine love able to warm the coldest of hearts. Ultimately, this is the responsibility and vocation of all the baptized; in the words of Jesus: "You are the salt of the earth.... You are the light of the world ... and your light must shine so brightly before men that they can see your good works, and glorify your Father who is in heaven" (Mt. 5:13–16).

It is in the great mystery of the communion of saints that we can find an answer to the perennial question of achieving unity; for in the Mystical Body only charity reigns, as well as the burning desire to see all God's children find their way to the glory of salvation in Jesus Christ, and a seat at the table of the eschatological banquet. True unity can only be found in the constant search for the truth, and in the recognition that it is a gift from God, not something obtained by human efforts alone. The victory of Jesus was a victory not in the triumphalist sense, but a victory achieved through suffering, humble service, and adherence to the divine will of the Father. And it is through imitation of the Lord that all Christians will one day partake of the Kingdom of God in its fullness.

My primary motivation for writing this book has been to delve deeply into the mystery of the Church, and more specifically, the binding of its members through the dogma of the Communion of Saints, a term used in the Apostles' Creed and frequently cited through the centuries by the Magisterium. I believe it is essential in this age of rationalism to rediscover a doctrine that Pope Francis has called "a very beautiful reality of our faith."[2] In the post-conciliar years, there arose a terribly damaging interpretation of Vatican II—the so called "spirit of the Council." This "Spirit of Vatican II" led to a variety of liturgical innovations and a watering-down or suppression of traditional devotions: those to the Blessed Virgin (the Rosary and Angelus), St. Joseph, and the Holy Souls were de-emphasized or abandoned. The veneration of saints and relics was deemed antiquated and not in keeping with the "spirit of the Council." Authentic private revelations were frowned upon, and the Church at times seemed to become more like an NGO than the Sacrament of Salvation for humanity.[3] It is essential that we discover anew the richness of the supernatural life of the Church, and of our relationship to those who have passed through this life into the City of God (cf. Heb. 12:22). For this is the antidote to the evils of sin and division present in the world: to see in each man and woman a true brother or sister created in the image of God. Just as Babel came to symbolize separation and disunity through the confusion of languages, so the Church, speaking one language of truth and love, offers the remedy—the means provided by God—for the restoration of unity. Although we will all one day make the final journey to the judgment seat alone, the reality is that we are all saved as a community. The parables of Jesus make this abundantly clear, as do certain references throughout Sacred Scripture describing the redeemed gathered together (cf. Matt. 25:31–34; Heb. 11:16; Is. 43:9).

It is perhaps a sad reality that in recent years this great doctrine has been somewhat forgotten among Catholics. And yet, how essential it is for us here on earth, in the theatre of a spiritual war, to

2. Pope Francis, "General Audience," October 30, 2014, www.vatican.va.

3. On this point of the Second Vatican Council and its various interpretations, it is worth reading the entire text of Pope Benedict XVI's last speech to the priests of the Diocese of Rome in which he explains in great depth the crisis wrought by a false reading of this great event in the life of the Church. Also noteworthy is his analysis of the theological development of the concepts of the "Mystical Body of Christ" and the "People of God" throughout the twentieth century. The entire text is available here: http://www.vatican.va/holy_father/benedict_xvi/speeches/2013/february/documents/hf_ben-xvi_spe_20130214_clero-roma_en.html.

invoke the powerful intercession of the saints in heaven and the holy souls in Purgatory. How essential it is for us to offer prayerful assistance to those same souls in Purgatory, hastening their entrance into Paradise. Christianity is not a private matter even if for many of us the spiritual life has a profoundly private intimacy; as St. John of the Cross famously wrote, "In the evening of our lives, we will be judged by love alone." That love must be transmitted to all as an authentic witness to the love of God and neighbor, for too often we hear only the cries of Abel echoing in our communities.

I hope this book will help in a small way to inspire Catholics *and* non-Catholics to accept the reality of the communion of saints as something almost tangible, to see that we are a part of the most beautiful mosaic of God's creation and destined one day to reign together in unending joy and divine love. The foundation of that eternal city is being laid now, and through baptism we have been invited to become co-workers, co-redeemers, at the service of humanity. May the Holy Spirit make our hearts burn within us ever more (cf. Lk. 24:32) for God and for all.

⮞ The Communion of Saints ⮜

Introduction

BEFORE VENTURING into the mystery of the Church within its
three levels—militant, suffering, and triumphant—we must first
explore the doctrine of the communion of saints itself in order to
understand what this entails for all its members, and how this
interchange of charity contributes to the growth of the Kingdom of
God.

The term "communion of saints" is found in the Apostles' Creed
directly after the profession of faith: "I believe in the Holy Spirit, the
holy catholic Church," and undoubtedly should be understood as
an extension of the teaching concerning the Church as the sacrament of salvation given to the world by its founder and head, Jesus
Christ. The Church was formed as the place in which the people of
God could grow in holiness under the sanctifying presence of the
Holy Spirit, and therefore is essentially a community, a family. We
read in the Acts of the Apostles:

> There was one heart and soul in all the company of believers; none
> of them called any of his possessions his own, everything was
> shared in common. Great was the power with which the apostles
> testified to the resurrection of our Lord Jesus Christ, and great was
> the grace that rested on them all. None of them was destitute; all
> those who owned farms or houses used to sell them, and bring the
> price of what they had sold to lay it at the apostles' feet, so that
> each could have what share of it he needed. (Acts. 4:32–35)

This text reveals how, in the aftermath of Pentecost, the early Christians were bound by a great love and concern for one another. A new
path had been opened by the message of Jesus, proclaimed especially
in the words recorded in St. John's Gospel: "I have a new commandment to give you, that you are to love one another; that your love for

one another is to be like the love I have borne you" (Jn. 13:34).[1] Notably, this teaching of the Lord was given after he had washed the feet of the Apostles at the Last Supper, giving them the supreme example of service and humility. If any of the apostles other than Judas had clung to the notion of the inbreaking of God's Kingdom occurring through a political revolution, the Lord had forcefully rejected this theory, insisting that love, mercy, and sacrifice would be the means employed to advance the final victory over the forces of evil. In the Upper Room he had admonished Peter for his obstinacy: "If I do not wash thee, it means thou hast no companionship with me" (Jn. 13:8). The paramount lesson for the disciples was that they were to love *"As I have loved you,"* rather than the poorer approximation of love that had hitherto existed under the Law.

In the New Testament we discover two Greek words describing love: *philia* and *agape*. *Agape* is the most commonly used term to describe divine love (or charity), love that ascends like incense to the throne of God. *Philia* is used to describe a lower form of love, based on friendship. Henceforth, Jesus's followers were to immerse themselves into his life by imitating *agape*: "[A]nd yet I am alive; or rather, not I; it is Christ that lives in me. True, I am living, here and now, this mortal life; but my real life is the faith I have in the Son of God, who loved me, and gave himself for me" (Gal. 2:20). The Christian faith was to be accepted as a gift; one that could not be allowed to remain within the "I," but extended to the "you."

Time and again in the Gospel accounts, the apostles had failed to grasp the full extent of what the Lord was demanding of them; per-

---

1. Although even Jesus himself refers to this teaching as a "new commandment," we may recall that in Leviticus we read: "Do not seek revenge, or bear a grudge for wrong done to thee by thy fellow-citizens; thou shalt love thy neighbor as thyself; thy Lord is his" (19:18). In what sense then is it a "new" commandment? In biblical language the word "new" denotes finality, completeness. Therefore it could be stated that Jesus is giving this teaching as the definitive way for the baptized to live, the blueprint for the community of believers awaiting the glorious return of the Lord. At the same time, he dismantles the logic of revenge: "You have heard that it was said, an eye for an eye and a tooth for a tooth. But I tell you that you should not offer resistance to injury; if a man strikes thee on thy right cheek, turn the other cheek also towards him" (Mt. 5:38–39).

haps it was the often violent history of Israel that had contributed to their lack of understanding, or the fact that they were living under the occupation of the Roman Empire. Whatever the reason, Jesus's mission was to turn worldly logic on its head and impress upon his followers the necessity of imitating his life, to be *ipse Christus*—Christ himself. In St. Mark's Gospel, we read how James and John had asked Jesus to grant them places at his right and left hand in the Kingdom, and his response was to direct them to what God demands:

> You know that, among the Gentiles, those who claim to bear rule lord it over them, and those who are great among them make the most of the power they have. With you it must be otherwise; whoever has a mind to be great among you, must be your servant, and whoever has a mind to be first among you, must be your slave. (Mk. 10:42–44)

In the primitive Church, powered by the divine love of the Holy Spirit and under the maternal care of the Holy Mother of God, we see the dawning of a new age of holiness. With Jesus's Ascension into heaven, where he presented a transfigured human nature to God the Father, a new, beautifully intimate, relationship with God is made possible for all the baptized. The Eternal Father is no longer inaccessible, for through the one universal mediation of his Son Jesus, He hears our prayers for ourselves and those dear to us. Just as the Passion, Death, and Resurrection of the Lord transformed vicious evil and cruelty into a wondrous act of love and mercy, so too would the persecution and martyrdom of the saints gradually transform the world from the empire of Satan into the Kingdom of Christ. In this way the binding of the communion of saints would become ever stronger as it entered more deeply into the mystical life of the Lord Jesus.

The *Catechism of the Catholic Church* explains that the term "communion of saints" has two closely linked meanings: "communion in holy things (*sancta*) and among holy persons (*sancti*)."[2] We know from the Acts of the Apostles that the faith was shared

---

2. *Catechism of the Catholic Church*, no. 948, www.vatican.va.

among the early Christians who met together to be nourished through the Word of God and the reception of Jesus in the Eucharistic Sacrifice:

> These occupied themselves continually with the apostles' teaching, their fellowship in the breaking of bread, and the fixed times of prayer, and every soul was struck with awe, so many were the wonders and signs performed by the apostles in Jerusalem. All the faithful held together, and shared all they had, selling their possessions and their means of livelihood, so as to distribute to all, as each had need. They persevered with one accord, day by day, in the temple worship, and, as they broke bread in this house or that, took their share of food with gladness and simplicity of heart, praising God, and winning favour with all the people. And each day the Lord added to their fellowship others that were to be saved. (Acts. 2:42–47)

Clearly, the first aspect of the doctrine of the "communion of holy things" was deeply entrenched in the heart of the Church from its birth. The Lord had shown in the miraculous feeding of the five thousand (cf. Matt. 14:13–21), and the similar miracle of the four thousand (cf. Matt. 15:32–38), that the people were to share what they had. The apostles in the first miracle had suggested to Jesus that he send the crowd away to buy food for themselves, but Jesus chose to display divine predilection by strengthening not only physically, but spiritually, the community gathered there. In a sense it was a foreshadowing of the Church on several levels. First, setting aside the fact that this was a stupendous sign of Jesus's own power, the incident prefigured the institution of the Holy Eucharist (the Lord would proclaim the doctrine of the Eucharist at Capernaum).[3] Secondly, the scene of the crowd on the grass with the Lord blessing the food and then having the disciples distribute the bread and the fish prefigures the Church as a community. Significant is the fact

---

3. "I myself am the living bread that has come down from heaven. If anyone eats of this bread, he shall live for ever. And now, what is this bread which I am to give? It is my flesh, given for the life of the world. Then the Jews fell to disputing with one another, how can this man give us his flesh to eat? Whereupon Jesus said to them, Believe me when I tell you this; you can have no life in yourselves, unless

that Jesus wanted nothing wasted, and that the scraps filled twelve baskets. Perhaps there is a deeper meaning here: the Lord's grace and mercy are always inexhaustible; we will never be lacking and there will always be more than enough. But as we spiritually mature those graces must not be "wasted" but nurtured through grafting oneself onto the vine: the Lord. Those twelve baskets filled with scraps would later become the altars from which the true *divine* food would be distributed.

We have therefore a basic structure, the nucleus of the Church, present in prophetic fashion. The Lord's divinity provides for his children while the disciples distribute in his name—the twelve baskets representing the foundation columns of the twelve apostles. Later, the Lord would remind the disciples of the significance of both miracles: "Have you no wits even now, or have you forgotten the five thousand and their five loaves, and the number of baskets you filled?" (Matt. 16:9–10). No doubt the apostles after Pentecost would have understood these signs Jesus gave in a new way through the working and instruction of the Holy Spirit, although naturally a theological understanding of the nature of the Church as a communion would take time to develop.

The Communion of holy things incorporates the entire variety of gifts given by God to the Church: communion of the sacraments, communion of charisms, and communion in charity. Concerning the sacraments, the Catechism states:

> The fruit of all the sacraments belongs to all the faithful. All the sacraments are sacred links uniting the faithful with one another and binding them to Jesus Christ, and above all Baptism, the gate by which we enter into the Church. The communion of saints must be understood as the communion of the sacraments . . . the

---

you eat the flesh of the Son of Man, and drink his blood. The man who eats my flesh and drinks my blood enjoys eternal life, and I will raise him up at the last day. My flesh is real food, my blood is real drink. He who eats my flesh, and drinks my blood, lives continually in me, and I in him. As I live because of the Father, the living Father who has sent me, so he who eats me will live, in his turn, because of me. Such is the bread which has come down from heaven; it is not as it was with your fathers, who ate manna and died none the less; the man who eats this bread will live eternally" (Jn.6:51–59).

name "communion" can be applied to all of them, for they unite us to God.... But this name is better suited to the Eucharist than to any other, because it is primarily the Eucharist that brings this communion about.[4]

The Sacraments are none other than the extraordinary presence of Jesus Christ; gratuitous gifts given through the power of the Holy Spirit, efficacious because it is the Lord himself who works through them. Not only are they ordered to the sanctification of the individual, but also to the community as a whole, for they increase the charity of the Church and propel its missionary activity to spread the Gospel to the ends of the earth. If sacramental life is the fulcrum of the ministerial Church, then charisms form a secondary channel of grace—spiritual gifts bestowed on the faithful for the continual renewal and growth of the Body of Christ. St. Paul eloquently describes how the Holy Spirit "breathes where he will" (cf. Jn. 3:8):

[A]nd yet there are different kinds of gifts, though it is the same Spirit who gives them, just as there are different kinds of service, though it is the same Lord we serve, and different manifestations of power, though it is the same God who manifests his power everywhere in all of us. The revelation of the Spirit is imparted to each, to make the best advantage of it. One learns to speak with wisdom, by the power of the Spirit, another to speak with knowledge, with the same Spirit for his rule; one, through the same Spirit, is given faith; another, through the same Spirit, powers of healing; one can perform miracles, one can prophesy, another can test the spirit of the prophets; one can speak in different tongues, another can interpret the tongues; but all this is the work of one and the same Spirit, who distributes his gifts as he will to each severally. (1 Cor. 12:4–11)

Although St. Paul speaks of the great variety of charisms that were energizing the Church in its earliest times, the list is not exhaustive; in fact a brief overview of the two thousand year history of the Catholic Church shows how the Holy Spirit has intervened time and again to reinvigorate missionary activity through the granting of new gifts. We could recall the spiritual giants of the

---

4. *Catechism of the Catholic Church*, no. 950, www.vatican.va.

medieval period such as St. Francis of Assisi and St. Dominic, the great mystics of the sixteenth century, the birth of ecclesial movements in the mid to late twentieth century, the countless martyrdoms of religious and lay alike, and even the beautiful witness of children such as St. Maria Goretti, Blessed Jacinta and Francisco Marto, and the Venerable Antonietta "Nennolina" Meo. In a certain way the Holy Spirit upsets the apple cart—or "creates a mess," to borrow the phrase of Pope Francis—but this mess is always designed to rouse the Church from inertia. In order to attract the gentile world, the Church must ever be young and vibrant, and so the Holy Spirit is constantly hovering over the waters of the Church, just as at the dawn of creation. It is important to stress however that we are not referring to a kind of parallel Church, where the ministerial and charismatic are competing against one another; no, the Lord specifically gave Peter the keys and the power to bind and loose.[5] Therefore the duty of the pope and bishops is to discern the authenticity of these gifts and incorporate them into the life of the Church, enhancing the unity and vibrancy of the faithful.

In what sense do charisms contribute to the communion of saints? The answer lies in the dual aspect of individual holiness and communal holiness—communal holiness in the sense that the Church increases its members down the centuries through the passing on of the Faith from one to another. In the First Letter of St. Peter we read:

> Make one another free of what is yours ungrudgingly, sharing with all whatever gift each of you has received, as befits the stewards of a God so rich in graces. One of you preaches, let him remember that it is God's message he is uttering; another distributes relief, let him remember that it is God who supplies him the opportunity; that so, in all you do, God may be glorified through Jesus Christ; to him be the glory and the power through endless ages, Amen. (1 Pt. 4:9–11)

A secondary aspect of communal holiness refers to the spiritual

---

5. "[A]nd I will give to thee the keys of the kingdom of heaven; and whatever thou shalt bind on earth shall be bound in heaven; and whatever thou shalt loose on earth shall be loosed in heaven" (Matt. 16:19).

goods known as the Church's treasury. Although we will return to this subject in more detail in a later chapter, let us quote from the Catechism at this point:

> The "treasury of the Church" is the infinite value, which can never be exhausted, which Christ's merits have before God. They were offered so that the whole of mankind could be set free from sin and attain communion with the Father. In Christ, the Redeemer himself, the satisfactions and merits of his Redemption exist and find their efficacy. This treasury includes as well the prayers and good works of the Blessed Virgin Mary. They are truly immense, unfathomable, and even pristine in their value before God. In the treasury, too, are the prayers and good works of all the saints, all those who have followed in the footsteps of Christ the Lord and by his grace have made their lives holy and carried out the mission in the unity of the Mystical Body.[6]

It has always been the teaching of the Church that individual gifts, although beneficial for the recipient, are always bestowed for the benefit of the entire Body of Christ. Thus we see how the sharing of these charisms draw into closer unity all the saints.[7] Of course, without love, these gifts would be worthless and instead of fostering unity would create division and discord. Therefore authentic charisms will always lead the recipients to place themselves at the service of God and his Church with no hidden agenda—as St John the Baptist proclaimed: "He must become more and more, I must become less and less" (Jn. 3:30).

Communion in charity forms the third aspect of communion in

---

6. *Catechism of the Catholic Church*, no. 1476–1477, www.vatican.va.

7. The Second Vatican Council and the renewal movement gave fresh impetus to the understanding and acceptance of these charisms while the post-conciliar popes have prayed for a fresh outpouring of the Holy Spirit. The Dogmatic Constitution *Lumen Gentium* taught: "Whether these charisms be very remarkable or more simple and widely diffused, they are to be received with thanksgiving and consolation since they are fitting and useful for the needs of the Church. Extraordinary gifts are not to be rashly desired nor is it from them that the fruits of apostolic labors are to be presumptuously expected. Those who have charge over the Church should judge the genuineness and proper use of these gifts, through their office, not indeed to extinguish the Spirit but to test all things and hold fast to what is good." (cf. 1 Thes. 5:12, 19–21) *Lumen Gentium*, 12, www.vatican.va.

holy things. The early Church Father Tertullian informs us that the pagans were converted to the true faith by witnessing this great charity among the Christians: "See how they love one another"[8] was their response. What must have struck the pagans more than anything in the early centuries after the Resurrection was the humble acceptance of persecution and martyrdom. Everything was done for love of God; nothing was too great a burden for them if it meant experiencing the liberating, transforming power of the Holy Spirit. The faithful embraced the cross willingly and lovingly, knowing that to enter the tomb with the Lord meant rising gloriously with him as well. This love of the Lord radiated out to the community at large so that for the baptized, they were no longer just neighbors on the same journey, but true brothers and sisters in Christ.

Pope Benedict XVI in his encyclical *Caritas in Veritate* describes charity in these terms:

> Charity is love received and given. It is "grace" (*cháris*). Its source is the wellspring of the Father's love for the Son, in the Holy Spirit. Love comes down to us from the Son. It is creative love, through which we have our being; it is redemptive love, through which we are recreated. Love is revealed and made present by Christ (cf. Jn. 13:1) and "poured into our hearts through the Holy Spirit" (Rom. 5:5). As the objects of God's love, men and women become subjects of charity, they are called to make themselves instruments of grace, so as to pour forth God's charity and to weave networks of charity.[9]

The New Testament continually shows the need for charity as proof and fruit of a profound spiritual life. In the life and teachings of Jesus we see how a narrow form of charity restricted to one's own clan is not enough. The parable of the Good Samaritan (cf. Lk. 10:30–37) demonstrates in a striking way that we are all brothers and sisters; nobody is excluded from God's love and nobody is excused from this duty to assist those in need by hiding behind religious or ethnic divides. The many instances of Jesus healing the sick or restoring life to the dead provide ample evidence of God's divine

---

8. Tertullian, *Apology*, no. 39, www.newadvent.org.
9. Pope Benedict XVI, *Caritas in Veritate*, no. 5, www.vatican.va.

mercy and of his desire to associate himself with the poorest of the poor (both materially and spiritually) and the despised and the vulnerable. All his works are charity. Jesus is *caritas-agape* personified. The parable of the Last Judgement as described in St. Matthew's Gospel takes us to the very heart of this message:

> Then the King will say to those who are on his right hand, Come, you that have received a blessing from my Father, take possession of the kingdom which has been prepared for you since the foundation of the world. For I was hungry, and you gave me food, thirsty, and you gave me drink; I was a stranger, and you brought me home, naked, and you clothed me, sick, and you cared for me, a prisoner, and you came to me. (Matt. 25:34–36)

The Christian of all times, and perhaps most especially ours, cannot forget that behind every human face lies the presence of God and of his looming judgment. How often have we turned a blind eye to some form of injustice no matter how great or trivial? How often have we thought "someone else can take care of that problem"? The reality is that these everyday situations that the Lord places before us are occasions to meet Jesus in the worries and sufferings of our brothers and sisters. In the world of the twenty-first century, it is no longer enough to shut the Church doors behind us and live in a comfort zone of what we know and have always done. Somehow, we need to grasp this notion of communion in charity with those asleep to the knowledge and love of the Lord in the geographical and existential peripheries of the world. Ultimately, conversions to the faith will come through great witness, through love and charity. This is no mere philanthropic sentiment, but a decisive choice to manifest this great communion between God, ourselves and our neighbor.

So far we have discussed one of two strands of this dogma, *communion in holy things*. There is also a second great aspect: the *communion of holy persons*. The term *holy persons* refers to all the baptized, for in baptism all are incorporated into the life of Christ—they are born again. By being immersed into the water, they symbolically descend into the tomb of the Lord and then in the rising out of the water they become a new creature, freed from the stain of original sin and accepted into the family of the Church. From the moment of this initiation, the newly baptized begins a journey that has no end. It is a journey that will no doubt involve much suffering and hardship, but also continual grace for as St. Paul says: "Surely you know that your bodies are the shrines of the Holy Spirit, who dwells in you. And he is God's gift to you, so that you are no longer your own masters" (1 Cor. 6:19). The further sacraments of initiation—Confirmation and the Holy Eucharist—in a sense seal that initial covenant between God and the elect by increasing grace in the soul, and allowing the Holy Spirit to purify it while gradually bringing charity to perfection. In this way the Word of God is planted in rich soil (cf. Matt. 13:23) and yields abundant fruit.

At the end of earthly life, the human soul is destined for one of two definitive places: heaven for the just, and hell for the damned. For the just who are not yet stripped of all that hinders their ability to experience the immense light of God, a temporal spiritual reality exists called Purgatory in which the soul is able to rid itself of human weaknesses: pride, arrogance, impurity, selfishness, envy. The soul is healed of every vice that on earth caused a wound in its relationship with the Holy Trinity. In this way the Lord has mercifully provided what could almost be called a retreat in eternity, but one far more intense than those we are used to attending on earth. For in this retreat, the soul has already glimpsed the burning love of God at the individual judgment and is confronted by the absolute clarity of its sins. The soul-searching it must undergo in Purgatory cannot be compared with anything it has experienced before; it must detach itself from what could be a lifetime of filth, or just the last traces of dirt that sullied its white robe (cf. Rev. 7:14).

The Mystical Body of Christ therefore consists of three levels: the Church Militant (*ecclesia militans*) on earth, the Church Suffering (*ecclesia patiens*) in Purgatory and the Church Triumphant (*ecclesia triumphans*) reigning in heaven. All three are part of the same Body, with Christ as its head, and each lives in unity of love and charity. Again we return at this point to the key word at the heart of this doctrine: communion, in Greek *koinonia*. *Koinonia* actually means "participation" rather than "community"; therefore it opens up a deeper understanding of the mystery of the communion of saints.

To *participate* implies that we are not mere spectators within a community of which we are passive members, but rather we are immersed in the lives of others. We are bound by our love and concern for one another and by our desire to help each other carry the cross: to be Simon of Cyrene for one and all.

In what sense does this interchange of love between the three levels of the Mystical Body of Christ take place? St. Paul, in his First Letter to the Corinthians wrote: "If one part is suffering, all the rest suffer with it; if one part is treated with honour, all the rest find pleasure in it" (1 Cor. 12:26). Reciprocal giving and receiving exist between all the members of the one Church, but there are specific tasks given to each in order to give glory to God.

The Church Militant has been placed directly in the midst of a spiritual war. It exists to extend the victory already accomplished by Jesus on Calvary by snatching away from Satan the souls still stained by original sin. Pope Pius XII, in his encyclical *Mystici Corporis Christi*, taught that although Jesus could have bestowed all the graces won through his Passion directly on humanity, he willed instead to incorporate his children in the saving work of redemption by establishing a visible Church. Thus, the Lord created a situation where his followers could learn to imitate him, becoming co-redeemers through the offering up of their prayers and sufferings.[10] This charity of the faithful on earth not only encompasses one another, but also extends to the suffering souls in Purgatory. It has been the teaching of the Church throughout its history that the temporal punishments of those undergoing purification in Purgatory can be alleviated by their brothers and sisters still fighting the forces of evil on earth. In this way the bond of love existing between those on either side of eternity is strengthened. Whereas these first two aspects of the Church Militant involve the positive emptying of oneself for another, a third aspect exists in which roles are reversed; the faithful on earth express their need for divine assistance by

---

10. "As the Word of God willed to make use of our nature, when in excruciating agony He would redeem mankind, so in the same way throughout the centuries He makes use of the Church that the work begun might endure." Pope Pius XII, *Mystici Corporis Christi*, Encyclical Letter, June 29, 1943, www.vatican.va.

invoking the powerful intercession of the saints reigning in heaven. As prayers ascend to the throne of glory, so at the behest of God, blessings continually flow in the other direction, in an unbroken stream of grace and peace linking time and eternity. The saints in heaven become our protectors, jealously watching over the faithful in battle.

Although magisterial teaching on the intercessory role of the holy souls is scarce,[11] it has been taught by various saints throughout the ages that they can assist the Church Militant; notable among these luminous figures are St. Pio of Pietrelcina and St. Josemaria Escriva. It is not unreasonable to suggest that these souls have a certain knowledge of the spiritual assistance being offered for them by the faithful on earth and therefore would be ardent in their desire to return the favor. How much knowledge they have is an open question, but later in the book we will put flesh on the bones of this particular area of doctrine by seeing from the mystical life of certain saints how deep this union between the *ecclesia militans* and the *ecclesia patiens* really is.

Thus far we have examined the doctrine of the communion of saints in general and how the mutual interchange of love is the hallmark of the community of believers. We are now able to look in detail at the three levels of the Mystical Body of Christ and hopefully discover the beauty and greatness of the Church. Although at times the Church Militant is disfigured by the sins of its members which then spill over into the inevitable purification required in Purgatory, we cannot allow the evils to overshadow the truth that the Church is the Bride of Christ, that he willed its birth at Pentecost and through it lies the key that opens the door to immortality and transfiguration.

It is my ardent hope that reading this book will cause people to

---

11. Pope Leo XIII granted an indulgence on December 14, 1889 for the recitation of various prayers, one of which is also addressed to the holy souls themselves: "I beseech you to respond to this offering which I make to you, and obtain for me from God, *with whom you are so powerful* on behalf of the living, that I may be freed from all dangers of soul and body . . . obtain for us peace of heart; assist us in all our actions; succor us in all our spiritual and temporal needs." *Acta Sanctae Sedis* (1889–90), 744, www.vatican.va.

love the Church more, desire the sanctification of its members more and, above all, pray that those who do not see the Church as their home will open their hearts to the truth and so become part of a family that will one day live in perfect union with the Holy Trinity. Yes, we are dealing with a great mystery, but one in which we must seek to immerse ourselves, to perceive the role God has given each of us in salvation history. Jesus has entrusted to each of us the task of bringing the lost and wounded into his presence. There is no greater mission in life than this. We should not understand our reward in heaven as anything other than seeing our brothers and sisters enjoying the beatific vision in the great company of saints and the glory of God illuminating all in the triumph of divine love.

PART I

The Church Militant

～1～

The Eternal Mystery Awakens

Listen, then, to my voice, and keep your covenant with me; and I, to whom all the earth belongs, will single you out among its peoples to be my own. You shall serve me as a royal priesthood, as a consecrated nation; tell the Israelites this. (Ex. 19:5–6)

NO STUDY of the origins of the Church can be made without tracing its biblical roots all the way back to the Old Testament. There is a hermeneutical perspective in which the Old Testament must be understood in the light of its fulfilment in the New Testament, while the New must be seen as the sealing of the covenant God made with his chosen people in the Old. At the heart of both is the person of Jesus Christ, the Word of God who proclaims the truth and *is* the Truth. All texts from both Testaments must be read as if centered on him, for the entire span of salvation history proceeds under the gaze of the Savior.

We are told by St. John at the beginning of his Gospel in no uncertain terms: "At the beginning of time the Word already was" (Jn. 1:1). Profound words, which echo Jesus's own statement to the Jews concerning his divine and eternal presence as described in chapter eight of the same Gospel:

> As for your father Abraham, his heart was proud to see the day of my coming; he saw, and rejoiced to see it. Then the Jews asked him, Hast thou seen Abraham, thou, who art not yet fifty years old? And Jesus said to them, Believe me, before ever Abraham came to be, I am. (Jn. 8:56–58)

By using the name *I am*, just as God had done when he commissioned Moses to lead the first exodus out of Egypt (cf. Ex. 3:14), Jesus places himself equal to God. At the same time he supersedes Moses

21

by prophesying his own Passover that would bring true liberation, a liberation far greater than that wrought at the Red Sea—a liberation from death:

> Then Jesus said to them, When you have lifted up the Son of Man, you will recognize that it is myself you look for, and that I do not do anything on my own authority, but speak as my Father has instructed me to speak. . . . Believe me when I tell you this; if a man is true to my word, to all eternity he will never see death. (Jn. 8:28, 51)

Therefore, a picture emerges from Sacred Scripture that Jesus is present as the Word, the divine *Logos* who from eternity enters into time, to shape it according to his will and to eventually bring to completion the promises made to his people. In this light, we can consider the origins of the Church, knowing that the Old Testament is linked to the New through the gradual saving action of Christ Jesus. The Church is the Sacrament of Salvation that is prefigured in the words of the prophets and born out of the merciful heart of God as the seed and initial stage of the Kingdom of God in its fullness. St. Jerome, the great biblical scholar and Church Father, offers a beautiful insight on this point:

> When I read the Gospel and find there testimonies from the Law and from the Prophets, I see only Christ; I so see Moses and the Prophets and I understand them of Christ. Then when I come to the splendor of Christ Himself, and when I gaze at that glorious sunlight, I care not to look at the lamplight. For what light can a lamp give when lit in the daytime? If the sun shines out, the lamplight does not show. So, too, when Christ is present the Law and the Prophets do not show. Not that I would detract from the Law and the Prophets; rather do I praise them in that they show forth Christ. But I so read the Law and the Prophets as not to abide in them but from them to pass to Christ.[1]

From the moment of Adam and Eve's fall in the Garden of Eden, God began the slow, gentle process by which humanity could rise

---

1. St. Jerome, Tract. in Marc., 9:1–7, cited in *Spiritus Paraclitus*, Encyclical Letter of Pope Benedict XV, www.vatican.va.

again; a process which would gradually draw man away from Satan's evil influence to the influence of his Son, who would be prefigured in a series of prophets and kings. In this opening chapter, we explore the origin and typology of the Church as seen in the Old Testament in order for us to grasp the great foresight of God, and to marvel at the wisdom of his actions in bringing to fruition a work of mercy that humanity did not deserve. In this way, we will discover that the Church did not come into being as a kind of afterthought on God's part at the time of Jesus's public ministry, but rather was conceived in eternity as the means chosen to extend salvation to the entire world.

The opening pages of Genesis recount the story of the seven days of creation, of all God's beautiful works gradually taking shape and culminating in a creature fashioned in the Lord's own image—man. But as he was not to be alone (cf. Gen. 2:18), God took a rib from the sleeping Adam, and created Eve, mother of all the living. From this point the tiny seed of a community emerges which is to love God and share in his divine life in Eden, the Garden of perfection. However, by listening to the serpent's lies and desiring to become like God (cf. Gen. 3:5), they reject the communion willed by the Lord and so are exiled from Eden. Significantly though, when God discovers their sin he first rebukes the devil, rather than Adam and Eve, and prophesies the battle to come throughout history, and the eventual victory of good over evil.[2] It is in the path taken by Adam's sons that we see the divergence and division that would come to mar humanity's relationship with God and with each other. Cain

---

2. St. Irenaeus of Lyons developed the concept that this was the prophecy of a future redeemer who would crush the head of the serpent. In his great work *Adversus Haereses* he writes: "He has therefore, in His work of recapitulation, summed up all things, both waging war against our enemy, and crushing him who had at the beginning led us away captives in Adam, and trampled upon his head, as you can perceive in Genesis that God said to the serpent, 'And I will put enmity between you and the woman, and between your seed and her seed; He shall be on the watch for (*observabit*) your head, and you on the watch for His heel.'" (*Adversus Haereses* bk V, ch. 21.1) St Jerome's Vulgate translation adds a Marian perspective by using the word "she" for the epicene form in Genesis 3:15, thus opening up a new doctrinal avenue for the co-redemptive role played by the Blessed Virgin in the redemption of mankind.

killed his brother Abel, and in doing so fostered a line of immorality[3] that would end with the great flood, while Adam's third son, Seth, founded a new line that would be faithful to God. Seth's descendants included Enoch, who we are told "walked with God" (Gen. 5:24)[4] and Noah, who would be commanded by the Lord to build an Ark to preserve the line of faithful descendants.

Noah: Blessing Through Obedience

It is through Noah, and the dramatic events surrounding his life, that we uncover the first interventions of God that draw us closer into the mystery of salvation through Christ. These interventions are typological: they are events and signs that prefigure the salvific actions of Jesus and his Church. The first of these events concerns the great flood as recounted in Genesis, chapter six. We read:

> And now God found that earth was full of men's iniquities, and that the whole frame of their thought was set continually on evil; and he repented of having made men on the earth at all. So, smitten with grief to the depths of his heart, he said, I will blot out mankind, my creature, from the face of the earth, and with mankind all the beasts and the creeping things and all that flies through the air; I repent of having made them. (Gen. 6:5–7)

As Noah found favor with God, he, his wife and their three sons and daughters in law were spared the divine punishment. Not only that, God made a covenant with them before the flood came; one that was to be confirmed once the waters had receded:

> Here is a covenant I will observe with you and with your children after you, and with all living creatures, your companions, the

---

3. Lamech, one of Cain's descendants, took two wives and killed a young man, imitating the evil of his ancestor and boasting of his murderous ways: "For Cain, sevenfold vengeance was to be taken; for Lamech, it shall be seventy times as much" (Gen. 4:24).

4. It is this Enoch whom God took away (cf. Gen 5:24) that the Church Fathers taught would return with Elijah to convert the Jews during the reign of the Antichrist and in preparation for the second coming of Christ; a teaching confirmed by God in the mystical revelations, *Scivias*, of St. Hildegard of Bingen, Doctor of the Church.

birds and the beasts of burden and the cattle that came out of the Ark with you, and the wild beasts besides. Never more will the living creation be destroyed by the waters of a flood; never again a flood to devastate the world. This, God said, shall be the pledge of the promise I am making to you, and to all living creatures, your companions, eternally; I will set my bow in the clouds, to be a pledge of my covenant with creation. When I veil the sky with clouds, in those clouds my bow shall appear, to remind me of my promise to you, and to all the life that quickens mortal things; never shall the waters rise in flood again, and destroy all living creatures. There, in the clouds, my bow shall stand, and as I look upon it, I will remember this eternal covenant; God's covenant with all the life that beats in mortal creatures upon earth. Such was the pledge God gave to Noe of his promise to all living things. (Gen. 9:9–17)

This covenant is the beginning of a new relationship between God and his people. Its goal is to readmit humanity into the interior life of the spirit, to bring to fulfilment the words Jesus spoke to the woman of Samaria at Jacob's well: "but the time is coming, nay, has already come, when true worshippers will worship the Father in spirit and in truth; such men as these the Father claims for his worshippers" (Jn. 4:23).

The entire story of Noah and the flood is rich in typological matter that point toward baptism and regeneration through the Church. Noah himself is a type of new Adam, one who, we are told, "walked with God" (Gen. 6:9).[5] From him, salvation history in a sense begins anew. The wood of the tree of life from which Adam and Eve had eaten, causing their downfall, now becomes salvific for Noah and his seven companions in the form of the Ark, which is in itself a figure of the Church and an embryonic communion of saints. Outside, the raging waters wash away all filth, destroying those who had given themselves to iniquitous ways (the flood, in its cleansing work is a type of baptism). Meanwhile, Noah's family in the Ark represent a community of the faithful saved from the fate of

---

5. The same phrase was used to describe Enoch, emphasizing perhaps the mystical nature of both these holy men, which set them apart from others.

their contemporaries.[6] The famous axiom "*Extra Ecclesiam nulla salus*"—"Outside the Church there is no salvation," which has been taught by the Church since its earliest days, finds in the story of Noah's Ark an important reference point, because we see that God spared nobody outside the Ark.[7] There was to be no halfway house, no second chance for those eventually swept away; one was either for God or against God and in that Ark, the Lord was symbolically recreating humanity in order for it to be sent out anew—with the rainbow as the sign that would remind all of the existence of the new covenant.[8]

There is one further point worth considering that links the beginning of God's covenant to its end within salvation history. In St. Luke's Gospel, in the eschatological discourse, the Lord Jesus warns his disciples of the events to come at the end of time. Jesus draws a parallel between the days immediately before the great flood and the time preceding his second coming:

> [T]he Son of Man, when his time comes, will be like the lightning which lightens from one border of heaven to the other. But before that, he must undergo many sufferings, and be rejected by this

6. St. Justin Martyr in his *Dialogue with Trypho* sees an eschatological significance to Noah escaping the judgement of God during the flood; for as the Ark saved Noah, Christ, at the end of the world will save from his just judgement those who had been regenerated through baptism and repented of their sins—essentially those remaining in the "Ark" of the Church. See *Dialogue with Trypho*, no. 138, www.newadvent.org.

7. Although this doctrine will be discussed later in the book, it should be stressed that the Catholic Church teaches that it is possible to be saved even if one is not visibly a member of the Church. The point being that in God's mysterious yet merciful design, all those who are saved, Catholic or not, find salvation through Jesus Christ—head of the Mystical Body, the Church, and the *only* key through which the door to eternal life can be unlocked.

8. On this point, it comes to mind how God has never revoked his promise made to Noah and his progeny. A particular moving remembrance of this covenant occurred during the visit of Pope Benedict XVI to Auschwitz on May 28, 2006. In his address, he asked these questions: "In a place like this, words fail; in the end, there can only be a dread silence—a silence which is itself a heartfelt cry to God: Why, Lord, did you remain silent? How could you tolerate all this?" After the Pope had finished his speech and the Jewish Kaddish prayer for the dead had been sung, the rain clouds parted to reveal a beautiful rainbow.

generation. In the days when the Son of Man comes, all will be as it was in the days of Noe; they ate, they drank, they married and were given in marriage, until the day when Noe went into the ark, and the flood came and destroyed them all. (Lk. 17:24–27)

What is the conclusion to be drawn here? There is a divine prophetic warning that just as nobody was prepared or watchful in Noah's time, the same circumstances would occur at the end. Reading Jesus's words on two levels, we can also discover anew the typology of Noah from the standpoint of the apostasy to come in the last days. On the one hand, the Lord clearly foresees a state of decadence and worldliness that afflicts humanity in general. But if we also take into account his words recorded later in Luke's Gospel: "But ah, when the Son of Man comes, will he find faith left on the earth?" (Lk. 18:8), we can also suspect they refer to the shipwreck of the faith from those who have abandoned the Ark that is the Church. The duty therefore of all Christians is to stay awake to the signs of the times, living in a state of constant preparation not only for our individual judgements, but for the general judgement at the Lord's final coming.[9]

If the story of Noah and the Ark speaks of the necessity of baptism and the future realization of the Church as the sole means of salvation, the typology of faith needed to live in communion with God is amply demonstrated in the life of the great Patriarch Abraham, an exemplary model of faithfulness throughout the ages. We read in Genesis chapter 12:

> Meanwhile, the Lord said to Abram, Leave thy country behind thee, thy kinsfolk, and thy father's home, and come away into a land I will shew thee. Then I will make a great people of thee; I will bless thee, and make thy name renowned, a name of benediction; those who bless thee, I will bless, those who curse thee, I will curse, and in thee all the races of the world shall find a blessing. (Gen. 12:1–3)

---

9. The issue of recognizing the eschatological signs of the times primarily from the prophetic voice of recent popes is dealt with in my previous book, *Heralds of the Second Coming, Our Lady, the Divine Mercy and the Popes of the Marian Era from Bl. Pius IX to Benedict XVI* (Tacoma: Angelico Press, 2013).

Abraham: Blessing Through Faith

At the heart of the covenant between God and man, for a truly reciprocal relationship to exist we need the three theological virtues; faith, hope and charity (cf. 1 Cor. 13:13). These virtues, gifts of the Holy Spirit, take root in the soul and enable it to respond to the call of God by living the commandments and orienting its life towards the supernatural. In Abraham, we have the figure of a man who lived the first of these virtues, foreshadowing the faith of the Church. He is asked to set out on a journey to a place he does not know; he is told that from him a great nation will rise and his descendants will be as many as the grains of sand on the seashore (cf. Gen 22:17). It is fitting to contemplate and marvel at the absolute trust and faith required on his part to accept what God was asking of him. The journey was into the unknown—into darkness. But Abraham allowed the path to be illuminated by the total radicalness of his response—his faith that what God was promising would come to pass. In the Letter to the Hebrews it is stated:

> And he to whom the name of Abraham was given shewed faith when he left his home, obediently, for the country which was to be his inheritance; left it without knowing where his journey would take him. Faith taught him to live as a stranger in the land he had been promised for his own, encamping there with Isaac and Jacob, heirs with him of a common hope; looking forward all the while to that city which has true foundations, which is God's design and God's fashioning. (Heb. 11:8–10)

Where can we see the Church prefigured in this? It is in the individual *and* communal journey to the promised land of the Kingdom of God. For all of us are called to live by faith and hope, and at times the darkness of sin seems to halt that pilgrimage. But as Abraham went with the blessing of God, so too does the Church, striving for the fulfilment of the promise to be realized when the heavenly Jerusalem finally descends at the end of time (cf. Rev. 21:2). Even in the early Church, the youthful Christian community considered itself "alien" to the world it had to live in and referred to its populated gatherings in the cities as "parishes," in Greek *pároikoi*, meaning a colony of foreigners. Thus we see a strong desire to follow the path trod by Abraham in striving to be "in the world but not of the world" while fixing our gaze on the prize to come.

Abraham's greatness, his holiness, consists in an entire life lived as one continuous act of faith. This is born out of several other significant events: the mediation with God over Sodom and Gomorrah, the miraculous birth of Isaac, and the sacrifice of Isaac. In the story of Sodom and Gomorrah, which is recounted in chapter 18 of Genesis, we see the intercessory role of Abraham[10] which is typological of Christ's one universal mediation with the Father, and the intercession of the Church. As Abraham was the chosen one, the father of all nations, it fell to him to intercede on behalf of a sinful humanity. In the text of Genesis, immediately before the story of Sodom and Gomorrah unfolds, we read of the meeting between Abraham and God at the Oak of Mamre. God appears in the form of three men, which undoubtedly is the first manifestation of the Holy Trinity, and Abraham is given the promise of bearing a Son to his wife Sarah (the significance of which will be discussed later). It is at the end of this meeting that we see the prefiguring of Abraham as a type of Christ. God considers whether to involve Abraham in the heart of the conflict between good and evil:

> And now the men rose up, and turned towards Sodom, Abraham going with them to put them on their way. And the Lord said, Should I hide my purpose from Abraham, this man who is destined to give birth to a people so great and so powerful? This man through whom all the nations of the world are to find a blessing? Have I not chosen him as one who will teach his children and all his race after him to follow the paths which the Lord shews them, and to do what is just and right, winning him the fulfilment of all the Lord has promised him? So the Lord told him, The ill repute of Sodom and Gomorrah goes from bad to worse, their sin is griev-

---

10. Until Abraham was 99 years old, he was known as Abram, but God changed his name as he was to become the "father of a throng, such is the multitude of nations" (Gen. 17:5). Throughout salvation history the names of people were changed in order to denote a significant role or event: Abraham's wife Sarai became Sarah (Gen. 17:15), Jacob became Israel after wrestling with the Lord (cf. Gen. 32:28), and Simon Became Peter, the rock on which the church would be built (Jn. 1:42).

ous out of all measure; I must needs go down to see for myself whether they have deserved the ill report that has reached me or not; I must know for certain. And Abraham stood there in the Lord's presence, as the men turned and went on towards Sodom. (Gen. 18:16–22)

The crucial point is that Abraham stays with the Lord and begins a dialogue of intercession for the potentially good people in those cities:

Suppose there are fifty innocent men in the city, must they too perish? Wilt thou not spare the place to save fifty such innocent men that dwell there? Never that, thou wilt not destroy the innocent with the guilty, as if innocence and guilt were all one; that is not thy way, that is not how the Judge of the whole earth executes justice! And the Lord told him, If I find fifty innocent citizens in Sodom, I will spare the whole place to save them. (Gen. 18:24–26)

The boldness with which Abraham confronts the Lord is truly striking. Could we not see in this a risk of provoking the anger of God? But it is precisely in a deep intimacy with the Lord that we can and must take risks, because that is what the Lord wants; for in bargaining with God—without ever forgetting his divine majesty—we show him how much we trust and believe. It is the way two people in a loving relationship converse; formality exists between those who are acquainted but not in love. Returning to the dialogue between God and Abraham, the bargaining continues as Abraham suggests there may be fewer righteous people; perhaps only forty-five, then forty, then thirty, then twenty until finally he suggests there might only be ten found worthy of salvation from the chastisement to come. In response, God grants that if ten can be found Sodom will be spared. The prayer of Abraham mirrors Jesus's words on the Cross: "Father, forgive them; they do not know what it is they are doing" (Lk. 23:34).

The Patriarch intercedes not only for the just but for the sinners as well, and in this way demonstrates the divine mercy of God who desires not death but repentance and conversion. His mission then becomes prophetic, anticipating the salvific role of Jesus where he will take on our sin (cf. 2 Cor. 5:21) before destroying its chains

upon the cross in an act of total self-giving. The Church is prefigured in the intercession of Abraham, for, through the power of the
Holy Spirit, the people of God implore the Lord for spiritual blessings to descend instead of the rigors of his justice.

The two other aspects of Abraham's life which concern us relate to
his son Isaac. God made a promise to him that he would have an
heir: "to me (Abram added) thou hast given no children, so that all
the heir I have is a slave born in my house. Whereupon the Lord sent
word to him, this man shall not succeed thee; thou shalt have an heir
sprung from thy own body" (Gen. 15:3–4). The promise was that
Sarah would give birth to a son, even though she was barren and in
old age. God granted this miraculous birth when Abraham was 100
and Sarah 90. From a typological viewpoint, we can see a foreshadowing of the birth of Jesus. Sarah stands as a type of Mary and Isaac
as a type of Christ. Mary gave birth despite her virginity and Sarah
gave birth despite her age and in both cases God chose what, in
human eyes, would be weakness.[11] Sarah also resembles Mary in her
faith that this miracle would be accomplished—even if both she and
Abraham had laughed at the idea (cf. Gen. 17:17, 18:12).[12]

Just as significant as Isaac's birth was God's command that Abraham offer him up as a sacrifice. Isaac was the promised son who
would continue the line of the covenant established with Abraham,
as the Lord said: "for indeed it is through Isaac that thy posterity
shall be traced" (Gen. 21:12). In the testing of Abraham that followed, the Lord gave a proof of his love and mercy as well as the
true revelation of his own Fatherhood—even if several millennia
would follow before the glorious mystery was realized in its fullness.
God revealed his intentions to Abraham in this way: "Take thy only
son, thy beloved son Isaac, with thee, to the land of Clear Vision,
and there offer him to me in burnt-sacrifice on a mountain which I

11. Of course there is a direct parallel between Sarah and St. Elizabeth, who
would give birth to St. John the Baptist while in old age.

12. Isaac means "laughter," and the name has been read by the Fathers of the
Church as a foreshadowing of that supernatural joy which would come at the Savior's birth 2000 years later, and the new covenant. See St. Augustine, *Civitate Dei*,
bk XVI, ch. 31, and Clement of Alexandria, *Paedagogus* (The Instructor), bk I, ch. 5,
both available at www.newadvent.org.

will shew thee" (Gen. 22:2). Abraham did as he was instructed, but as he was about to strike Isaac, the Angel of the Lord cried out and stopped him. Because of this great faith and acceptance of God's will, he was promised the defeat of his enemies and as many descendants as there are grains of sand on the seashore. Once again in this story, there is a richness of meaning and foreshadowing of future mysteries. The figure of Isaac is clearly seen to be a forerunner of Jesus as the only son who is to be sacrificed as an offering pleasing to the Father, while Abraham is a figure of God the Father himself, who does not deny the offering of his only son.

The divine predilection of the Father is revealed in that he stops short of allowing the sacrifice of Isaac, something that he would not do centuries later even when his own Son prayed "My Father, if it is possible, let this chalice pass me by; only as thy will is, not as mine is" (Matt. 26:39). The ram that is sacrificed by Abraham then truly becomes a symbol of Christ crucified and a foreshadowing of the immense love of the Father for his adopted children. The fact that this takes place on a mountain—which tradition associates with the meeting of God and his people—confirms the proposition that this event is one of the great manifestations of God's mysterious plan. It is as if he wished to reveal something of his merciful nature—a counterbalance to the just judgment displayed in the flood, the destruction of Sodom and Gomorrah, and the dispersal of the people building the Tower of Babel.

There is one final aspect of this story that goes to the very heart of the faith of Abraham and the Church. It concerns the resurrection and God's power to bring it about. The Letter to the Hebrews puts it in these terms:

> Abraham shewed faith, when he was put to the test, by offering up Isaac. He was ready to offer up an only son, this man who had made the promises his own, and received the assurance, it is through Isaac that thy posterity shall be traced. God, he argued, had the power to restore his son even from the dead; and indeed, in a hidden sense, he did so recover him. (Heb. 11:17–19)

It is apparent that Abraham's knowledge of what the promise entailed was profoundly theological in the sense that it transcended a basic belief that he would inherit a physical land that his descendants would enjoy. We know this in part from Jesus's own words in his discourse with the Jews after the woman had been caught committing adultery: "As for your father Abraham, his heart was proud to see the day of my coming; he saw, and rejoiced to see it" (Jn. 8:56). In what sense did he see the Lord's Day? Without doubt, the understanding that what he was experiencing in his life were figures, symbols of future realities that would shape salvation history. In this context he would have understood that for Isaac to die, and yet be the means for the continuation of his faithful line, a resurrection would have had to occur. It would be pure speculation to consider what amount of knowledge Abraham had concerning the true nature of the promise given to him, but the fundamental point is that he had faith in abundance that whatever form or direction the plan of God took, his faith would be rewarded with the ultimate realization of the Father's will. St. Irenaeus of Lyons teaches how the old covenant given to Abraham finds its fulfilment in the future resurrection of the dead:

> If, then, God promised him the inheritance of the land, yet he did not receive it during all the time of his sojourn there, it must be, that together with his seed, that is, those who fear God and believe in Him, he shall receive it at the resurrection of the just. *For his seed is the Church*, which receives the adoption to God through the Lord, as John the Baptist said: "For God is able from the stones to raise up children to Abraham" (Lk. 3:8). Thus also the apostle says in the Epistle to the Galatians: "But you, brethren, as Isaac was, are the children of the promise" (Gal 4:28). And again, in the same Epistle, he plainly declares that they who have believed in Christ do receive Christ, the promise to Abraham thus saying, "The promises were spoken to Abraham, and to his seed. Now He does not say, and of seeds, as if [He spoke] of many, but as of one, and to your seed, which is Christ" (Gal. 3:16).[13]

Abraham is truly our father in faith and the prototype of a faith for which we are all called to pray. Of course faith is a gift, belief in the

---

13. St. Irenaeus of Lyons, *Adversus Haereses*, bk V, ch. 32.2, www.newadvent. org.

Holy Eucharist is a gift, belief in the resurrection is a gift, but to be truly pleasing to God it is a virtue that must be nurtured.

In terms of the intercession of the Church and its members, perhaps a fitting image to cling to is Abraham's meeting at the Oak of Mamre. God appears to Abraham in the form of three men. The three men then leave to go and see what is happening in Sodom. Abraham walks alongside them, rather than remaining where he is in partial or total ignorance of the situation. He wants to be close to the Lord, to try to influence him for the benefit of his brothers and sisters languishing in the filth of immorality. In the communion of saints, this is the only acceptable attitude to have, because ultimately Abraham's actions were the lesson God wanted to teach us.

Moses: Blessing Through Divine Strength

Thus far, we have seen how the Church, and Christ its head, have been prefigured in various ways from the dawn of salvation history with two essential elements: baptism and faith. These two elements stand out from the scriptural text as essential means to grow in holiness under the roof of the "Ark," the Church. We now turn towards perhaps the pre-eminent type of Christ, Our Lord: Moses, the great prophet, who conversed with God. It is with Moses and the Passover from Egypt that a third constitutive element of the Church is prophesied: a communion of faithful.

As with the story of Abraham's sacrifice of Isaac, Moses also encounters God on a mountain, at Horeb where he is given the great task of leading the Israelites out of Egypt:

> And here the Lord revealed himself through a flame that rose up from the midst of a bush; it seemed that the bush was alight, yet did not burn. Here is a great sight, said Moses, I must go up and see more of it, a bush that does not waste by burning. But now, as he saw him coming up to look closer, the Lord called to him from the midst of the bush, Moses, Moses; and when he answered, I am here, at thy command, he was told, Do not come nearer; rather take the shoes from thy feet, thou art standing on holy ground. Then he said, I am the God thy father worshipped, the God of Abraham, and Isaac, and Jacob. And Moses hid his face; he dared

34

not look on the open sight of God. I have not been blind, the Lord told him, to the oppression which my people endures in Egypt, I have listened to their complaints about the cruelty of the men who are in charge of their work. I know what their sufferings are, and I have come down to rescue them from the power of the Egyptians; to take them away into a fruitful land and large, a land that is all milk and honey, where the Chanaanites dwell, and the Hethites, and the Amorrhites, and the Pherezites, and the Hevites, and the Jebusites. (Ex. 3:2–8)

Moses is then given the command to lead the exodus away from Pharaoh's grasp: "Up, I have an errand for thee at Pharaoh's court; thou art to lead my people, the sons of Israel, away out of Egypt" (Ex. 3:10).

Although it is not necessary to recount the entire story of the Passover and the parting of the Red Sea, it is of paramount importance that we study these events in the light of Christ and his Church. Firstly, we can understand the situation of the Israelites under the yoke of bondage as a symbol of the entire history of humanity's struggle against sin and the Devil. Moses is the intercessory figure who resembles Christ; the Israelites, the chosen ones, are the forerunners of the gentile world. Pharaoh is a type of antichrist, one of several throughout the Old Testament.[14] The last of the plagues that God sent into Egypt was the death of each first born son; but the Israelites were to be spared from this punishment by performing a sacrificial rite whereby a lamb, one year old without blemish, was to be eaten either one household on its own, or if the family was too small, together with neighbors. The blood of the lamb was then to be put on the doorposts and lintel while the angel tasked with bringing this chastisement across the land would "pass over" these houses knowing that they were marked by God (cf. Ex. 12:1–13). There are several typological occurrences within the Passover meal that relate to the future sacrifice of Jesus and the remem-

14. King Nebuchadnezzar, whose army plundered Jerusalem leading to the Babylonian exile in 586 BC, would be one such figure, as would Antiochus Epiphanes who profaned the Temple and commanded the Israelites to abandon their religion. (1 Mac. 1:41–43)

brance of it passed down the centuries through the Holy Sacrifice of the Mass.

The paschal lamb, as in the case of the ram sacrificed by Abraham, is a type of Christ. Dr. Lawrence Feingold, an expert on biblical typology, sees great significance in the days of preparation for the sacrifice. He explains:

> The paschal lamb is a clear type of Christ, as witnessed by John the Baptist: "Behold the Lamb of God." Each family was to take a "lamb without blemish, one year old" on the tenth day of Nisan. On the fourteenth day he was to be offered. What is the significance of the tenth and fourteenth day? There is a beautiful typology with the events of Holy Week. Christ chose to enter triumphantly into Jerusalem on Palm Sunday. Why did He choose that day? It seems that this was the tenth of Nisan (assuming that Holy Thursday was the fourteenth of Nisan). As the paschal lamb was chosen five days before its sacrifice, so the Lamb of God solemnly entered the household of Jerusalem on that same day, in preparation for His Sacrifice.[15]

The blood on the doorposts once again points us in the direction of baptism, for as the angel knew to spare those within, so too through the saving blood of Christ are the baptized saved from their sin. The blood on the doorposts represents the blood of Christ. Another quite different aspect concerns the change of God's action from the Old to the New Testament. As we have just read, the angel did not go into the houses of the Israelites, but in the new covenant, with baptism, Jesus desires to enter through the door: "It is those I love that I correct and chasten; kindle thy generosity, and repent. See where I stand at the door, knocking; if anyone listens to my voice and opens the door, I will come in to visit him, and take my supper with him, and he shall sup with me" (Rev. 3:19–20). If the angel is the executioner of God's wrath in the Old, then Jesus the Lamb, is executioner of God's mercy in the New.

The typology of the Passover meal encompasses more than just the knowledge that Jesus is the true paschal lamb; it foreshadows

---

15. Dr. Feingold's great work on biblical typology and the mystery of Israel and the Church is available from Miriam Press, and at www.hebrewcatholic.net.

the Holy Eucharist, and the unity of the Church gathered round this great sacrament of love. Pope Benedict XVI points out in the second volume of his *Jesus of Nazareth* trilogy that Jesus did not celebrate the Passover meal in Holy Week in the sense of the one prescribed to Moses; rather the Last Supper became his new Passover: that with the knowledge of his impending death, it was the moment for the new to supersede the old. At the heart of both the Passover meal in its original form and the Last Supper where the Lord gave his Body, Blood, Soul and Divinity under the appearance of bread and wine, is the passion and death of Jesus. Both types of meal led to an exodus from slavery; in the case of the Israelites, freedom to walk towards the Promised Land, and in the case of the Last Supper and its anticipation of the Sacrifice of the Cross, liberation from all evil and entrance into the true promised land of the Father. St. Leo the Great explains the revealing of this great mystery from the old covenant to the new in these terms:

> For the things which had long been promised under mysterious figures had to be fulfilled in all clearness; for instance, the True Sheep had to supersede the sheep which was its antitype, and the One Sacrifice to bring to an end the multitude of different sacrifices. For all those things which had been divinely ordained through Moses about the sacrifice of the lamb had prophesied of Christ and truly announced the slaying of Christ. In order, therefore, that the shadows should yield to the substance and types cease in the presence of the Reality, the ancient observance is removed by a new Sacrament, victim passes into Victim, blood is wiped away by Blood, and the law-ordained Feast is fulfilled by being changed.[16]

Of course in both instances of the Passover meal and the Last Supper, the act of eating is a communal one. For the Israelites, they were commanded to eat in the house, in small family units among themselves; while at the Last Supper, the Lord gathered to himself his apostles—the future pillars of the Church. St. Cyprian saw God's command to the Israelites to eat only within the house as a

---

16. Pope St. Leo the Great, "Sermon 58," no.1, available at www.newadvent.org.

type of the Church, in a similar symbolism to Noah's Ark.[17] The unity of the Church in the communion of saints is certainly prefigured in the Passover meal, for the salvific action of the angel takes place while they eat together, consuming the source of the sacrifice. Noteworthy also is the fact that down the centuries the prayer of praise known as the "Great Hallel" (Psalm 136/135) has been sung at the end of the Passover meal; it is a prayer of thanksgiving for the marvel of God's mighty works through salvation history, and one that foreshadowed the prayer of praise offered by the saints in the Mystical Body of Christ.

The story of the Exodus continues with the miraculous parting of the waters through the Red Sea. Again there is a very similar typology to that of the great flood; the Lord allows his chosen ones to escape through the water, while evil is swept away by the waters that pour over the evildoers. On the other side of the Red Sea, the Israelites are able to look back with joy to see their captors destroyed, and at last freedom is theirs. The waters tell two different stories in this incredible event; on the one hand, biblical imagery has seen water as a power of sin and death, while on the other hand it also speaks of new life. For Pharaoh and his oppressive army the sea meant being swallowed up in their own evil; their adherence to the use of witchcraft and worship of alien gods precluded them from passing from spiritual death to life.[18] For the Israelites this symbol of baptism led to a new beginning, a new stage on the journey to the Promised Land. Even though they sang the great canticle of praise to God in the aftermath of their triumph (cf. Ex. 15:1–19), they had not yet reached their final destination, and for Christians it is the same. Baptism is the initiation of true life in Christ, but not the guarantee of salvation. It is still possible to ruin the grace, the pledge of salvation through a life of self-centered evil.

Pope Benedict XVI also sees the sea that the Israelites crossed as analogous to the Church's voyage through time:

---

17. See St. Cyprian of Carthage, *On the Unity of the Church*, no. 8, available at www.newadvent.org.

18. Pharaoh's magicians tried to mimic the plagues as described in chapters 7–9 of Exodus through their use of witchcraft.

There is a surprising parallel to the story of Moses's song after Israel's liberation from Egypt upon emerging from the Red Sea, namely in the Book of Revelation of Saint John. Before the beginning of the seven last plagues imposed upon the earth, the seer has a vision of something "like a sea of glass mingled with fire; and those who had conquered the beast and its image and the number of its name, standing beside the sea of glass with harps of God in their hands. And they sing the song of Moses, the servant of God, and the song of the Lamb. . . ." (Rev. 15:3) This image describes the situation of the disciples of Jesus Christ in every age, the situation of the Church in the history of this world. Humanly speaking, it is self-contradictory. On the one hand, the community is located at the Exodus, in the midst of the Red Sea, in a sea which is paradoxically ice and fire at the same time. And must not the Church, so to speak, always walk on the sea, through the fire and the cold? Humanly speaking, she ought to sink. But while she is still walking in the midst of this Red Sea, she sings—she intones the song of praise of the just: the song of Moses and of the Lamb, in which the Old and New Covenants blend into harmony. . . . She is standing on history's waters of death and yet she has already risen. Singing, she grasps at the Lord's hand, which holds her above the waters. And she knows that she is thereby raised outside the force of gravity of death and evil—a force from which otherwise there would be no way of escape—raised and drawn into the new gravitational force of God, of truth and of love.[19]

Although the concept of a community has already been unearthed from Genesis and Exodus, it has mainly revolved around small groups. Now however, with the Israelites free as a people, the next stage of God's covenant is revealed. It happens in the wilderness of Sinai when God calls Moses from the mountain:

Here Moses went up to meet God, and the voice of God came to him from the mountain, a message to the race of Jacob; to Israel's sons proclaim it: You have seen for yourselves what I did to the Egyptians, how I carried you as if on eagle's wings, and took you up into my care. Listen, then, to my voice, and keep your covenant

19. Pope Benedict XVI, "Homily for the Easter Vigil," April 11, 2009, www.vatican.va.

with me; and I, to whom all the earth belongs, will single you out among its peoples to be my own. You shall serve me as a royal priesthood, as a consecrated nation; tell the Israelites this. (Ex. 19:3–6)

So for the first time with the entire community of Israel present facing the mountain, God reveals his intention to create a communion of people who will love and serve him, and in return become a great and holy nation. This is the great prophetic foreshadowing of the communion of saints, a Kingdom of priestly people who will love God and neighbor. What was required on the part of Israel was fidelity to God and his laws.

Although the Ten Commandments were already written in the human heart from the beginning through natural law and conscience, God gave them again to Moses written on stone tablets in the aftermath of their acceptance and obedience to his proposal of making them a "treasured possession." Significantly, the Israelites were told to prepare themselves for two days, and on the third day the Lord would reveal his commandments.[20] The entire event, which was a true theophany, took place with an apocalyptic atmosphere: peals of thunder, lightning, loud trumpet blasts and a smoking mountain. The commandments themselves can be understood as a gift on the Lord's part, a sort of moral compass which will allow

---

20. The significance of this lies in the comparison of 50 days from the first Passover to the Law being given, and 50 days from Jesus's resurrection to Pentecost. St. Augustine explains: "Read the book of Exodus, and observe the number of days between the first passover and the giving of the Law. God speaks to Moses in the desert of Sinai on the first day of the third month. Mark, then, this as one day of the month, and then observe what (among other things) the Lord said on that day: 'Go unto the people, and sanctify them today and tomorrow, and let them wash their clothes, and be ready against the third day; for the third day the Lord will come down in the sight of all the people upon Mount Sinai.' (Exodus 19:10–11) The Law was accordingly given on the third day of the month. Now reckon the days between the 14th day of the first month, the day of the passover, and the 3rd day of the third month, and you have 17 days of the first month, 30 of the second, and 3 of the third—50 in all. The Law in the Ark of the Testimony *represents* holiness in the Lord's body, by whose resurrection is promised to us the future rest; for our receiving of which, love is breathed into us by the Holy Spirit." St. Augustine, "Letter 55," no 16.30, available at www.newadvent.org

Israel to develop a deep personal relationship with him, and allow for the peaceful existence of their nation. As long as they obey God, their enemies would be their footstool and the Lord's blessings would be upon them. The order of the Commandments is structured in such a way as to guide the recipient in the path of sanctity, whereby God is worshiped above all else, and then below that is given the teaching on the correct mode of existence among themselves: honoring father and mother, not killing, not committing adultery etc. Understood in this way, the laws of God are not restrictive, but liberating in that they open the heart to divine charity which binds the communion of God and his people ever closer, while symbolizing the nature of future communion in heaven. Even if the weakness of sin damages that process, the commandments are and always will be the bedrock of a peaceful co-existence among peoples.

As this chapter is concerned only with developing an overview of the plan of God from the Old Testament to the New, it is not possible to look in detail at every instance in which the Church is prefigured; that would require a huge volume in itself. But before we move further in salvation history, we need to look at the role of Moses himself and how he is a type of Christ. First and foremost, Moses, like Jesus, was a man of prayer. He understood clearly that to be God's chosen leader, to be the intercessor for all Israel, he would have to live in the most intimate union with the Lord. As with Christ, Moses prayed not only for his own people, but for his enemies; for when God was sending the plagues to Egypt, he interceded for Pharaoh (Ex. 8:9–10). Other instances of his power as a mediator concern his prayer for the people who complained, leading God to send fire to the outskirts of the camp: "and when Moses prayed to the Lord, the fire died down" (Num. 11:2). He asked the Lord to heal his sister Miriam who had been punished with leprosy (Num. 12:10–15), and he prayed before God not to destroy the people after they had threatened a revolt in the aftermath of the scouting of the land of Canaan (Num. 14:19). One of the most significant events concerns the forty days and nights that Moses spent in fasting and contemplation, while waiting to receive the Tablets of the Law. Below, at the foot of the mountain, the people had grown weary of waiting, so they turned to Aaron: "fashion us gods, to be our leaders. We had a man to lead us, this Moses, when we came away from Egypt; but there is no saying what has become of him" (Ex. 32:1). At the precise moment that Moses was acting in his exalted role of mediator, the people were committing the great sin of apostasy. When Moses was told by God of their unfaithfulness and his anger blazed against them, he prayed:

> Oh let the storm of thy anger pass; pardon thy people's guilt! Remember thy servants Abraham, Isaac and Israel, and the oath thou didst swear by thy own name: I will make your posterity countless as the stars in heaven, and give them all this land of which I spoke to you, to be their everlasting home. (Ex. 32:12–13)

The Lord relented and did not inflict the great punishment. Moses seems to have recognized the strength of God's mercy as did Abraham before him. Even though justice demands retribution, for Moses, his life of prayer led him to understand that God wanted to release his mercy rather than judgment, and in this way Moses's mediation anticipated in a profound way the mediation of Jesus. Significant also was the way Moses called to mind the ancient covenant God had made; perhaps we can see here his desire to remind the Lord of the great plan of salvation that could only be accomplished if the chosen people were spared.

If we delve a little deeper into the typological role of Moses as a forerunner of Jesus Christ, we are confronted by two wonderful episodes of intercession that undoubtedly foreshadow the Cross: the fashioning of a bronze serpent (Num. 21:4–9), and the battle between Israel and Amalek's forces (Ex. 17:8–16). In the first case, the Israelites were complaining. They asked God and Moses: "Why didst thou ever bring us away from Egypt, only to die in the desert? We have neither bread nor water here; we are sick at heart, sick of the unsatisfying food thou givest us" (Num. 21:5). At this, God sent fiery serpents which brought death to many in Israel. The people recognized they had sinned and asked Moses to intercede for them. In response, the Lord told Moses to mount a bronze snake on a standard and if anyone was bitten, they could look at it and be saved.

The comparison is obvious here between Moses and Jesus; but whereas Moses's standard only allows physical healing, the Cross of Jesus saves from spiritual death and opens the gate to everlasting life. Jesus himself links the two salvific events in his discourse with Nicodemus: "And this Son of Man must be lifted up, as the serpent was lifted up by Moses in the wilderness; so that those who believe in him may not perish, but have eternal life" (Jn. 3:14–15). We may ask, why did the Lord instruct Moses to use a serpent? On the face of it, it does seem slightly confusing. Perhaps the answer lies in its symbolism. We know Satan, in the form of a snake, led Adam and Eve to sin; he was the cause of our downfall. By nailing the snake to the standard, in prophetic fashion the Lord was foretelling how Jesus on the Cross would become "sin" (2 Cor. 5:21), would take it all upon himself, and in doing so would destroy the reign of the serpent forever. It is not the snake on the standard that saves, but his impotence in being fixed to it that effects the miraculous healing.

The second story is just as significant. In Exodus, chapter 17 we read:

> And while they were at Raphidim, the Amalecites came and offered the Israelites battle. So Moses said to Josue, Muster me an army, and go out to fight against Amalec; I will take my stand tomorrow on the hill top, with the miraculous staff in my hand. And Josue did as Moses bade him, going out to do battle with Amalec, while Moses, Aaron and Hur went up to the hill top. Whenever Moses lifted up his hands, Israel had the better of it; only when he rested for a little did the victory go to Amalec. But now Moses's arms grew weary; so they found him a stone to sit on and bade him be seated on it; then, one on each side, Aaron and Hur kept his hands lifted up. In this way, the strength of his arms held out until set of sun, while Josue routed Amalec, and all the forces Amalec could rally, at the sword's point. (Ex. 17:8–13)

Once again the symbolism is very powerful. Although Joshua (Josue) leads the army, it is Moses, arms outstretched like Our Lord on the Cross who is truly leading the fight. But there is more to it than that. The name *Joshua* is a variant of *Yeshua* which is the Hebrew spelling of Jesus, therefore the Fathers saw in Joshua the presence of Jesus symbolized at the forefront of the battle, which explains why Moses was in the position he was, rather than on his knees imploring God's saving help.[21] After Moses's death, it was Joshua himself who as a figure of Christ led Israel into the Promised Land. His praises are sung in the Book of Sirach:

> Next to Moses in the line of prophets comes Josue the son of Nave, that fought so well. With him, name and renown are one; who is more renowned for the deliverance he brought to God's chosen people, beating down the enemies that defied him until Israel made their land its own? What fame he won by those valiant blows he dealt, hurling his armed strength at city after city! What chieftain had ever stood his ground so manfully? And still the Lord brought enemies to confront him. (Sir. 46:1–4)

The final point that we need to consider in this short exposition on the life and work of Moses concerns a prophecy found in Deuteronomy that a new Moses will come sometime in the future:

> No, the Lord thy God will raise up for thee a prophet like myself, of thy own race, a brother of thy own; it is to him thou must listen. Was it not thy own plea, that day when all were publicly assembled at mount Horeb, that thou mightest hear the voice of the Lord thy God no longer, have sight of that raging fire no longer, lest it should be thy death? And the Lord told me, All that they have said is well said. I will raise up for them a prophet like thyself, one of their own race, entrusting my own message to his lips, so that he may instruct them at my bidding. (Deut. 18:15–19)

In the last chapter of Deuteronomy, we read how Moses ascended Mount Nebo and was shown by God all the lands that he had prom-

---

21. St. Justin Martyr in his *Dialogue with Trypho* states: "When the people waged war with Amalek, and the son of Nave (Nun) by name Jesus (Joshua), led the fight, Moses himself prayed to God, stretching out both hands, and Hur with Aaron supported them during the whole day, so that they might not hang down when he got wearied. For if he gave up any part of this sign, which was an imitation of the cross, the people were beaten, as is recorded in the writings of Moses; but if he remained in this form, Amalek was proportionally defeated, and he who prevailed by the cross. For it was not because Moses so prayed that the people were stronger, but because, while one who bore the name of Jesus (Joshua) was in the forefront of the battle, he himself made the sign of the cross." (ch. 90) See also Tertullian, *Against Marcion*, bk III, ch. 18, available at www.newadvent.org.

ised Abraham, Isaac and Jacob. Significantly though, the Lord said: "I have granted thee the sight of it; enter it thou mayst not" (Deut. 34:4). Moses then died and was buried in a valley in the land of Moab. A few verses later we again come across a reference to the prophecy of the new Moses: "There was never such another prophet in Israel as Moses; what other man was the Lord's familiar, meeting him face to face?" (Deut. 34:10) At the crux of this prophecy is the issue of God not allowing Moses to cross over into the Promised Land. But why? Moses's great task was to present the Old Law; he was bound up in preparing the people for the fulfilment of God's promise, rather than seeing it through. For the complete work of the Lord to be revealed in the fullness of time (Gal. 4:4), a new Moses would be needed. Pope Benedict XVI in his landmark first volume of *Jesus of Nazareth* compares the two "Moses" and why the second superseded the first:

> At this point, though, we need to recall another remarkable story that the Book of Exodus recounts concerning Moses's relationship to God. There we are told that Moses asked, "I pray thee, show me thy glory" (Ex. 33:18). God refuses his request: "You cannot see my face" (Ex. 33:20). . . . As he passes, God covers Moses with his own hand, but he withdraws it at the end: "You shall see my back; but my face shall not be seen" (Ex. 33:23). . . . In terms of the present question, the main point is that although Moses's immediate relation to God makes him the great mediator of Revelation, the mediator of the Covenant, it has its limits. He does not behold God's face, even though he is permitted to enter into the cloud of God's presence and to speak with God as a friend. The promise of a "prophet like me" thus implicitly contains an even greater expectation: that the last prophet, the new Moses, will be granted what was refused to the first one-a real, immediate vision of the face of God.[22]

In the life of Moses, therefore, we encounter a reflection of the life of Christ as mediator, prophet, miracle worker and legislator. As in the case of a house being built on sure foundations, Moses was God's architect laying them in preparation for the eventual coming

---

22. Pope Benedict XVI, *Jesus of Nazareth* (London: Bloomsbury, 2007), 5.

of the Savior, who would replace the Old Covenant with the New. Jesus, the new Moses, would be recognized as fulfilling the prophecy of Deuteronomy in various instances in the New Testament. For example, when he performed the miracle of the loaves, the crowd exclaimed joyfully: "Beyond doubt, this is the prophet who is to come into the world" (Jn. 6:14).[23] Later, after Pentecost, St. Peter and St. Stephen would also make reference to it in Acts 3:22–23, and Acts 7:37 respectively. The three instances of God the Father vocally glorifying the work of his Son (Lk. 3:22, Lk. 9:35 and Jn. 12:28) could also be seen as sealing the identity of the new Moses as the head of the new community founded on grace and truth (cf. Jn. 1:17).

In the reflections we have made so far, from the point of view of the chosen people, one disconcerting attitude is prevalent: they complain. In spite of all the marvels of God in liberating them, they do not seem to have the law written in their hearts as the Lord would want; faith seems to be in short supply. One of the great lessons we learn through meditating on these stories is the great patience God has with them. They are taught like babies who are given small amounts of milk at a time; they cannot cope with anything more. Jesus implies that things had not improved even in his day, referring to their attitude when the Pharisees questioned him on why Moses allowed divorce: "It was to suit your hard hearts that Moses allowed you to put your wives away; it was not so at the beginning of things" (Matt. 19:8). Still, even though unfaithfulness on their part often marred the relationship between themselves and God, he did not revoke the covenant, instead continuing to send prophets who would instruct them in the ways of the Lord. The plan of salvation was therefore set and would not be altered, for the prophet Malachi said: "In me, the Eternal, there is no change, and you, sons of Jacob, are a people still" (Mal. 3:6).

Before closing this chapter, there are two further prophetic elements of the Old Testament that need exploration which will broaden our understanding of the mystery of the Holy Church of

---

23. Perhaps the crowd also understood this miracle as relating to the miraculous falling of bread from heaven as recounted in Exodus, chapter 16. In this way they would have recognized Jesus as the "prophet," the new Moses.

God, as prefigured in the former Covenant. The first concerns the Tabernacle containing the Ark of the Covenant and the Temple of Solomon as types of the presence of Jesus Christ and his community of faithful. The second concerns the work of the prophets in proclaiming a new Covenant where God would replace a heart of stone with a heart of flesh (cf. Ezek. 36:26).

Tabernacle and Temple: Blessing Through the Divine Presence

When God created the Old Law, giving it to Moses on Mount Sinai, not only did He give the Ten Commandments, but also a series of instructions concerning how He was to be worshiped by the community of Israel. He told Moses: "I mean them to build me a sanctuary, so that I can dwell among them" (Ex. 25:8). After giving very specific instructions on how it was to be built, God said: "Thence will I issue my commands; from that throne of mercy, between the two cherubs that stand over the ark and its records, my voice shall come to thee, whenever I send word through thee to the sons of Israel" (Ex. 25:22). The Ark of the Covenant was to contain three precious things: the two stone tablets containing the Ten Commandments, the jar of manna and the Staff of Aaron that sprouted and blossomed upon his election as high priest.[24]

Moses was also commanded to construct a Tabernacle, in which the Ark would be housed, and a court made of fine linen curtains and bronze pillars. Once completed, the Lord God would dwell within the Tabernacle and would accompany Israel on its journey to the Promised Land. The Tabernacle was divided by a veil and consisted of two parts; the "sanctuary" and the "inner sanctuary" (cf. Ex. 26:33). God dwelt behind the veil in the inner sanctuary where the Ark was kept while on the other side of the veil was the table of the showbread,[25] the golden Menorah,[26] and the Altar of Incense.

If we briefly look at the contents of the Ark of the Covenant, we see how they symbolize the figure of Christ as the true high priest.

---

24. See Num. 17:10 and Heb. 9:4.

25. The holy bread that was placed on the table every Sabbath as an offering to God and subsequently eaten by the priests.

26. A lampstand made of pure gold that contained seven lamps.

The Ten Commandments are the rule of the Old Law, the blueprint for living in communion with God. But with Jesus who in himself encapsulates this true life with God (cf. Rom. 6:10) we find the new law; not that it does away with the old, but rather fulfils it, bringing it to perfection through the Beatitudes. Therefore the two stone tablets, cornerstones of the Old law, foreshadow the new cornerstone, Christ (cf. Acts. 4:11). The jar of Manna speaks of Jesus, the divine bread, who gives his life for the world and spiritual food for the journey, while the Staff of Aaron foretells Jesus as the supreme high priest who offers what the Levitical priests could not, that is, a perfect sacrifice. This last point is of great significance because it is a prophecy of the future sacrifice offered by the priests of the Church in Holy Mass, and one that does not come from a human line, as in the case of Aaron's priesthood, but rather from a divine one, in the order of Melchizedek.[27]

27. Melchizedek first appears in Genesis 14:18, after Abram had defeated Chodorlahomor and other kings allied with him: "Melchisedech, too, was there, the king of Salem. And he, priest as he was of the most high God, brought out bread and wine with him, and gave him this benediction, On Abram be the blessing of the most high God, maker of heaven and earth, and blessed be that most high God, whose protection has brought thy enemies into thy power. To him, Abram gave tithes of all he had won." The Letter to the Hebrews would later inform us that Melchizedek was without lineage, "no name of father or mother, no pedigree, no date of birth or of death; there he stands, eternally, a priest, the true figure of the Son of God" (Heb.7:3). In Melchizedek, we see a pagan King who in a sense, like Jesus, did not have a priesthood that was connected to the Law; in fact that law had not yet been given. Therefore, he symbolizes an eternal priesthood, one which is above the weaknesses of Levitical priests. The Letter to the Hebrews states: "Such was the high priest that suited our need, holy and guiltless and undefiled, not reckoned among us sinners, lifted high above all the heavens" (Heb.7:26). The essential difference then between the priesthood of Aaron and the Priesthood of the New Covenant is that in the Old, the sacrifices were not capable of being salvific; they had to be repeated constantly in order to appease God. Ultimately, a true mediation was not possible because of original sin; in the same way as Moses could not look at the face of God in his full glory. In the new priesthood, however, the priest shares in the ministry of Christ by making present each day his perfect sacrifice on Calvary: "Now the minister, by reason of the sacerdotal consecration which he has received, is truly made like to the high priest and possesses the authority to act in the power and place of the person of Christ himself (*virtute ac persona ipsius Christi*)." *Catechism of the Catholic Church*, no. 1548, www.vatican.va.

The entire court itself was typological of the physical Church in that not only did God reside there in the Tabernacle (as Jesus does in the Blessed Sacrament, Body, Blood, Soul and Divinity), but the court was also the place where an altar was erected in order for the sacrifices to be offered. In Leviticus chapter nine we see a foreshadowing of the community of the mystical body:

> Then he stretched out his hands over the people, and blessed them; and so, the sacrifice done, the atonement for faults, the burnt-sacrifice, and the welcome-offering, he came down from the altar. After this, both Moses and Aaron went into the tabernacle that bears record and blessed the people as they came out. Whereupon the glory of the Lord shone out upon the whole multitude, and suddenly the Lord sent down fire, which consumed the burnt-sacrifice, and all the fat that lay on the altar. At the sight, the whole people raised a cry of praise, and fell face to ground in worship. (Lev. 9:22–24)

The Temple of Jerusalem, built by King Solomon the son of King David, is the other great prefigurement of the Church. The Lord's will was that a permanent place of worship would be built once the Israelites had reached the promised land and destroyed all the false idols found therein (cf. Deut. 12:5). In the aftermath of David's capture of Jerusalem from the Jebusites, he desired to build a temple in which to house the Ark of the Covenant, but God, through the prophet Nathan, responded by prophesying his own house building, the House of David, a dynastic line from which would come the Messiah, the everlasting ruler:

> So, when thy days are ended, and thou art laid to rest beside thy fathers, I will grant thee for successor a son of thy own body, established firmly on his throne. He it is[28] that shall build a house to do my name honour. I will prolong for ever his royal dynasty. . . . Through the ages, far as thy thought can reach, dynasty and royalty both shall endure; thy throne shall remain for ever unshaken. (2 Sam. 7:12–13, 16)

---

28. A reference to Solomon, who would build the Temple.

Although God promises a line of descendants to David, the central point of this text is not to promise a kind of divine seal on a political kingdom that would last for all time, but instead a new type of spiritual kingship. Rather than David building a house, it is the Lord's work: "and this too the Lord promises, that he will grant thy line continuance" (2 Sam. 7:11). In this way we see two elements converge in the messianic figure: He is both high priest and king. He *is* the Temple; as Jesus himself prophesied: "Destroy this temple, and in three days I will raise it up again" (Jn. 2:19). The Jews said: "This temple took forty-six years to build; wilt thou raise it up in three days? But the temple he was speaking of was his own body" (Jn. 2:20–21).

One of the great foreshadowings of the communion of saints came in the requirement that three pilgrimages a year be made to the Temple in Jerusalem.[29] This underscored the necessity of unity of worship and the offering of sacrifices. The bonds of love between God and his communion of faithful could grow within the confines of the Temple where the liturgical actions would prefigure those of the Christian communities of the New Covenant. Jerusalem was now the point of reference for the sanctification of Israel and the bridge between two covenants; unfortunately, time and again Israel would betray their God and cause the desecration and destruction of the temple. However with the reign of King David, himself a type of Christ as prophet and king, Jerusalem becomes in a sense the center of history pointing not only to the establishment of the New Covenant on Calvary but also to its eschatological fullness in the New Jerusalem (cf. Rev. 21:2).

The Holy Prophets: Blessing Through the Spirit

As salvation history progressed through the ages, there was a constant tension between God and his people. The Israelites certainly didn't understand the nature of following God's will at all times, for time and time again as we have seen, there were transgressions,

---

29. Passover, Shavuot [Pentecost] and Sukkot [Tabernances] Tabernacles.

apostasy and betrayal. God in his great mercy gave Israel a series of prophets to guide them along the path of faithfulness and love; but the role of the prophet was not a kind of soothsayer, someone who would be predicting dates and times of events. Rather, it was to point out the faults, the sins of the chosen ones and promote the true path of holiness that would enable them to live faithfully the Covenant the Lord had made with them. Therefore, the prophets carried out a constant ministry of calling for repentance so that God's anger could be appeased and blessings instead of punishment could fall like dew on all Israel.

As we have seen throughout this chapter, the Church Militant was prefigured in a variety of ways and through the prophetic life of various people. Everything was pointing towards something greater: the advent of the Messiah and his New Covenant. For the prophets, this was the other essential part of their ministry: to prophesy the coming of a new time of grace and holiness that would replace and supersede the Old Law. One of the most significant elements of this message was the promise that God's people would come from all nations. If we remember, Israel was a single nation, chosen from the mysterious design of the Lord. They didn't do anything to earn this blessing; it was simply a gratuitous gift from heaven. Now God was lifting the veil on his divine plan to extend salvation to the entire world, on a universal level; in one word: catholic.

It is the prophet Isaiah who began to preach about the expansion of salvation from one nation to all in his beautifully poetic language:

> And now, here is my servant, to whom I grant protection, the man of my choice, greatly beloved. My spirit rests upon him, and he will proclaim right order among the Gentiles. He will not be contentious or a lover of faction; none shall hear his voice in the streets. He will not snap the staff that is already crushed, or put out the wick that still smoulders; but at last he will establish right order unfailingly. Not with sternness, not with violence; to set up right order on earth, that is his mission. He has a law to give; in the far-off islands men wait for it eagerly. (Is. 42:1–4)

Isaiah understood very clearly the magnitude of the message he was given;[30] not only the vision of the "suffering servant" and his sacrifice (cf. Is. 53:1–12), but also the fruit of the immolation of Christ. This fruit would be the gathering of a redeemed people: "I have appointed thee to be the light of the Gentiles, in thee I will send out my salvation to the furthest corners of the earth" (Is. 49:6). The invitation to accept the hand of God for the gentile world is also apparent in his writings:

> So many athirst; who will not come to the water? So many destitute; who will come and get him food, get wine and milk free, no price to be paid? ... Summons of thine shall go out to a nation thou never knewest; peoples that never heard of thee shall hasten to thy call; such the glory thy God, the Holy One of Israel, has bestowed on thee. (Is. 55:1, 5)

As with all the prophets, Isaiah was insistent on the need for repentance as a prerequisite for the correct disposition of the soul in preparation for the coming of the Savior. He talked of valleys being raised, and mountains laid low; in essence he was saying: prepare! Make a straight road for the Lord to meet us in the dust of our sin!

In terms of the prefiguring of the Lord's mystical body, his Church, we can turn to chapter two of Isaiah. He speaks of the Lord's mountain that will rise above all other mountains: "all nations will flock there together. A multitude of peoples will make their way to it, crying, Come, let us climb up to the Lord's mountain-peak, to the house where the God of Jacob dwells; he shall teach us the right way, we will walk in the paths he has chosen" (Is. 2:2–3). This prophecy tells us that the power of the Lord's grace will attract the gentile world to seek the truth of God's Word. Isaiah would return to the glory of Zion in chapter sixty by proclaiming that the light of God would dispel the darkness of sin and become the dawning of a new day.

---

30. The Book of Isaiah contains more than the writings of the original prophet who lived in the eighth century BC. Also contained therein are the writing of his successors, notably "Deutero-Isaiah," who was responsible for chapters 40–55, written some two centuries after Isaiah himself.

If we read carefully through the many chapters of Isaiah, we are presented not only with the truth of the first coming of Jesus and the establishment of his Church, but also the consummation of the world at the end of time (Is. 65:17–25). It is a visionary book that gives comfort and hope that evil will not prevail, that even though man brings about his own downfall time and time again, ultimately goodness and truth will be victorious through the working of God's grace. St. Jerome certainly saw Isaiah's ability to penetrate the very mystery of salvation history: "He was more of an Evangelist than a Prophet, because he described all of the Mysteries of the Church of Christ so vividly that you would assume he was not prophesying about the future, but rather was composing a history of past events."[31]

One of the other great messages foretold by several Old Testament prophets was the coming of the Holy Spirit, and with him and through him, a new holiness that would be manifested from the heart through faith and love. This would be the central pillar of the New Covenant as prophesied by Jeremiah:

> A time is coming, the Lord says, when I mean to ratify a new covenant with the people of Israel and with the people of Judah . . . I will implant my law in their innermost thoughts, engrave it in their hearts; I will be their God, and they shall be my people. (Jer. 31:31, 33)

The writing of the law on the heart, of placing it within, is to be seen as a decisive change for humanity. No longer is the law of God a set of rules and regulations that instruct but don't necessarily penetrate the inner core of man; rather now it is as if the "cage" of the soul has been opened allowing the freedom of God's presence to enter in. Not only that: with the coming of the Holy Spirit and the Eucharistic presence of Jesus, the body and soul of mortal man become the temple of the Lord[32] so that the human and the divine are active in a fusion of love that increases our capacity to reach the heights of holi-

---

31. St. Jerome, *Prologue to Isaiah, The Lives of the Holy Prophets* (Buena Vista: Holy Apostles Convent Publications, 1998), 101.
32. Cf. 1 Cor. 6:19.

ness. The entrance of Trinitarian love in the soul becomes the foundation of sanctifying grace, as we read in St. Peter's Second Letter:

> See how all the gifts that make for life and holiness in us belong to his divine power; come to us through fuller knowledge of him, whose own glory and sovereignty have drawn us to himself! Through him God has bestowed on us high and treasured promises; you are to share the divine nature, with the world's corruption, the world's passions, left behind. (2 Pet. 1:3–4)

The prophet Ezekiel also spoke of the coming of the Holy Spirit (Ez. 11:19, Ez. 36:26), while portraying the Lord as a shepherd who would take care of the flock himself (Ez. 34:11–16). This representation of the Lord was impressed greatly in the hearts of the early Christian community after Pentecost, and the early images of Jesus the Good Shepherd are still to be seen in the Roman Catacombs to this day. The prophet Joel also prophesied the divine activity of the Holy Spirit in the Church: "And afterwards? Afterwards I will pour out my spirit upon all mankind, and your sons and daughters will be prophets. Your old men shall dream dreams, and your young men see visions; everywhere servants of mine, handmaids of mine, inspired to prophesy!" (Joel. 3:1–3)

Of course, it was only after Pentecost that this vision would become a reality. Significantly though before that, the Gospels tell us that Jesus had instructed the apostles about the coming of the Holy Spirit (Jn. 15:26), and also had opened their hearts to see his divine life foretold through the psalms[33] and the writings of the prophets. This second aspect only occurred after his glorious resurrection and therefore the Lord wanted them to truly understand the entire mystery of the Passover he had accomplished; one they were now witnesses to. On the road to Emmaus he scolded the two disciples for not accepting and understanding:

> Then he said to them, too slow of wit, too dull of heart, to believe all those sayings of the prophets! Was it not to be expected that the

---

33. For a detailed understanding of the prophetic nature of the Psalms, it is extremely beneficial to study the general audiences of St. John Paul II and Pope Benedict XVI that ran from 2001 to 2006, all available at www.vatican.va.

Christ should undergo these sufferings, and enter so into his glory? Then, going back to Moses and the whole line of the prophets, he began to interpret the words used of himself by all the scriptures. (Lk. 24:25–27)

When the Apostles were assembled later, Jesus appeared and reiterated the truth of the prophets: "This is what I told you, he said, while I still walked in your company; how all that was written of me in the law of Moses, and in the prophets, and in the psalms, must be fulfilled. Then he enlightened their minds, to make them understand the scriptures" (Lk. 24:44–45).

As this chapter draws to a close, we can now proceed with a greater knowledge and understanding of the hidden mystery of the Catholic Church, the mystical body of Christ on earth. Everything revealed in the Old Testament is about preparation. Preparation for the full revelation of God's might; not in the parting of the Red Sea, or the miraculous events surrounding the journey of Israel to the Promised Land, but in the resurrection from the dead of Jesus Christ and the path to full communion with God. With the birth of the Church at Pentecost and the new law of love that is the gift of the Holy Spirit, the communion of saints becomes a reality that begins to mirror the love and communion of the Triune God. The Church is now seen as the true "mountain of God" that all the saints must climb together, supporting one another where necessary until the summit is reached by the last one. It is from this perspective that we should strive to love the Church and our brothers and sisters in this great communion of saints.

✤ 2 ✤

Today Salvation
Has Come To This House

The Jews would not let the bodies remain crucified on the sabbath, because that sabbath day was a solemn one; and since it was now the eve, they asked Pilate that the bodies might have their legs broken, and be taken away. And so the soldiers came and broke the legs both of the one and of the other that were crucified with him; but when they came to Jesus, and found him already dead, they did not break his legs, but one of the soldiers opened his side with a spear; and immediately blood and water flowed out. (Jn. 19:31–34)

IN THE BOOK of Genesis we recall that God created man in His own image, on the sixth day of creation; the last and greatest creature in God's stupendous design. In the second account of the beginning of humanity,[1] we read that God, seeing that Adam needed a helper, a companion to share his life with, sent him into a deep sleep and then proceeded to open his side. From there he took a rib and, fashioning flesh around it, created Eve, the mother of all humans. On the Cross of Calvary a similar event of unfathomable proportions took place. Shortly after the Savior of the World had passed from this life, the Roman soldier known by tradition as Longinus thrust his spear into the side of Jesus's lifeless body, and in the testimony of St. John: "immediately blood and water flowed out. He who saw it has borne his witness; and his witness is worthy of trust. He tells what he knows to be the truth, that you, like him, may learn to believe" (Jn. 19:34–35).

---

1. Gen. 2:15–25.

In that moment, while the Lord slept his sleep of redemptive death, he provided us all with a "helper"; even more than that, a Mother—the Church. In fact the blood and water which flowed from Jesus's pierced side represent the new life: baptism and the Eucharist.[2] From the Cross therefore, the sacramental life of the Church is born; everything that prefigured this moment from Noah to Moses and beyond, now finds its fulfilment in the Sacrifice on the Cross. History now takes a decisive change of direction. No longer does humanity consist of a nomadic people that wander through time with no lasting place of comfort, and subject to the dominion of the evil one. No, from Jerusalem a fresh path of hope is trodden; one that will lead multitudes of disciples to spread the good news of the death and resurrection of Jesus to the ends of the earth and the end of time itself.[3]

In this chapter, we will delve into the mystery of the Church as *the* Sacrament of salvation for humanity. We will seek to look into the heart of Jesus to discern his will for the community that would make up the Church. There are questions that need to be addressed in order for us to appreciate the beauty and mystery at work in the mystical body of Christ: what is the relationship between the Lord and the Church? Can we say "yes" to Jesus but "no" to the Church? What is the relationship between the Church and the Kingdom of

2. In reference to the famed image of Divine Mercy, the Lord Jesus explained to St. Faustina Kowalska: "The two rays denote Blood and Water. The pale ray stands for the Water which makes souls righteous. The red ray stands for the Blood which is the life of souls. These two rays issued forth from the very depths of My tender mercy when My agonized heart was opened by a lance on the Cross." St. Maria Faustina Kowalska, *Divine Mercy In My Soul* (Stockbridge, MA: Marian Press, 2005), n. 299.

3. Pope Benedict XVI relates an old story that symbolizes the restoration of man to God from the original Tree of Knowledge to the Tree of Life; Jesus Christ: "There is an ancient tradition that the wood of the Cross was taken from a tree planted by Adam's son Seth over the place where Adam was buried. On that very spot, known as Golgotha, the place of the skull, Seth planted a seed from the tree of the knowledge of good and evil, the tree in the midst of the Garden of Eden. Through God's providence, the work of the Evil One would be undone by turning his own weapons against him." Benedict XVI, "Homily at the Latin parish church of the Holy Cross—Nicosia," June 5, 2010, www.vatican.va.

God? These are all questions that are central to the mission of the Church and by implication, all its members.

From the Law to Grace

If we want to truly focus on the Church from the perspective of the communion of saints, then we need to take ourselves back to its origins on the banks of the River Jordan. It was there, even before the Lord had begun his public ministry, that a community of faith had formed around the greatest of the prophets: John the Baptist. This supremely important figure, whose own life was heralded by no less than the Archangel Gabriel,[4] had been preaching a stern message of repentance in preparation for the imminent coming of the Savior. Around him had gathered an expectant people: "Thereupon Jerusalem and all Judaea, and all those who dwelt round Jordan, went out to see him, and he baptized them in the Jordan, while they confessed their sins" (Matt. 3:5–6.) We also know that two of the future apostles were also disciples of John: Andrew the brother of Peter, and by tradition, John (Jn. 1:35–37).

John the Baptist, the day after having testified to seeing the Spirit come down on Jesus in the form of a dove, pointed out the Lord to his disciples as he walked past: "Look, this is the Lamb of God," and immediately they followed Jesus. In answer to the disciples' question "where dost thou live?" (Jn. 1:38) Jesus replied: "Come and see" (Jn. 1:39). There are several noticeable things here: the disciples of John do not hesitate to leave him and follow Jesus; it is as if there is some mysterious attraction to the figure of Jesus. But why? What seems most likely is a combination of their absolute trust in the knowledge of the prophet John, their innocence as faithful Jews expectantly awaiting the coming of the Messiah, and the total attraction of the divine countenance of Jesus. Unlike the blinded

---

4. "[A]nd from the time when he is yet a child in his mother's womb he shall be filled with the Holy Ghost. He shall bring back many of the sons of Israel to the Lord their God, ushering in his advent in the spirit and power of an Elias. He shall unite the hearts of all, the fathers with the children, and teach the disobedient the wisdom that makes men just, preparing for the Lord a people fit to receive him" (Lk. 1:15–17).

Pharisees who were caught up in their own pride and arrogance, these two disciples were living a humble existence whereby they could, to some extent at least, accept the message of the prophets that the Redeemer's arrival was imminent. Furthermore, immediately after staying with Jesus, Andrew went and found Simon his brother and presented him to the Master. At this point we see for the first time the nucleus of the future mystical body: Jesus looked at Simon and said: "Thou art Simon the son of Jona; thou shalt be called Cephas" (Jn. 1:42). Simon will become Peter, the rock on which the Church is built.

In a sense this day of meeting becomes the day where the Old Testament draws to a close, and the New opens up. As Jesus walks past John the Baptist, there is a symbolic passing of time from expectation of the future to fulfilment in the present. As John is the last of the great prophets, when the Lord passes in front of him he exclaims "Look, this is the Lamb of God" to his disciples, and his mission gradually draws to a close, ending in glorious martyrdom. Romano Guardini expounds on John the Baptist's mission in these terms:

> It was John's mission—and greatness—to proclaim the advent of the Kingdom. Nor was he in any way unworthy to do so, he who "even from his mother's womb" was filled with the Holy Spirit (Lk. 1:15). It could only mean that his particular vocation was to lead the way to the promised realm, to direct others to it, but in some special sense to remain without. One is reminded of Moses close to death, standing on Mount Nebo and looking down on the promised land. He is not allowed to enter ... everything in him (John) cried out to be with Christ, in that Kingdom of God about to dawn in Messianic abundance, ushering in the new creation. For us its bliss is unimaginable, but for the prophet, who had felt it deeply, it was the object of his most powerful longing. Yet he was not allowed to enter.[5]

From this point, as the divine light of Jesus begins to shine more brightly over Israel, another symbolic act takes place: the Lord chooses his twelve apostles as the foundation stones of the new

---

5. Romano Guardini, *The Lord* (London: Longmans, 1956), 24.

Israel. The calling of twelve apostles is significant in that it recalls the twelve tribes of Israel, which were the ancient divisions of the Jewish people originating from Jacob's sons. Whereas with Israel, the twelve tribes represented a single nation, the twelve apostles are pillars of the New Israel—the eschatological Israel. Again, as with Jesus's symbolic passing by John the Baptist, this momentous act tells us in no uncertain terms that the time of the Kingdom is here, and it recalls the prophetic words spoken by Ezekiel: "I mean to restore Jacob from exile, the Lord God says, and extend my mercy to the whole race of Israel; the honour of my name demands it" (Ez. 39:25).

What we must consider as vitally important at such an early stage in the public ministry of Jesus is his desire to form a community around him. At no time throughout the Gospels do we get the impression that he seeks to accomplish the redemption of the world in a solitary existence almost as if he had never left the eternal presence of his Father in heaven. Actually the opposite happens: the Lord wants to gather a communion of love around him, one that will bear witness to the truth, and in time fan the flame of the Gospel of divine love. The calling of the apostles is noteworthy in particular because it is not members of the religious hierarchy that are chosen, but rather a group of men from everyday working backgrounds, a lower social class that includes fishermen, a tax collector and a thief. One might be tempted to question Jesus's judgement. What was he thinking? Was he a social anarchist who was intent on forming some sort of rebel band of brothers? Or was something else at work in his choice? The answer lies in his prayer life. St. Luke tells us:

> It was at this time that he went out on to the mountain-side, and passed the whole night offering prayer to God, and when day dawned, he called his disciples to him, choosing out twelve of them; these he called his apostles. Their names were, Simon, whom he also called Peter, his brother Andrew, James and John, Philip and Bartholomew, Matthew and Thomas, James the son of Alphaeus, and Simon who is called the Zealot, Jude the brother of James, and Judas Iscariot, the man who turned traitor. (Lk. 6:12–16)

No doubt that night of prayer consisted of God the Father affirming the choice of his Son. In fact, as Jesus came to do the Will of God, we can be certain that they were the Father's choice just as much as the Son's.[6] Perhaps we can understand the choice of the apostle's characters as evidence of the grace and mercy of God in shaping the new covenant in a way which contradicts the ways of the world. For just as God formed Adam from the earth, so too does he fashion the apostles from the earth—the earth of lowliness and sin. If we look back over the two thousand years of the Catholic Church we can admire the great wisdom of God in granting the twelve apostles[7] this task of announcing the redemptive work of Jesus Christ; for who could have foreseen how a group of this kind could have been the "engine room" for a new movement, one that would in time even swallow up the Roman Empire if it was a purely human endeavor?

Unity and Love in the Heart of the Church

There is a certain sense of urgency when we reread the biblical texts pertaining to the calling of the Apostles, an urgency that comes from the imminence of an eschatological breakthrough whereby an old creation, an old order, is about to be overthrown forever. It is within this divine framework that the twelve are to plough the fields of humanity, sowing the word of God and administering the sacraments of salvation, in continuation of the redemptive work of the Lord. The number twelve also has a universal dimension: "This can be understood from the symbolic value that the numbers have in the Semitic world: twelve results from the multiplication of three, a perfect number, and four, a number that refers to the four cardinal points, hence, to the whole world."[8]

The great mission entrusted to the Apostles, and passed down the

6. "Christ therefore was sent forth by God, and the apostles by Christ. Both these appointments, then, were made in an orderly way, according to the will of God." "Letter to the Corinthians," ch. 43, St. Clement of Rome, available at www.newadvent.org.

7. We may recall that after Judas had betrayed Jesus and hanged himself (Matt. 27:5), Matthias was chosen to take his place. (Acts. 1:26)

8. Benedict XVI, "General Audience on Apostolic Tradition," May 3, 2006, www.vatican.va.

centuries through their successors, the bishops, lies in their fidelity to the living Tradition of the Church. This Tradition, not to be confused with "traditions," customs, etc., is the active presence of God and his teachings within the communion of the faithful. At its heart is the Holy Spirit who keeps the Church ever young in its proclamation of the Gospel message: inviting new methods of evangelization, and imparting a continuously rich appreciation of the mystery of our salvation, while the inexorable march of time leads ever closer to its end. Within this consoling truth of faith, we discover that the universality of the Church exists within a dual aspect: we are united as a family of believers not only throughout the world, but also throughout time from Pentecost to Judgment Day.

In a sense, this communion of the Church is a mirror of the perfect union of the Holy Trinity. Even allowing for human frailties and the constant stain of sin, the people of God are called to imitate the love and peace that exists in the Father, Son and Holy Spirit. St. Paul affirmed this when he wrote to the Christians at Corinth: "The grace of our Lord Jesus Christ, and the love of God, and the imparting of the Holy Spirit be with you all. Amen" (2 Cor. 13:13). The "imparting" or "communion" of the Holy Spirit is the glue that binds the grace and mercy offered by the Father and Son; it is His guidance that has led the Church through tempestuous times in its history, from schisms and scandals to persecutions. Without this divine assistance of the Paraclete, the Church would in a sense be rudderless; it would no longer be the unifying force that speaks prophetically of a future world of glory free from decay and death.

It is in the Gospel and letters of St. John that we perhaps gain a greater understanding of the communion of love willed by God for the Church. The great high priestly prayer of Jesus recounted in chapter 17 of his Gospel gives us remarkable insights into this truth; for having already set in place the hierarchical structure of the Church through the appointment of apostles, with Peter as its head (cf. Matt. 16:18), the Lord broadens the vision of the future Church by pleading no fewer than four times for his Father to grant unity to all his disciples. The question that surely needs to be asked at this point is why does Jesus repeat this particular intention? It cannot be solely a measure of his desire for the Father to answer it in a positive manner; after all, the prayer of Jesus is a perfect reflection of the will of his Father anyway. No, we must see it as a summons for the Church of all times to seek unity at all costs. The profound words of this great prayer express the anguish and foreknowledge of One who knows what interior and exterior battles the Church will face in the centuries to come. The prayer is without a doubt also directed at us. Communion of love and service would be an irresistible attraction to the pagan world, but on the other hand disunity would be the poison that would leave evangelization severely harmed—the absolute antithesis of the unity of the Triune God.

In the First Letter of St. John, we are presented with both these opposing forces that have characterized the past two millennia both within the Church and without. At the heart of the Letter is a treatise on how to live an authentic Christian life of charity and truth. The holy Apostle's emphasis on being "sons of God" (cf. 1 Jn. 3:1) invites us to contemplate the grandeur of what baptism procures for us: it is not simply an invitation to be guests of the Father's Kingdom. To be children of God is to be in the most intimate communion with him, to live within the Heart of Jesus and as a temple of the Holy Spirit. If the commandment to love God is the apex of faith, then the commandment to love one another is its logical extension, for in loving our neighbor, we follow the path of Jesus who came not to be served but to serve (cf. Matt. 20:28). St. John emphasizes this point several times in the letter, expressing succinctly the new demands of the Gospel message:

> Beloved, I am not sending you a new commandment; it is an old commandment, which you were given from the very first; what was the message to which you listened long ago but this same commandment, now grown old? And yet it is a new commandment I am sending you, now that it is verified in him and you; the darkness has passed away now, and true light shines instead. He who claims enlightenment, and all the while hates his brother, is in darkness still. It is the man who loves his brother that lives in light; no fear of stumbling haunts him. The man who hates his brother is in the dark, guides his steps in the dark without being able to tell where he is going; darkness has fallen, and blinded his eyes. (1 Jn. 2:7–11)

St. John later touches on the great mystery of this teaching, reflecting on its eternal consequences: "Beloved, we are sons of God even now, and what we shall be hereafter, has not been made known as yet. But we know that when he comes we shall be like him; we shall see him, then, as he is. Now, a man who rests these hopes in him lives a life of holiness; he, too, is holy" (1 Jn. 3:2–3).

There is also a stark, almost apocalyptic, warning that the Apostle delivers which harks back to the plea of Jesus in the high priestly prayer. John speaks of the enticements of this passing world[9] from which the baptized are not exempt, and he adds:

> My sons, this is the last age of time. You have been told that Antichrist must needs come; and even now, to prove to us that it is the last stage of time, many Antichrists have appeared. They came of our company, but they never belonged to our company; if they had belonged to it, they would have persevered at our side. As it is, they were destined to prove that there are some who are no true companions of ours. (1 Jn. 2:18–19)

The warning is absolutely clear. It is not enough to be a baptismal "passport" holder in the community of the mystical body. We can be antichrists even within the confines of the Church. History confirms this, as do the present evils within the Church—evils that Pope Benedict XVI stated were causing greater harm than those external. The path of conversion is one that will never end, and is precisely why the great sacraments of Confession and the Holy Eucharist are there to increase the sanctity not only of the individual, but the community together, as a true bond of love, giving fulfilment to the two great commandments of loving God and one another.

The Mystery of Christ and His Church

At this point we can turn our attention to the question of Jesus's relationship with the Church, and the pressing, contemporary issue

---

9. "I have given them thy message, and the world has nothing but hatred for them, because they do not belong to the world, as I, too, do not belong to the world. I am not asking that thou shouldst take them out of the world, but that thou shouldst keep them clear of what is evil" (Jn. 17:14–15).

of whether we can live an authentic Christian life without partaking of the sacramental life of the Church.

One of the greatest images we have from the Gospels is that of the Vine and the branches (cf. Jn. 15). It is a parable that speaks of the visitation of God among his people, of the entering into history of Christ, who wills to graft humanity onto himself:

> I am the true vine, and it is my Father who tends it. The branch that yields no fruit in me, he cuts away; the branch that does yield fruit, he trims clean, so that it may yield more fruit. You, through the message I have preached to you, are clean already; you have only to live on in me, and I will live on in you. The branch that does not live on in the vine can yield no fruit of itself; no more can you, if you do not live on in me. I am the vine, you are its branches; if a man lives on in me, and I in him, then he will yield abundant fruit; separated from me, you have no power to do anything. If a man does not live on in me, he can only be like the branch that is cast off and withers away; such a branch is picked up and thrown into the fire, to burn there. (Jn. 15:1–6)

The image of the Vine, rich in symbolism, goes back far into the history of Israel. The prophet Isaiah had applied it to Israel itself: "Alas, it is the house of Israel that the Lord called his vineyard; the men of Juda are the plot he loved so" (Is. 5:7). This cherished plant would sadly produce rotten fruit (cf. Is. 5:4) and therefore, as Jesus taught in the parable of the wicked tenants (cf. Mt. 21:33–43), the vineyard would be given to another people. This new vineyard would succeed where the previous one had failed because the Vine would ensure that through a divine vitality, the branches would be able to grow year after year, spreading ever further and producing abundant fruit. Reflecting on this image, we discover that the Vine, Jesus himself, is the source of its life. Without him the branches would die. The Lord is insistent that without us abiding in him and him in us then we are destined to be thrown on the fire. Therefore, we see before us only two options which speak of eternal realities: heaven or hell. As Jesus is the only gateway to the Father, we have to be grafted onto the Vine, the mystical body of Christ—even if only at the very least, in an indirect way. There is no separate vine, and therefore no other possible way of being saved.

To return briefly to the parable of the wicked tenants, we are given unequivocal evidence that places Jesus as head of the Church, the new Israel. After recounting the story of how the Eternal Father's servants (the prophets), and finally his own Son were put to death for trying to obtain the produce at vintage time, Jesus asked the chief priests and elders this question: "what will the owner of the vineyard do to those vine-dressers when he returns?" They answered him, "He will bring those wretches to a wretched end, and will let out the vineyard to other vine-dressers, who will pay him his due when the season comes" (Matt. 21:40–41). What happens next is in essence the revelation of the divine identity of Him who stands before the wicked tenants (the chief priests). The Lord responds to their answer by placing himself at the heart of the Old Testament prophecy concerning the Messiah: "Have you never read those words in the scriptures, the very stone which the builders rejected has become the chief stone at the corner; this is the Lord's doing, and it is marvellous in our eyes?" (Matt. 21:42)[10]

What becomes apparent upon reflection on these texts is that the Church cannot be anything other than a divine institution. The Cornerstone is not simply man made but heavenly by nature.[11] As already noted in the imagery of the Vine, the branches cannot exist without a greater power to feed them. Sanctifying grace and the sacramental life of the Church form the divine sustenance which holds the Church in existence. The insistence of the Lord that we abide in him in an interconnection with all the other branches tells us that we cannot go it alone; it is not God's will. To place oneself in a situation of saying yes to Jesus but no to the Church is quite contradictory. The mystery of the Church is bound to the mystery of Christ

10. The psalm quoted by the Lord is 118 (117): 22.

11. St. Paul explains: "Mankind begins with the Adam who became, as Scripture tells us, a living soul; it is fulfilled in the Adam who has become a life-giving spirit. It was not the principle of spiritual life that came first; natural life came first, then spiritual life; the man who came first came from earth, fashioned of dust, the man who came afterwards came from heaven, and his fashion is heavenly. The nature of that earth-born man is shared by his earthly sons, the nature of the heaven-born man, by his heavenly sons; and it remains for us, who once bore the stamp of earth, to bear the stamp of heaven" (1 Cor. 15:45–49).

himself, for we see a divine and human element in both. Even if the human element of the Church cannot match the perfect human state of the Savior, the command to love impels it to strive towards the perfection of the heavenly city: "But you are to be perfect, as your heavenly Father is perfect" (Matt. 5:48).

The terrible scandals of recent years have certainly damaged the reputation of the Church and, without doubt, left many questioning their own obedience to its teachings. The temptation is to walk away, to no longer accept that this could possibly be a divine institution. But is this truly the correct way of understanding the Church? Did the Lord ever promise a sort of utopia this side of eternity? The New Testament provides plenty of evidence that the Church never was and never would be free from the corruption of sin within its members. It should be noted that Peter, even after his triple denial of Jesus, was to remain as the Lord's choice to lead and govern the Church as the first pope. Unlike Judas, Peter repented and grasped the mercy offered by the Lord and through a profound conversion served the Lord until martyrdom.

The key to understanding the Church, therefore, is divine mercy; for without mercy there would be no Incarnation, no Passion, no victory over the devil, no redemption. The mission of the Church is nothing less than an extension of the Incarnation of the Lord of history, Jesus Christ. As Jesus himself, the divine physician, healed the spiritual and physical ills of humanity, so too does the Church through its administering of the sacraments and its mediation with God. Struggling to see past the terrible sins of its members is no doubt extremely difficult for some, but perhaps this temptation can be seen as a summons to practice humility and mercy for those who have gravely betrayed their vocation. The horrendous sufferings of Jesus demand that we fall silent without throwing any stones; the glory of the Cross has overcome even the greatest filth Satan can hurl at it. In some way large or small, we are all part of that filth, dirtying the beautiful garment of the Church, but we must look within ourselves rather than to the left or the right for betrayal. At times we all hold the hammer and nails, we all press the crown of thorns deeper into the Sacred Head of Jesus; we all pierce that merciful Heart through gossip, slander and a multitude of other sins.

The pontificate of Pope Francis has certainly reinvigorated the Church, especially in the essential aspect of self-examination. The emphasis on recognizing our own sinfulness and the constant need for mercy has struck a chord throughout the Catholic world (although it should be stated that Pope Benedict XVI frequently spoke of this reality as well). Francis has on several occasions referred to the Church as a "field hospital," and in a sense that sums up perfectly the contemporary situation.

Speaking to the parish priests of Rome, the Holy Father explained this in his own inimitable style, one that has become so characteristic of his papacy:

> Today we can think of the Church as a "field hospital." Excuse me but I repeat it, because this is how I see it, how I feel it is: a "field hospital." Wounds need to be treated, so many wounds! So many wounds! There are so many people who are wounded by material problems, by scandals, also in the Church.... People wounded by the world's illusions.... We priests must be there, close to these people. Mercy first means treating the wounds. When someone is wounded, he needs this immediately, not tests such as the level of cholesterol and one's glycemic index.... But there's a wound, treat the wound, and then we can look at the results of the tests. Then specialized treatments can be done, but first we need to treat the open wounds. I think this is what is most important at this time. And there are also hidden wounds, because there are people who distance themselves in order to avoid showing their wounds closer.... The custom comes to mind, in the Mosaic Law, of the lepers in Jesus's time, who were always kept at a distance in order not to spread the contagion.... There are people who distance themselves through shame, through shame, so as not to let their wounds be seen.... And perhaps they distance themselves with some bitterness against the Church, but deep down inside there is a wound.... They want a caress! And you, dear brothers—I ask you—do you know the wounds of your parishioners? Do you perceive them? Are you close to them? It's the only question....[12]

12. Pope Francis, "Address to the Parish Priests of the Diocese of Rome," March 6, 2014, www.vatican.va

Of course, the field hospital without a doctor—especially for the most serious wounds—is rather pointless; it would have no healing effect. The Church is the same; it could not function as *the* sacrament of salvation without the divine physician as its head, and consequently in trying to separate Jesus from the Church, we essentially cut away the entire edifice on which Christianity was founded. In this age of rationalism and relativism, a school of thought exists in which we place ourselves as autonomous from anyone else. Our conscience—well-formed or not—undertakes moral decisions and makes arbitrary judgments which do not necessarily take into account the fundamentals of moral law handed down through a great spiritual heritage. The extreme form we find today even rejects the notion of God; we could say that for many He is irrelevant—a myth. One negative consequence of this attitude is the loneliness of despair that grips society. Charity diminishes, and a community formerly built on service for one another slowly ebbs away. The Church is the antidote to this flawed view of life. By saying yes to Jesus we are saying yes to love. Yes to the poor. Yes to the work of co-redemption. In other words we *are* saying yes to the Church. One of the most compelling arguments for this truth stems from the conversion of St. Paul on the road to Damascus. As he was blinded by the brilliant light, he heard a voice saying: "Saul, Saul, why dost thou persecute me?" (Acts. 9:4) The significance of the question cannot be underestimated. Saul responded by asking "Who art thou, Lord?," and the Lord's answer reiterated his original question: "I am Jesus, whom Saul persecutes." Why did the Lord not refer to his Church rather than himself? It is because the Church and Christ are one—they form one body, one subject. In this theological premise, the Church community is not akin to a group of election canvassers who promote the teachings or policies of the Lord—they are the active members of one body (cf. 1 Cor. 12:12–13).[13]

13. Pope Pius XII explains: "As the nerves extend from the head to all parts of the human body and give them power to feel and to move, in like manner our Savior communicates strength and power to His Church so that the things of God are understood more clearly and are more eagerly desired by the faithful. From Him streams into the body of the Church all the light with which those who believe are

In addressing this present critical situation of the multitudes that have left the Church, especially in western Christianity, we can make our own the words of St. Bernard of Clairvaux who lived through similar times of distress, but who understood that to reject the Church was to reject Christ himself:

> The garments of Christ are being divided, the sacraments of the Church torn to shreds. But the tunic of Christ remains whole for it has no seam, having been woven all in one piece from the top. The tunic of Christ is the unity of the Church which does not admit of being torn or divided. What has thus been woven, what the Holy Spirit has thus unified, cannot be torn up by men. Though they sharpen their tongues like serpents and draw their stings of ingenuity to disturb the peace of the Church, yet, because they are the gates of hell, they shall never prevail against her. If you are indeed her son, if you recognize her as your mother, do not desert her in danger, do not withdraw your support from her in trouble.[14]

A Kingdom Not of This World

One final point for our consideration in this chapter concerns the relationship between the Church, the Kingdom of Christ and the Kingdom of God. These theological terms, although containing various meanings, speak of the mysterious unity that exists between them, a unity in which the communion of saints finds its joy and holiness. In the Vatican II Dogmatic Constitution *Lumen Gentium* we read:

> When Jesus, who had suffered the death of the cross for mankind, had risen, He appeared as the one constituted as Lord, Christ and eternal Priest, and He poured out on His disciples the Spirit promised by the Father. From this source the Church, equipped with the gifts of its Founder and faithfully guarding His precepts of charity, humility and self-sacrifice, receives the mission to proclaim and to spread among all peoples the Kingdom of Christ and

---

divinely illumined, and all the grace by which they are made holy as He is holy." Pope Pius XII, Encyclical Letter, *Mystici Corporis Christi*, June 29, 1943, www.vatican.va.

14. St. Bernard of Clairvaux, *The Letters of Saint Bernard of Clairvaux* (Kalamazoo, MI: Cistercian Publications, 1998), 326.

of God and to be, on earth, the initial budding forth of that kingdom. While it slowly grows, the Church strains toward the completed Kingdom and, with all its strength, hopes and desires to be
united in glory with its King.[15]

In drawing back this curtain of mystery so to speak, we need look no
further than Jesus himself. In his divine person, we find the fullness
of the Kingdom: the perfect image and glorification of God and the
absolute crown of holiness. In essence Christ *is* the Kingdom. The
entire basis of his public ministry was to proclaim the coming of this
kingdom and to invite humanity to enter into it through baptism
and repentance. When we reread the passage of Jesus's discourse
with Pontius Pilate, we discover the true nature of his kingship. It is
not of this world,[16] not political, not revolutionary, not secular. At
its heart, the Kingdom is concerned with the divinization of man;
the reclaiming of God's creation from the murderous hands of
Satan. Truth, love and sacrifice are its attributes; completely illogi-
cal, insane to the values of the world, which is why Pilate brushed
aside the words of the Lord: "What is truth?" (Jn. 18:38). Pilate did
not have the courage to enquire as to what truth entailed. His heart
was closed; perhaps the consequence of his formation in a brutal
kingdom built on fear and oppression.

The discourse between Jesus and Pilate highlights the fundamental difference between the old order and the new. We need to consider that Pilate was being confronted by a religious figure who was
claiming kingship without an army or a political manifesto. For
Jesus, he had come into the world to bear witness to the truth, to
reveal the face of his Father. He hadn't come to bring about some
sort of rapture that would remove the subjects of his kingdom from
reality here and now. No, the essence of the Kingdom of Christ from
the beginning of the fullness of time (cf. Gal. 4:4) was to draw
humanity back to the truth, because in doing that humanity would
begin to reflect the holiness and love of God in a way that had not
happened before. The prophecy of the Lord given to the woman of
Samaria demonstrates the necessary disposition needed to enter

15. *Lumen Gentium,* no. 5, www.vatican.va.
16. Jn. 18:36.

this spiritual kingdom: "but the time is coming, nay, has already come, when true worshippers will worship the Father in spirit and in truth; such men as these the Father claims for his worshippers" (Jn. 4:23).[17] From the very first moment of the Incarnation of the Divine Word in the womb of the Blessed Virgin Mary, the presence of Jesus infuses a new life of grace for humanity. He bestows a Kingdom through the power of his transcendent Spirit, a freedom from the chains of sin whereby Man is drawn into a hitherto unheard-of intimacy with the Creator. It is through the power of the Holy Spirit that the heart and conscience begin to dwell within the realm of Christ. St. Paul explains:

> Only, as before, the Spirit comes to the aid of our weakness; when we do not know what prayer to offer, to pray as we ought, the Spirit himself intercedes for us, with groans beyond all utterance: and God, who can read our hearts, knows well what the Spirit's intent is; for indeed it is according to the mind of God that he makes intercession for the saints. (Rom. 8:26–27)

The action of grace within the soul brings about an ontological change; the Kingdom begins to develop from within in such a powerful way that St. Augustine is able to proclaim: "You were more inward than the most inward place of my heart and loftier than the highest."[18] St. Augustine was essentially mirroring St Paul's words: "and yet I am alive; or rather, not I; it is Christ that lives in me" (Gal. 2:20). The reclaiming of God's Kingdom rests upon the notion that God wills to recreate humanity into a community of saints that are fully immersed in the life of the Spirit; for only through this same Spirit could disobedience be turned into obedience and error

---

17. Pope Benedict XVI explains: "God is the criterion of being. In this sense, truth is the real 'King' that confers light and greatness upon all things. We may also say that bearing witness to the truth means making creation intelligible and its truth accessible from God's perspective.... Let us say plainly: the unredeemed world consists precisely in the failure to understand the meaning of creation, in the failure to recognize truth; as a result, the rule of pragmatism is imposed, by which the strong arm of the powerful becomes the god of this world." Pope Benedict XVI, *Jesus of Nazareth, Holy Week: From the Entrance into Jerusalem to the Resurrection* (San Francisco: Ignatius Press, 2011), 193.

18. St. Augustine, *Confessions* (London: Sheed & Ward, 1948), 37.

be replaced by truth. The Kingdom of Christ therefore is the active participation in the divine life and one that extends to all spheres of life.

What then of the relationship between the Church and the Kingdom? As we have seen, the Kingdom of Christ *is* Christ on the one hand, due to the spiritual nature of his reign; for possessing Christ is to possess his Kingdom. But we can also say that the Kingdom of Christ is the Church. *Lumen Gentium* states:

> To carry out the will of the Father, Christ inaugurated the Kingdom of heaven on earth and revealed to us the mystery of that kingdom. By His obedience He brought about redemption. The Church, or, in other words, the kingdom of Christ now present in mystery, grows visibly through the power of God in the world.[19]

It is important to note that for many Fathers of the Church and theologians of the medieval period, there was precious little difference between the terms "Church" and "Kingdom." More recent times however have led to greater reflection in this area. From an eschatological perspective, the Church and the Kingdom are one and the same, but the nature of the Church within history, as opposed to the Kingdom that transcends time, is where we discover a subtle difference. The Church is not an end unto itself; it exists to spread the good news of the Kingdom, to proclaim the Lord's year of favor. We could say that the Church is the visible presence of the Kingdom of Christ in the world.

Within this framework, there is obvious tension between the temporal and eternal realities which concern the pilgrim Church. We know from the Second Vatican Council's documents that the faithful are called to transform society by looking after the poor and the widow, by practicing justice and mercy—all beautiful virtues that prepare us for the glory of heaven for which we yearn.[20] In practicing the faith in this way, the Church remains firmly rooted in a historical context, it fulfils the mandate given by Jesus prior to his ascension into heaven, and professes its faith by giving witness to

---

19. *Lumen Gentium*, 3, www.vatican.va.
20. *Lumen Gentium*, 35 and *Gaudium et Spes*, 27, www.vatican.va.

the truth. Essentially, the outward signs are proof of the inward existence of the mystery of the Kingdom. On the other hand, the Church cannot but look towards the eschatological realities of life with its Lord and King; even as it traverses the sea of history, it must always cling to the words of the Savior: "In the world, you will only find tribulation; but take courage, I have overcome the world" (Jn. 16:33). For just as Christianity would be dead without the Resurrection, so too would the Church, without the hope of final salvation.

It is in this hope that the pilgrim Church, the Kingdom of Christ and the Kingdom of God finally converge as one, unified and triumphant realm of glory. Although we will look deeper into this great mystery in Part III concerning the Church Triumphant, suffice it to say that the goal of the Church and Christ Jesus is to bring to completion the consummation of the world and the final overthrow of Satan. Even if the devil has been defeated definitively through the Passion, Death and Resurrection of the Lord, his evil influence continues to wreak havoc and destruction on a universal scale. He continues to espouse a false freedom that promotes an inward, selfish autonomy that is happy to trample on the poor and the weak. It is the complete antithesis of the communion of saints and the unity of love in the Kingdom of God.

"Today, salvation has been brought to this house" (Lk. 19:9). With these words we understand that we live within that "today." It is the day of the Church, the time of preparation for the moment when Jesus will hand over the Kingdom to his Father:

> [J]ust as all have died with Adam, so with Christ all will be brought to life. But each must rise in his own rank; Christ is the first-fruits, and after him follow those who belong to him, those who have put their trust in his return. Full completion comes after that, when he places his kingship in the hands of God, his Father, having first dispossessed every other sort of rule, authority, and power; his reign, as we know, must continue until he has put all his enemies under his feet, and the last of those enemies to be dispossessed is death. God has put all things in subjection under his feet; that is, all things have been made subject to him, except indeed that power which made them his subjects. And when that subjection is complete, then the Son himself will become subject

to the power which made all things his subjects, so that God may
be all in all. (1 Cor. 15:22–28)

There can be no greater incentive to be part of this glorious future
than to see the Church, the Kingdom of Christ, as our home. It is
the safe harbor in this time of great spiritual storms. It is the refuge
from despair and the dominance of sin in our lives. The Church is
the home for everyone without exception, and even though the
crosses of daily life are at times extremely heavy, we are never asked
to carry them alone. That the Lord is there, not only alongside us
but within us, is of course without question; but he has willed that
the communion of saints be a creative force within salvation history, sustaining us with prayer and charity. If the world could accept
this premise, then the Kingdom of Christ would begin to illuminate
even the darkest caverns of human existence.

ᔧ 3 ᔤ

The Maternal Gift of God

While he was still speaking to the multitude, it chanced that his mother and his brethren were standing without, desiring speech with him. And someone told him, Here are thy mother and thy brethren standing without, looking for thee. But he made answer to the man that brought him the news, Who is a mother, who are brethren, to me? Then he stretched out his hand towards his disciples, and said, Here are my mother and my brethren! If anyone does the will of my Father who is in heaven, he is my brother, and sister, and mother.

(Matt. 12:46–50)

OUR DELIBERATIONS thus far have led us to ascertain that the Church is a family: a living, breathing entity that thrives on love of God and neighbor. Love is the fuel that increases holiness in its members and leads the Church Militant to resemble more closely the divine perfection of its Lord and Savior. But what makes this a family? Can it be said that a community made up of 1.2 billion members really constitutes a family? Doesn't a family need a father *and* mother to exist in the first place?

In this chapter we will reflect on the mysterious but beautiful relationship between the Church as Mother, and the Mother of the Church—Blessed Mary ever Virgin. In seeking to grasp the essence of this mystery we will perhaps gain a greater understanding of the perfect nature of the Church as Christ's bride, and why the weak human element of the visible Church is in constant need of a maternal presence. If God has deigned to grant his children two spiritual mothers, then we must reflect on the reasons why, and its implications for our spiritual growth.

The Perfect Marriage

The great early Church Father Saint Cyprian tells us: "He can no longer have God for his Father, who has not the Church for his mother."[1] In proclaiming this message, St. Cyprian emphasizes the profound familial nature of the Church. It exists under the loving care of a Father and Mother. If the children of the Covenant are to be reborn in the Spirit then consequently there is need for a Mother to give birth to them.

In what sense therefore can we refer to the Church as Mother? If the so called "domestic Church," the individual family unit, exists to bring to fruition God's command: "Increase and multiply" (Gen. 1:28), and therefore generates children to partake in the rich tapestry of creation, the Church exists to elevate these same children from a natural to a supernatural order of grace, and just as the natural family needs a mother, so too does the supernatural family. We cannot move beyond this theological supposition without acknowledging that the Father and Mother are somehow betrothed to one another. Everything rests on their absolute faithfulness to one another. The Old Testament portrays the actions of God as One who desires to take Israel as his Bride; he seeks her faithfulness and reciprocal love.[2]

---

1. St. Cyprian of Carthage, Treatise 1, "On the Unity of the Church," www.new advent.org.

2. Pope Benedict XVI explains how God manifests the two different types of love in his search for matrimony with his people Israel. It is a quite startling teaching that reveals the burning furnace of love that dwells within the Triune God, a love that cannot be contained within: "The term agape, which appears many times in the New Testament, indicates the self-giving love of one who looks exclusively for the good of the other. The word eros, on the other hand, *denotes the love of one who desires to possess what he or she lacks and yearns for union with the beloved.* The love with which God surrounds us is undoubtedly agape.... *But God's love is also eros.* In the Old Testament, the Creator of the universe manifests toward the people whom he has chosen as his own a predilection that transcends every human motivation. The prophet Hosea expresses this divine passion with daring images such as the love of a man for an adulterous woman (cf. 3:1–3). For his part, Ezekiel, speaking of God's relationship with the people of Israel, is not afraid to use strong and passionate language (cf. 16:1–22). These biblical texts indicate that eros is part of God's very Heart: *the Almighty awaits the 'yes' of his creatures as a young bridegroom that of his bride.*" Pope Benedict XVI, "Message for Lent 2007," November 21, 2007, www.vatican.va.

The Prophet Isaiah tells us of this truth in these terms: "Husband now thou hast, and the name of him is the Lord of hosts, thy creator; he, the Holy One of Israel, that will now be called God of the whole earth, makes thee his own" (Is. 54:5). Even confronted by the adulterous nature of Israel, the folly of God is such that love impels Him to forgive; to stretch out his arm and offer once again his hand in marriage. Of course, as we have discovered thus far, the Israel of the Old Testament could not be faithful, therefore the true betrothal could only take place once the Passover of the Lord had been accomplished. The Gospels clearly portray Jesus as the Bridegroom, the Father of this community of faith.[3] St. John the Baptist had referred to himself as the "bridegroom's friend" (Jn. 3:29); the "best man," who rejoiced at hearing the voice of the bridegroom, while Jesus, in response to a question as to why John's disciples fasted but his did not, replied decisively:

> Can you expect the men of the bridegroom's company to go fasting, while the bridegroom is still with them? As long as they have the bridegroom with them, they cannot be expected to fast; but the days will come when the bridegroom is taken away from them; then they will fast, when that day comes. (Mk. 2:19–20)

In these texts, we see that Jesus desires to place himself firmly within the tradition of the Old Testament prophecies and that the entire span of salvation history is nothing more than a love story between God and his people, a quest for marriage.

From the moment of Adam's fall in Eden, a process begins in which all are invited to participate in the communion of saints. God does not brood over the rejection of His love, but instead, immediately almost "betrays" the *eros* that dwells within his Godhead. Many of us, even if we eventually forgive a betrayal or offense—even the tiniest, cannot let go of the opportunity to scowl, to rub salt into the wound, until we have "benefited" from exacting a little vengeance. For God, that is not the case. In the moment of

---

3. We may recall that Isaiah refers to Jesus as "Father of the world to come" (Is. 9:6).

the greatest possible betrayal there is no sense of retribution for punishment's sake; on the contrary, the path is opened to future union again, albeit with the necessity of suffering—as a mysterious consequence of rejecting God's divine protection.

The parables of Jesus are a noteworthy addition to the evidence that nothing less than a wedded union between Christ and his Church is at the center of God's will and the salvific plan. The parable of the Wedding Feast (Matt. 22:1–14) tells us how God turned to the pagans after Israel had rejected his invitation to the wedding banquet. It is important to note how God sent his servants to find good *and* bad alike: "You must go out to the street-corners, and invite all whom you find there to the wedding" (v.9). The lesson is that the Kingdom is not there for those who considered themselves perfect—as the Pharisees would have presumed—but for the sinner, tax collector and prostitute. All are invited without exception. We are told that the wedding hall was filled with guests (v.10). Is this not an image of the gathering of the communion of saints within the royal palace of the King and Bridegroom? The parable takes us a step further when a guest is discovered not wearing a wedding garment (v.11). In his apparently extreme treatment in being removed from the wedding hall and bound hand and foot, we are reminded that certain conditions need to be met if we are to be admitted to this eternal feast. Conversion and a life of grace are the garments more resplendent than those of Solomon. Conversely, the fate of the guest provides us with the sobering prospect that there is no other proposal on offer, no other option other than the dark bitterness of a self-inflicted loneliness that deliberately rejects communion. If that were not the case, then the guest would have been free to leave unbound, able to search for another feast.

The second parable recounted in St. Matthew's Gospel is that of the ten bridesmaids. Again the betrothal of the Lord to his people is at the heart of the story, although it is laced with an eschatological significance. Five bridesmaids were foolish and did not have enough oil for their lamps for the moment when the Bridegroom arrived. The essence of the parable is that the Christian life must be one of constant vigilance while awaiting the definitive moment when the marriage will reach the perfection of love in the Kingdom of God.

Even though the love of the Bridegroom is perfect, the Church Militant and suffering cannot yet offer that perfect love in return. But the patience of Jesus allows *agape* to grow through the power of the Holy Spirit until the "Yes" of the Bride imitates perfectly the "Yes" of the Bridegroom. Although there are other passages within Sacred Scripture that reinforce the theology of a marriage between God and His Church,[4] for our purposes we now have the foundations in place to look at the spiritual maternity of the Church and Mary its Mother.

As the nascent Christian community began to reflect more deeply on the matrimonial relationship between Christ and his Bride, the natural theological development was to see the maternal instincts of the Church as an extension of the paternal instincts of the Father. The term "Mother Church" began to be used frequently in second- and third-century Patristic Literature. St. Augustine, Origen, Tertullian, St. Clement of Alexandria and St. Irenaeus among others all used the term to describe her essential disposition. For these great writers, the motherhood of the Church followed the same path as a natural mother; they bore their children from the womb, nourished them with food and drink, cared for them with a precious bond of love and educated them in preparation for future life. From the moment of baptism,[5] Mother Church's obligation

---

4. Although the Wedding of Cana is not directly related to the image of the betrothal of Jesus to his Church as we find in the parables, nevertheless the fact it was chosen by the Lord for his first miracle draws our attention to its significance. The "fullness of time" had arrived and Jesus, by working his grace within the context of a marriage, was proclaiming the arrival of the true Bridegroom. Everything about Cana is "new": The new marriage, the new wine, the new mediation of the Blessed Virgin. It is on a certain level giving fulfilment to the great prophetic Psalm 96: "Sing the Lord a new song; in the Lord's honour, let the whole earth make melody! Sing to the Lord, and bless his name; never cease to bear record of his power to save. Publish his glory among the heathen; his wonderful acts for all the world to hear" (Ps. 96:1–3).

5. The baptismal font itself was to find typological significance in the ecclesiology of St. Augustine: "Although even now before ye are born, ye have been conceived of His seed, as being on the eve of being brought forth in the font, the womb as it were of the Church" ("Sermo VI on the Lord's Prayer in the Gospel of St. Matthew," http://www.ccel.org/ccel/schaff/npnf106.vii.viii.html). Also in Sermo 216 we

would be to form her children into the image and likeness of Christ the Lord—even if that would need to include not only the *positive* elements of sacramental nourishment and the study of *lectio divina*, but also the necessary *negative* element of correction from error. We are all aware that the spoiled child is the one who is pandered to by their parents, who lacks discipline and an awareness of the needs of others; for the spiritual life, with eternity at stake, we can better understand the need for a strong Mother who ensures that her brood do not follow this path, but rather embrace the virtues that lead to sanctification.

At this point, let us look at several examples from the Fathers that will serve to illustrate this discussion. St. Cyril of Jerusalem, in advice to his catechumens, or baptismal candidates, writes:

> And if ever thou art sojourning in any city, inquire not simply where the Lord's House is (for the sects of the profane also make an attempt to call their own dens houses of the Lord), nor merely where the Church is, but where is the Catholic Church. For this is the peculiar name of this Holy Body, the mother of us all, which is the spouse of our Lord Jesus Christ, the Only-begotten Son of God (for it is written, As Christ also loved the Church and gave Himself for it [Eph. 5:25, and all the rest]) and is a figure and copy of Jerusalem above, which is free, and the mother of us all (Gal. 4:26); which before was barren, but now has many children.[6]

St. Clement of Alexandria in his *Paedagogus* c.198, displays great wisdom and insight concerning the mystery of how the Church is at

---

read: "Ecce uterus matris Ecclesiae, ecce ut te pariat, atque in lucem fidei producat, laborat in gemitu suo. Nolite vestra impatientia viscera materna concutere, et partus vestri ianuas angustare. Popule qui crearis, lauda Deum tuum: lauda, qui crearis, lauda Dominum tuum." (Behold the womb of our mother the Church; Behold how she gives you birth, brings you forth into the light of faith, and groans in her labor pains. Do not disturb your mother's womb with your impatience and restrict the entrance of your birth. You people who are begotten, praise your God: praise, you who are begotten, praise your Lord.) http://www.augustinus.it/latino/discorsi/discorso_273_testo.htm.

6. St. Cyril of Jerusalem, *The Catechetical Lectures of St. Cyril, Archbishop of Jerusalem* (Oxford: John Henry Parker, 1839), 252.

once Virgin *and* Mother, proclaiming her ability to provide spiritual "milk" to her children:

> O mystic marvel! The universal Father is one, and one the universal Word; and the Holy Spirit is one and the same everywhere, and one is the only virgin mother. I love to call her the Church. This mother, when alone, had not milk, because alone she was not a woman. But she is once virgin and mother—pure as a virgin, loving as a mother. And calling her children to her, she nurses them with holy milk, viz., with the Word for childhood. Therefore she had not milk; for the milk was this child fair and comely, the body of Christ, which nourishes by the Word the young brood, which the Lord Himself brought forth in throes of the flesh, which the Lord Himself swathed in His precious blood.[7]

Tertullian also employed the image of a "nursing" mother in his *Ad Martyras*, addressed to those facing the ultimate test of faith:

> Blessed Martyrs Designate,—Along with the provision which our lady mother the Church from her bountiful breasts, and each brother out of his private means, makes for your bodily wants in the prison, accept also from me some contribution to your spiritual sustenance.[8]

So we discover that the image of the Church as Mother was one that was loved by the early Christian writers. In a sense, we can understand the image as emerging out of the newness of Christianity. The first converts were like babies: they didn't possess the plethora of Christian literature that we have the luxury of benefitting from, or the biblical exegesis that would give a profound interpretation to Sacred Scripture. For the Fathers like St. Augustine, this vision of the Church would reveal the true essence of the Mystical Body of Christ: the Mother who teaches, feeds and suffers when her children rebel and seek to destroy the communion of the Church. If the Church was truly a mother, then she would take to heart every aspect of the lives of her children, and from that point of view, the early Christians could feel the paternal charity of the Father mani-

7. St. Clement of Alexandria, *The Paedagogus,* bk. 1, ch. 6, www.newadvent.org.
8. Tertullian, *Ad Martyras,* ch. 1, www.newadvent.org.

fested in the maternal presence of the Mother: "gentle to some, severe to others; to none an enemy, to all a mother."[9]

A Mother Teaches Her Children

A question arises from this beautiful image: does the maternity and virginity of the church only relate to the divine Institution itself or does it encompass the faithful at a grass roots level? The answer to this question is directly related to the dogma of the communion of saints and the necessity of participating in the threefold mission of Christ: Priest, Prophet and King. Through baptism, the gift of faith is freely given; not something to hide away, but to be passed on like a torch bearer. The path to holiness presupposes that the promises made at the font are kept and constantly renewed. If the soul is receptive to the promptings of the Holy Spirit, then the maternal nature of the Church is able to grow through the individual by displaying the same charity and mercy that exemplifies the role of a mother. In fact, what we are really saying is that Jesus is born anew in every heart that embraces the maternal element, and just like the Church, he wishes to reveal the Christ to those in darkness. If Jesus is "born" in the heart of the Christian, then the Christian truly replicates the Church as Mother. Not only that, he becomes almost the Church in miniature, what Origen called the *anima ecclesiastica*.[10] St. Peter Damien explains thus:

> The cohesive force of mutual charity by which the Church is united is so great that she is not merely one in her many members but also, in some mysterious way, present in her entirety in each individual. So true is this that we rightly consider the Church as the unique Spouse of Christ and yet rightly believe that through this Sacramental mystery the Church is fully present in each individual.[11]

9. St. Augustine, *On the Catechising of the Uninstructed*, ch. 15, 23, www.newadvent.org.

10. Cf. Origen, "Homilies on the Song of Songs" (1:10).

11. St. Peter Damien, *Dominus Vobiscum*, ch. 5, cited in: Henri de Lubac, *Catholicism* (London: Burns & Oates, 1962), 288–289.

Through this evolution of faith, the communion of saints becomes energized through the gradual maturation of each member so that the faithful on earth begin to advance towards the holiness of those in heaven—and indeed this is most wonderfully discovered in the lives of the canonized saints who are true icons of the *Ecclesia Mater.* If we return to the Gospels, we discover a passage that illustrates perfectly what we have been reflecting upon. St. Matthew tells us:

> While he was still speaking to the multitude, it chanced that his mother and his brethren were standing without, desiring speech with him. And someone told him, Here are thy mother and thy brethren standing without, looking for thee. But he made answer to the man that brought him the news, Who is a mother, who are brethren, to me? Then he stretched out his hand towards his disciples, and said, Here are my mother and my brethren! If anyone does the will of my Father who is in heaven, he is my brother, and sister, and mother. (Matt. 12:46–50)

Some have seen in these words of Jesus a kind of rebuke to his Mother. But that is not the case. In fact the Lord wishes to broaden the understanding of his listeners to explain the new relationship that he has come to make possible. The communion of saints that Jesus desires to gather round him is not dependant on family ties but rather on adherence to the divine will. It is a brief sketch of the "school of holiness" that found greater expression in the Beatitudes.[12] This is the new family of which the Church is Mother and the individual is Mother. We also discover in the words of Jesus his intent to question those around him about how they view one another. By asking "Who is my brother?" he indirectly sows the question in the heart of those around him in much the same way as he did with the parable of the Good Samaritan. In the Kingdom of God there is no room for cliques or arbitrary choices where God's children are concerned; we are all children of the Eternal Father and all required to dismantle the barriers that separate us from loving one another.

12. Matt. 5:3–12.

But what of virginity? In what sense do we understand the term as relating to the Church? Can it be possible to speak of the Church in such terms while acknowledging the filthy stains of sin that afflict even the hierarchy? In order to answer these questions convincingly, we must delineate the two specific elements that make up the Church. In the previous chapter, we reflected upon the truth that the Church is a divine institution, pure and perfect in its continuation of the work of the Lord Jesus. It cannot be anything other because it was born from the pierced side of the Savior and exists because it is the one means of salvation. In that sense it must be described as indefectible. Pope Pius XII teaches us:

> Certainly the loving Mother is spotless in the Sacraments by which she gives birth to and nourishes her children; in the faith which she has always preserved inviolate; in her sacred laws imposed on all; in the evangelical counsels which she recommends; in those heavenly gifts and extraordinary grace through which with inexhaustible fecundity, she generates hosts of martyrs, virgins and confessors.[13]

However, the Pope makes clear the reality of sin that pervades all its members on earth:

> And if at times there appears in the Church something that indicates the weakness of our human nature, it should not be attributed to her juridical constitution, but rather to that regrettable inclination to evil found in each individual, which its Divine Founder permits even at times in the most exalted members of His Mystical Body, for the purpose of testing the virtue of the Shepherds no less than of the flocks, and that all may increase the merit of their Christian faith.[14]

In order to gain a greater understanding of this paradox we can turn to the great Milanese bishop, St. Ambrose. In his writings we find a unique and curious phrase that describes his ecclesiology: *Casta Meretrix*—"The Chaste Whore." This somewhat startling

---

13. Pope Pius XII, *Mystici Corporis Christi*, 66, June 29, 1943, www.vatican.va.
14. Ibid.

expression traces its Ambrosian roots back to the story of Rahab[15] found in the Book of Joshua. A brief outline of the story will suffice for contextual purposes. Joshua had sent two spies to reconnoitre the land of Jericho. They lodged in a house belonging to Rahab, a prostitute. The King of Jericho was informed that two Israelite spies had stayed there and ordered Rahab to bring them out. Rahab, while insisting they had left, had actually hidden them on the roof. Later she approached the two men and asked them to spare her and her family, knowing that Israel would soon destroy the entire city. They agreed: "Keep our secret, said they, and our lives shall answer for yours. When the Lord makes us masters of thy country, we will remember and spare" (Josh. 2:14). They told her to hang a scarlet cord from her window (the same one they would use to escape) so that when the army besieged the city, they would know to spare Rahab's house. This all came to pass and Rahab and her entire family were spared by Joshua. From that day they dwelt in the company of Israel (cf. Josh. 6:25).

For St. Ambrose, Rahab is a type of the Church, a prophetic figure that unites the gentile world with that of Israel:

> Rahab—who as a *type* was a prostitute, but as a *mystery* is the Church—showed in her blood, the future sign of Universal Salvation amid the world's carnage; she does not refuse to unite herself with numerous fugitives, and is all the more chaste in the extent to which she is closely joined to the greater number of them; she is the immaculate virgin, without a wrinkle, uncontaminated in her modesty, plebeian in her love, a chaste whore, a barren widow, a fecund virgin.[16]

15. The Church came to realize very quickly the symbolism attached to Rahab. St. Matthew saw fit to place her in the genealogy of Jesus along with only three other women (Tamar, Ruth and Bathsheba), while her virtues are praised in the Letter to the Hebrews and the Letter of St. James. Various Patristic theologians also explored her significance, among them St. Clement of Rome, St. Cyprian, Origen, St. Justin and St. Irenaeus.

16. St. Ambrose, *Expositio evangelii secundum Lucam*, 3:23, cited in Cardinal Giacomo Biffi, *Casta Maretrix: An Essay on the Ecclesiology of St. Ambrose* (London: The Saint Austin Press, 2000), 19.

Although this quote could almost seem to create misunderstandings, the essential point that Ambrose stresses concerns Rahab's openness to the truth that God resides in the chosen people of Israel. Therefore, she welcomes them into her home; in fact she *saves* them; she acts like a prototype of the Church. She, a gentile, creates the opportunity for the process of salvation history to move forward through a good and courageous act. The "plebeian" love of the Church is such that prostitutes and the gravest sinners are called to participate in God's saving love just as much as anyone else. Rahab also prophetically reveals the three theological virtues of the Church: faith, hope and charity: faith that she would be spared from the destruction of Jericho (cf. Heb. 11:31), hope that a new beginning would emerge for her family through the blessing of God's servant, Joshua, and charity through her protection of the two spies.

Through the story of Rahab, Ambrose goes on to explain the virginity of the Church in these terms: "The Church is a fecund virgin because she has given birth to the multitude, as the fruit of her love; not, however, through the intervention of concupiscence."[17] Along these lines, we can also see the symbolism of the scarlet cord that saves both the men and Rahab the prostitute. It is like the umbilical cord through which the precious blood of Christ gives eternal life to all. Both Israel and the gentile Church benefit from it.

The term *Casta Meretrix* exemplifies the seemingly contradictory truth of the Church. But therein lies the grandeur and mystery of God. The Church is chaste and yet is home to a multitude of sinners. Her virginity derives from the absolute faithfulness to her Lord and Bridegroom. If she is "*meretrix*," symbolically, Ambrose is stressing she is the mother of all without exception. She will go into the slums and the peripheries of the world to search out and find those who can be regenerated in her womb. Her great desire is to pass onto her children the virginity of soul that she herself possesses, that she may present them to the Lord with "no stain, no wrinkle, no such disfigurement . . . spotless" (Eph. 5:27). Now that we have explored the maternal nature of the Church as Mother, we

17. Ibid., 22.

can turn our attention to the Mother of the Church: our Mother, the mirror image of the Church in its perfection.

Mary the Maternal Masterpiece

In the Book of Revelation, chapter 12, we are presented with a vision that serves as a substantial biblical foundation for our contemplation of the Mother of all saints. We read:

> And now, in heaven, a great portent appeared; a woman that wore the sun for her mantle, with the moon under her feet, and a crown of twelve stars about her head. She had a child in her womb, and was crying out as she travailed, in great pain of her delivery. Then a second portent appeared in heaven; a great dragon was there, fiery-red, with seven heads and ten horns, and on each of the seven heads a royal diadem; his tail dragged down a third part of the stars in heaven, and flung them to earth. And he stood fronting the woman who was in childbirth, ready to swallow up the child as soon as she bore it. She bore a son, the son who is to herd the nations like sheep with a crook of iron; and this child of hers was caught up to God, right up to his throne, while the mother fled into the wilderness, where God had prepared a place of refuge for her, and there, for twelve hundred and sixty days, she is to be kept safe . . . the great dragon, serpent of the primal age, was flung down to earth; he whom we call the devil, or Satan, the whole world's seducer, flung down to earth, and his angels with him. . . . So the dragon, finding himself cast down to earth, went in pursuit of the woman, the boy's mother; but the woman was given two wings, such as the great eagle has, to speed her flight into the wilderness, to her place of refuge, where for a year, and two years, and half a year she will be kept hidden from the serpent's view. Thereupon the serpent sent a flood of water out of his mouth in pursuit of the woman, to carry her away on its tide; but earth came to the woman's rescue. The earth gaped wide, and swallowed up this flood which the dragon had sent out of his mouth. So, in his spite against the woman, the dragon went elsewhere to make war on the rest of her children, the men who keep God's commandments, and hold fast to the truth concerning Jesus. (Rev. 12:1–6, 9, 13–17)

One of the reasons why this passage is appropriate at this point is that it relates both to the Church as Mother and the Blessed Virgin herself. Tradition and the Magisterium have both clearly taught this interpretation. For the Church, clothed with the light of Christ, has faced the continual persecution of the Devil since its inception. It has sought refuge in the desert, close to the solitude of God, detached from the world of vice. As Mother, it continually gives birth to Christians; encouraging them even to the point of martyrdom.

Primarily though, we must see in the "Woman" the glorious figure of Mary. As we reflected earlier, we know that the Church is Mother because of her relationship to the Bridegroom. As Mary is the Mother of Jesus, and he the Bridegroom, logic tells us that Mary must also be Mother of the Church. In Revelation 12 we are told that the child she gave birth to was taken immediately up to God, thus emphasizing the divine nature of the baby. The image of the Woman however, in mariological terms, also bears something of heavenly glory and royalty. Firstly, Mary appears as a sign in the sky, clothed with the Sun and wearing a crown. She is in the throes of childbirth. This clearly reminds us of the uniqueness of Mary's relationship to her Son—that she is "full of grace" as the Archangel Gabriel proclaimed (Lk. 1:28). Not only that: the pain of labor and delivery pertains to her sufferings at the foot of the Cross when she participated in an extraordinary way in the plan of redemption for her children. Mary is clothed with God's own divine light; her sinless state and total acceptance of God's will allow her to be bathed in this transfiguring brightness. Under her feet the moon resides, a symbol of mortality, which the Blessed Virgin has conquered with her Son. The crown signifies her maternity and queenship over the communion of saints, symbolically represented by the twelve stars. In essence we are shown the marvellous truth about Mary; she is both *Theotokos* (Mother of God) and *Mater Ecclesiae* (Mother of the Church). If the later passage from this text (concerning the woman who takes flight into the desert) relates more to the Church, we can still see the figure of Mary the mother who never leaves the Church abandoned but remains within it as a secure refuge from Satan; as the vision relates, she does not remain in the heavenly realm somewhat removed from our reality but is with her children in the midst of battle. It recalls the "Protoevangelium" from Genesis chapter 3 in which God announces that he will put enmity between the serpent and the woman.[18]

It is no coincidence that the maternal and salvific mystery of Mary spans our entire salvation history from Genesis to Revelation; for without her assent at the Annunciation, God's eternal plan would have never materialized. The Second Vatican Council document *Lumen Gentium* contains a beautiful eighth chapter in which the role of Mary is explored:

> Predestined from eternity by that decree of divine providence which determined the incarnation of the Word to be the Mother of God, the Blessed Virgin was on this earth the virgin Mother of the Redeemer, and above all others and in a singular way the generous associate and humble handmaid of the Lord.... This maternity of Mary in the order of grace began with the consent which she gave in faith at the Annunciation and which she sustained without wavering beneath the cross, and lasts until the eternal fulfillment of all the elect. Taken up to heaven she did not lay aside this salvific duty, but by her constant intercession continued to bring us the gifts of eternal salvation. By her maternal charity, she cares for the brethren of her Son, who still journey on earth surrounded by dangers and cultics, until they are led into the happiness of their true home.[19]

In order for us to meditate on this profound mystery, we must ascertain in what way Mary exercises her divine motherhood within the Church; to what extent does she mold her children into the com-

---

18. St. John Paul II sensed a dramatic intensity of this conflict as he explained to priests of the Pauline Fathers on June 19, 1983: "Our times are in need of this action [the growth of the order and their charism through the Holy Spirit], because they are times of great struggle. The late Cardinal Stefan Wyszynski, who was your spiritual brother, spoke often of it. Many times he said, using the Latin words: '*Non est nobis colluctatio adversus carnem et sanguinem, sed adversus principes . . . tenebrarum harum*' (Eph. 6:12). In the period of these great struggles, Mary is given to us as a sign. 'A woman clothed with the sun with the moon under her feet, and on her head a crown of twelve stars' (Rev. 12:1); thus says John in the Book of Revelation. In the period of this great struggle with the '*principes et potestates . . . tenebrarum harum*,' a powerful illumination is required, *more powerful than at any other time*, of the power of the Holy Spirit, through his most pure Spouse." www.vatican.va.

19. *Lumen Gentium*, 61, 62, www.vatican.va.

munion of saints? We can see a quite clear distinction between the motherhood of Mary and that of the Church; for with Mary it concerns a perhaps more personal and interior form which affects the individual soul in the ascent to holiness. This occurs unceasingly through the distribution of graces that is part of Mary's maternal mediation; for just as she formed the humanity of Jesus, so too does she form the humanity of the faithful. We can see evidence of this throughout the history of the Church: the great pilgrimages to Marian shrines, the regular apparitions pleading for penance and conversion (especially in recent centuries) and the increased expounding of Mariology in the papal magisterium. It is even correct to say that in the Church, the Marian principle takes precedence over the Petrine because in Mary we have the spotless Church, the pinnacle of mystical union with Jesus. On the other hand, the Petrine ministry exists to safeguard the faith and unity of the Church Militant that strives to imitate Mary's Fiat.

Even before the hierarchical structure was formulated, the Church existed in the Immaculate Heart of Mary; she was the first and most exquisite tabernacle for the Incarnate God. However, Mary didn't allow this divine love that consumed her soul to remain enclosed, but rather embraced the maternal role that God had carved out for her. This explains why she went in haste to visit Elizabeth; perhaps even in the earliest days of pregnancy the Holy Spirit began to awaken in her the spiritual maternity that would prove pivotal for the sanctification of countless souls throughout the centuries.[20]

Mother of the Interior Life: I am All Thine

If we return to Holy Scripture for a moment, three particular texts

---

20. Significantly, Elizabeth, through the inspiration of the Holy Spirit, almost anticipates the divine motherhood of Mary in its duality by proclaiming "Blessed art thou among women, and blessed is the fruit of thy womb. How have I deserved to be thus visited by the mother of my Lord?" (Lk. 1:42–43) Of even greater significance is that the unborn child, John, also perceived the Virgin Mother's arrival and leapt for joy upon hearing her voice. Is there not a lesson for us in this age of abortion on demand that an unborn baby was the first person to hail Mary's presence and by implication that of the divine child?

form a mariological thread that reveals the divine motherhood of Mary in relation to the Church. They are the Annunciation (Lk. 1:26–38), the words of Jesus upon the Cross: "Woman, this is thy Son" (Jn. 19:26), and the descent of the Holy Spirit at Pentecost (Acts. 2:1–4).

At the Annunciation, the Archangel Gabriel didn't at first use the name "Mary," but instead called her "full of grace"; emphasizing the fact that Mary is without sin, full of every spiritual blessing of God (cf. Eph. 1:3). The new title revealed to Mary her unique vocation that was conceived in the mind of God before creation even began. By responding to the divine messenger: "Behold, the handmaid of the Lord; let it be done unto me according to thy word," the Blessed Virgin was formally dissolving her own will into the divine will and allowing herself to become the chosen vessel, the active co-operator with her Son in our redemption. By accepting to become the Mother of God, she was saying yes to become Mother of his mystical body also.

Mary's perpetual virginity also needs to be explored briefly within this context. Why is it important? The idea of virginity for the sake of the Kingdom, declares the prophetic, God-given gift whereby the virgin, rather than rejecting sexual intimacy as something evil, voluntarily sacrifices it so as to be more conformed to the likeness of Christ, the chaste bridegroom. The *eros* is able to be transformed more freely into *agape* and thus becomes a beautiful sign of the Church in glory. In Mary, we have the supreme example of this fact; so perfect, that the Holy Spirit found her soul irresistible and the only possible dwelling for the Word incarnate. We could almost assume a silent "dialogue" of spirit must have occurred between the Eternal Father and his daughter in her childhood. Notwithstanding her astounding humility, Mary must have sensed she was somehow different from those around her, even as a young girl. Of course, we may state without hesitation that she would never have considered herself sinless until the Archangel Gabriel announced it to her, but all the same, something inspired her to consecrate her life to God with a vow of perpetual virginity. Therefore, the "dialogue" in a sense was God saying "you are my chosen daughter" and Mary responding "*Totus tuus*"—I am all thine!

So the Annunciation was the revelation to the Blessed Virgin of her spiritual maternity—one that will never cease, and one that was to be marked by anguish and pain. Suffering would never be far away; grief would torment her soul not only in the terrible sufferings of Jesus, but in the individual lives of her children torn asunder by sin. All this was prophetically announced to Mary by Simeon in the Temple: "as for thy own soul, it shall have a sword to pierce it" (Lk. 2:35). It seems certain that Our Lady already knew—at least to some extent—the road she had taken, but Simeon, informed by the Holy Spirit, confirmed it. It in a sense confirms her role as co-redemptrix: if the pierced heart of Jesus opens the path of salvation to all, then the pierced soul of Mary forms a union of redemptive suffering that weds the divine and human in cancelling original sin.[21] Christ is the new Adam, Mary the new Eve.

This naturally takes us to the second pertinent text: the Lord's maternal gift to the Church given in his final moments of agony. In St. John's Gospel we read: "And Jesus, seeing his mother there, and the disciple, too, whom he loved, standing by, said to his mother, Woman, this is thy son. Then he said to the disciple, this is thy mother. And from that hour the disciple took her into his own keeping" (Jn. 19:26–27). Our attention is immediately drawn to the Lord's use of the term "Woman." Why did Jesus refer to his Mother in this way? Was it not somewhat strange in the context of his imminent death? The answer is laden with rich mariological/ecclesiological significance. The reference to "Woman" takes us in two biblical directions spanning the beginning and end of history: Eve, the first woman and mother of all; and the Woman of Revelation chapter 12, the mother of redemption. What Jesus does upon the Cross is present to humanity, and more specifically the Church, the "new" woman, the new Eve. We must remember that it was not the first time he referred to her in that way. At the wedding at Cana

---

21. Pope Pius XI explains: "From the nature of his work the Redeemer ought to have associated his Mother with his work. For this reason we invoke her under the title of Co-Redemptrix. She gave us the Savior, she accompanied him in the work of the Redemption of mankind." Pope Pius XI, "Papal Allocution to Pilgrims of Vicenza," November 30, 1933, *L'Osservatore Romano*, Dec. 1, 1933.

when Mary said to Jesus "They have no wine left," Jesus replied: "Nay, woman, why dost thou trouble me with that? My time has not come yet" (Jn. 2:3–4). That episode anticipated the Sacrifice of Calvary, but interestingly, even at this first miracle, Jesus desired to assert immediately the prominence of this "woman," not as a peripheral figure but as central to the key events of God's plan. In asking the question: "woman, why dost thou trouble me with that?" Jesus implies the maternal mediation of Mary; in fact we can glean from Mary's own approach to Our Lord that she was already aware of this fact; it is hard to imagine that Mary did not understand the use of the term "woman" in reference to herself and to Eve. Suffice it to say, the incident at Cana, at the outset of Jesus's public ministry, reveals the *mediatrix of all graces*, the woman of regeneration who places herself between God and humanity and the bridge that allows Jesus to cross over to us, bringing forth salvation.

Returning to the scene at Calvary, the original Greek version of the text concerning the disciple taking Mary into his home gives us a rather deeper meaning than the English: *eis tà ìdia*—"took her unto his own," or "into his inner life." This suggests a far more powerful understanding of Jesus's words. If the "home" refers to a temporal shelter for Mary, then the "inner life" speaks of something directed far more at the apostle John—and by extension to every one of us. It is an invitation to accept the maternal mediation of the Mother of the Lord. If at Cana only the first traces of Mary's motherhood were revealed, at the foot of the Cross they blossom into that fullness willed by God. It is not by accident that the final act of Jesus before achieving our redemption was to bequeath his Mother to the disciples; it needs to be seen in the context of the imminent birth of the Church from the pierced side of the Lord. Mary is to be for the mystical body, both mother and prototype: the image of perfection and holiness, and as the dispenser of graces, a necessary help for those seeking the true path.[22] Far from a shelter being prepared

---

22. St. Pius X explains: "It cannot, of course, be denied that the dispensation of these treasures is the particular and peculiar right of Jesus Christ, for they are the exclusive fruit of His Death, who by His nature is the mediator between God and man. Nevertheless, by this companionship in sorrow and suffering already men-

for Mary, her divine Son ensures that it is the community of aspiring saints that is blessed by *her* refuge.

In the bitter sufferings of Calvary, Simeon's prophecy comes full circle: The piercing of Mary's Immaculate Heart and mystical crucifixion, coupled with the renunciation of maternal rights over her Son[23] lead to a new form of spiritual maternity where the "thoughts of many hearts shall be made manifest" (Lk. 2:35).[24] It could be said that these thoughts relate to Mary's victory over the influence of Satan in souls; for as Eve welcomed the evil one by desiring to become like God, Mary saw herself as the *handmaid* of the Lord and therefore restored (through her *Fiat*) the original equilibrium between God and man.

Her new expression of motherhood would allow her to mold the children of God into saints who worship in spirit and truth. In the First Letter to the Corinthians, we find a similar expression to that of Simeon which seems to add weight to this interpretation: "Whereas, if some unbeliever or some uninstructed person comes in when all alike are prophesying, everyone will read his thoughts, everyone will scrutinize him, all that is kept hidden in his heart will

tioned between the Mother and the Son, it has been allowed to the august Virgin to be the most powerful mediatrix and advocate of the whole world with her Divine Son.... Mary, as St. Bernard justly remarks, is the channel (Serm. de temp on the Nativ. B.V. De Aquaeductu n. 4); or, if you will, the connecting portion the function of which is to join the body to the head and to transmit to the body the influences and volitions of the head—we mean the neck. Yes, says St. Bernardine of Sienna, 'she is the neck of Our Head, by which He communicates to His mystical body all spiritual gifts' (Quadrag. de Evangel. aetern. Serm. x., a. 3, c. iii.)." Pope Pius X, Encyclical Letter *Ad diem illum Laetissimum*, February 2, 1904, www.vatican.va.

23. Pope Benedict XV affirms: "She gave up her Mother's rights over her Son to procure the salvation of mankind, and to appease the divine justice, she, as much as she could, immolated her Son, so that one can truly affirm that together with Christ she has redeemed the human race." Benedict XV, *Inter Sodalicia*, March 22, 1918, *Acta Apostolicae Sedis* 10, 1918, 182.

24. The *Catena Aurea* of St. Thomas Aquinas contains various interpretations from the Fathers for this intriguing text. Gregory of Nyssa suggests that through the events of the Passion and Resurrection, man's evil intentions should be corrected "for doubts are quickly superseded by certainty." St. Thomas Aquinas, *Catena Aurea Vol. 3: St Luke* (Southampton: The Saint Austin Press, 1997), 91.

be revealed; and so he will fall on his face and worship God, publicly confessing that God is indeed among you" (1 Cor. 14:24–25). In Mary, we marvel at the faithful prophetess who bears witness to Jesus through a singular grace-filled life; in her sufferings we are confronted by the reality of what our desire to become "like God" has done. In her divine motherhood, we are taught at the school of faith, hope and charity. "Secret thoughts" are changed from darkness to light.

The third text of this mariological thread takes us to the scene in the upper room awaiting the descent of the Holy Spirit at Pentecost:

> Coming in, they went up into the upper room where they dwelt, Peter and John, James and Andrew, Philip and Thomas, Bartholomew and Matthew, James the son of Alphaeus and Simon the Zealot, and Judas the brother of James. All these, with one mind, gave themselves up to prayer, together with Mary the mother of Jesus, and the rest of the women and his brethren. (Acts 1:13–14)

Again, as at the Annunciation, the key figures altering the course of history are the Holy Spirit, and his Spouse, the Blessed Virgin. It is in this arena—the cenacle of Jerusalem—that we find the maternal mediation of Mary imploring the coming of the Paraclete upon the Apostles and the new-born Church. We could say that here the two motherhoods converge; Mary becomes the visible and unparalleled maternal icon of the *Ecclesia Mater*. The Apostles are in a certain sense led by Mary's faith and prayer, undoubtedly a source of hope and comfort in the confusing days after the Passion, Resurrection and Ascension. In Mary, they still see the indescribable light of Jesus active and resplendent. It would surely not have gone unnoticed to them that she lived a profoundly mystical life pervaded by the continuous presence of God, and perhaps they sensed that in the days before Pentecost the Blessed Virgin was entering a sort of second "annunciation" in preparation for the birth of the Church. The stark contrast between their fear and her calm would have also left an indelible mark on them; it would be a decisive lesson for the future: in a deep union with God, prayer destroys fear.

One of the most striking elements of the New Testament is that Mary is rarely heard. Perhaps it was to ensure that the focus remained fully on the Incarnate Word and his mission, until such time as the Church could reflect theologically on this "new Woman" without the danger of a distorted view taking precedence over reality. However, the silence does tell us something of Mary and her extraordinary relationship with the Holy Spirit. It speaks of an inner recollection whereby her spirit was in constant harmony with the Divine Spirit, never discordant but always beautiful. However, we shouldn't assume Mary was a sort of forerunner of an enclosed nun; she was active in the commotion of daily life as we discover from the Gospels. Her life was undoubtedly one of real simplicity: holiness rooted in the commandments, far removed from the fake humility of the Pharisees. No, for Mary, silence meant pondering all these mysterious events (cf. Lk. 2:19) with the wisdom and knowledge given her by her Spouse. Her heart was always open and thus she was able to navigate the joys and sufferings within the perspective of the divine will.

Mary, Spouse of the Holy Spirit

At this point, it is beneficial to peruse the mariological teachings of the great Marian apostle, St. Maximilian Kolbe. He meditated at length on the relationship between the Blessed Virgin and the Holy Spirit, seeking to discover the extent to which Mary mirrors His divine holiness. In the context of the communion of saints, this will help us gain a greater appreciation of why Mary is the Queen of Saints, the pre-eminent member of this family and the "cause of our joy."[25] St. Maximilian's radical Mariology is rooted in the idea that in all creation there is a similitude to God the creator:

> Everything that exists, outside of God himself, since it is from God and depends upon him in every way, bears within itself some semblance to its Creator . . . because every created thing is an effect of the Primal Cause. . . . Would not "conception" be an exception to this rule? No, there is never any exception.[26]

This question and answer is quite astounding; the implication is

25. Cf. *Litany of Our Lady.*
26. H.M. Manteau-Bonamy, O.P., *Immaculate Conception and the Holy Spirit* (Kenosha: Prow Books/Franciscan Marytown Press, 1977), 2–3.

that a former "conception" must have taken place before creation existed; but where and to whom? St. Maximilian explains:

> And who is the Holy Spirit? The flowering of the love of the Father and the Son. If the fruit of created love is a created conception, then the fruit of divine Love, that prototype of all created love, is necessarily a divine "conception." The Holy Spirit is, therefore, the "uncreated, eternal conception," the prototype of all the conceptions that multiply life throughout the whole universe.[27]

The Polish saint was greatly influenced by the title "Immaculate Conception." He pondered the fact that the Immaculate Conception was not simply a process but rather a person; for Mary had said to St. Bernadette in Lourdes "I am the Immaculate Conception." Her nature was therefore Immaculate, a pure vessel for all the virtues. The Holy Spirit, we can presume, in his eternal thought, saw the creation of Mary's soul as resembling his own "eternal conception" and rejoiced at the day he would set her soul ablaze with his own love (that of the Father and Son). If we understand humanity as the pinnacle of God's creation, then we can view the Spirit's descent at the beginning of time as a foreshadowing of the moment of Mary's Conception; for with that miraculous event, the new creation entered into time.

St. Maximilian takes us a step further into their holy intimacy. He actually finds the term "spouse" inadequate to describe the bond of love:

> The Third Person of the Blessed Trinity never took flesh; still our human word 'spouse' is far too weak to express the reality of the relationship between the Immaculata and the Holy Spirit. We can affirm that she is, in a certain sense, the incarnation of the Holy Spirit.[28]

We need to state categorically that the Saint is not suggesting Mary is the Holy Spirit in human form; on the contrary, he desires to stress the unique relationship that allows Mary to be the mediatrix of grace, and all through the benevolence of the Holy Spirit. He also

27. Ibid., 3.
28. Ibid., 50.

makes reference to the Holy Spirit as "*quasi-incarnatus*" but clarifies exactly what he means:

> The Holy Spirit is in the Immaculate as the Second Person of the Most Holy Trinity is in Jesus, but with this difference: There are in Jesus two natures, the divine and human, and one sole person, the divine. The nature and person of the Immaculate are distinct from the nature and person of the Holy Spirit.[29]

For St. Maximilian Kolbe, the holiness of Mary stems from a rapturous love that fills every fibre of her being. It has dwelt within her from the moment of conception and will forever remain so. Because of this inner divine influence, the fruitfulness of the Holy Spirit is manifest through her actions: Mary becomes his agent within the communion of saints, using all the sanctifying tools at her disposal, and all in perfect conformity to the divine will. In union with St. Louis de Montfort, St. Maximilian understood Mary's role as pivotal until the end of time; he saw the spread of devotion to her Immaculate Heart as the surest means of reinvigorating evangelization, and ultimately crushing the serpent's head.

Relating this intense Mariology to the communion of saints, we cannot fail to see that Mary sits in an exalted position at the right hand of her Son. For every member of the Mystical Body she is both Mother and heroine; the embodiment of perfect sanctity and the quickest way to finding Jesus.[30] The entire communion of Saints benefits from Mary's spiritual motherhood precisely because of her salvific influence in each individual. She is not like the class teacher who knows only half the students' names. Rather, all are known to her intimately. If all souls have been bought and paid for (cf. 1 Cor. 6:20) then along with Jesus, Mary owns a "share," an "investment" that she desires to see matured in eternity. This very personal and interior aspect of Mary's spiritual motherhood is one of the main reasons why many Catholics have such love and devotion to her. Accepting to be a child of Mary is to enter more profoundly into the

---

29. Br. Francis M Kalvelage, *Kolbe: Saint of the Immaculata* (San Francisco: Ignatius Press, 2002), 113.

30. *See* St. John Paul II's "Homily at Fatima," May 13, 2000, www.vatican.va.

of Father, Son and Holy Spirit *and* praising the magnificent plan of God who desired to send a new Eve into the world, one who would not only reverse and repair what was lost by the first Eve, but would take under her mantle every child of God as her own. For this we can never thank her enough.

To return to the original question posed at the beginning of this chapter, we hopefully now have a clearer image of the Church as a family. We need to perhaps discern how we can manifest in our own lives that maternal nature of the Mystical Body, because in doing so we are activating the virtues of hope and love in ourselves and those on the peripheries of life. In a world smoldering in the ashes of despair and sadness, the forces of the Church need to rise up to proclaim that a new light is dawning on the horizon of history.[31] The Church Militant exists to be a mother to all, pouring the sacramental ointment on the wounds of her children and encouraging those outside the family to enter under her care. If we picture the scene of Jesus's outstretched arms on the Cross as a sign of his embrace of the entire world within his redemptive act, we should see a comparable image of the mother with outstretched arms ready to clasp her child. The Church is that mother. In some way, this image needs to be promoted as an antidote to the prevailing opinion in secular society (and even within the Church to some extent) that the Institutional Church is archaic and irrelevant, somewhat cold-hearted. Just as we all owe our existence to a mother, so we should preach the message that for eternal life, we also need this Holy Mother. The promotion of love and mercy will, with the help of the Holy Spirit, open hearts and minds to the entire truth: to see that the world has nothing to offer but decay and death. As the Mother holds the key to a happiness and peace that transcends this life, she is able to guarantee that her spiritual family is reunited in a divinized form in the Kingdom of God. That is the primary message that must be shouted from the rooftops.

---

31. "In her prophetic role, whenever peoples cry out to her: 'Watchman, what of the night?' (Is. 21:11), the Church wants to be ready to give a reason for the hope she bears within her (cf. 1 Pet 3:15), because a new dawn is breaking on the horizon (cf. Rev. 22:5)." Pope Benedict XVI, Apostolic Exhortation, *Africae Munus*, no. 30, www.vatican.va.

❧ 4 ❧

Master, What Must I Do?

You are no longer exiles, then, or aliens; the saints are your fellow cit-
izens, you belong to God's household. Apostles and prophets are the
foundation on which you were built, and the chief corner-stone of it
is Jesus Christ himself. In him the whole fabric is bound together, as it
grows into a temple, dedicated to the Lord; in him you too are being
built in with the rest, so that God may find in you a dwelling-place
for his Spirit. (Eph. 2:19–22)

IN OUR QUEST to unravel the mystery of the Communion of
Saints as pertaining to the Church on Earth, we have reached an element of utmost importance, one that concerns each of our lives
individually and collectively. I am referring to the call to holiness
that is imprinted on the soul at the moment of baptism. Until now,
we have reflected upon the formational and maternal nature of the
Church that is directed from the divine to the human. In this chapter, I would like to focus on the notion of "saints" within the context
of the New Testament. Can we refer to ourselves as saints? What is
its true meaning? How do we venture forward aspiring sanctity
while struggling with the consequences of original sin? Pondering
these questions will allow us to look afresh at the baptismal promises we made or that were made on our behalf, and hopefully,
encourage us to break free from the despondency that can easily
grip our spiritual lives in the midst of the tribulations of life. For
those brothers and sisters who may not yet be part of the Church, I
hope they too will find in this chapter a source of encouragement to
seek the loving friendship of Jesus and a place at his table.

Saints of the First Resurrection

It is significant that from the earliest days of the Church after Pentecost, the term "saint" was being applied to the faithful. In the account of St. Paul's conversion we read how Ananias, during his vision of the Lord complained: "Lord, many have told me about this man, and all the hurt he has done to thy saints at Jerusalem" (Acts 9:13). In the same chapter, we read how St. Peter "visited the saints everywhere" (Acts 9:32). It is with St. Paul however that the term gains greatest traction; it becomes a frequent form of greeting in his Letters:

> From Paul, by God's will an apostle of Jesus Christ, and Timothy, who is their brother, to the Church of God which is at Corinth and to all the saints in the whole of Achaia; grace and peace be yours from God, our Father, and from the Lord Jesus Christ. (2 Cor. 1:1)[1]

The great Apostle also encourages a more intimate greeting in several Letters: "greet one another with the kiss of saints." Similar expressions are also found in 1 Cor. 16:20, 1 Thess. 5:26 and Rom. 16:16. This greeting, so close to the "sign" or "kiss" of peace used in the Latin and Eastern Liturgies, shows a bond of love that united Christians under the influence of the Holy Spirit. In fact, St. Peter refers to this as the "Kiss of fellowship" (cf. 1 Pet. 5:14).[2] Alongside

---

1. Very similar expressions are found at the opening of the Letters to the Ephesians, Philippians, and Colossians.

2. Interestingly, through patristic sources, we discover that the kiss of peace formed a part of the earliest Church liturgies. St. Justin tells us: "Having ended the prayers, we salute one another with a kiss" (St. Justin, *First Apology*, no. 65). He then describes the offertory procession leading to the Eucharistic Prayer and Consecration of the bread and wine. St. Cyril of Jerusalem gives a profound exposition of the true meaning of this act: "Then the Deacon cries aloud, 'Receive ye one another; and let us kiss one another.' Think not that this kiss is of the same character with those given in public by common friends. It is not such: but this kiss blends souls one with another, and courts entire forgiveness for them. The kiss therefore is the sign that our souls are mingled together, and banish all remembrance of wrongs. For this cause Christ said, If you are offering your gift at the altar, and there rememberest that your brother has anything against thee, leave there your gift upon the altar, and go your way; first be reconciled to your brother, and then come and offer your gift. The kiss therefore is reconciliation, and for this reason holy." (St. Cyril of Jerusalem, *Catechetical Lecture no.*23), 3, www.newadvent.org.

these beautiful salutations, there are many others instances where St. Paul[3] describes the Church as a community of saints. But why?

The answer to this question lies in the very clear understanding of the early Christians that they were a part of something new: "new" in the biblical sense, that is with an eschatological orientation, directed to final perfection. With this in mind, coupled with an expectation of the imminent arrival of the Lord's second coming, these communities strived to conform their lives as closely as possible to Christ's. It wasn't enough for them to be passive bystanders who accepted baptism but little else; no, for these disciples, a burning zeal consumed them even to the point of martyrdom. They relished the opportunity to show that holiness was available to all without exception. We may consider that this aspiration was easier to understand in the nascent Church because of the proximity to the central events of salvation history and also due to the pure clarity of truth, unlike today where the fog of relativism and rationalism has crept into the lives of the faithful.[4] On the other hand, the vicious persecution they had to endure no doubt reinforced the reality of a great spiritual struggle becoming manifest, of which they were now central figures. It is not difficult to see the appeal of imitating their victorious King and Savior, for Jesus's words about laying down one's life for love[5] would have surely been known as the benchmark for the highest degree of sanctity even before the canonical gospels had been disseminated.

To return then to the use of the term "saints," we see that it forms part of the *already* and *not yet* of the Church; *already*, in the sense

3. St. Jude also uses the term (v. 3).

4. On this point, Pope Benedict XVI gave a little-noticed but strikingly prophetic warning by evoking St. Paul's prophecy of the last days in his Second Letter to Timothy: "This makes the words of the Apostle sadly appropriate for our own time, when he warned Timothy of the day in which 'people will not put up with sound doctrine, but having itching ears, they will accumulate for themselves teachers to suit their own desires, and will turn away from listening to the truth and wander away to myths'" (2 Tim. 4:3). Pope Benedict XVI, "Address to Participants in the Meeting of the Christian/Centrist Democrat International," September 22, 2012, www.vatican.va.

5. "This is the greatest love a man can shew, that he should lay down his life for his friends" (Jn. 15:13).

that by virtue of baptism we are immersed in the life and death of the Lord and become part of his Mystical Body, and *not yet*, because we have not finished the race that must be run to its completion (cf. 2 Tim. 4:7). Only in the glory of heaven will the expression reach its full potential. Perhaps after two thousand years, and the filth that has somewhat disfigured the Church, we find the use of this term a little uncomfortable to say the least. But that doesn't obscure the fact that to profess the Catholic faith is to take on the mantle of the early Christians in zeal, fortitude and holiness. St. Paul in his Letter to the Ephesians proclaims:

> Blessed be that God, that Father of our Lord Jesus Christ, who has blessed us, in Christ, with every spiritual blessing, higher than heaven itself. He has chosen us out, in Christ, before the foundation of the world, to be saints, to be blameless in his sight, for love of him; marking us out beforehand (so his will decreed) to be his adopted children through Jesus Christ. (Eph. 1:3–5)

If we have been chosen to be blameless in the Lord's sight, we may ascertain that the initiative is not ours but God's. He alone, through the power of the Holy Spirit, instills within us a desire for holiness, and secure in that knowledge, we may be confident that this is not an insurmountable mountain to climb by ourselves, but eminently possible, as long as we seek a constant interior renewal, with a heart open to the graces God desires to give us. We should therefore understand that we *are* saints in a very real sense, but saints of the *novitiate* rather than the fulfilment.

In the Letters of St. Paul, we find a number of references linking the concept of holiness and communion together, almost as if anticipating the more extensive "communion of saints" doctrine that would be formulated later.[6] It is in the context of his missionary journeys that we can understand his linking of the two elements. Holiness was now a viable option for the pagan world, but for it to bear fruit the gentiles would need to accept that God's will was for a community to grow together, rather than a Christian individualism

---

6. St. Nicetas of Remesiana, a friend of the great poet St. Paulinus of Nola, appears to have been the first theologian to use the term "communion of saints" in his *Explanatio Symboli* 10 (P.L. 52, 871).

that remained behind closed doors. He wanted to ensure that the totality of the Gospel was preached as opposed to a "pick and choose" redaction. In this way St. Paul could leave a flourishing community behind, fully equipped to continue the evangelization of neighboring territories while he pressed ahead to where the Holy Spirit took him. Looking at St. Paul's teachings on sanctification and communion, we discover the perennial timeliness of his message and a theological treasure trove that instruct us in the art of becoming saints.

In the Letter to the Romans chapter 12, the new law of love is expounded upon; it is holiness through self-sacrifice and charity:

> And now, brethren, I appeal to you by God's mercies to offer up your bodies as a living sacrifice, consecrated to God and worthy of his acceptance; this is the worship due from you as rational creatures. And you must not fall in with the manners of this world; there must be an inward change, a remaking of your minds, so that you can satisfy yourselves what is God's will, the good thing, the desirable thing, the perfect thing.... The spiritual gifts we have differ, according to the special grace which has been assigned to each.... Each must perform his own task well; giving alms with generosity, exercising authority with anxious care, or doing works of mercy smilingly. (Rom. 12:1–2, 6, 8)

It is worth reflecting on that opening plea (v. 1) expressed by St. Paul because it reveals the *Christological imitation* that he desired to impress upon those seeking sanctification. We need firstly to remember that for the Apostle, Jesus *was* the new Temple. Through his sacrificial Death and Resurrection, the old Temple had been made redundant by the perfect sacrifice of the eternal High Priest; as the Letter to the Hebrews states: "He has opened up for us a new, a living approach, by way of the veil, I mean, his mortality. A great priest is ours, who has dominion over God's house" (Heb. 10:20–21). True imitation would necessitate offering ourselves as holy temples where everything imperfect would be abolished, while sacrificing our lives in the work of co-redemption; as we read in Colossians: "I am glad of my sufferings on your behalf, as, in this mortal frame of mine, I help to pay off the debt which the afflictions of Christ still leave to be paid" (Col. 1:24).

The Pauline theology of the "Body of Christ" also traces its root to this idea. Why? Because for St. Paul the Church exists as a communion of fellowship and love; each member and their particular charisms form a specific function that is willed by God for the greater good of the entire Church. In this way the vitality of the "Body" is manifest and the unique importance of each individual is guaranteed. This explains why the call to holiness is one from which nobody is exempt; were that not the case, spiritual gangrene would soon tear into the Body. The Church would no longer be the Mystical Body of Christ if it did not imitate its Lord in an individual and collective sense.

There is a second unifying element of this Body from which, according to St. Paul, the faithful derive their sanctity; namely the reception of the Holy Eucharist—Jesus himself. To receive the Lord is the greatest sign of unity among the brethren and the means of sanctifying the Church, deepening the awareness of its own mystery as the Body of Christ—not a replica, but truly *the* Body. In the Eucharistic banquet the spousal love of God and His people is renewed constantly; the words found in the Letter to the Galatians express this beautiful reality perfectly: "and yet I am alive; or rather, not I; it is Christ that lives in me" (Gal. 2:20). By striving to live *within* the confines of the Church we are able to offer our lives as a "living sacrifice" of praise and thanksgiving; the Christological imitation becomes the model for all who seek to share in the sanctity of the Body of Christ. In the Eucharistic presence we allow Jesus to increase the likeness of his divinity upon our souls, thus conforming ourselves ever more to the pattern of his life and death.

Continuing with the Letter to the Romans, St. Paul delineates the essence of the second commandment to love one's neighbor:

> Your love must be a sincere love; you must hold what is evil in abomination, fix all your desire upon what is good. Be affectionate towards each other, as the love of brothers demands, eager to give one another precedence. I would see you unwearied in activity, aglow with the Spirit, waiting like slaves upon the Lord; buoyed up by hope, patient in affliction, persevering in prayer; providing generously for the needs of the saints, giving the stranger a loving welcome. Bestow a blessing on those who persecute you; a bless-

ing, not a curse. Rejoice with those who rejoice, mourn with the mourner. (Rom. 12:9–15)

Other texts also speak of this new law where grace transforms man, loosening the bonds of sin, paving the way for a new humanity to take hold. In the Letter to the Ephesians we are told to be "always humble, always gentle; patient too" (Eph. 4:2) while "eager to preserve that unity the Spirit gives you, whose bond is peace" (Eph. 4:3). St. Paul always urges humility and truth when dealing with one another, in imitation of the Lord who came to serve with meekness:

> Fill up my cup of happiness by thinking with the same mind, cherishing the same bond of charity, soul knit to soul in a common unity of thought. You must never act in a spirit of factiousness, or of ambition; each of you must have the humility to think others better men than himself, and study the welfare of others, not his own. Yours is to be the same mind which Christ Jesus shewed. (Phil. 2:2–5)

The Holy Spirit: Supreme Sanctifier

One of the great theological developments found in St. Paul's Letters concerns the pivotal action of the Holy Spirit in the life of the Christian. For the Apostle, the Holy Spirit is the driving force of sanctification, the divine inspiration for everything good that proceeds from the souls of the faithful. As we have already stated, in Pauline theology, charisms were considered of great importance for the unity of the Body of Christ, and in the First Letter to the Corinthians we see the origin of these special gifts:

> Just as no one can be speaking through God's Spirit if he calls Jesus accursed, so it is only through the Holy Spirit that anyone can say, Jesus is the Lord; and yet there are different kinds of gifts, though it is the same Spirit who gives them.... The revelation of the Spirit is imparted to each, to make the best advantage of it ... but all this is the work of one and the same Spirit, who distributes his gifts as he will to each severally. (1 Cor. 12:3–5, 7, 11)

Logically, if the Holy Spirit is the source of all these gifts, then the spiritual benefit that the Church gains from them is also his concern. His will is that a serene humility reign at the center of this communion ensuring that envy and jealousy do not create disunity. Even if the range of charisms is great, and some extraordinary, in the rank of holiness it is not the type of gift that bestows sanctity— rather the way it is carried out. Is it for love? Prestige? Or vainglory? These are the questions that the Holy Spirit continually asks the beneficiaries of his generosity, and the Church attains an increased binding of the *sanctorum communio* to the extent that its faithful ponder these questions and act upon them in a spirit of love and self-sacrifice.

Looking at the specific nature of the Holy Spirit, two great attributes stand out: love and communion. He is the uncreated love and communion of the Father and the Son, an endless source of unity, harmony and creativity; a divine person who exists as the fruit of inexhaustible love between Father and Son. Is it possible that St. Paul, reflecting upon the divine affinity between the three Persons of the most Holy Trinity, saw the Holy Spirit operating in a similar way in his relationship with the Church? It certainly appears to be the case because in a Pauline sense the Holy Spirit not only inspires acts of charity in the Christian, but becomes the secret visitor who resides in the depths of the soul, notably through the sacraments of Baptism and Confirmation. By inspiring the soul to love from within, the Divine Spirit gradually impresses the image of love and communion that he himself partakes in with the Father and Son and therefore divinization begins to take effect little by little.[7]

We have reached a point in our discussion of Pauline theology

---

7. Hans Urs Von Balthasar has some very interesting thoughts on this aspect that are well worth sharing, especially for those who struggle to pray to the Holy Spirit: "This Spirit is breath, not a full outline, and therefore he wishes only to breathe through us, not to present himself to us as an object; he does not wish to be seen but to be the seeing eye of grace in us, and he is little concerned about whether we pray to him, provided that we pray with him, 'Abba, Father,' provided that we consent to his unutterable groaning in the depths of our soul. He is the light that cannot be seen except upon the object that is lit up: and he is the love between Father and Son that has appeared in Jesus." Hans Urs von Balthasar, *Explorations in Theology*, vol. 3, *Creator Spirit* (San Francisco: Ignatius Press, 1993), 111.

where our thoughts naturally turn to the influence of the Holy Spirit in the life of prayer. In a famous passage from his Letter to the Romans, we read:

> Only, as before, the Spirit comes to the aid of our weakness; when we do not know what prayer to offer, to pray as we ought, the Spirit himself intercedes for us, with groans beyond all utterance: and God, who can read our hearts, knows well what the Spirit's intent is; for indeed it is according to the mind of God that he makes intercession for the saints. (Rom. 8:26–27)

A most striking element of this teaching is that St. Paul does not see prayer as a one-way conversation in which we speak and God listens. In fact as we examined earlier, holiness is a gift of God and therefore, the ability to pray must also be a gift. Without this divine assistance we would be searching for something or someone of whom we know nothing. Fortunately for us, the Lord does not leave us with spiritual blindness; he instigates always without fail: "the Lord must lead, and man follow" (Hos. 11:10). In the text just cited from Romans, we see evidence of this: the Holy Spirit resides within the temple of the Christian soul "coming to our aid." We are told he intercedes for us when our weaknesses mean either we cannot express our thoughts clearly to God, or our prayers are lacking in conviction and strength. In these moments, the Holy Spirit in a sense almost takes on a similar role of mediation to that of Jesus. By that I mean he appears to stoop down from his glory and ministers on our behalf to our Father in heaven; as St. Paul taught:

> Those who follow the leading of God's Spirit are all God's sons; the spirit you have now received is not, as of old, a spirit of slavery, to govern you by fear; it is the spirit of adoption, which makes us cry out, Abba, Father. The Spirit himself thus assures our spirit, that we are children of God. (Rom. 8:14–16)

Of course, we must also say that as the Holy Spirit guarantees our freedom,[8] we need to be receptive to his call deep within us. His

---

8. The Spirit we have been speaking of is the Lord; and where the Lord's Spirit is, there is freedom. (2 Cor. 3:17)

burning love invites us to allow him to intercede within us; for without our own will to enter into a communion with him we cannot ascend the mountain of the Lord and experience the grace of transformation. For St. Paul, the Holy Spirit also acts to help us understand that within the Mystical Body we truly have become sons and daughters of God, heirs to His Kingdom and divine life. The Paraclete encourages us to call out "Abba, Father" knowing that this isn't a pious wish but the most consoling truth. In fact to truly embrace the Catholic faith it is essential to speak intimately with the Father; yes to never forget his divine majesty, but in humility to constantly show him that we desire to live as His faithful children in imitation of Jesus our brother. As the Holy Spirit is the love of Father and Son, he is the perfect guide of the soul who can instill confidence and sanctity, allowing a true communion to develop between God the Father and His adopted children.[9] With the correct disposition on our part, theory becomes a reality and the Father's Kingdom becomes the homeland we yearn for.

Before moving on from the precious teachings of this great Apostle, let us look briefly at his suggestions for living our lives as saints on earth. He gathers various aspects of prayer that are relevant to the differing circumstances that Christians find themselves in, both individually and as a community. In the Letter to the Ephesians we read: "Let your contentment be in the Holy Spirit; your tongues unloosed in psalms and hymns and spiritual music, as you sing and give praise to the Lord in your hearts. Give thanks continually to God, who is our Father, in the name of our Lord Jesus Christ" (Eph. 5:18–20). Similar words are found in the Letter to the Colossians in which he adds: "Whatever you are about, in word and action alike, invoke always the name of the Lord Jesus Christ, offering your thanks to God the Father through him" (Col. 3:17). The message that St. Paul wants to convey is that life must be a continuous act of

---

9. St. Paul lists the effects of the Holy Spirit specifically in the Letter to the Galatians: "Whereas the spirit yields a harvest of love, joy, peace, patience, kindness, generosity, forbearance, gentleness, faith, courtesy, temperateness, purity" (Gal. 5:22–23).

worship. Nothing we do, say or think should be done unless it is done for the glory of the Father; for musicians every note should be played in thanksgiving and offered out of love, for the surgeon, every incision of the scalpel.

In this sense, our very existence and all it entails can become sanctified through love; there is no need to compartmentalize our spiritual life as if needing to set an alarm clock for when it is time to pray. Of course this is not to devalue specific periods of prayer; on the contrary, living day to day with God at the center of everything should increase our desire to spend the more intimate moments with him in an ever increasingly mystical way. And the fruit of this loving exchange? Anxiety is erased, and the peace of the Lord imbues the soul even in the most trying circumstances. St. Paul urges this as a central pillar of the faith: "Use every kind of prayer and supplication; pray at all times in the spirit; keep awake to that end with all perseverance; offer your supplication for all the saints" (Eph. 6:18).

One of St. Paul's most insistent teachings on the spiritual life (which stems undoubtedly from his theology of the Mystical Body) was to realize that the "body" of the Christian was no longer under the influence of the old order, but of the new. An ontological change had occurred through baptism which meant that all converts had "put on the person of Christ" (Gal. 3:27). With that in mind, he set about molding a primal "theology of the body" in which the purity of God would be reflected in the "new" liberated human body. In this way, body and soul would both partake in the life of prayer: "glorify God by making your bodies the shrines of his presence" (1 Cor. 6:20). St. John Paul II intuited the Pauline link between purity and piety in a way that is most beneficial to this discussion:

> Among these gifts, known in the history of spirituality as the seven gifts of the Holy Spirit (cf. Is. 11:2, according to the Septuagint and the Vulgate), the one most congenial to the virtue of purity seems to be the gift of piety (*eusebeia, donum pietatis*). If purity prepares man to "control his own body, as something holy and held in honour" (1 Thess. 4:3–5), piety, which is a gift of the Holy Spirit, seems to serve purity in a particular way. It makes the human sub-

ject sensitive to that dignity which is characteristic of the human body by virtue of the mystery of creation and redemption.[10]

Although piety is distinct from prayer, it is the foundation stone on which a meaningful spiritual life can be built; prayer becomes a consequence of the fertility wrought by this gift. If we return to the passage from the First Letter to the Thessalonians (4:3–5), St. Paul impresses upon his readers that it is not enough to pray with the soul but remain bound by impurity. He sees the virtue of temperance as a prerequisite for the sanctification of the body. Of course, everything the Apostle teaches is geared towards promoting the imitation of Jesus; for if the Sacred Body of the Lord was (and always will be) absolute perfection in purity and chastity, the Mystical Body would have to be likewise. This explains why in several Letters this element of Pauline theology is so vigorously taught:

> You must not, then, allow sin to tyrannize over your perishable bodies, to make you subject to its appetites. You must not make your bodily powers over to sin, to be the instruments of harm; make yourselves over to God, as men who have been dead and come to life again; make your bodily powers over to God, to be the instruments of right-doing. Sin will not be able to play the master over you any longer; you serve grace now, not the law. (Rom. 6:12–14)

And again, writing to the Ephesians:

> As for debauchery, and impurity of every kind, and covetousness, there must be no whisper of it among you; it would ill become saints; no indecent behaviour, no ribaldry or smartness in talk; that is not your business, your business is to give thanks to God. (Eph. 5:3–4)

Should we view this anthropological understanding as a negative or positive? On the one hand it is a stern rebuke which appears to be wholly negative in its consequences: One continuous "No!" for those catechumens being instructed in the faith, but on the other

---

10. St. John Paul II, General Audience, "The Pauline Doctrine of Purity as Life According to the Spirit," *L'Osservatore Romano*, Weekly Edition in English, March 23, 1981, 9.

hand it is positive because it clearly defines what does and does not lead to holiness. The truth is spoken; the holy Apostle uncovers the evil that would rather hide in the shadows of the soul; he reminds us that grace has replaced sin as the master within. As usual with St. Paul, we see a boldness that challenges anyone who meditates upon his words. He doesn't do gray areas; on the contrary he presents truth and falsehood with a brilliant clarity that demands a definitive choice of our will.

There are several ways in which the body shares in the prayer of the soul. We can think of the acts of blessing oneself, kneeling in adoration, the laying on of hands and anointing with oil. Even temptations against physical purity become prayer when evil is rejected. In a wider context, the parable of the Last Judgment (Matt. 25:31–46) presents a list of physical deeds which are essentially acts of prayer when done with love of God and neighbor; they manifest the inner workings of grace in the soul, thus allowing an opportunity for the body to partake in the life of the spirit.

Suffering must also be seen in the light of prayer, because it becomes salvific when accepted in loving submission to the will of God. We need look no further than the Lord's suffering in the Garden of Gethsemane: "My Father, if it is possible, let this chalice pass me by; only as thy will is, not as mine is" (Matt. 26:39). From that moment when Jesus's precious blood fell from his body, until the lance pierced his side upon the Cross, his body was tormented in the crucible of suffering. The complete offering up of his holy body meant that holiness was now possible for our own lowly body. The ultimate fruit of this divine gift is martyrdom, the supreme witness of this new sanctity of the body because in the act of self-giving, the martyr brings love to perfection in the most radical way; the desire for total communion with God is affirmed and the body now enters into the most profound union of prayer with the soul. There is also a prophetic element to this selfless act; the martyr looks with hope to the day when body and soul will be reunited in a glorious form, when prayer will be brought to perfection.

From St. Paul's eschatological thought concerning the resurrection of the dead, we can see why the body forms such an integral part of his theology. Encompassing two related spheres, the rising of the *complete* Mystical Body in glory in the *"civitate Dei,"* and the individual rising for each of the saved, the teachings reveal the richness and depth of the recapitulation of creation that God willed from the beginning of salvation history. In the First Letter to the Thessalonians, we have confirmation of this dual aspect: "So, when our Lord Jesus Christ comes with *all his saints,* may you stand boldly before the presence of God, our Father, in holiness unreproved. Amen" (1 Thess. 3:13). And later he says, "So may the God of peace sanctify you wholly, keep spirit and soul and body unimpaired, to greet the coming of our Lord Jesus Christ without reproach. The God who called you is true to his promise; he will not fail you" (1 Thess. 5:23–24).

For St. Paul, to have stressed only the sanctification of the soul would have left the truth of God only half told; the resurrection of the human being will happen in its totality—both body and soul; therefore the body deserves the same attention as the soul. The message we glean throughout his Letters is one of hope and expectation in the definitive victory: that as Christ reigns in a glorious body we too will arrive at this same destination one day, but only on the condition that the Christian life is taken seriously and that its demands are met every day. The Apostle reminds us that we are in a spiritual battle against the forces of evil, but that the final triumph is already secured through the Death and Resurrection of the Lord and it is through the power of His grace that we will be saints of the transfiguration.

At this point, let us look at the Gospel message concerning the notion of saints within the Church Militant. Although the expression originated with St. Paul, the ideal is nonetheless clearly defined in the teachings of Jesus. For even before the Church had become a functioning entity, the Lord had instructed the Apostles *and* the people in the new life of the spirit; they now had a Shepherd who would lead them in the path of sanctification.

The Beatitudes: Spirit of the New Law

Perhaps the closest we come to seeing a "charter for the saints" on earth is revealed in the Beatitudes that Jesus proclaimed at the Sermon on the Mount.[11] These great teachings complementing the Ten Commandments give a new perspective on the interior disposition that must be nurtured in the soul for true life to develop.[12] If the Commandments are to be seen as the minimum requirement expected to fulfil the Law and remain within the friendship of God, the Beatitudes are the revelation of what is possible through the positive energy of love. They don't contradict in any way the laws given to Moses, but rather surpass them because the general rule of *avoidance* that is found in the Decalogue is replaced by a desire to *act*, to take the initiative in the quest for perfection. Spiritual stagnation, which is possible even if the commandments are kept, is not an option if the Beatitudes are lived as the "Christian's identity card."[13]

The Sermon on the Mount reveals Jesus as the new Moses—the new law giver. The Lord ascended the mountainside just as Moses did, rightly taking his place in close proximity to God, but with a striking difference. Moses *received* the Law, but Jesus, with divine authority *gave* the law himself. In this way, the definitive vision of God's desire for man was presented. Jesus though, of course was very clear that the Commandments were not now a redundant, antiquated relic of a bygone era; on the contrary, they had been enriched:

11. "Blessed are the poor in spirit; the kingdom of heaven is theirs. Blessed are the patient; they shall inherit the land. Blessed are those who mourn; they shall be comforted. Blessed are those who hunger and thirst for holiness; they shall have their fill. Blessed are the merciful; they shall obtain mercy. Blessed are the clean of heart; they shall see God. Blessed are the peace-makers; they shall be counted the children of God. Blessed are those who suffer persecution in the cause of right; the kingdom of heaven is theirs. Blessed are you, when men revile you, and persecute you, and speak all manner of evil against you falsely, because of me. Be glad and light-hearted, for a rich reward awaits you in heaven; so it was they persecuted the prophets who went before you" (Matt. 5:3–12).

12. Pope Benedict XVI provides the foundation for our understanding of the Beatitudes: "In the biblical tradition, the beatitude is a literary genre which always involves some good news, a 'gospel,' which culminates in a promise." Pope Benedict XVI, "Message for World Day of Peace," January 1, 2013, www.vatican.va.

13. Pope Francis, "Morning Meditation in the Chapel of the Domus Sanctae Marthae," June 9, 2014.

Do not think that I have come to set aside the law and the prophets; I have not come to set them aside, but to bring them to perfection. Believe me, heaven and earth must disappear sooner than
one jot, one flourish should disappear from the law; it must all be
accomplished. (Matt. 5:17–18)

Returning to the Beatitudes themselves, they actually present an
image of Jesus himself; they are a reflection on his inner life and
consequently they become for the Christian what the piano is for
the pianist. In what sense therefore do they represent Jesus? We see
in the first Beatitude his poverty; born in a stable in Bethlehem, a
refugee in Egypt, a King who unlike the fox has no place to lay his
head (cf. Matt. 8:20). The Lord's patience, meekness and piety is
evident throughout the Gospels, for example rebuking James and
John who thought of sending down fire upon the Samaritans who
would not receive Jesus (cf. Lk. 9:54). In the mourner, we see Jesus
weeping over the death of Lazarus and more significantly over the
city of Jerusalem: "And as he drew near, and caught sight of the city,
he wept over it, and said: Ah, if thou too couldst understand, above
all in this day that is granted thee, the ways that can bring thee
peace! As it is, they are hidden from thy sight" (Lk. 19:41–42). For
those who hunger for holiness, justice and peace, the Lord's entire
life is one continuous testament to those yearnings. The Beatitude
concerning mercy recalls to mind the treatment of the woman
caught committing adultery; for those bound by the Old Law there
was only one option: death by stoning. But for Jesus, the epitome of
mercy, his will was twofold. On the one hand, repentance and a
chance of conversion for the woman which in turn could, with the
grace of God, lead to the life of a saint; while on the other hand, for
those condemning her, a lesson in self-examination of conscience
which would lead to mercy rather than judgment flowering in the
soul. As the Lord taught: those who forgive will be forgiven; those
who practice mercy will receive mercy.

Blessed are the clean of heart; they will see God. This Beatitude is
the apex of all the Beatitudes. Why? Because without the purity of
heart, of intention, the soul of the Christian remains lifeless; it is
unable to withstand the light of God. In Jesus, we see clearly that
purity which is often so elusive for us. In St. John's Gospel we read:

"What, Philip, Jesus said to him, here am I, who have been all this while in your company; hast thou not learned to recognize me yet? Whoever has seen me, has seen the Father" (Jn. 14:9). Everything that Jesus accomplished in his mission on earth was pure: pure love, pure mercy, pure humility, pure sacrifice. Each and every act of his will was oriented towards restoring communion between his Father and his adopted children. His purity of heart was such that he could speak those words to Philip; the communion was total and unconditional between Father and Son, and within Jesus's interior *and* exterior holiness, the glory of God shone brightly.

In the penultimate Beatitude, *Blessed are the peace-makers*, we discover the true extent of Jesus's Kingship, he is King of a new order; not like the repressive authoritarian monarchs that have littered history, but one of peace and charity. Isaiah prophesied precisely this fact: "Ever wider shall his dominion spread, endlessly at peace; he will sit on David's kingly throne, to give it lasting foundations of justice and right; so tenderly he loves us, the Lord of hosts" (Is. 9:7). The heavenly chorus of angels that greeted the Savior's birth also bore testament to the bearer of eternal peace: "Glory to God in high heaven, and peace on earth to men that are God's friends" (Lk. 2:14). In reconciling the world to God (cf. 2 Cor. 5:19) Jesus was overthrowing a false peace built on political power and replacing it with the inner peace that comes from union with God. In this way, the process of universal restoration that St. Peter spoke of in the Porch of Solomon (Acts. 3:21) was initiated, one that would eventually lead to the second earthly paradise of everlasting peace.

The final Beatitude, *Blessed are the persecuted,* in a sense unveils the Christological impression *par excellence*. The Old Testament prophecy of the Suffering Servant (Is. 53:1–12) finds in Jesus's Passion and Death its sorrowful fulfilment. Salvation history is now centered on the persecution of the Lord, on the rejection he suffered by his own people. Through divine love, Jesus immerses himself in the most acute pain and suffering that can be experienced in the world. He embraces our own humanity to its very core, with the exception of sin, and thus binds himself to us wholeheartedly. Suffering takes on a new meaning; the King crowned with thorns becomes the Brother of all who suffer. If suffering is still evil, it nevertheless is transformed by *agape* and becomes the currency that purchases our redemption. This Christological image gives us a unique insight into God's mysterious and radical form of Kingship, because we discover that his throne is the Cross; that the royal garment is not that given mockingly by the soldiers, but actually his precious blood that robes him in regal splendor. Before the scene, in reality, we can only remain speechless; gazing at the God-Man in humble adoration, continually seeking to understand a love that knows no bounds even in the midst of the vilest hatred.

From our reflections thus far, the humanity of Jesus is seen to be the point of reference for living the Beatitudes, the portrait of supreme holiness that every saint of the novitiate aspires to. Let us now look with a sharper focus on the relevance of the Beatitudes for ourselves, striving to be *ipse Christus*.

When delivering the Sermon on the Mount, the Lord began each Beatitude with the word "blessed," meaning "happy." The Greek original in the New Testament however uses a word: "*makarioi*" which "refers to the distinctive religious joy which comes to persons from their share in the salvation of the kingdom of God."[14] Understood in this context, the happiness is not superficial or temporal but is borne out of communion with God and solidarity with one's neighbor. This spiritual joy stems from the outright rejection of worldly temptations: money, possessions, power, and all that is ephemeral. Instead the Lord proclaims "blessed" those who seek the true path towards heaven; those who embrace the Christian life as a "sign of contradiction" (cf. Lk. 2:34). For entry into the Kingdom of God, it is truly a blessing to be poor, humble and pure in heart, even if the world sees this as madness and a sign of weakness. It is the path of humble service, of sacrificial love that cannot be understood other than through the grace of God.

St. Paul describes the paradox that is presented by the "blessedness" of living the beatitudes when writing to the Corinthians:

14. James Francis Cardinal Stafford, "Address to the Catenian Association," May 14, 2005, www.vatican.va.

To right and to left we must be armed with innocence; now honoured, now slighted, now traduced, now flattered. They call us deceivers, and we tell the truth; unknown, and we are fully acknowledged; dying men, and see, we live; punished, yes, but not doomed to die; sad men, that rejoice continually; beggars, that bring riches to many; disinherited, and the world is ours. (2 Cor. 6:7–10)

In another passage, he explains succinctly the reason for this supernatural joy: ". . . we carry about continually in our bodies the dying state of Jesus, so that the living power of Jesus may be manifested in our bodies too" (2 Cor. 4:10). We can therefore understand that the blessing consists in the ability to project the countenance of Christ in our own lives; through the ebb and flow of human existence, and in this way ensuring that the lures of the world do not break the bonds of love, even if concupiscence and temptation are never far away.

Towards the end of St. Matthew's account of the Sermon on the Mount, he relates words of Jesus that present a profoundly Christological backdrop to this interpretive key: "Whoever, then, hears these commandments of mine and carries them out, is like a wise man who built his house upon rock" (Matt. 7:24). The implication is that Jesus is the rock, the hope that does not fail us, the perfect embodiment of the beatitudes; and for us, the more authentic way this vision is lived, the more evangelical our discipleship will be, and the perfection of the Father will become the most sought after treasure.

When we look closely at the Beatitudes, we notice that each begins and ends with a promise. As we have seen, to be "blessed" is a promise, one which seems to have a dual meaning: on the one hand spiritual joy even amidst the tribulations of this life, and on the other hand an indicator of future eschatological glory. At the end of each, there are also more specific promises: for the poor in spirit, they will inherit the Kingdom of heaven; for the mourner, they shall be comforted, and the patient, they will inherit the land. Jesus did not leave the disciples with a half revelation; he wanted them to see the prize of living the beatitudes and therefore revealed the ultimate goal of each. The aim of this surely was to redefine in the minds of the listening crowds the notion of power and victory; not as they perhaps believed (that Jesus was the revolutionary political leader about to set Israel free), but in a way that would reveal Jesus's spiritual Kingship and their own calling to be saints, uprooting the logic that had prevailed until then.[15]

Although it is not my intention to study in detail each of these promises, suffice to say that they all speak of fulfilment; fulfilment that can only come from God's gift, rather than the antithetical promises that are worldly in nature. We should however be careful to note that the promises do not present a utopian vision of the future. The Lord was resolute in his teaching that to live the Christian life meant persecution and suffering would be constant companions. Evil would remain until the end of the world (cf. Matt. 13:24–30). However, even if the promises have a profoundly eschatological nature that transcends history, they do also refer to the here-and-now through the *Sanctorum Communio*. By participating in the Mystical Body, the fruits of these promises are bestowed upon us; eternity enters into time through the definitive triumph of the Cross allowing the very real foretaste of these end time promises. A prime example of this, most relevant to our discussion, would be the promise of comfort to those who mourn. Where do we find compelling evidence of this? Precisely in the communion of saints, in the knowledge that prayer, sacrifice and the offering of indulgences for our departed brothers and sisters keeps a fusion of love alive between the Church Militant and Suffering. Comfort comes through faith, that life or death makes no difference to being part of

15. In fact, when we read the rest of the Sermon on the Mount, this interpretation seems ever more plausible; for Jesus went on to give a great wealth of instruction that would have astounded those listening: the concept of committing adultery with the heart (Matt. 5:28) (enforcing the beatitude of purity), replacing revenge with forgiveness (Matt. 5:38–40) (the beatitude of mercy), loving your enemy (Matt. 5:44) (the beatitude of peace-makers) and the teaching on secrecy of almsgiving and prayer (Matt. 6:3–6) (the beatitude thirsting for holiness.) The presentation of the "Our Father" in the first person plural, points toward an appreciation of the communion of saints (on earth) praying together as one body *and* with Jesus himself. The petitions directed to the Father foster a desire to see the *immediate* and *future* shaped by God's primacy in the world and indirectly, a more radical response to the demands of the beatitudes, thus a spiritual vision of the promises emerge.

the true Vine: "Yet it is of living men, not of dead men, that he is the God" (Mk. 12:27).

Romano Guardini touches on the eschatological element of the promises that in a sense confirm the communal holiness of the saints at the descent of the New Jerusalem:

> In the Beatitudes something of celestial grandeur breaks through. They are no mere formulas of superior ethics, but tidings of sacred and supreme reality's entry into the world. They are the fanfare to that which St. Paul refers in the eighth chapter of his Roman epistle when he speaks of the growing glory of the children of God, and what the last chapters of the Apocalypse suggest in their reference to the new heaven and new earth.[16]

At this point, we should ask ourselves the question: how do we view these promises? What effect would a serious reflection on them have for our spiritual life? Even within the context of the Beatitudes, a danger still lurks that would nullify the graces received without the proper disposition. Isn't it the case that for the aspiring saint rewards don't really matter? Our sole aim has to be nothing less than possessing Jesus forever. Every other desire dissipates into nothingness, as if irrelevant. The Lord desires that we view the promises within him and through him; for to see them in any other way is to fall into a narcissistic mentality that loses the primary focus of clothing ourselves with the garment of Christ. We may recall the concept of liberation theology that leaned heavily towards a Marxist ideology; seemingly presenting itself as a form of millenarianism,[17] promising the poor possession of the land and an exit from poverty. In this case, true liberation, the true promise of the Lord was distorted; salvation took on a temporal meaning and in doing so, became a false promise that originated in the mind of man rather than God.

Perhaps the most positive way to look towards the fulfilment of the promises is through the prism of hope. In moments of spiritual darkness, they remind us that Jesus will have the last word in his-

---

16. Romano Guardini, *The Lord* (London: Longmans, 1956), 73.

17. *See* "Interview of the Holy Father during the flight to Brazil," May 9, 2007, in which Benedict XVI specifically refers to liberation theology as a form of millenarianism.

tory, that in spite of the continual assault of evil, the saints will prevail through the justice and mercy of God. The Kingdom of God will come in its fullness; Jesus-peace, Jesus-mercy, Jesus-pure image of God. Our delight will be to see the promises issuing forth from the heart of Jesus, glorious and victorious. Until that day of salvation arrives, the aspiring saint must continually relearn the beatitudes so that the canvass of our soul becomes the setting where the Lord's brush strokes paint an image of sanctity akin to his own.

Before we conclude this chapter, there is one further passage from the Gospels that deserves our attention. It concerns the account of the man who desired to know the requirements of entry into eternal life. The story is related in the three Synoptic Gospels,[18] but we will restrict ourselves to the version given by St. Mark:

> Then he went out to continue his journey; and a man ran up and knelt down before him, asking him, Master, who art so good, what must I do to achieve eternal life? Jesus said to him, why dost thou call me good? None is good, except God only. Thou knowest the commandments, Thou shalt not commit adultery, Thou shalt do no murder, Thou shalt not steal, Thou shalt not bear false witness, Thou shalt not wrong any man, Honour thy father and thy mother. Master, he answered, I have kept all these ever since I grew up. Then Jesus fastened his eyes on him, and conceived a love for him; in one thing, he said, thou art still wanting. Go home and sell all that belongs to thee; give it to the poor, and so the treasure thou hast shall be in heaven; then come back and follow me. At this, his face fell, and he went away sorrowing, for he had great possessions. And Jesus looked round, and said to his disciples, with what difficulty will those who have riches enter God's kingdom! (Mk. 10:17–23)

This dialogue between the Lord and the rich man captures the very essence of holiness, its demands and consequences. It is significant that the man, even though he admitted to keeping the commandments, still perceived something was missing. Perhaps he sensed deep within his soul a "rigidity" that actually constrained his spiritual development through an overreliance on the moral aspect of the commandments, at the expense of a true relationship with God

18. Matt. 19:16–22, Lk. 18:18–24.

and neighbor. We can presume that his question arose with the genuine desire to go beyond the pharisaical falsification of sanctity, and that in Jesus he saw the perfect reflection of God's goodness. Without realizing it, the man was asking to be enlightened on the beatitudes—the prescriptions for a saint.

Jesus's reply reinforces the teachings given in the Sermon on the Mount: he invites the man to sell everything and give it to the poor. In this way he promises to make the man truly rich, for in rejecting all material possessions he inherits the freedom to ascend towards perfect charity. Not only that. There is an invitation to follow Jesus once materialism is banished from the man's aspiration—but why only after? The reason stems from the radical nature of Jesus's call. The Lord always asks for a "yes" or "no"; sitting on the fence in a passive manner is not enough. We may recall the severe warning addressed to the Church in Laodicea: "I know of thy doings, and find thee neither cold nor hot; cold or hot, I would thou wert one or the other. Being what thou art, lukewarm, neither cold nor hot, thou wilt make me vomit thee out of my mouth" (Rev. 3:15–16).

To live as a disciple means to imitate Jesus and that can only truly happen when we conform our will to his; when we reject the earthly treasures in favor of those divine. We see in the life of St. Francis of Assisi the absolute acceptance of this call. He embraced the totality of the Lord's demands—and all with divine love, stripping himself bare of everything that could be construed as a hindrance to following Jesus. By living the beatitudes in such a complete way, the great Seraphic Father was able to become a perfect icon of the Lord and therefore the love that emanated from within was not really his own but that of the Son of God.

The question that was asked: "what must I do to achieve eternal life?" is one that must forever be the locus of our spiritual life. We must always seek the fundamental precepts that create saints and allow space for God in every moment of our existence. The lofty requirements needed seem unreachable to many, but actually that is not the case. Real holiness in the mind of God is carrying out everyday duties with love of God and neighbor. Everything is done for the glory of God and the salvation of our brothers and sisters. Of course, there are many different vocations within the Mystical Body.

Some are called to great acts of Christian heroism—we can think of the martyrdom of Christians in Iraq and Syria—but for most, it is the ordinary, even mundane journey through life that is laden with opportunity for growth in holiness. Love is the key to the saint; it is the characteristic of all saints, and without it, no matter how pious appearances may be, the Christian life remains an illusion.

For the Church of the twenty-first century, the notion of saints presented in the New Testament needs to be reflected upon; we need to return to the root cause of our joy, Jesus Christ, as the first Christians did. Perhaps the Church has become over-reliant on strategies, allowing the focus to drift away from a personal encounter with the Lord—one bound by a burning love. In the following chapter, we will look to the contemporary situation of the Church Militant, and especially the magisterium of Pope Francis as a natural progression from this chapter. But to conclude this important area of theology, I would like to quote St. Thérèse of Lisieux, who understood in a most astounding way the truth that to be a saint is quite simply to love:

> Charity gave me the key to my vocation. I understood that if the Church has a body composed of different members, the noblest and most necessary of all the members would not be lacking to her. I understood that the Church has a heart, and that this heart burns with Love. I understood that Love alone makes its members act, that if this Love were to be extinguished, the Apostles would no longer preach the Gospel, the Martyrs would refuse to shed their blood.... I understood that Love embraces all vocations, that Love is all things, that it embraces all times and all places ... in a word, that it is eternal! To be love in the heart of the Church. Then in the excess of my delirious joy, I cried out: "O Jesus, my Love, at last I have found my vocation, my vocation is Love! ... Yes, I have found my place in the Church, and it is you, O my God, who have given me this place ... in the heart of the Church, my Mother, I will be Love! ... Thus I shall be all things: thus my dream shall be realized!!!"[19]

---

19. St. Therese of Lisieux, *Spiritual Canticle*, prologue 3, 2.

5

A Poor Church for the Poor

If anyone deludes himself by thinking he is serving God, when he has not learned to control his tongue, the service he gives is vain. If he is to offer service pure and unblemished in the sight of God, who is our Father, he must take care of orphans and widows in their need, and keep himself untainted by the world. (Jam. 1:26–27)

THE EVENTS OF February and March 2013 will, in the annals of the Catholic Church, always have a great historical significance. With the resignation of Pope Benedict XVI on February 28, the first papal abdication in six centuries and the subsequent election of Cardinal Jorge Mario Bergoglio on March 13, a new chapter opened in the history of the papacy. The Church was blessed with the first South American Pontiff, who took the name Francis.[1]

---

1. The Pope related the reason behind choosing the name Francis in a speech to journalists shortly after his election: "During the election, I was seated next to the Archbishop Emeritus of São Paolo and Prefect Emeritus of the Congregation for the Clergy, Cardinal Claudio Hummes: a good friend, a good friend! When things were looking dangerous, he encouraged me. And when the votes reached two thirds, there was the usual applause, because the Pope had been elected. And he gave me a hug and a kiss, and said: 'Don't forget the poor!' And those words came to me: the poor, the poor. Then, right away, thinking of the poor, I thought of Francis of Assisi. Then I thought of all the wars, as the votes were still being counted, till the end. Francis is also the man of peace. That is how the name came into my heart: Francis of Assisi. For me, he is the man of poverty, the man of peace, the man who loves and protects creation; these days we do not have a very good relationship with creation, do we? He is the man who gives us this spirit of peace, the poor man.... How I would like a Church which is poor and for the poor!" Pope Francis, "Audience to representatives of the communications Media," March 16, 2013, www.vatican.va.

Although the papacy as an institution defends the faith and teachings of the Church throughout history, nevertheless the occupants of the Chair of St. Peter possess their own charisms and wisdom that at times shed greater light on matters pertaining to the times in which they live. For St. Pius X it was the restoration of all things in Christ as the antidote to a menacing modernism. For St. John Paul II fighting the evils of communism, it was the freedom and dignity of man as God had designed. For Pope Benedict XVI it was the conviction that love, faith and reason would reveal the truth concerning Jesus Christ as the Savior of the world in a post Christian culture. But what of Pope Francis in the early years of his papacy? Do we yet perceive a theme that is central to his magisterium?

Although much has already been written about Francis concerning a variety of theological positions and the two Synods on the family, it is not my intention to enter into these polemics; in this final chapter of part one, I would rather venture into the teachings of the Pope, seeking to ascertain his thought concerning the vocation of the baptized, and the necessity of the Church in removing all that hinders its ability to show Jesus Christ to the world. Essentially then, we will seek to cut through the controversies and reveal the true intention of this Pope, because he has much to teach us in the quest to become authentic members of the communion of saints.

The Danger of Spiritual Worldliness

Before we look in detail at the magisterium of Pope Francis, it is worth recalling a theme that Pope Benedict XVI focused on during his pontificate. It relates to the dangers that threaten the faith:

> As for the new things which we can find in this message today [the third secret of Fatima], there is also the fact that attacks on the Pope and the Church come not only from without, but the sufferings of the Church come precisely from within the Church, from the sin existing within the Church. This too is something that we have always known, but today we are seeing it in a really terrifying way: *that the greatest persecution of the Church comes not from her enemies without, but arises from sin within the Church,* and that the Church thus has a deep need to relearn penance, to accept purifi-

cation, to learn forgiveness on the one hand, but also the need for justice.[2]

Again in a homily for the Feast of Saints Peter and Paul, he returned to the same theme:

> Indeed if we think of the two millenniums of the Church's history, we may note as the Lord Jesus had foretold (cf. Mt. 10:16–33) that trials for Christians have never been lacking and in certain periods and places have assumed the character of true and proper persecution. Yet, despite the suffering they cause, they do not constitute the gravest danger for the Church. *Indeed she is subjected to the greatest danger by what pollutes the faith and Christian life of her members and communities, corroding the integrity of the Mystical Body, weakening her capacity for prophecy and witness, and marring the beauty of her face.*[3]

Although commentators on the fringes have tried to show a rupture between the papacies of Benedict and Francis, the evidence actually shows that Pope Francis has taken this thread of Ratzingerian thought (consciously or unconsciously) and developed it as the focal point of his magisterium. He continually addresses many areas of the spiritual life of Christians that need urgent attention, and for what reason? Because he desires to change the mentality that too often prevails in the Church: one of mediocrity and narcissism. In Francis's view, the only possible response to the challenges and tribulations of this epoch is to return to the heart of Christianity: salvation through Jesus Christ, the embracing of his mercy, and an acceptance that we are sinners aspiring to become saints, through the humble daily service of humanity.

The similarity of the thought expressed by both Benedict and Francis stems from the exposing of a hypocritical form of Christianity that seeks to show outward piety while concealing a connivance with evil in a variety of forms: impurity, slander, judgmentalism, spiritual petrification, envy and vainglory to name just a few. In this

2. Pope Benedict XVI, "Interview of the Holy Father Benedict XVI with the Journalists during the flight to Portugal," May 11, 2010, www.vatican.va.

3. Pope Benedict XVI, "Homily at Mass for the Feast of Saints Peter and Paul," June 29, 2010, www.vatican.va.

way sin pollutes the Church, spreading like an infectious disease and making the work of evangelization less credible to an agnostic and skeptical gentile world. In essence it is a variant of pharisaism, of which we know Jesus was so critical.

A good starting point for this discussion can be found in Francis's very first homily at the *Missa Pro Ecclesia* the day after his election, in which he warns of a counterfeit Catholicism:

> We can walk as much as we want, we can build many things, but if we do not profess Jesus Christ, things go wrong. We may become a charitable NGO, but not the Church, the Bride of the Lord.... When we do not profess Jesus Christ, the saying of Léon Bloy comes to mind: "Anyone who does not pray to the Lord prays to the devil." When we do not profess Jesus Christ, we profess the worldliness of the devil, a demonic worldliness.[4]

These are striking words that offer evidence that this Pope was not so much chosen for a renovation of the Roman Curia, as for a renewal of spiritual values that would allow nobody to lie comfortably in a cosy Christianity that shuns the Cross. The reference to the devil was the first of many that would become, to the disquiet of some, a hallmark of this pope's magisterium.[5] The principle of "spiritual worldliness" in the mind of the Pontiff is the quintessential temptation that the faithful must confront. It could almost be described as the antithesis of the Beatitudes: a perverted inversion that seeks to replicate the temptations Jesus faced in the wilderness, those of pleasure in materialism, power, and the rejection of the Kingdom of God for our own interests. Pope Francis spoke at length on this subject during a visit to Assisi on the Feast of St. Francis in 2013:

> Someone could ask: "Of what must the Church divest herself?" Today she must strip herself of a very grave danger, which threatens every person in the Church, everyone: the danger of worldliness. The Christian cannot coexist with the spirit of the world, with the worldliness that leads us to vanity, to arrogance, to pride.

---

4. Pope Francis, "Homily for the Missa Pro Ecclesia," March 14, 2013, www.vatican.va.

And this is an idol, it is not God. It is an idol! And idolatry is the gravest of sins! . . . Worldliness hurts us. It is so very sad to find a worldly Christian, sure—according to him—of that security that the faith gives and of the security that the world provides. You cannot be on both sides. The Church—all of us—must strip herself of the worldliness that leads to vanity, to pride, that is idolatry. . . . Jesus himself told us: "You cannot serve two masters: either you serve God or you serve mammon" (cf. Mt. 6:24). In mammon itself there is this worldly spirit; money, vanity, pride, that path . . . we cannot take it . . . it is sad to erase with one hand what we write with the other. The Gospel is the Gospel![6]

The obvious question that needs addressing therefore is what vision does Pope Francis have for the Church? Undoubtedly, he desires to see the Mystical Body as an irresistible force to those on the outside, through the authentic witness of Christians who are not afraid to get their hands dirty. In an interview with Fr. Antonio Spadaro, S.J., he shared his thoughts on this matter:

I see clearly, that the thing the church needs most today is the ability to heal wounds and to warm the hearts of the faithful; it needs

5. Interestingly, on this point we have evidence that the Cardinals in the conclave had begun to look towards Bergoglio on Saturday, March 9 after his dramatic speech in the penultimate pre-conclave congregation. With Bergoglio's permission, the Cardinal of Havana, Jaime Lucas Ortega y Alamino quoted the future pope's thoughts in a Chrism Mass homily back in Cuba: "When the Church does not come out from itself to evangelize it becomes self-referential and gets sick (one thinks of the woman hunched over upon herself in the Gospel). The evils that, in the passing of time, afflict the ecclesiastical institutions have a root in self-referentiality, in a sort of theological narcissism. In Revelation, Jesus says that he is standing at the threshold and calling. Evidently the text refers to the fact that he stands outside the door and knocks to enter. . . . But at times I think that Jesus may be knocking from the inside, that we may let him out. The self-referential Church presumes to keep Jesus Christ within itself and not let him out." . . . "The Church, when it is self-referential, without realizing it thinks that it has its own light; it stops being the 'mysterium lunae' and gives rise to that evil which is so grave, that of spiritual worldliness (according to De Lubac, the worst evil into which the Church can fall): that of living to give glory to one another." Sandro Magister, "The Last Words of Bergoglio Before the Conclave," http://chiesa.espresso.repubblica.it/articolo/135048 4?eng=y (accessed December 27, 2014).

6. Pope Francis, "Meeting with the Poor Assisted of Caritas," October 4, 2013, www.vatican.va.

nearness, proximity. . . . I dream of a church that is a mother and shepherdess. The church's ministers must be merciful, take responsibility for the people and accompany them like the good Samaritan, who washes, cleans and raises up his neighbor. This is pure Gospel. . . . Instead of being just a church that welcomes and receives by keeping the doors open, let us try also to be a church that finds new roads, that is able to step outside itself and go to those who do not attend Mass, to those who have quit or are indifferent. The ones who quit sometimes do it for reasons that, if properly understood and assessed, can lead to a return. But that takes audacity and courage.[7]

The Crisis of Humanity

As we have already seen, one of the most pressing concerns for the Pope is the galvanization of the Church towards a concern for the poor, the marginalized and the refugee. He doesn't however see this from the viewpoint of mere philanthropy, but rather from the conviction that caring for the impoverished is a prophetic witness to the love of God and neighbor, and a testament to the virtue of hope; Christ is the point of reference in any work of fraternal charity that emanates from the saints. The Holy Father reflected on this in a Pentecost address to Ecclesial Movements when recounting his experiences as a confessor in Argentina. He stated how he would ask several questions:

And when you give alms, do you touch the hand of the person you are giving them to or do you toss the coin at him or her? This is the problem: the flesh of Christ, touching the flesh of Christ, taking upon ourselves this suffering for the poor. Poverty for us Christians is not a sociological, philosophical or cultural category, no. It is theological. I might say this is the first category, because our God, the Son of God, abased himself, he made himself poor to walk along the road with us.[8]

---

7. Pope Francis, "A Big Heart Open to God," www.http://americamagazine.org/pope-interview (accessed December 27, 2014).

8. Pope Francis, "Pentecost Vigil with Ecclesial Movements," May 18, 2013, www.vatican.va.

There is also an eschatological element of this issue that should not be overlooked, one that Pope Francis has repeatedly affirmed already. It concerns the reality of a final judgment that is approaching.[9] The parable that describes this unique event, found in Matthew chapter 25, forms the basis for Pope Francis's thought. If we recall, the parable presents the scene of all humanity gathered together: the sheep on the Lord's right, and the goats destined for hell on his left. Jesus in a sense presents the consummation of the Beatitudes to those on his right, the harvest of their charity. He reveals the truth taught by the Church throughout the ages, that his presence is to be found in the poorest:[10]

> For I was hungry, and you gave me food, thirsty, and you gave me drink; I was a stranger, and you brought me home, naked, and you clothed me, sick, and you cared for me, a prisoner, and you came to me.... Believe me, when you did it to one of the least of my brethren here, you did it to me. (Matt. 25:35–36, 40)

Pope Francis calls our attention to the reality that each one of us, without exception, will be confronted by the voice of the just judge on that climacteric day. He reminds us that we already know the criteria by which we will be judged: that of living the Beatitudes, the

9. In my previous work, *Heralds of the Second Coming*, published in the week of Pope Benedict XVI's resignation, I had talked of the need for the Church to strip itself of pomp and political power in order to ready itself for the last times: "The Church at the end must be pure and chaste; it must resemble St. John the Baptist who ate only locusts and honey in the wilderness." This was in reference to St. Hildegard of Bingen, Doctor of the Church, who foresaw in a series of papal approved visions, the five successive ages until the end of the world, one of which accurately described the loss of the Papal States many centuries before it occurred. Could it be that Pope Francis senses, as did his recent predecessors, the signs of the Lord's return emerging in ever greater clarity and thus deems it necessary to preach a message of evangelical poverty as the greatest form of spiritual preparation? Stephen Walford, *Heralds of the Second Coming: Our Lady, the Divine Mercy and the Popes of the Marian Era from Bl. Pius IX to Benedict XVI* (Angelico Press, 2013), 161, 214–215.

10. St. Peter Chrysologus captures the heart of this teaching beautifully: "The hand of the poor person is Christ's treasury, since whatever the poor person receives, Christ receives." (Sermon VIII. 4) Peter, William B. Palardy, *St. Peter Chrysologus: Selected Sermons*, vol. 2, (Washington, DC: The Catholic University of America Press, 2004), 44.

gateway to sanctity. To forget the weakest is a scandal, a grave sin; it is to bypass the modern-day "mangers" for fear of upsetting our own conscience:

> I have said that the poor are at the heart of the Gospel; they are present there from beginning to end. In the synagogue at Nazareth, Jesus made this clear at the outset of his ministry. And when in Matthew 25 he speaks of the latter days, and reveals the criterion by which we will all be judged, there too we find the poor. There is a danger, a temptation which arises in times of prosperity: it is the danger that the Christian community becomes just another "part of society," losing its mystical dimension, losing its ability to celebrate the Mystery and instead becoming a spiritual organization, Christian and with Christian values, but lacking the leaven of prophecy. When this happens, the poor no longer have their proper role in the Church. This is a temptation from which particular Churches, Christian communities, have suffered greatly over the centuries; in some cases they become so middle class that the poor even feel ashamed to be a part of them. It is the temptation of spiritual "prosperity," pastoral prosperity. No longer is it a poor Church for the poor but rather a rich Church for the rich, or a middle class Church for the well-to-do.[11]

The Holy Father has a great gift for cutting through theological concepts, presenting the truth in such a way that it simply cannot be ignored. His criticism above concerning the "spiritual prosperity" of a middle class cafeteria Catholicism will ring true for many. The reality is that a sense of the mystical has been lost in past decades, having the effect of weakening the ties between the natural and supernatural order. As a consequence of this, sin, judgment and the eternal realities—the so-called last things—have been swept under the carpet, allowing a comfortable laissez-faire attitude to prevail where the conscience becomes ever more insensitive to the spiritual needs of ourselves and others. Pope Francis obviously senses the need to rouse the Church out of this dormancy before it is too late:

11. Pope Francis, "Meeting with the Bishops of Korea," August 14, 2014, www.vatican.va.

"It is a human crisis: it is the human person that is in crisis! Man himself is in danger of being destroyed! But man is the image of God! This is why it is a profound crisis!"[12]

By refocusing the Church on the reality of the Last Judgment, the Pope is not scaremongering but reminding us all that much indeed will be expected of Christians, especially Catholic Christians who benefit from the sacraments. The task is to love and forgive, to show faith through good works, with no other incentive than to see the lives of others changed through the joy of giving. In this way the brilliance of the Light that will descend on the clouds one day will not blind those who profess the true Faith, but illuminate their own sanctity. This is the meaning of Pope Francis's frequent stinging criticisms of Catholics. He may appear very harsh at times, but it is because he wants a Church bursting at the seams with saints, a Mystical Body that resembles as closely as possible the holiness of its Bridegroom:

> Dear brothers and sisters, may looking at the Last Judgement never frighten us: rather, may it impel us to live the present better. God offers us this time with mercy and patience so that we may learn every day to recognize him in the poor and in the lowly. Let us strive for goodness and be watchful in prayer and in love. May the Lord, at the end of our life and at the end of history, be able to recognize us as good and faithful servants.[13]

One of the great innovations of this Pontificate is the daily meditations given by Francis at his early morning Mass. By following the Scriptural readings of the yearly cycle, he has been able to expound on many themes that perhaps would otherwise remain relatively unexplored. Again, everything is taught with the intention of shaping a Catholicism that is totally authentic and free from any hypocrisy.

For instance the Holy Father has spoken many times already on the evil of gossip in the gravest terms: "every time we judge our

---

12. Pope Francis, "Pentecost Vigil with Ecclesial Movements," May 18, 2013, www.vatican.va.

13. Pope Francis, "General Audience," April 24, 2013, www.vatican.va.

brother in our hearts or worse when we speak badly of them with others, we are murdering Christians."[14] On a previous occasion he had broached the subject in a similar way: "we are used to gossip, to spreading rumors, and we often transform our communities as well as our family into 'hell' where this kind of crime that leads to killing one's brother and sister with one's tongue is manifest."[15] Gossip, slander, envy, jealousy are all frequent themes in these meditations that form an anti-gospel; the gospel of spiritual worldliness. The Holy Father is always careful to explain how these poisons seep into the life of Christians, and how they are reflected in the biblical texts. By doing this he sets before us a sort of compendium for the self-examination of conscience.

As we briefly saw earlier, the devil is never far away from the thoughts of Pope Francis. It is most significant, because even in the short period of this papacy, the truth of the existence of Satan appears more often than in all the other recent papacies in their entirety. What should we read into this? Without doubt, it stems from the belief of the Holy Father that to warn is to protect:

> The Church has the courage of a mother who knows she must defend her children against the dangers which arise from Satan's presence in the world, in order to lead them to the encounter with Jesus. A mother always protects her children. This defence also calls for vigilance: to be watchful for the snares and seduction of the Evil One. Because even though Satan was defeated by God, he always returns with his temptations; we know it, we are all tempted, we have been tempted and we are tempted. Satan comes "like a roaring lion" (1 Pt. 5:8), the Apostle Peter says, and it is up to us not to be naïve, but to be vigilant and to resist, steadfast in the faith. To resist with the counsel of Mother Church, to resist with the help of Mother Church, who like a good mama always accompanies her children at difficult times.[16]

14. Pope Francis, "From gossip to love of others," *L'Osservatore Romano*, Weekly ed. in English, September 18, 2013, 38.

15. Pope Francis, "The Threat of Gossip," *L'Osservatore Romano*, Weekly ed. in English, September 4, 2013, 36.

16. Pope Francis, "General Audience," September 3, 2014, www.vatican.va.

A Satanic Onslaught

The Holy Father, in union with his great predecessors, understands the nature of the apocalyptic battle being waged in this epoch. At the center of this struggle is Satan, the father of lies who seeks to destroy the communion of saints as much as he can on earth. In the words of the Pope, he "doesn't cast flowers on us but flaming, poisonous arrows."[17] In a homily on the existence of the devil, the Pontiff explained how the temptations of the Evil One draw us away from the life of holiness, both as an individual and as a community of love, and all through the power of seduction that had wounded Adam and Eve:

> The devil's temptations have three main characteristics, and we have to be aware of them in order to not to fall into his trap. First: the temptation begins subtly but then it grows and increasingly grows stronger. Then it infects someone else . . . it spreads to another and seeks to take root in the community. Finally, to calm the soul, it seeks to justify itself. In short: it grows, spreads and justifies itself.[18]

Two episodes from the Gospels show how self-justification can rip through an entire community, easing the conscience while seeking to destroy the work of God. In the first, when Jesus was in the Synagogue at Nazareth (Lk. 4:16–30), the crowd, after having been astonished by the Lord's wisdom, allowed Satan to tempt them into dismissing him as a crank. Collectively, they allowed pride and envy to cloud their judgment of him. No doubt his words pierced their hearts, but instead of choosing the path of repentance and renewal, they opted for the easier path of erasing him and his message. In that way no challenge needed to be met; no inner searching for the truth; the sorry chapter could be closed almost before it had begun.

The second episode concerns the religious authorities of the Sanhedrin who desired to kill Jesus. Their arrogance led to their own

17. Pope Francis, "A Beautiful Struggle," *L'Osservatore Romano*, Weekly ed. in English, November 7, 2014, 45.

18. Pope Francis, "The Devil exists," *L'Osservatore Romano*, Weekly ed. in English, April 18, 2014, 16.

blindness of Scripture; even as Isaiah's prophecy of the Suffering Servant was being fulfilled before their very eyes. Caiaphas the High Priest had spoken the prophetic words: "you do not reflect that it is best for us if one man is put to death for the sake of the people, to save a whole nation from destruction" (Jn. 11:50). The others agreed; their self-justification soothing any troubles within. A conformism feeding on each other's corruption had led to the rejection of the true Son of God, through the power of diabolical persuasion.

Along with the teachings on demonic methods of temptation, the Holy Father has also given instruction in the ways of averting the influence of Satan in our lives. During a meditation in the *Domus Sanctae Marthae* Chapel in October 2013 he spoke on the subject:

> There is no shadow of a doubt. A battle exists, a battle in which the eternal salvation of us all is at stake. There are no alternatives, even if at times we hear about "pastoral proposals" that seem more accommodating. No! Either you are with Jesus or you are against him.... We must always be vigilant against the deception and seduction of the evil one.... We can ask ourselves: Do I keep watch over myself? Do I guard my heart? My feelings? My thoughts? Do I guard the treasure of grace? Do I protect the Holy Spirit's presence within me? ... This is the devil's strategy: you become a Christian, go forward in your faith, and I will leave you alone; I will leave you in peace. But then, once you have grown accustomed to it, are no longer watchful and feel secure I will return.... Please, let's not do business with the devil, the devil is on the first page of the Bible and he is still there on the last, when God has his final victory.[19]

Freedom through Grace

If the more progressive, liberal side of Catholicism were under the impression that Pope Francis was sent by the Holy Spirit to redefine

---

19. Pope Francis, "How to Rout the Demon's Strategy," *L'Osservatore Romano*, Weekly ed. in English, October 18, 2013, 42.

revealed truth and deliver a new updated form of Christianity, then his teachings on the devil should instill a healthy dose of reality. It is one of the great intrigues of this Pontificate that he will not allow himself to be stereotyped by anyone. Labels mean nothing to him: Liberal, Traditionalist or Conservative; all have felt the full force of his criticism, and why? Because for Jorge Mario Bergoglio, the only matter of importance is the full, unconditional response to the Gospel; in heaven there won't be "mansions" for each group, only the communion of saints that exist as one body built on love—divine love.

It is interesting to note how much has been written about this Pope already from so many quarters both within the Church and without. For those within, often the essays come with a certain amount of head scratching because he *appears* contradictory, but that is precisely the point. He wants to create a mess; he wants Catholics to come out of their self-made pigeonholes where rash judgments are made, and experience the liberation that comes from the most radical form of Christianity, that of St. Francis of Assisi. Too often, in the mind of the Pope, Christians develop an interior disposition where avenues are closed that should be open to God's grace; that safety in one form of the spiritual life is detrimental to the overall plan of God. As an example from his own life, he humbly recounted how at one time he viewed the Charismatic Renewal Movement with suspicion, but "converted" after realizing that the Holy Spirit was working through them. The fruits bore testament to the presence of God within these communities, opening up new creative possibilities for the Church.

The temptation to Paganism (or modern forms of it) has also been targeted by the Argentine Pontiff. In a speech to Brazilian Bishops, warning of several temptations concerning missionary discipleship, he stated:

> The Pelagian solution. This basically appears as a form of restorationism. In dealing with the Church's problems, a purely disciplinary solution is sought, through the restoration of outdated manners and forms which, even on the cultural level, are no longer meaningful. In Latin America it is usually to be found in small groups, in some new religious congregations, in exaggerated

tendencies toward doctrinal or disciplinary "safety." Basically it is static, although it is capable of inversion, in a process of regression. It seeks to "recover" the lost past.[20]

He also returned to the theme in his Apostolic Exhortation, *Evangelii Gaudium*:

> The other [form of spiritual worldliness] is the self-absorbed promethean neopelagianism of those who ultimately trust only in their own powers and feel superior to others because they observe certain rules or remain intransigently faithful to a particular Catholic style from the past. A supposed soundness of doctrine or discipline leads instead to a narcissistic and authoritarian elitism, whereby instead of evangelizing, one analyzes and classifies others, and instead of opening the door to grace, one exhausts his or her energies in inspecting and verifying. In neither case is one really concerned about Jesus Christ or others. These are manifestations of an anthropocentric immanentism. It is impossible to think that a genuine evangelizing thrust could emerge from these adulterated forms of Christianity.[21]

What is the Pope actually saying here? Is this an attack on Traditionalism within the Church? Without doubt it calls into question the attitudes of some within the movement, but of course it would be totally wrong to stigmatize all with these criticisms. It has to be said that he is correct in many of his concerns; there certainly exists a rigidity of thought that is extremely judgmental to other expressions of Catholic faith—the Charismatic renewal or the gatherings for World Youth Day being examples that have attracted plenty of criticism. Another example is the negative attitude towards natural family planning, which is often judged to be little better than artificial contraception. Then there is the erroneous understanding of the function of a bishop who often appears to be more akin to a political governor wielding power, rather than a gentle shepherd and servant of Jesus Christ.

---

20. Pope Francis, "Address to the Leadership of the Episcopal Conferences of Latin America," July 28, 2013, www.vatican.va.

21. Pope Francis, Apostolic Exhortation, *Evangelii Gaudium*, November 24, 2013, www.vatican.va.

The security provided by rules and regulations creates an atmosphere that is inward looking, that is fearful of change. It is as if there exists an attempt to "imprison" the work of the Holy Spirit, to call into question almost anything after 1960 as an "innovation" or "rupture." In this way, the real theological understanding of Tradition—as something alive and active here and now—is conveniently discarded, and the very ones who profess to uphold Tradition end up being the ones who deny it.[22]

But is the Pope saying rules can be ignored? Certainly not, but it is the reliance on them, the strictness of interpretation that is called into question. As an example, we could take the true teaching on mortal sin.[23] There is at times little distinction in a rigorist position of what constitutes a mortal sin. In the desire to "analyze or classify others," as Pope Francis said, harsh judgments are often meted out to those struggling in sinful situations. There is little interest in the possibility that someone has not given their full consent to an act of grave matter, or even had full knowledge of the seriousness of the sin. Mercy seems to be in short supply it has to be said; perhaps this explains why the Divine Mercy devotion seems to be rather frowned upon in traditionalist circles. I am sure that those of us who have been regular attendees of the extraordinary form of the Mass are sadly familiar with these sentiments.

22. In terms of liturgical renewal, it is interesting to read a passage from Pope Pius XII's Encyclical *Mediator Dei*, written in 1947—long before Vatican II: "The use of the Latin language, customary in a considerable portion of the Church, is a manifest and beautiful sign of unity, as well as an effective antidote for any corruption of doctrinal truth. In spite of this, the use of the mother tongue in connection with several of the rites may be of much advantage to the people. . . . The same reasoning holds in the case of some persons who are bent on the restoration of all the ancient rites and ceremonies indiscriminately. The liturgy of the early ages is most certainly worthy of all veneration. But ancient usage must not be esteemed more suitable and proper, either in its own right or in its significance for later times and new situations, on the simple ground that it carries the savor and aroma of antiquity. The more recent liturgical rites likewise deserve reverence and respect. They, too, owe their inspiration to the Holy Spirit, who assists the Church in every age even to the consummation of the world. They are equally the resources used by the majestic Spouse of Jesus Christ to promote and procure the sanctity of man." Pope Pius XII, *Mediator Dei*, nos. 60–61, November 20, 1947, www.vatican.va.

23. *Catechism of the Catholic Church*, no. 1857, www.vatican.va.

We must stress that Pope Francis is not against those who cherish the ancient form of the Mass, or those who worship the Lord through traditional devotions. What he seeks to do is purify it, removing the stench of hypocrisy and thus displaying the full beauty of it. Praying with the heart, offering alms with the heart, is worshiping in spirit and in truth. The joy of being part of this great symphony of praise and thanksgiving is surely the distinguishing feature we desire to project, rather than the continual angst that sometimes appears to be a traditionalist hallmark. A heart open to God's grace is one that does not put restrictions on the activity of the Holy Spirit but rejoices in the freedom to go where the Lord wills.

The Era of Divine Mercy

Perhaps the greatest theme to date in the magisterium of Pope Francis is the promotion of God's mercy,[24] and in that sense he is continuing the legacy of St. John Paul II, who promoted the devotion to the Divine Mercy as revealed by the Polish mystic, St. Faustina Kowalska.[25] Not only did St. Faustina's compatriot canonize her, but he also acceded to the request that Jesus expressed through her, namely giving the Second Sunday of Easter the title of Divine Mercy Sunday. Our present Holy Father wasted no time in proclaiming this greatest attribute of God, when only four days into his pontificate, he preached on the subject in his first Sunday Angelus address:

> This is the best thing we can feel: it changes the world. A little mercy makes the world less cold and more just. We need to understand properly this mercy of God, this merciful Father who is so patient.... Let us remember the Prophet Isaiah who says that

24. Pope Francis's proclamation of an *Extraordinary Jubilee Year of Mercy* to begin on the Feast of the Immaculate Conception, December 8, 2015, bears testimony to the importance he places on this marvel of God.

25. Of great significance is the motto Pope Francis has beneath his Coat of Arms. It reads: *"miserando atque eligendo,"* which translates as: "by having mercy, by choosing him." It is taken from a homily by the Venerable Bede on St. Matthew's Gospel: "Jesus saw the tax collector and by having mercy chose him as an Apostle saying to him: Follow me."

even if our sins were scarlet, God's love would make them white as snow. This mercy is beautiful![26]

It is certain that Pope Francis feels very strongly the sense that this time, this era is a *Kairos*, that is, a special period of grace marked by mercy. He more than alluded to it in a speech to the priests of Rome during Lent 2014, in which he displayed a perfect unity of thought with the great Polish Pope:

> Thus we understand that we are not here to take part in a pleasant retreat at the beginning of Lent, but rather to hear the voice of the Spirit speaking to the whole Church of our time, which is the time of mercy. I am sure of this. It is not only Lent; *we are living in a time of mercy, and have been for 30 years or more, up to today. In the Church, everything is the time of mercy.* . . . Today we forget everything far too quickly, even the Magisterium of the Church! Part of this is unavoidable, but we cannot forget the great content, the great intuitions and gifts that have been left to the People of God. And Divine Mercy is one of these. *It is a gift which he gave to us, but which comes from above. It is up to us, as ministers of the Church, to keep this message alive*, above all through preaching and in our actions, in signs and in pastoral choices, such as the decision to restore priority to the Sacrament of Reconciliation and to the works of mercy.[27]

In the overall context of the communion of saints, mercy may seem somewhat remote, but truth be told, it is that foundation on which holiness is built. It generates goodness within us because it becomes a fruit of humility and repentance. If recognizing our own sinfulness is the first step on the road to sanctity, then mercy is the second; it is the acceptance of the Lord's forgiveness, and trust in his desire to cleanse us from all that stains the soul. Of course, as the Gospels inform us, the forgiveness we gain from heaven will be proportionate to the forgiveness and mercy we show to others. And if we embrace this path, it will create a ripple effect whereby mercy is

26. Pope Francis, "Angelus Address," March 17, 2013, www.vatican.va.

27. Pope Francis, "Address to the Parish Priests of the Diocese of Rome," March 6, 2014.

replicated among all the faithful; fellow pilgrims will no longer be acquaintances but true brothers and sisters; the Holy Souls in Purgatory will be bound to us by divinely inspired charity, and the Saints in heaven will shower us with an endless stream of graces won by their love for us. Mercy allows this source of love to grow, because bathing in the good done to us, impels us to act likewise and in that sense, a stream of mercy turns into a river and then an ocean. This has to be the vision for the Lord's Mystical Body, for without it the Church would be full of the introverted, with little compassion or empathy for the fate of others. That is not the route pointed out by the Lord; rather for us, the Lord's invitation is to become his friends, to share in the divine secrets together as a community.

Cardinal Christoph Schonborn explains the nature of this friendship, first between God and us and then to each other:

> The love that is friendship has two distinguishing characteristics: *benevolentia*, that is to say, willing the good of the other person; and *mutua amatio*, mutuality of love. Not every love has these qualities. Friendship presupposes a certain *equality*. There is no friendship without mutual exchange: "A friend is a friend to his friend [*amicus amico amicus*]," says Thomas [Aquinas] with Aristotle. "Talis mutua benevolentia fundatur super aliquam communicationem" (Such mutual good will is based on some kind of communication).[28]

As part of this theology of mercy, Pope Francis has often encouraged the faithful to frequent the Sacrament of Confession; in fact to emphasize the point, he publicly received the Sacrament himself in St. Peter's Basilica during Lent of 2014, much to the surprise of those present. He sees it as an absolutely essential element of any true conversion, as is proven by these thoughts expressed during a morning Mass:

> If being a sinner is only a word or a way of speaking, then we do not need God's forgiveness. But if it is a reality that enslaves us

---

28. Christoph Schonborn, *Loving the Church: Spiritual Exercises in the Presence of Pope John Paul II* (San Francisco: Ignatius Press, 1998), 166.

then we truly need the interior freedom and strength of the Lord. Paul shows us the way out, confess your sin and your tendency to sin to the community, do not hide it. This is the disposition which the Church asks of all of us, which Jesus asks of all of us: humbly to confess our sins.

Then, continuing in his own inimitable style, Francis addressed those who would prefer to seek forgiveness away from the Sacrament:

> It's easy. It's like confessing by email.... God is there, far away; I say things and there is no face to face, there is not a face to face encounter. But Paul confessed his weakness to his brothers face to face.... But if there is one thing that is beautiful, it is when we confess our sins in the presence of God just as they are. We always feel the grace of being ashamed. To feel ashamed before God is a grace.[29]

Before we leave the subject of mercy, we need to be clear that the *expectation* of mercy does not justify lessening efforts to refrain from sin. There appears to be an orchestrated campaign to portray Pope Francis as one who softens the seriousness of sin by preaching mercy, as if sin is somewhat relegated to a bygone era; or to put it another way, that mercy is available on tap no matter what. Of course the Holy Father promotes mercy for those who genuinely struggle from the effects of original sin, who want to rise from the mediocrity imposed by sin, on the other hand he rails against the corrupt and the arrogant; those who feel no need for mercy. In that sense he preaches as Jesus did: gentleness and patience for those who show humility in their weakness; righteous anger for those puffed up with pride.

A further point worth stressing here is that in the spiritual *Diary* of St. Faustina Kowalska, even though mercy is the dominant theme, the Lord Jesus does not in any way downplay the significance of sin; we are not presented with a caricature of Jesus where

---

29. Pope Francis, "The grace of being ashamed," *L'Osservatore Romano*, Weekly ed. in English, November 1, 2013, 44.

everything will be forgiven come what may, as if repentance was not a prerequisite. On the contrary, the entire message and devotion is placed within the context of the terrible events of the twentieth century, and the onset of the end times, with its tragic spiral of evil as described in St. John's Apocalypse—a point not lost on Popes John Paul II, Benedict XVI and now Francis.[30]

The Communion of Saints: Spiritual Fraternity

To conclude this chapter, let us look at what Pope Francis teaches us concerning the doctrine of the communion of saints. Even in the short duration of this pontificate, he has devoted two general audiences to the theme, ensuring that the significance of the dogma is not lost on the faithful. In the first audience, he concentrated on the expression: *communion among holy persons*:

> The Church, in her most profound truth, is communion with God, intimacy with God, a communion of love with Christ and with the Father in the Holy Spirit, which extends to brotherly communion. This relationship between Jesus and the Father is the "matrix" of the bond between us Christians: if we are intimately part of this "matrix", this fiery furnace of love, then we can truly become of one single heart and one single soul among us. For God's love burns away our selfishness, our prejudices, our interior and exterior divisions ... *our faith needs the support of others*, especially in difficult moments. If we are united our faith becomes stronger. How beautiful it is to support each other in the wonderful adventure of faith! I say this because the tendency to be closed and private has influenced the religious sphere as well, so much so that it often becomes difficult to ask for spiritual help from those [who] would share this Christian life with us. Who among us has not experienced insecurity, confusion and even doubt on our journey of faith?[31]

---

30. St. Faustina faithfully recorded the words of Jesus: "Speak to the world about My mercy; let all mankind recognize My unfathomable mercy. It is a sign for the end times; after it will come the day of justice." St. Maria Faustina Kowalska, *Divine Mercy In My Soul* (Stockbridge, MA: Marian Press, 2005), n. 848.

31. Pope Francis, "General Audience," October 30, 2013, www.vatican.va.

The Holy Father stresses the need for courage and humility to open ourselves up to the possibility of spiritual fraternity, for in that way a true sense of companionship is able to develop through the action of the Holy Spirit.

The Lord has left us a wonderful example of this truth, through the entrance of Christianity into Korea towards the end of the eighteenth century. The Gospel did not come to the Korean people through missionary activity; rather it came through the spread of books from China. There was a quest to discover the truth on an intellectual level, and this soon led the Koreans to experience the great delight of knowing the risen Lord through faith. It is unique in the history of the Church in that the foundations were entirely laid by a lay community. Even without priests and bishops for most of the first fifty years, the Church grew in a communion of love, *and* while suffering extreme persecution; it is estimated that there were some ten thousand martyrs by 1866. This is proof that as long as the love of the Holy Spirit remains at the heart of the community— even without recourse to Holy Mass and Confession—God is able to make the communion of saints a tangible reality, no matter how desperate or exceptional the circumstances.

Pope Francis continued his address by restating the constant teaching that the Church exists as one family: those on earth, in Purgatory and the blessed in Heaven; and it is through intercessory prayer that the channels of grace are opened.

In his second address on the *Sanctorum Communio*, the Pope turned to the communion of holy things, focusing especially on the Sacraments and Charisms:

> Each one of us, in fact, through Baptism, Confirmation and the Eucharist, is incorporated into Christ and united to the entire community of believers. Therefore, if on the one hand it is the Church that "makes" the Sacraments, on the other, it is the Sacraments that "make" the Church, that build her up, by generating new children, by gathering them into the holy people of God, by strengthening their membership. . . . Every encounter with Christ, who in the Sacraments gives us salvation, invites us to "go" and communicate to others the salvation that we have been able to see,

145

to touch, to encounter and to receive, and which is truly credible because it is love.[32]

The emphasis here on the sacramental life also touches on a similar theme found in the Pontiff's teaching: that it is an absurd dichotomy to love Jesus without the Church, to expect sanctification while living on the fringes of Christianity. To think outside the confines of the Mystical Body is to damage the witness of that communion willed by Christ. It is a "do it yourself" mentality that tempts one to circumvent the *sensus fidei*, in favor of an individualistic approach to matters of faith and morals.

The Holy Father links this with his cherished view that the Church is a Mother, and that it exists as a family, and as such, all should be within the bosom of the Church, able to participate in the rhythm of family life under the blessing and protection of the Eternal Father. Charisms also play their part within this ecclesiastical theology because they enable the family to grow in a variety of ways, fostering the communion that is driven by love:

> The charisms are important in the life of the Christian community, but they are always a means for growth in charity, in love, which St. Paul sets above the charisms (cf. 1 Cor. 13:1–13). Without love, in fact, even the most extraordinary gifts are in vain; this man heals people, he has that power, this other virtue . . . but does he have love and charity in his heart? If he does then all is well, but if he does not he is no servant of the Church. Without love no gift or charism could serve the Church, for where there is not love there is an emptiness that becomes filled with selfishness. And I ask myself: if we all were egotistical, could we live in communion and peace? No, it's not possible, that is why it is necessary that love unite us. Our smallest gesture of love benefits everyone! Therefore, to live out unity in the Church and communion in charity means not seeking one's own interests but sharing the suffering and the joy of one's brothers (cf. 1 Cor. 12:26), ready to carry the weight of the poorest and the weakest. This fraternal solidarity is not a figure of speech, a saying, but an integral part of the communion among

---

32. Pope Francis, "General Audience," November 6, 2013, www.vatican.va.

Christians. If we live it, we are a sign to the world, the "sacrament" of God's love.[33]

This, in a nutshell, captures the thought of Pope Francis: that to love and serve God is only possible when it is allied to a real concern for all God's children, especially the weakest. If we truly love God, then we love those he loves; it cannot work any other way. The First Letter of St. John, I believe, is a fitting reference point for anyone who wants to understand the charismatic figure of this first Jesuit Pope. It sums up perfectly what so much of his Magisterium is about, and if it was truly acted upon by large swathes of the faithful, we would begin to see pride crumble, long confessional lines, and a new awareness of the communion of saints that speaks of the most beautiful fraternity:

> This, then, is how God's children and the devil's children are known apart. A man cannot trace his origin from God if he does not live right, if he does not love his brethren. To love one another; that, from the first, was the charge given to you.... God has proved his love to us by laying down his life for our sakes; we too must be ready to lay down our lives for the sake of our brethren. And now, suppose that a man has the worldly goods he needs, and sees his brother go in want; if he steels his heart against his brother, how can we say that the love of God dwells in him? My little children, let us shew our love by the true test of action, not by taking phrases on our lips. That proves to us that we take our character from the truth, and we shall be able to satisfy our consciences before God. (1 Jn. 3:10-11, 16–19)

33. Ibid.

PART II

The Church Suffering

ༀ 6 ༀ

Purgatory:
The Merciful Invention of God

If any man has a claim against thee, come to terms there and then,
while thou art walking in the road with him; or else it may be that
the claimant will hand thee over to the judge, and the judge to the
officer, and so thou wilt be cast into prison. Believe me, thou shalt not
be set at liberty until thou hast paid the last farthing.

(Matt. 5:25–26)

NOW THAT WE have reflected upon the Church Militant, we can turn our attention to the Church that exists in the next life: *Suffering and Triumphant*. But before we examine the Church in Heaven, we need to meditate on the teaching and mystery of Purgatory, that state of purification where one is able to rid themselves of all the things they clung to through life that were contrary to the Gospel. We will endeavour to analyze various aspects of Purgatory in the second part of this triptych: an examination of the historical teachings derived from biblical sources, Tradition and the Magisterium, the Church Suffering as revealed in the general mystical tradition, the purgatorial doctrines of St. Catherine of Genoa and St. Therese of Lisieux, and an analysis of the spiritual fraternity that exists between *the ecclesia militans* and the *ecclesia patiens*.

Purgatory: The Historical Truth

In this opening chapter, it is essential that we place Purgatory within its rightful place as a dogma of the faith, far away from new age-type superstitions at one end of the spectrum, or the outright rejection of it from the other. There is no doubt that the modernist agenda that has crippled the Church in recent decades has also left an open wound in the supernatural sense of the faithful. Simply put, Purgatory has been somewhat relegated to the pews of devout souls who have remained focused through thick and thin on the reality of the Church beyond the grave. Homilies are rarely given that teach on the subject, or prayers encouraged for the dead; and for many Catholics, November is the only time when there is any real reflection on the last things. This intolerable situation has arisen even though popes have continued to teach on the subject regularly throughout the past century.

As a consequence of this, the entire doctrine of the communion of saints has become fragmented; funerals have become at times quasi-canonizations, with the deceased presumed to be resting in the wonder of the beatific vision rather than undergoing any kind of purification. Of course, the Liturgy of the Church does not see it that way, but the perception is that a sprinkling of protestant belief in immediate access to the Kingdom has crept in, which probably stems from the reluctance of priests to preach on Purgatory, and also due to the nature of eulogies and secular songs within the funerals themselves. In this way, a sort of "feel good factor" comes into play, which perhaps is designed to take away some of the terrible sorrow felt by the relatives, but in reality at the expense of the far greater truth that the deceased is very much alive, and quite possibly in need of their invaluable help now more than ever to reach the eternal joys awaiting them.

What I hope to do in some little way through these pages is to rekindle the fire of love that the Church on earth must have for the Church in Purgatory, to bring the Holy Souls back to the forefront of our prayer lives, and to realize that there are perhaps thousands, if not millions of them awaiting our loving assistance. They are like the frozen gathered around a fireplace, desperately hoping for some warmth, and God in his mercy has allowed us to provide it.

Before we look at Sacred Scripture for the truth concerning Purgatory, we will briefly survey the relevant dogmatic pronouncements made by the Catholic Church, since she alone has authority to interpret the Word of God, while acting as guardian of the

"Sacred deposit" of the faith.[1] This will then give us the solid foundation needed to proceed towards understanding the nature and reality of this place of purification.

The formulation of the Church's doctrine on Purgatory can be found in several Ecumenical Councils: the Second Council of Lyon (1274), the Council of Florence (1439–1445) and the Council of Trent (1545–1563). More recently, the Second Vatican Council has reaffirmed the teaching on Purgatory as infallible in the Dogmatic Constitution on the Church, *Lumen Gentium.*[2] In the Second Council of Lyon, we find confirmation not only of the existence of a state of purification, but also an exposition on the power of intercession within the communion of saints:

> Because if they die truly repentant in charity before they have made satisfaction by worthy fruits of penance for (sins) committed and omitted, their souls are cleansed after death by purgatorical or purifying punishments.... And to relieve punishments of this kind, the offerings of the living faithful are of advantage to these, namely, the sacrifices of Masses, prayers, alms, and other duties of piety, which have customarily been performed by the faithful for the other faithful according to the regulations of the Church.[3]

While the Council of Florence reiterated this teaching almost word for word in its sixth session held on July 6, 1439, it was the Council of Trent, when faced with the turmoil caused by the Protestant Ref-

---

1. The Catechism of the Catholic Church teaches: "The task of giving an authentic interpretation of the Word of God, whether in its written form or in the form of Tradition, has been entrusted to the living teaching office of the Church alone. Its authority in this matter is exercised in the name of Jesus Christ. This means that the task of interpretation has been entrusted to the bishops in communion with the successor of Peter, the Bishop of Rome.... The Church's Magisterium exercises the authority it holds from Christ to the fullest extent when it defines dogmas, that is, when it proposes, in a form obliging the Christian people to an irrevocable adherence of faith, truths contained in divine Revelation or also when it proposes, in a definitive way, truths having a necessary connection with these." *Catechism of the Catholic Church*, nos. 85, 88.

2. *Lumen Gentium*, ch. VII, no. 51.

3. Heinrich Joseph Dominicus Denzinger, *Enchiridion symbolorum, definitionum et declarationum de rebus fidei et morum*, 464, www.patristica.net.

ormation, that led the way in condemning the false teaching of Martin Luther, who denied the existence of the Church Suffering. On January 13, 1547 the sixth session opened in which the *Decree of Justification* was written to counter the threat posed by this erroneous theology. In the *Canons of Justification*, we encounter a fierce condemnation of the view that denies the necessary debt of temporal punishment to be paid by repentant sinners before entrance into Heaven:

> If anyone shall say that after the reception of the grace of justification, to every penitent sinner the guilt is so remitted and the penalty of eternal punishment so blotted out that no penalty of temporal punishment remains to be discharged either in this world or in the world to come in Purgatory before the entrance to the kingdom of heaven can be opened: let him be anathema.[4]

Shortly before the solemn closing of the Council of Trent in 1563, the Fathers issued several decrees that directly address the entire notion of the communion of saints which was being undermined by the protestant reformers in northern Europe. For now, we will only concern ourselves with the specific text concerning Purgatory:

> The holy Synod commands the bishops that they insist that the sound doctrine of Purgatory, which has been transmitted by the holy Fathers and holy Councils, be believed by the faithful of Christ, be maintained, taught, and everywhere preached.[5]

This decree was followed by those related to the invocation and veneration of saints, sacred images and indulgences, all of which we will return to in later chapters. Two years after the Council ended, Pope Pius IV issued the *Professio fidei Tridentina* in his Bull, *Iniunctum Nobis*, which was a Creed used frequently for the reconciling of converts and an oath of loyalty for errant theologians. In this document, we again see the placement of Purgatory as a dogma binding all the faithful without exception, its existence as real as heaven and earth. To be a loyal son or daughter of the Church, the state of final purification is a non-negotiable fact. Now that we have the author-

---

4. Ibid., 840.
5. Ibid., 983.

ity of Holy Mother Church to guide us, let us delve into this mystery from its revelation within the pages of the Bible, and Tradition.

The Church Suffering: Biblical Evidence

The Old Testament contains a magnificent example of the Jewish understanding that the prayers of the living can aid the dead in their journey towards communion with God. In the two Books of Maccabees we are presented with the figure of Judas Maccabeus, the leader of Jewish opposition to the Syrians; not only a great warrior, but also a powerful religious icon who rebuilt the Temple in Jerusalem after the persecution of Antiochus IV Epiphanes. In the Second Book of Maccabees, after recounting the victorious routing of Gorgias' army, we are told how Judas and his troops returned to the battlefield in order to retrieve the dead bodies of the fallen Jews. They discovered that each of the deceased was wearing a token, an amulet of the false gods of Jamnia under their shirts, in obvious defiance of the Law. We then read:

> And so they fell to prayer, pleading that the sin might go unremembered. Judas himself, their gallant commander, gave public warning to his men, of fault they should evermore keep clear, with the fate of these transgressors under their eyes. Then he would have contribution made; a sum of twelve thousand silver pieces he levied, and sent it to Jerusalem, to have sacrifice made there for the guilt of their dead companions. Was not this well done and piously? Here was a man kept the resurrection ever in mind; he had done fondly and foolishly indeed, to pray for the dead, if these might rise no more, that once were fallen! And these had made a godly end; could he doubt, a rich recompense awaited them? A holy and wholesome thought it is to pray for the dead, for their guilt's undoing. (2 Macc. 12:42–46)

Several elements of this text stand out with great importance. First, it should be noted that a century and a half before the birth of Jesus, the Jews were well acquainted with the idea that prayers for the dead were beneficial, and from this fact we can also state that they were aware that death did not necessarily bring about the perfection of the soul that would allow immediate communion with God. Second, and perhaps more interestingly, we see how Judas Maccabeus was using a primitive form of indulgence through almsgiving for the dead, when he sent an offering to Jerusalem. In essence, the Catholic doctrine of a final purification was already a part of the spiritual heritage of Judaism, even if the actual term "Purgatory" was not formulated until many centuries later.

Belief in Purgatory has often been challenged by various individuals and movements since the birth of Christianity. Arius, the fourth century heretic, believed prayers for the dead were of no avail, while the twelfth century *Apostolici* denied its existence. The *Albigenses*, *Waldenses*, and *Hussites* were also sects arising in the Middle Ages who shared this denial of Purgatory.

However with the Reformation doctrine of *Sola Scriptura*, this heresy became far more widespread under the influence of Luther, Calvin and Zwingli. So the question we must ask ourselves is: where can the doctrine of a final purification be found in the New Testament, and more specifically the teachings of Jesus? The following passage from St. Matthew's Gospel is a good starting point:

> If any man has a claim against thee, come to terms there and then, while thou art walking in the road with him; or else it may be that the claimant will hand thee over to the judge, and the judge to the officer, and so thou wilt be cast into prison. Believe me, thou shalt not be set at liberty until thou hast paid the last farthing. (Matt. 5:25–26)[6]

The "prison" we are told about cannot mean anything other than Purgatory;[7] for the Lord to speak of liberation from it after having paid the last farthing tells us it has a temporal character. All mainstream Christian denominations agree that for the damned in Hell there is no escape for all eternity, and for those in Heaven there is an eternity of happiness; therefore it cannot refer to anything else.

The Church Fathers also saw in this passage a vision of purification that awaited the tainted soul before it could enter the Holy City. Tertullian, in his treatise *Liber de Anima*, explains that the "last farthing" refers to the "very smallest offense that has to be recom-

---

6. The Parable is also related in Luke 12:58–59.

7. Of significance here is that the Greek term for "prison," *Phylake*, was also a contemporary term used to describe Hades.

pensed."[8] While St. Jerome in his *Letter to Demetrias* warns her that unless she constantly lives by her baptismal vows, she will not receive Christ the true light "till you have expiated your most trifling sins."[9] The common understanding among the Fathers is that the road to be walked relates to our journey through life and that the judge is certainly the Lord. The man with a claim has several meanings: the devil, those we injure and even our own conscience.

The entire parable is therefore related to man's inner struggle to live a life of perfection, to "come to terms" with God's grace through the humility to ask for forgiveness, and to live the beatitudes that we have already discussed. If even the tiniest speck of dirt remains on the soul after the individual judgement, the Lord tells us a prison awaits; "prison" in the sense that we do not yet possess the freedom to fly to God's eternal abode.

St. Matthew also records significant words of Jesus concerning the sin of blasphemy in which the implication for some form of temporal purification is evident:

> And now I tell you this; there is pardon for all the other sins and blasphemies of men, but not for blasphemy against the Holy Spirit. There is no one who blasphemes against the Son of Man but may find forgiveness; but for him who blasphemes against the Holy Spirit there is no forgiveness, either in this world or in the world to come. (Matt. 12:31–33)

The stand-out part of this text relates to the revelation that blasphemy against the Holy Spirit will not be forgiven either in *this world or the next*. The conclusion from this is that certain sins *can be* forgiven in eternal life—which must concern only venial sins— since Catholic doctrine states that unrepented mortal sins will lead a deceased person immediately into hell.

If this interpretation were not correct, why would Jesus have been so specific in making distinctions between this world and the next? In fact why mention the next world at all? This text also reveals the error of the protestant theology of Justification, because it is evident

8. Tertullian, *Liber De anima*, ch. 58, www.tertullian.org.
9. St. Jerome, Letter 130, http://www.ccel.org/ccel/schaff/npnf206.v.CXXX.html.

now that Christians do not necessarily have their sins blotted out at the moment of judgment; the admission has to be that some intermediate phase of expiation exists where forgiveness is allied to a catharsis of the soul.[10] St. Augustine in his theological masterpiece *City of God* states:

> For some of the dead, indeed, the prayer of the Church or of pious individuals is heard; but it is for those who, having been regenerated in Christ, did not spend their life so wickedly that they can be judged unworthy of such compassion, nor so well that they can be considered to have no need of it.[11]

Pope St. Gregory the Great in his *Dialogues*[12] also concurs with the exegesis of St. Augustine but also takes us a step further by linking the passage from St. Matthew to this critical text found in St. Paul's First Letter to the Corinthians:

> The foundation which has been laid is the only one which anybody can lay; I mean Jesus Christ. But on this foundation different men will build in gold, silver, precious stones, wood, grass, or straw, and each man's workmanship will be plainly seen. It is the day of the Lord that will disclose it, since that day is to reveal itself in fire, and fire will test the quality of each man's workmanship. He will receive a reward, if the building he has added on stands firm; if it is burnt up, he will be the loser; and yet he himself will be saved, though only as men are saved by passing through fire. (1 Cor. 3:11–15)

St. Gregory states that St. Paul, by using the images of wood, grass or straw is deliberately drawing our attention to venial sins that can be consumed with ease by the fire of final purification, whereas foundations built on iron, brass or lead, would have represented mortal sins that would not be remissible in Purgatory. St. Augustine, St. Jerome, St. Ambrose, St. Basil and Origen all share a similar view that St. Paul is referring to the final purification.

---

10. As we shall see later, the soul can do nothing any longer to accelerate this process through its own merit or volition.

11. St. Augustine, *Civitate Dei*, bk. XXI, 24, www.newadvent.org.

12. St. Gregory the Great, *The Dialogues of Saint Gregory the Great* (Merchantville: Evolution Publishing, 2010), 233.

St. Francis de Sales, Bishop and Doctor of the Church, whose life coincided with the immediate aftermath of the sixteenth century Reformation, also saw in this passage of Sacred Scripture a reference to purgatorial fire, albeit with a different but profound interpretation than St. Gregory's, on the meaning of the foundations:

> The Apostle uses two similitudes. The first is of an architect who with solid materials builds a valuable house on a rock: the second is of one who on the same foundation erects a house of boards, reeds, straw. Let us now imagine that a fire breaks out in both the houses. That which is of solid material will be out of danger, and the other will be burnt to ashes. And if the architect be in the first he will be whole and safe; if he be in the second, he must, if he would escape, rush through fire and flame, and shall be saved yet so that he will bear the marks of having been in fire. . . . The fire by which the architect is saved can only be understood of the fire of Purgatory.[13]

Moving away from St. Paul's theological approach, the First Letter of St. Peter presents us with a vivid image of the descent of Jesus in the immediate aftermath of his salvific death: "In his mortal nature he was done to death, but endowed with fresh life in his spirit, and it was in his spirit that he went and preached to the spirits who lay in prison" (1 Pet. 3:18–19).

Of course, this passage has to be understood in the sense that Jesus descended to "hell": not the state of eternal damnation, but the realm of the dead where all who merited eternal life awaited the coming of the divine King. This would include the "limbo of the just"[14] which the Lord called "Abraham's Bosom" (cf. Lk. 16:22), and almost certainly those undergoing purgatorial suffering, for they too were now part of the Mystical Body, the communion of saints.

---

13. St. Francis de Sales, *The Catholic Controversy* (London: Burns & Oates, 1909), 373.

14. All those who from the time of Adam and Eve onwards had completed any necessary period of expiation, and therefore possessed the perfection required to experience the beatific vision of God. In the First Book of Samuel, we are told how Saul visited the witch of Endor and asked her to summon the spirit of Samuel. Upon doing so, Samuel said: "Why hast thou disturbed my rest?" (1 Sam. 28:15).

St. Thomas Aquinas held the view that Christ did visit each of the various "hells," but makes a very careful distinction in explaining the manner of these descents. He suggests that the Lord manifested his presence in two distinct ways: through *effect* and *essence*. In *essence*, Jesus's soul *only* visited the souls of the just, and that, "interiorly by grace." But through *effect*, he descended to the hell of the damned to shame them for their wickedness; to those in Purgatory, he gave the hope of approaching glory and those holy brothers and sisters detained solely on account of original sin, he "shed the light of eternal glory."[15]

As we have seen, Sacred Scripture does give us the evidence for belief in Purgatory even for those non-Catholics who do not accept the teaching authority of the Church. The question must also be asked as to why there is no teaching of Jesus within the Gospels condemning the practice of praying for the dead, if the Judaic tradition seen in 2 Maccabees was a futile one. We know that the Lord corrected the Jewish attitude towards marriage and divorce, therefore it is inconceivable that he would have ignored a doctrine central to the mystery of eternal life. We would also presume that Jesus was familiar with the *Kaddish*, the Jewish prayer for the dead and the general customs that followed bereavement. As the Son of God, mercy and truth personified, the Lord would not have allowed a false doctrine to develop if the justice of God did not demand it.

Purgatory in the Patristic Era

Before we look deeper into the reasons for Purgatory's existence, a brief survey of early Christian Tradition will help to reinforce the idea that as a doctrine, the Church Suffering was already in the hearts of the faithful from the earliest centuries of Christianity. The great Dominican theologian, Fr. Reginald Garrigou-Lagrange, tells us that there are two distinct periods in Christian Tradition that explore the theology of a final purification: the first four centuries,

---

15. St. Thomas Aquinas, *Summa Theologica*, Part 3, Q. 52.2, www.newadvent. org.

where implicit references are made by a variety of Fathers,[16] and a later period beginning with St. Augustine which explored the various fundamentals of Purgatory as a place of expiation for sin, laying the foundations for its eventual dogmatic definition.

The concept of atonement for sin can be traced back to one of the earliest texts of Christianity, known as the *Shepherd of Hermas*.[17] In this tract, dated to roughly the end of the first or the early second century, a series of visions were given to a Roman slave called Hermas in which he saw the Church as a Tower, built with living stones symbolizing the faithful. In Book One, Hermas asks the Lady in the vision if those stones who are cast away from the Tower can find a place once more within the construction. The Lady replies:

> They may repent . . . but they cannot come into this tower; but they shall be placed in a much lower rank; and this after that they shall have been afflicted, and *fulfilled the days of their sins*. And for this cause they shall be removed, because they have received the word of righteousness; and then they shall be translated from their afflictions.[18]

Although this passage does not present conclusive proof concerning a supranatural purgation, it does seem to imply it, with the reference to the days of sins being fulfilled, which would lead one to consider the arrival of death. Added to that the mention of "afflictions," punishments in other words, that will be ended at some point, and we have the basic doctrine of Purgatory present. It is also worth noting that we are told the repentant shall be "placed" in a lower rank, as if they have no choice in the matter. We can sense therefore that this does not refer to the individual soul actively looking (through

---

16. This first period of theological development also includes evidence of practical piety on behalf of the earliest Christians for the Church Suffering; the Roman Catacombs from the third century display inscriptions asking God to refresh the souls of the dead, and to bestow his eternal light upon them.

17. St. Irenaeus called this work "Scripture," while Origen believed it was divinely inspired. St. Athanasius, while stating it was not strictly canonical, nevertheless thought it very useful for instruction in the Faith. See, *The Genuine Epistles of the Apostolic Fathers* (Hartford: Parsons And Hills, 1836), 283–284.

18. Ibid., 307–308.

free will) to atone for sin while in the body on earth; rather it is a transitional state beyond the tomb.

In Book Three, there is another significant passage, in which Hermas questions whether the duration of punishment corresponds to the duration of self-indulgence and deceit. Again, without explicit reference as to when this occurs, there is a clue that provokes thoughts in this purgatorial direction. Towards the end of the dialogue, the Angel tells Hermas: "Whosoever therefore have delivered themselves over to such pleasures, are thus punished; because that *when they had life*, they rendered themselves liable to death."[19] Concerning the actual question, the Angel informs us that the duration of punishment is substantially longer than the length of sin itself, which perhaps corresponds to the seriousness of sin, coupled with the damage it causes to the Body as a whole:

> An hour of pleasure is terminated within its own space: but one hour of punishment has the efficacy of thirty days. Whosoever therefore enjoys his false pleasure for one day, and is one day tormented, that one day of punishment is equivalent to a whole year's space.[20]

Another very early text of profound insight is the *Martyrdom of Perpetua and Felicity* (c. AD 202), which includes several visions granted to St. Perpetua concerning her deceased brother, Dinocrates. In the first vision, he was in a gloomy place, parched and filthy looking. He was trying to reach a fountain of water to quench his thirst but was unable to. St. Perpetua recounts how she prayed for him day and night while in prison in order to lessen his sufferings. In a second vision, now benefitting from Perpetua's powerful intercession, Dinocrates had been freed from his punishments:

> I saw that that place which I had formerly observed to be in gloom was now bright; and Dinocrates, with a clean body well clad, was finding refreshment. . . . And when he was satisfied, he went away from the water to play joyously, after the manner of children, and I

19. Ibid., 371.
20. Ibid., 370.

awoke. Then I understood that he was translated from the place of punishment.[21]

Significantly, St. Perpetua recalls how before receiving these mystical experiences, she had been prompted to think of Dinocrates during prayer, something that had not occurred to her before. From this we can deduce that the Holy Spirit was the instigator for a deeper sense of remembrance; not one based on fading memories, but one where the deceased is made present through prayer. Even if as we have seen, the Old Testament bore witness to a concern for the souls of the dead, perhaps in these early Christian writings we can see how God opened up a new theological chapter—the *Sanctorum Communio*—where the Church was gradually enlightened on its unitary wholeness.[22]

The early Patristic era provides us with several other passages of importance for this discussion: Tertullian in *De Corona* informs us that: "As often as the anniversary comes round, we make offerings for the dead as birthday honours,"[23] while in St. Clement of Alexandria's *Stromata* we read:

> Accordingly the believer, through great discipline, divesting himself of the passions, passes to the mansion which is better than the former one, viz., to the greatest torment, taking with him the characteristic of repentance from the sins he has committed after baptism. He is tortured then still more—not yet or not quite attaining what he sees others to have acquired.[24]

Clement also took up the Pauline doctrine of purification through fire by taking the basis of Gnostic thought on *paideia*[25] and reinterpreted it by focusing on a gradual spiritual ascent towards the King-

---

21. *The Passion of the Holy Martyrs, Perpetua and Felicity*, ch. 2, 4, www.newav ent.org.

22. A very detailed historical and analytical study of the phrase *Sanctorum Communio* can be found in Stephen Benko's excellent resource: *The Meaning of Sanctorum Communion* (Naperville: Alec R. Allenson, Inc., 1964).

23. Tertullian, *De Corona*, ch. 3, www.newadvent.org.

24. St. Clement of Alexandria, *Stromata*, bk VI, ch. 14, www.newadvent.org.

25. The Greek concept of education in which the non-elect would be consumed by a fire of judgment. However the Gnostics believed they would be spared this through the water of Baptism and the breeze of the Spirit.

dom: "But we say that the fire sanctifies not flesh, but sinful souls; meaning not the all-devouring vulgar fire but that of wisdom, which pervades the soul passing through the fire."[26] Origen too reflected on the necessity of a burning purgation: "All therefore must come to the fire; all must come to the melting furnace,"[27] although his theological premise known as universal reconciliation (*apokatastasis*) whereby *all* would be saved from damnation was rejected by St. John Chrysostom among others. St. Gregory of Nyssa, one of the great Eastern Fathers, followed a similar path in recognizing that for man, a route towards divinization existed even if the irrational pressure of the passions had disfigured the soul of the faithful:

> After his departure out of the body, he gains knowledge of the difference between virtue and vice, and finds that he is not able to partake of divinity until he has been purged of the filthy contagion in his soul by the purifying fire.[28]

The practice of prayer for the dead is evident in many texts of this era. St. John Chrysostom, another Eastern Father of great importance, explains thus:

> Help him as far as possible, not by tears, but by prayers and supplications and alms and offerings. For not unmeaningly have these things been devised, nor do we in vain make mention of the departed in the course of the divine mysteries, and approach God in their behalf, beseeching the Lamb Who is before us, Who takes away the sin of the world—not in vain, but that some refreshment may thereby ensue to them.[29]

He continues by referring to the Holy Sacrifice of the Mass being offered on their behalf; and that, at the ordinance of the Holy Spirit.

---

26. *Stromata*, bk. VII, ch. 6, www.newadvent.org.

27. Origen of Alexandria, "Homily on Exodus VI," Ronald E. Heine, *Origen: Homilies On Genesis and Exodus* (Washington, DC: Catholic University of America Press, 1982), 290.

28. St. Gregory of Nyssa, "Sermon on the Dead," William A. Jurgens, *The Faith of the Early Fathers*, vol. 2 (Collegeville: Liturgical Press, 1979), 58.

29. St. John Chrysostom, "Homily 41 on First Corinthians," 8, www.newadvent. org.

St. Ephrem, St. Epiphanius, St. Basil and St. Cyril of Jerusalem also encourage prayer for the dead.[30]

From this evidence, deriving from some of the most influential figures of the post-apostolic age, we can say for certain that a theology of the dead was already firmly rooted in the spiritual life of the Church. There was no sense that Christians were to be ushered into heaven come what may; on the contrary, as we see with so many saints throughout the ages, the stain of sin haunted them like a shadow and therefore humility instilled in them a healthy dose of reality. The chances of arriving at the judgment seat in perfect condition were rather slim, and based on the words of Sacred Scripture, a cathartic possibility could be explored, applicable to the next life.

With the advent of St. Augustine's brilliant theology, we see the dawn of a new understanding in the truth of this dogma. The four essential elements that constitute the Church Suffering now become visibly present in Patristic teaching: Purgatory exists as a place; souls can no longer gain merit for themselves; the souls detained there can be aided by the Church Militant, and Purgatory will cease to exist at the Last Judgment. In Augustine's *Enchiridion*, he refers to several of these issues:

> Therefore, it is in this life that all the merit or demerit is acquired, which can either relieve or aggravate a man's sufferings after this life. No one, then, need hope that after he is dead he shall obtain merit with God which he has neglected to secure here. . . . Nor can it be denied that the souls of the dead are benefited by the piety of their living friends, who offer the sacrifice of the Mediator, or give alms in the church on their behalf. But these services are of advantage only to those who during their lives have earned such merit, that services of this kind can help them.[31]

In *Civitate Dei*, Augustine speaks of the duration of Purgatory; for

---

30. The *Apostolic Constitutions* (c. AD 380), a type of manual for liturgical and private worship, bears witness to the centrality of devotion to the souls of the dead in these terms: "Let us pray for our brethren that are at rest in Christ, that God, the lover of mankind, who has received his soul, may forgive him every sin, voluntary and involuntary, and may be merciful and gracious to him, and give him his lot in the land of the pious." (Treatise 8.41), www.newadvent.org.

31. St. Augustine, *Enchiridion*, 110.

by its very nature of temporality, it must cease to exist at some stage in the future:

> But temporary punishments are suffered by some in this life only, by others after death, by others both now and then; but all of them before that last and strictest judgment.[32]

And again several chapters later he reinforces the point:

> Whoever, therefore, desires to escape eternal punishment, let him not only be baptized, but also justified in Christ, and so let him in truth pass from the devil to Christ. And let him not fancy that there are any purgatorial pains except before that final and dreadful judgment.[33]

As we have already seen, Pope Gregory the Great followed in the theological footsteps of Augustine, not only in the understanding of a purging fire of liberation from evil, but also in the view that Purgatory would serve no purpose after the end of the world.[34] Interestingly, this great Pope adds a mystical dimension to his doctrine of Purgatory, one that recalls the vision seen by St. Felicity.

He relates two fascinating episodes:[35] the first occurred in the city of *Centumcellis*, whereby a priest was befriended by a man at the baths who would look after him. After a while the priest decided to offer him a gift of "two singing breads"[36] for his kindness. At this, the man revealed that he was dead and was doing his Purgatory at the same place he had worked while alive. He asked the priest to offer the bread to God for his release and to intercede for him. Before vanishing, he informed the priest that if he did not appear the next time he visited the baths, he would know that his prayers had been answered. And this is exactly what occurred later.

The second vision formed the basis for the famed thirty Gregorian Masses for the deceased, a well-known powerful aid to the

---

32. St. Augustine, *Civitate Dei*, Bk. XXI, ch. 13, www.newadvent.org.
33. Ibid., ch. 16, www.newadvent.org.
34. St. Gregory the Great, *The Dialogues of Saint Gregory the Great* (Merchantville: Evolution Publishing, 2010), 233.
35. Ibid., 249.
36. Understood to be two unconsecrated hosts.

Holy Souls frequently used until recent times. Pope Gregory tells us how a dying monk called Justus informed his lay friend Copiosus that he had betrayed the vows of holy poverty by hiding three gold crowns among his medications. When Gregory (who had been the founding monk at the monastery) became aware of the scandal, he ordered the prior to place Justus in solitary confinement and after his death not to bury him with the monks but in a "dunghill." Justus repented; but 30 days after his death, Gregory began to think of his probable purgatorial sufferings and asked Pretiosus the prior to ensure that 30 Masses were offered on consecutive days for Justus' soul. On the thirtieth day, Justus appeared to Copiosus filled with joy at his release from Purgatory.

Of course, private revelations can never be placed on a par with the teachings derived from Scripture, Tradition and the Magisterium. But when authentic, these experiences can add a depth of understanding that perhaps is not revealed through the ordinary means. For instance: the nature of purgatorial sufferings and their whereabouts or the disposition of souls who remain there. Do they experience joy or sorrow or a mixture of both? Is the fire real or spiritual? These are all questions that we will seek to answer in the following chapter.

We can speculate as to the reason why Pope Gregory felt the need to recount these mystical events in his *Dialogues*. Perhaps it was simply to allow the supernatural to speak for itself. After all, by its nature, Purgatory is a mysterious part of the Mystical Body, and without God's generosity in allowing these visions to occur, it is unlikely that devotion to the souls of the Church Suffering would have been so firmly rooted in the faithful over so many centuries, much in the same way that Marian apparitions have often rejuvenated the Church. One need only think of the incredible conversions after the Virgin's appearances to St. Juan Diego in Guadalupe, Mexico. Through these manifestations of the dead, the *ecclesia patiens* seems that much closer to us; Purgatory is no longer an abstract proposition but the invention of merciful love.

St. Caesarius of Arles (AD 470–543), following the theological method of Augustine, contemplated the nature and length of sufferings endured by those in Purgatory:

Let no one say this, dearest brethren, because that fire of Purgatory will be more difficult than any punishment in this world can be seen or imagined or felt. . . . How does anyone know whether he is going to pass through that fire days or months or perhaps even years?[37]

The Bishop of Arles was also keen to instruct on how to lessen or even avoid the purification in the next life. He warns against committing serious sins, but if done, the absolute necessity of repentance. The practice of good works as a healing remedy against temporal punishment caused by venial sin is also encouraged: visiting the sick and prisoners, recalling to harmony the discordant, fasting and "washing the feet of guests."[38] However for mortal sins confessed, Caesarius calls for harsher penance: "tears and crying and groaning"[39] added to prolonged fasting and public penance. He also suggests we should mourn for our soul in the same way we would mourn the loss of a family member. In essence, he teaches that Purgatory can be carried out at least to some extent in this life, the suffering being less intense this side of eternity.

Now that we have explored the truth of Purgatory, a reality that cannot be ignored from Sacred Scripture and Tradition, we can examine more closely the reason for its existence. Is it vindictive punishment from a cruel God, or the meeting place between justice and mercy? We will also look at why the Protestant understanding of Justification does not suffice to eliminate the necessity of post-mortem purification, if a soul presents itself to the Lord at their individual judgment in a state of imperfection.

The Manifestation of the Father's Mercy

In order to fully understand the necessity of Purgatory, we need to reflect upon the perfect justice of God and its implications for humanity. The parable of Lazarus and the rich man (Lk. 16:19–31)

---

37. St. Caesarius of Arles, Sermon 179, *The Fathers of the Church, St. Caesarius of Arles, Sermons,* vol. 2 (Washington DC: The Catholic University of America Press, 1964), 453.

38. Ibid.

39. Ibid., 455.

exemplifies this truth perfectly: Lazarus is comforted in the Bosom of Abraham after a life of poverty and suffering, while the rich man reaps the rewards of his opulence and selfishness in the fires of hell. The order of justice demands that choices taken in this life will have eternal consequences; God who is its ultimate arbiter will not sanction an alternate court of double standards.[40] In fact, the entire span of salvation history speaks of this: Adam and Eve's fall demanded justice from God, and thus they were expelled from the Garden of Eden, their sin so great that only the Sacrifice of God himself could make the atonement needed.

Moving to the other end of the spectrum, we see the scene of the Last Judgment, where final sentence will be pronounced by the supreme Judge. Therefore, we can see that all our actions have a positive or negative effect, and they are constantly under the scrutiny of the just Judge, Christ himself. As we have already stated, mortal sin, the "sin that kills" (1 Jn. 5:16) leads to damnation if left unrepented. But what about the thousands of venial sins that wound the soul but don't ultimately destroy it?

The crux of the matter concerns several issues: the state of the soul at the moment of judgment, the trail of devastation it possibly left behind on earth as a consequence of evil actions, and the administration of justice on the part of God. The reality for most people, even "good" Catholics benefiting from the sacraments, is that at life's end, a certain amount of filth will have left their eschatological wedding garment soiled; and nobody would want to enter the banquet dressed like that. The Book of Revelation tells us in no uncertain terms: "Nothing that is unclean, no source of corruption or deceit can ever hope to find its way in" (Rev. 21:27).

The question has to be asked: if Purgatory did not exist, how could the justice of God be administered in a truthful way for those who escaped the flames of hell but had spent a lifetime trampling on others? What of the justice demanded by those who are prefig-

---

40. Jesus reminds us of this in the parable of the Widow and the Unjust Judge: "will not God give redress to his elect, when they are crying out to him, day and night? Will he not be impatient with their wrongs? I tell you, he will give them redress with all speed" (Lk. 18:7–8).

ured in the parable of the Widow? To answer these questions we must return to biblical sources. The key factor is that at no time does the Lord give any indication that Christians will have a free pass into heaven on account of being passive disciples; on the contrary he warns that complacency in the spiritual life can have the most tragic ramifications:

> The kingdom of heaven will not give entrance to every man who calls me Master, Master; only to the man that does the will of my Father who is in heaven. There are many who will say to me, when that day comes, Master, Master, was it not in thy name we prophesied? Was it not in thy name that we performed many miracles? Whereupon I will tell them openly, you were never friends of mine; depart from me, you that traffic in wrong-doing. (Matt. 7:21–23)

The parable of the Sower also warns in a similar fashion:

> And the grain that fell among the briers stands for those who hear it, and then, going on their way, are stifled by the cares, the riches, and the pleasures of life, and never reach maturity. (Lk. 8:14)

Finally, in the Book of Revelation, we encounter the most severe rebuke of all, addressed initially to the Church in Laodicea, but in reality, to the Universal Church:

> I know of thy doings, and find thee neither cold nor hot; cold or hot, I would thou wert one or the other. Being what thou art, lukewarm, neither cold nor hot, thou wilt make me vomit thee out of my mouth. (Rev. 3:15–16)

Now, as the Lord's own words show that those who *could* consider themselves Christians, but guilty of mortal sin, can be excluded from the Kingdom forever, it stands to reason that those Christians guilty of less serious sin, or repented mortal sin, cannot expect immediate admittance to the beatific vision. If we acknowledge that divine justice allows eternal punishment for the most serious sins, we should expect a similar (albeit less harsh) exercise of justice for all other sins. This is exactly where the Lord's reference to the *Phylake*, the prison of Hades (Matt. 5:25), directs us, as well as the teaching that sins can be forgiven in the world to come (Matt. 12:32).

The question that naturally follows is this: would punishment after death for those already assured of salvation be mere revenge on the part of God, or would it form part of a divine judicial system where equilibrium is restored? The answer again lies in the demands of God's justice; for if the law of love is violated, some form of reparation must be made either in this life or the next. There can be no greater example of this than the Lord's own Passion and Death; any meditation on his terrible sufferings can lead to only one conclusion: that the price to be paid for sin is enormous. But even if Jesus has paid that price in the most perfect way, the obligation for us to do the same remains ever present. We have been redeemed, but not yet saved. We have to make our own contribution to the coffers of satisfaction.

St. Paul is very clear on this critical point. In his Letter to the Colossians, we read: "Even as I write, *I am glad of my sufferings* on your behalf, as, in this mortal frame of mine, *I help to pay off the debt which the afflictions of Christ still leave to be paid*, for the sake of his body, the Church" (Col. 1:24). This is a statement of great clarity, proving beyond doubt that reparation is necessary for the individual; and theologically, it fits in beautifully with the concept of the communion of saints, because as St. Paul states, it may be offered on behalf of and for the benefit of others.

Natural reason also tells us that reparation has to be made when evil has been committed.[41] It is common to all peoples that a just and proportionate punishment may be handed out to those who deserve it, and if that is the case for the duration of our earthly exile, why should it be any different after death? On reflection, it is *more* important that a state of purgation exists after death for several reasons: firstly, it allows the completion of divinization without which the beatific vision is a false hope; and secondly, it ensures that nobody escapes justice ultimately, not even those who elude it on

---

41. Pope Leo XIII, in several encyclicals, speaks of "natural reason" as a prelude to truths revealed by Christ: "Hence it is that certain truths which were either divinely proposed for belief, or were bound by the closest chains to the doctrine of faith, were discovered by pagan sages with nothing but their natural reason to guide them." Leo XIII, *Aeterni Patris*, August 4, 1879, www.vatican.va. See also the Encyclical *Quod Auctoritate*, no. 4, December 22, 1885.

earth. Within these two parameters are revealed the true nature of Purgatory: the place where God's justice and mercy embrace.

Psalm 84 conveys this perfectly: "See, where mercy and faithfulness meet in one; how justice and peace are united in one embrace! Faithfulness grows up out of the earth, and from heaven, redress looks down" (Ps. 84:11–12). If this passage refers primarily to God himself, we can still see within it overtones of his mysterious design to see justice done. On the other hand, we should be careful not to overstate the temporal punishment aspect at the expense of mercy. Purgatory exists first and foremost as an invention of merciful love; it is a fruit of the redemption, the bridge that most of us will need to cross in order to reach the safe shores of the New Jerusalem.

St. John Paul II describes God's mercy in his Encyclical *Dives in Misericordia* as: "the most stupendous attribute of the Creator and of the Redeemer,"[42] and it is within this context that Purgatory must be understood. In a certain way, it is an extension of the salvific work of the Lord; for Jesus knows that the path we take towards heaven is often crooked, littered with mistakes and betrayals of varying degrees. But in spite of this he offers us a merciful sanctuary away from temptation and sin. Alone, the soul can finally come face to face with its contradictory desires, the devil's veil of deceit torn apart. If temporal suffering is still punishment, nonetheless it is also mercy, because it rids the soul of everything that hinders the ascent to sanctification. Let us never imagine the *Church Suffering* as a place akin to a concentration camp or earthly prison; as we stated earlier, it is a retreat in eternity, but one where the soul has already glimpsed the prize. Divine mercy is victorious in Purgatory because it is filled with those included in the Book of Life. Yes, the souls are ill, but they are recovering strength thanks to the benevolence and love of God. We can be sure that there is no soul in that place who won't be thankful for its existence for all eternity.

---

42. St. John Paul II, Encyclical Letter *Dives in Misericordia*, 13, November 30, 1980, www.vatican.va. This expression does not mean that God's other attributes are inferior to mercy. Rather, mercy is the attribute most manifest in creation and salvation history; a point the Pope clarifies earlier in the Encyclical.

The Protestant Question

Before we conclude this chapter, we need to address the Protestant objection to Purgatory which derives from its theology of Justification. The Lutheran teaching states that humanity is incapable of cooperating in its own salvation.[43] Everything necessary for the individual's salvation has been accomplished by Jesus Christ; the Lord's Sacrifice has satisfied the justice of God in such an absolute way that all sins have been atoned for, rendering a life of repentance and renewal superfluous. Temporal punishment has no place in this concept of God's justice, just as salvation through faith alone requires no good works in order to reach the Kingdom of heaven.[44]

Of course the problem with this theory is that even taking the Bible alone, we have the Lord's own teaching that good works are meritorious and that temporal punishments exist. Jesus instructs us to imitate his life. We can think of the command to "wash each other's feet" (Jn. 13:14); to "sell what you have and give alms" (Lk. 12:33). Rewards are promised for meritorious acts: "Give, and gifts will be yours; good measure, pressed down and shaken up and running over, will be poured into your lap; the measure you award to others is the measure that will be awarded to you" (Lk. 6:38).

However, this last sentence reveals something else: it shows that the application of God's judgment will be based on our own adherence to the requirement of performing good works. St. James uses rather stern language to reinforce this point: "Thus faith, if it has no deeds to shew for itself, has lost its own principle of life" (Jam. 2:17), and again: "Body separated from spirit is a dead body, and faith separated from good deeds is a dead faith" (Jam. 2:26).

Concerning the notion of temporal punishment, the Lord not only speaks of its reality, but also explains how it will be administered differently, depending on individual circumstances:

---

43. See the "Joint Declaration on the Doctrine of Justification," www.vatican.va.

44. There is no suggestion that Protestants do not value good works; one only need think of the accomplishments of the Salvation Army in serving the poor. It is the theological principle that good works have no merit in attaining heaven that is at the heart of Lutheran doctrine.

Yet it is the servant who knew his Lord's will, and did not make ready for him, or do his will, that will have many strokes of the lash; he who did not know of it, yet earned a beating, will have only a few. Much will be asked of the man to whom much has been given; more will be expected of him, because he was entrusted with more. (Lk. 12:47–48)

Personally, I find this passage the most exacting in the entire canon of Scripture. It leaves us in no doubt of the demands placed on Christians, especially Catholic Christians who are nourished by the Body and Blood of the Lord and continually receive grace and mercy in the Sacrament of Confession. The Lord has entrusted the treasure of faith to us and expects us to utilize it for the growth of the Kingdom. There is without question a warning here that recalls the passages we have already discussed in relation to Christian complacency; namely that a just punishment will await those disciples who remain tepid and who are content to watch history pass by without much regard for God or neighbor.

It seems logical to state that if we deny the need for Purgatory, we are in a sense calling into question divine justice itself. God governs through a judicial process that allows mercy to be granted but never at the expense of truth. It is evident from Scripture that reparation in some form or another must be made in order for divine justice to be properly carried out. We can think of several instances where this occurred: Adam's life of toil after eating from the Tree (Gen. 3:17), King David's suffering at the death of his son after committing adultery with Bathsheba (2 Sam. 12:16–19), and the blinding of St. Paul on the road to Damascus (Acts 9:8–9). But it is not only God's justice that comes under scrutiny in the Lutheran rejection of Purgatory; free will and conscience also are compromised. But why would this be?

The problem occurs when Protestants do not clearly distinguish between the God-given freedom of each individual soul to act as they wish, and the righteousness of Christ who "rules"[45] their sin. If we look at this from the perspective of natural reason, the dilemma becomes more obvious. Let us imagine a soul has lived on earth

---

45. "Joint Declaration on the Doctrine of Justification," no. 29, www.vatican.va.

with a great love of money, so much so that the plight of the destitute was continually ignored. When death arrives, and the soul departs the body, does it retain the same attitude of selfishness, or does the Justification of Jesus extend to not only forgiving sin, but also effecting an immediate and complete change of character? A positive answer to the second part of this question seems mere fantasy; it reduces the autonomy of the soul and makes free will more or less redundant if heaven awaits immediately with no questions asked. If God has given us liberty to act, then we must accept that we take that baggage with us to the judgment and beyond. God is no puppet master; He respects our choices even if He knows a long purification may be necessary in order to reach perfection.

Conscience would also be a wasted gift because what need would there be to utilize it, if the mere acceptance of faith in Christ Jesus was the only prerequisite to reach salvation? St. James tells us that the devils have belief in God (cf. Jam. 2:19); therefore a moral and spiritual life is necessary, while St. Paul says: "you must work to earn your salvation, in anxious fear" (Phil. 2:12).

Divine justice can have little or no fear to anyone who believes that faith alone will open the gates of paradise. On the contrary, conscience actually tells us that good works *are* necessary because it is the light of God within our soul that instructs us in the way of acting: the Father's call to imitate his Son. Many of us will recall times where laziness got the better of us until our conscience roused us to make the effort to help someone. Conscience and free will guarantee that when we arrive at the judgment seat of God, we get what we deserve. We will not see a Jesus who tells us our sins didn't really matter that much; rather we will see the holes in his hands and feet, and the reality will hit home. In shame we will desire to flee to Purgatory, away from the sight of a holiness we cannot dare to behold. And once there, even amid the suffering, we will be thankful for its existence; for without it where could we hope to go?

7

Ascent through Fire:
The Mystical Tradition Speaks

He will receive a reward, if the building he has added on stands firm;
if it is burnt up, he will be the loser; and yet he himself will be saved,
though only as men are saved by passing through fire.

(1 Cor. 3:14–15)

IN OUR DELIBERATIONS thus far, we have seen how the Church Suffering is a perfectly logical truth of faith. It has firm foundations from both the Old and New Testament, Tradition and natural reason. It stems from the conviction that sin must be atoned for and that the sinner must accept responsibility for his actions and make reparation either in this life or the next. In such a way is divine justice made manifest. Purgatory also makes complete sense in that it allows the soul an opportunity to be purged of all evil inclinations it had sought happiness in while on earth. It filters out the filth, allowing divine grace to envelop the soul ready for its entrance into eternal glory. Perfection comes at a price; for just as the most skilled carpenter must work hard to achieve the best results, so must the soul. Indeed, it is far better to accept all the sufferings that afflict us through life and offer them to the Father in union with the Son; but nevertheless, a final, merciful state of being will allow sanctification to become a reality if needed.

Now that we have been able to examine the basic doctrine of Purgatory from the great theologians and saints of the past, we can venture into the mystical realm, seeking answers to questions such as: What is the nature of suffering there? Where is it located? What do the visions of the saints tell us about the mind-set of those detained there? We will also look to see what element of interaction there is within the communion of saints, specifically directed from the Holy Souls to the Church Militant. We will navigate this mysterious path through the writings and ecstasies of various saints; those blessed with supernatural charisms that illuminate our understanding of the Church Suffering, inspiring us to help them in whatever way possible. I should also state that rather than leafing through a whole multitude of saints' experiences concerning Purgatory, as in the case of several books including Fr. Schouppe's fascinating *Purgatory: Explained by the Lives and Legends of the Saints*, I have decided to focus on a specific few that will give us all the insights necessary for the purposes of this book.

St. Hildegard of Bingen, Doctor of the Church

We begin our survey of these blessed souls with one of the greatest, yet strangely least known mystics of the Church's history: St. Hildegard of Bingen (1098–1179). A professed nun of the Order of Saint Benedict, she was declared a Doctor of the Church by Pope Benedict XVI on October 7, 2012, on account of her outstanding achievements, as the Holy Father himself explained:

> This great woman truly stands out crystal clear against the horizon of history for her holiness of life and the originality of her teaching. And, as with every authentic human and theological experience, her authority reaches far beyond the confines of a single epoch or society; despite the distance of time and culture, her thought has proven to be of lasting relevance.[1]

St. Hildegard's main works describing many of her visions are contained in three distinct volumes penned over thirty years: *Scivias*, the *Liber Vitae Meritorum* and the *Liber Divinorum Operum*. We see within them an extraordinary panoramic view of the history of salvation from the beginning of creation to its consummation in the new heaven and new earth. As part of this theological triptych, the concept of purification is dealt with at length, especially in the latter

---

1. Pope Benedict XVI, *Apostolic Letter declaring St. Hildegard of Bingen a Doctor of the Church*, October 7, 2012, www.vatican.va.

two volumes. In fact, St. Hildegard leaves us with perhaps the most remarkable and fullest treatment of Purgatory in the entire mystical tradition of the Church.

The *Liber Vitae Meritorum,* or *The Book of Life's Merits,* composed between 1158 and 1163, is based around thirty-five vices and their opposing virtues. It seeks to focus on the necessity of repentance, penance and Christian morality for union with God. St. Hildegard includes sections that are penitential in character, in which she sees the purgatorial sufferings that emerge from each particular vice. This is then followed by advice as to how to escape those agonies by performing penance on earth. The great mystic also informs us of the revelation of God concerning the nature of Purgatory; one which follows the patristic theological thoughts we have already evaluated:

> And I heard a voice from the living light saying to me: These things which you see are true. As you see these things, so they are, and there are more things. For the torments of these punishments cleanse these souls who, living in this changing world, have earned in a non-changing way the cleansing of their sins through punishment. But these torments have not cleansed them from the death which comes to the body; these torments do not prevent them from being weighed in the world by the divine scourges of the merciful God. But these torments will cleanse them unless they are snatched away from these punishments by the labors of men or by the virtues of the holy ones which God works in those men when they call upon the piety of divine grace.[2]

Hildegard gives vivid descriptions of the scenes she encounters in these visions: pits, lakes and mountains, while the familiar purgative fire is also present. Foul smelling marshes along with a host of creatures (vipers, worms, scorpions and toads) also add to the general sense of terror.[3]

---

2. Hildegard of Bingen, *The Book of the Rewards of Life* (*Liber vitae meritorum*) (New York: Oxford University Press, 1994), 47.

3. As with many of St. Hildegard's visions, there is a rich symbolism reminiscent of the Old Testament prophets. Pope Benedict XVI points this out in the Apostolic Letter of October 7, 2012: "Hildegard's language, characterized by an original

The *Liber Divinorum Operum* written between 1163 and 1173 offers an even greater exposition of Purgatory, where geographical and geological elements come to the fore. In the fifth of ten visions, Hildegard sees the globe divided into five regions: east, west, north, south and center. To put the entire vision in context, humanity is symbolized by the earth's form: the four outer parts give the earth sufficient weight for its stability, while the middle part maintains the earth in its place. Hildegard then explains: "This means that we human beings who are symbolized by the earth are strengthened and brought to our soul's salvation by the five senses that stimulate us to everything we need."[4] Explanations are then given concerning the positive aspects of each region and how they relate to the various senses.

In part six of this immense vision, Hildegard turns her attention to the plight of those who are to be redeemed after the soul's liberation from its body, yet who must undergo punishment because of their guilt. To the western part, punishment is administered for venial sin; to the south, atonement for grave sins, for those who chose vice over virtue. In the "corner of virtue" situated between the east and the south are found the most terrible punishments: "fiery and stormy powers of the air and other tortures by which the evilest deeds of murderers, robbers, thieves and similar individuals are punished."[5] The northern part purges those who enjoyed sins of the flesh, and those who committed apostasy against the Catholic faith: "stinking dampness, death-causing odors and smoke as well as other

---

and effective style, makes ample use of poetic expressions and is rich in symbols, dazzling intuitions, incisive comparisons and evocative metaphors." In a Letter to Saint Bernard, the Rhenish mystic reveals something of her extraordinary charism: "Father, I am greatly disturbed by a vision which has appeared to me through divine revelation, a vision seen not with my fleshly eyes but only in my spirit . . . Through this vision which touches my heart and soul like a burning flame, teaching me profundities of meaning, I have an inward understanding of the Psalter, the Gospels, and other volumes." *The Letters of Hildegard of Bingen*: vol. 1, trans. Joseph L. Baird and Radd K. Ehrman (New York: Oxford University Press, 1994), 27–28. 1994), 27–28.

4. Hildegard of Bingen, *The Book of Divine Works* (Santa Fe: Bear &Company, 1987), 155.

5. Ibid., 160.

tortures."[6] Hildegard stresses that all punishments are correctly measured by divine justice. The greatest punishments are reserved for those who show disdain towards the virtues and instead opt for a life of self-centered debauchery.

In the vision, mention is made of sturdy mountains that defend the earth from the horrors of these purgatorial regions, and in a sense, there is symbolized the very real connection between the physical earth and the spiritual state of Purgatory. Reading the entire vision from a purely literal standpoint, it is as if these two worlds co-exist, are bound together in a corporeal way, but if we view it metaphorically, the reality becomes more evident. The terrors stem from abuses caused by man himself: fire out of control is deadly, water in the form of a flood destroys, abuses of sexuality lead to terrible diseases. In essence, the natural world that is given as a gift becomes the source of punishment when mankind rebels against the parameters set by God. Understood in this way, the vision brings the truth of Purgatory sharply into focus; far from being a product of an overactive imagination, it spells out the danger of separating oneself from the path laid out by the Lord, which can only lead to destruction. The mountain which so often reminds us of God's presence in this case "protects" the good earth (those striving to live the divine will) from the destructive powers caused by personal and communal sin.

We also encounter these "earthly" temporal punishments in one of Hildegard's medicinal works, the *Causae et curae* (Causes and Cures c. 1150s) which adds a somewhat new dimension to the understanding of purgatorial suffering. The book follows much of the German mystic's theology through a cosmological approach where humanity is the summit of creation—a microcosm of the macrocosmic universe.[7] Within this framework, Hildegard promotes a holistic approach to human health allied to the *viriditas*, or

---

6. Ibid., 161.

7. In the *Causae et Curae*, Book One, St. Hildegard writes: "O man, look to man. For man has the heavens and earth and other created things within him. He is one, and all things are hidden within him." Hildergardis, *Causae et curae*, (Leipzig: In aedibus B.G. Teubneri, 1903), 2.

"greening power" of nature. In the final section, thoughts turn towards the purification "*De purgatoriis poenis*":

> There are some unquenchable fires in the air, which are kindled through diverse actions of men; for these fires which should have been for human glory, become punitive fires through men's evil deeds. So they descend to some places on earth, and there congregate, where too some rivers rise and flow forth, that draw heat and ardor from those fires, so that also by God's judgment some souls are tested in the fires and in the waters. But some streams from these waters at times flow into diverse regions among men— streams that are always hot, because they derive from the unquenchable fires. ... And the earth and mountains and stones which that fire has touched will always remain burning, till the last day; and in those places that burn thus, streams sometimes rise that are hot with the same fire and flow warm ... and these waters do not harm the men who use them for bathing in, but make them healthy, for the heat of the streams assuages the excessive heat in human beings and consumes their disordered humours.[8]

Taken in the context of a work devoted to cures for human ailments, we see how this great saint places Purgatory not only as a just punishment applied through God's divine judgment, but also as a therapeutic remedy for the maladies of body and soul. Hildegard seems to be describing thermal springs that emanate from volcanic activity, and in this imagery we have the juxtaposition between the healing and punitive aspects of Purgatory. We also discover how Hildegard integrates her cosmological approach into a supernatural order; God, man and nature all meet in the channels of divine mercy. For man, his journey to God comes through the active participation in creation where "Purgatory" can be carried out through daily suffering, or if necessary, symbolically through the "fire" and "water" of the next world.

Although the majority of St. Hildegard's mystical revelations are contained in her books, she also left about four hundred letters, some of which contain visions and prophetic admonishments to those in secular and ecclesiastical authority. Of great significance to

8. Ibid., 233.

our discussion, though, concerns a letter in which the mystic reveals the punishments endured by a particular soul after its death and judgment. She describes seeing the soul being sent to an arid region in the North where venomous scorpions arrive from the South and ferocious wild boars from the East. A house is also visible. The visionary recounts the unfolding scene thus:

> This soul was whirled about, here and there, by a huge whirlwind, and blown around in the midst of a great abundance of straw,[9] flying like thatch torn from a roof and destroyed. After it had been out in this way by the whirlwind, it was thrown into that house ... and, there, it was subjected to such fierce fire that it glowed like red-hot iron. Then, it was thrown among the poisonous scorpions, which punctured it with their venom, and, afterward, among the wild boars, which took great bites out of it. Thus on account of its instability and its false and deceiving way of life, this soul suffered the afflictions of the whirlwind, in company with that straw, and on account of certain hidden sins, which were very grievous, it was tortured by the fire in that house, and on account of its continually duplicitous tongue, it suffered the poison of the scorpions, and on account of its raping (as I learned in the true vision), it was torn among the boars.[10]

At the end of the vision, Hildegard informs us that the soul was a religious, who had been saved through the discipline of the Rule, and the physical infirmities sent by God. However, the nature of its wickedness would mean it would spend a great length of time suffering these purgatorial chastisements.

As with the other texts we have considered, perhaps the main conclusion we can draw is that Purgatory, in the mystical teachings of this great Doctor of the Church, is a reality that reflects the failure of humanity to draw on the God-given graces to transform itself individually and creation in general. It speaks of the gravity of sin, of the consequences of betraying God, and the natural law that guides our conscience. This sin not only affects the soul, but also

9. In *Scivias*, Hildegard explains that straw refers to those who negate and reject the Catholic faith.

10. Hildegard of Bingen, *The Personal Correspondence of Hildegard of Bingen*, ed. Joseph L. Baird (New York: Oxford University Press, 2006), 126–127.

seeps into the material world, as we read in the *Liber vitae meritorum*:

> And I heard a great voice from the elements of the world, saying to the [Cosmic] Man: "We cannot run and complete our course as we have been taught by our master, for humans overturn us like the millwheel with their depraved works—so we reek with pestilence and hunger for all justice." But the Man replied, "I will sweep you clean with the broom, and in the meantime, I will torture humans until they return to me. . . . And as often as you are polluted, so often I will purify you with the torment of your polluters."[11]

Despite the evils that sully the body and soul, St. Hildegard's revelations on the *Church Suffering* tell us that God's illustrious plan to deliver humanity from the chains of the devil will finally be realized even if further purification is necessary in the afterlife. Her theology of purgation needs to be understood in the overall context of her writings: a "global synthesis of the Christian faith."[12] This synthesis reveals God's love manifested in creation; in His desire to reveal Himself through nature, and especially in the life of His Son. The punishments first meted out to Adam and Eve and then extended to all humanity allow a way back towards life with God through suffering and repentance. All of God's actions throughout salvation history are geared towards repairing the damage caused by the first sin, and Purgatory takes its rightful place within that framework of justice and mercy.

St. Teresa of Avila, Doctor of the Church

If St. Hildegard of Bingen came to define the female mystical tradition of the Middle Ages, then St. Teresa of Avila (1515–1582) would do the same for the period of the Renaissance and beyond. Her profound theology has left its mark not only on the Church as an institution, but in the lives of individual Catholics throughout the past five centuries, especially through her teachings on prayer, spiritual

---

11. St. Hildegard of Bingen, *Liber vitae meritorum*, III, 2–3.

12. Pope Benedict XVI, *Apostolic Letter Proclaiming St. Hildegard a Doctor of the Church*, October 7, 2012, www.vatican.va.

ascent and final perfection. Pope Francis recently stated: "Teresa of Jesus does not recommend many things to us, only three: love for each other, detachment from everything, and to have true humility, 'which, although I put it last, is the most important of the three and embraces all the rest' (*The Way of Perfection* 4, 4)."[13]

Teresa's mystical gifts came to her through a "passive" reception of God's grace which was distinct from her own efforts in the spiritual life; in fact she describes in her autobiography, *Life*, a sort of rebirth in the Spirit:

> This is another, new book from here on—I mean another, new life. The life dealt with up to this point was mine; the one I lived from the point where I began to explain these things about prayer is the one God lived in me—according to the way it appears to me—because I think it would have been impossible in so short a time to get rid of so many bad habits and deeds. May the Lord be praised who freed me from myself.[14]

St. Teresa was blessed with a rich variety of mystical experiences: the Lord Jesus often appeared to her; she was clothed in a robe of purity by the Blessed Virgin and St. Joseph; she experienced the pains of hell and was tormented by Satan. St. Teresa also glimpsed the glory of heaven; she conversed with certain saints and was also given knowledge of the state of souls. All these visions and revelations revealed to her the supernatural reality of the communion of saints: the perfect love of the blessed and their intercession for the Church Militant,[15] and the plight of the Holy Souls in Purgatory.

13. Pope Francis, "Message to The Bishop of Avila on the occasion of the opening of The Teresian Jubilee Year," October 15, 2014, www.vatican.va.

14. St. Teresa of Avila, *Collected Works*, vol. 1: *The Book of Her Life, Spiritual Testimonies, Soliloquies* (Washington DC: ICS Publications, 1976), 200–201.

15. Of particular note in St. Teresa's writings is the power and influence of St. Joseph: "It is an amazing thing the great many favors God has granted me through the mediation of this blessed saint, the dangers I was freed from both of body and soul. For with other saints it seems the Lord has given them grace to be of help in one need, whereas with this glorious saint I have experience that he helps in all our needs and that the Lord wants us to understand that just as He was subject to St. Joseph on earth—for since bearing the title of father, being the Lord's tutor Joseph could give the Child command—so in heaven God does whatever he commands." Ibid., 79–80.

Throughout the many writings of St. Teresa, the existence of Purgatory is never far away; her sense of closeness to those detained there is palpable. We do not have the spectacular imagery that is found in St. Hildegard's visions; instead, we discover personal encounters with the dead, and reflections on how to avoid purification in the next life by embracing it in this. In *The Way of Perfection*, composed for the twelve novices of the Carmel of St. Joseph in Avila, St. Teresa exhorts her sisters to follow the path of the Suffering Servant:

> Let us praise God; let us force ourselves to do penance in this life. How sweet will be the death of one who has done penance for all his sins, of one who won't have to go to Purgatory! Even from here below you can begin to enjoy glory! . . . Sisters, let us beseech God that if therefore we are to receive sufferings, they will be received here below. For, with the hope of being freed from them, we can bear them here willingly, and we will not lose His friendship and grace.[16]

Prayer, in the Spanish mystic's teaching, is the other currency that allows one to pay the debt in the next life. St. Teresa encourages the community to not concern themselves so much with escaping the purgatorial flames, but instead, channelling their prayers towards advancing the Kingdom of Christ on earth:

> If you are uneasy because you think your sufferings in Purgatory will not be shortened, know that by this prayer they will be; and if you must still pay some debts, so be it. What would it matter were I to remain in Purgatory until judgment day if through my prayer I could save even one soul? How much less would it matter if my prayer is to the advantage of many and for the honor of the Lord. Pay no attention to sufferings that come to an end if through them some greater service is rendered to Him who endured so many for us.[17]

St. Teresa's own powers of intercessory prayer are evident in her

16. St. Teresa of Avila, *Collected Works*, vol. 2: *The Way of Perfection, Meditations on the Song of Songs, The Interior Castle* (Washington, DC: ICS Publications, 1980), 195.
17. Ibid., 50.

mystical experiences with the Holy Souls.[18] We discover the love that binds the Communion of Saints in a powerful way that should serve to inspire our own efforts to release these brothers and sisters from their sufferings. This charitable concern ultimately stemmed from the deep-rooted friendship Teresa cultivated in the Heart of Jesus; for in her profoundly mystical work, *The Interior Castle*, the saint reveals the true secret of holiness:

> I only wish to inform you that in order to profit by this path and ascend to the dwelling places we desire, the important thing is not to think much but to love much; and so do that which best stirs you to love . . . it doesn't consist in great delight but in desiring with strong determination to please God in everything, in striving, insofar as possible, not to offend Him, and in asking Him for the advancement of the honor and glory of His Son and the increase of the Catholic Church.[19]

St. Teresa understood perfectly well that pleasing the Lord, in part, consisted of immersing herself in the *Sanctorum Communio*; that through divine love, God expected every disciple to assist His children, especially those far from His grace, and the entire company of the Church Suffering. In her autobiography, a window is opened revealing this mystery, on an individual level, of those undergoing purification in Purgatory. In one instance, St. Teresa recounts how a brother-in-law had died suddenly without having the chance to go to confession. It was then revealed to her in prayer that her sister would also die in the same way. With permission from Teresa's confessor the Saint was able to visit her sister and instruct her in the habit of regular confession. Consequently, her sister died only eight days after her last confession and remained in Purgatory only a very short time: "I don't think more than eight

18. St. Teresa informs us of this fact in her autobiography: "The Lord has granted me so many favors by freeing souls from Purgatory and doing other noteworthy things that I would tire myself and tire whoever reads this if I mentioned them all." St. Teresa of Avila, *Collected Works*, vol. 1: *The Book of Her Life, Spiritual Testimonies, Soliloquies* (Washington, DC: ICS Publications, 1976), 344.

19. St. Teresa of Avila, *Collected Works*, vol. 2: *The Way of Perfection, Meditations on the Song of Songs, The Interior Castle* (Washington, DC: ICS Publications, 1980), 319.

days passed when the Lord appeared to me after I received Communion and wanted me to see how He brought her to glory."[20]

On another occasion, this great mystic reveals how, upon learning of the death of a former provincial, she pleaded to the Lord for him, offering up all the merits of her life to date, and asking Jesus to make up through his own merits what would be necessary for this man's entry into heaven:

> While beseeching the Lord for this as best I could, it seemed to me that person came out from the depths of the earth at my right side and that I saw him ascend to heaven with the greatest happiness. He had been well advanced in years, but I saw him as only about thirty, or even less I think, and his countenance was resplendent. This vision passed very quickly; but I was so extremely consoled that his death could never cause me any more sorrow, although I saw persons who were filled with grief over his loss since he had been generally highly esteemed. The consolation my soul experienced was so great I couldn't worry about him, nor could I doubt that it was a vision; I mean that it was not an illusion. No more than fifteen days had passed since his death.[21]

St. Teresa also gives two instances of religious whom she had known at different times, and who both appeared to her soon after death. In the first case, a "great servant of God" as Teresa called her, had been dead for a day and a half when she suddenly appeared next to the Spanish saint ascending towards heaven; this at the exact moment a nun along with Teresa were reciting a reading from the Office of the Dead for her. In the second case, Teresa saw an apparition of a holy friar during Mass and she understood that he had escaped Purgatory altogether. His death, it was later revealed, had occurred at the exact time she saw him.[22] Interestingly, St. Teresa revealed that in all the visions she had seen, only this friar, the great St. Peter of Alcantara, and a Dominican priest had managed to avoid Purgatory.

---

20. St. Teresa of Avila, *Collected Works*, vol. 1: *The Book of Her Life, Spiritual Testimonies, Soliloquies* (Washington DC: ICS Publications, 1976), 302.

21. Ibid., 340.

22. Ibid., 340–341.

Another remarkable account related in the *Book of Foundations* concerns Teresa's dealings with a "distinguished" young man[23] who offered the saint a fully paid house and large garden in which she could found a monastery in Valladolid. Teresa accepted gratefully this generous offer. Two months later, the man's health deteriorated leading first to a loss of speech and then soon after, death. The saint then tells how Jesus informed her that this man's soul had been in great jeopardy, but he had received mercy on account of his service in honor of the Blessed Virgin, through the offering of this house. However, he would not leave Purgatory until the first Mass had been offered in the new monastery. In Teresa's own words: "I was in prayer one day in Medina when the Lord told me to hurry because that soul was suffering very much. Although I didn't have the means available, I set to work and entered Valladolid on the feast of St. Lawrence."[24] St. Teresa hastily arranged for workmen to begin building a Church, and permission was sought from the Bishop for Mass to be offered there. Through the mercy of the Lord, the Mass that released the young man from Purgatory was offered on the grounds before the Church was actually built:

> When the priest came with the Blessed Sacrament to the place where we were to receive Communion and I approached to receive it, the gentleman I mentioned appeared beside him, his face joyful and resplendent. With hands folded, he thanked me for what I had done so that he could leave Purgatory and go to heaven.[25]

St. Teresa concluded the episode by stating that the man had found himself in spiritual danger because he had become somewhat engrossed in the world, even though he had performed many good deeds.[26] It is a reminder of the Lord's words found in St. Matthew's

23. The man in question was Don Bernardino de Mendoza, brother of the Bishop of Avila, who died in February 1568 in Ubeda, Spain. See, *The Collected Works of St. Teresa of Avila*, vol. 3: *The Book of Her Foundations and Minor Works* (Washington, DC: ICS Publications, 1985), 420.

24. Ibid., 145.

25. Ibid., 145–146.

26. It seems that the Mass was offered in August 1568, soon after St. Teresa had arrived in Valladolid on August 10. Therefore, Don Bernardino de Mendoza had spent about six months in Purgatory.

Gospel: "A man cannot be the slave of two masters at once; either he will hate the one and love the other, or he will devote himself to the one and despise the other. You must serve God or money; you cannot serve both" (Matt. 6:24).

In the mystical life of this Doctor of the Church, the presence of Satan and his legion was often a trial that God allowed her to experience, both for the spiritual benefit of herself and for others. Her visions expose the truth of a spiritual war being waged for souls, a fight for the eternal destiny of humanity. St. Teresa reveals the power of holy water in several mystical encounters; in one, she states how devils seemed to be choking her and that by sprinkling holy water around they had collectively left her "as though they were being thrown down a precipice."[27] In a second instance we see a diabolical attempt at stopping the Saint from concluding her prayerful intercession for the Church Suffering:

> I shall only mention what happened to me on the night of All Souls: while I was in the oratory after having recited a nocturn and while saying some very devotional prayers that come at the end, a devil appeared on the book so that I couldn't finish the prayer. I blessed myself, and he went away. When I began again to recite the prayers, he returned. I believe it was three times I began, and until I threw holy water at him I couldn't finish. I saw that some souls left Purgatory at that instant; little must have been lacking to their freedom, and I wondered if he had aimed at preventing this.[28]

Looking at the communion of saints through the lens of this great mystic, several factors should attract our attention: the closeness we must feel on an individual level to those suffering in Purgatory; that these holy souls are not just statistics but real people whose lives perhaps intermingled with our own; that prayer, mortification and the offering of illness for them will yield powerful results, not only lessening their purification, but instigating their total liberation. Finally, we clearly see that God's will is that we do everything we can to help them; we have been given the tools needed to accomplish

---

27. St. Teresa of Avila, *Collected Works*, vol. 1: *The Book of Her Life, Spiritual Testimonies, Soliloquies* (Washington, DC: ICS Publications, 1976), 267.
28. Ibid., 267–268.

this. In St. Teresa of Avila, we see the perfect charity of the communion of saints made manifest in her complete offering of herself for
the glory of the most Holy Trinity, and the salvation of souls.

St. Mary Magdalen de Pazzi

If the Lord graced the Carmelites of Spain with the extraordinary
mysticism of St. Teresa of Avila, then he did no less for the Carmelites of Italy in the same period by sending St. Maria Maddalena
de Pazzi (1566–1607). This daughter of Florence, though not sharing
the same universal fame as Teresa of Avila, nonetheless shared a very
similar mystical path in which she conformed herself to Jesus
through a profound interior union marked by suffering and great
charity.

Her earliest years bore witness to the supernatural and a yearning
for the Lord. She received Holy Communion for the first time on
March 25, 1576, and within a few days had made a vow of virginity.
Her desire to love God in an ever increasing way led her to join the
Carmel of St. Mary of the Angels at Borgo San Frediano, where on
January 30, 1583 she received the Carmelite habit and the name of
Sr. Mary Magdalene. Within a year, she had fallen gravely ill and
upon request was allowed to make her profession without further
delay.

From this point, St. Mary Magdalen's mystical life entered a new
and profuse phase in which the Lord granted her many revelations
and extraordinary visions. These have been handed down in the
form of various writings: *The Forty Days, The Dialogues, Probation,
Revelations and Knowledge* and the *Renovation of the Church*.[29] Several biographies of the Saint have also documented the miraculous
occurrences that pervaded her life in the Carmel.

As with St. Teresa of Avila, Purgatory and its detainees were ever
present in the mystical life of Maria Maddalena de Pazzi. This concern was the fruit of a love that knew no bounds. It was the doctrine

---

29. St. Mary Magdalen's revelatory discourses were recorded by her fellow nuns.
She herself actually burned notebooks detailing the visions from her period of probation until her confessors forbade it. It appears that for the Italian mystic, written
words could not convey the extraordinary dialogue between herself and the Word.

of the communion of saints taken off the page and lived as God would have it lived: no forgetfulness, no apathy, no token gestures; only pure charity for their cause, a fiery love that surely burned no less than that which consumed those very same holy souls. And what would account for so great a love? The explanation is quite simple. These heroes of the faith breathed in the Holy Spirit endlessly; it was not their own poor love but *agape*, the love of God, a love that is restless until God's will is fulfilled.

In Saint Mary Magdalene's *Dialogues* we sense this great love for the holy souls:

[N]ow amorous Word, although a lot should be done to regenerate and renew the body of your holy Church—and this is why you called me at the beginning—, nonetheless, since I do want to understand something about you, now I am not going to examine all the others but I shall focus on those blessed souls of Purgatory who are shut up, so to speak, in a prison. But blessed be those who go down there, and blessed me if I eventually go down there. But since I have offered all the other members of the holy Church to the Father and to you too, Word, now I want to offer this only to you, immensely pure and simple Word. . . . And what shall I offer you for these people? Oh, I shall offer you Mary's white and red, red and white milk. And her breasts will be like two springs from which milk will flow down to these blessed souls, cooling down the flames and nourishing them with milk, which will soothe their constant thirst for your vision. And you Word, sending also your blood to them, will adorn them with it and attract them to you. Thus we'll be able to say . . . this blood adorns these blessed souls as spring adorns flowers and boughs.[30]

At this point, St. Mary Magdalene saw Jesus sprinkling his precious blood over the souls which caused them to ascend to heaven while she joyfully proclaimed the great generosity of the Lord.

Like St. Teresa of Avila, St. Mary Magdalene saw her close relatives suffering in Purgatory. We read accounts involving both her brother and mother. In the case of her brother, who died in June 1587, the

30. Maria Maddalena de Pazzi, *Selected Revelations* (Mahwah: Paulist Press, 2000), 153–154.

mystic was shown him suffering terrible torments. After praying intensely for him while in rapture, St. Mary Magdalene informed the Mother Superior of the sad reality and extent of purgatorial punishment: "O Mother! Great, indeed, are the pains which the souls suffer in Purgatory! I would never have thought them to be so intense, had God not given me some light in regard to them."[31]

Her love for these souls was so immense that she struggled to bear the burden of living on earth while yet knowing and conversing with them. Several days after this initial vision, while walking in the garden with the other nuns, St. Mary Magdalene was enlightened on a certain structure in Purgatory. She described seeing various places where punishments were allotted: for religious, for hypocrites; then for the ignorant, disobedient, impatient, liars, ambitious, proud, the avaricious and the ungrateful. The nuns present were aware of the terrible anguish of the saint during this experience: her expressions of horror, her pleading with eyes raised to heaven. The sad spectacle left several nuns in tears, but significantly, the Carmel from that day offered ever more fervent prayers to God for the release of these holy souls. As for St. Mary Magdalene's brother, he was soon released thanks to the efficacy of her prayers.

St. Mary Magdalene's mother, Maria Buondelmonti de Pazzi, by reputation a very humble and devout soul, departed this life during Advent, 1590. It is related by Fr. Fabrini in his biography that the Saint knew of the moment of her death because of an unusual pain in her heart coupled with a strong desire to kneel and pray for her. It was later however, during the recitation of the *Miserere*, that the Carmelite mystic became rapt in ecstasy and beheld the vision of her mother's soul in Purgatory: "very cheerful and contented, as though little children were removing the flames from around her, and the tears of the poor who were weeping over her death gave her great relief in those pains."[32] The saint's guardian angel then revealed the "indescribable glory" which her mother would soon

---

31. St. Mary Magdelen, *The Life of St. Mary Magdelen de Pazzi, Compiled by Rev. Placido Fabrini* (Philadelphia: Isoleri, 1900), 91.

32. Ibid., 110.

possess, thanks to the charity she had shown to her neighbors in life. Fifteen days later, on the eve of the Nativity of the Blessed Virgin and after much prayer and sacrifice from her devoted daughter, Maria de Pazzi left Purgatory for the everlasting peace of heaven, in a glorious scene related by St. Mary Magdalene's fellow nuns:

> She understood, in a new ecstasy, how her soul on the morning of that same day, at the hour corresponding to that in which it had left her body, had flown up to heaven; and she saw it, all joyful, glancing at the side of the Word, and there it stopped, as at the time of death it possessed God in the act of charity. She had already seen how her patron Saints had carried her soul into heaven like an eagle, how St. Catherine adorned it with a habit of blood, St. Agnes with various flowers, and St. John the Baptist placed on her head a crown.[33]

We could speculate as to why the Lord allowed these two great mystics to see their own relatives suffering in Purgatory; of course it could be nothing more than the opportunity to help their own flesh and blood. But could we not also see a deeper meaning in the context of the *Sanctorum Communio* that takes us back to the Lord's question in St. Matthew's Gospel: "Who is a mother, who are brethren, to me?" (Matt. 12:48) On this theological basis, the whole company of Purgatory becomes my brother, sister and mother. The binding through divine love is such that our concern for each individual holy soul is no less than if it were an immediate family member. The communion of saints cannot be truly lived in its most radical way unless the members of the Mystical Body on earth recapture a boundless love and compassion for the deceased. This means a restoration of devotion to the Church Suffering, and a greater self-examination of conscience that on the one hand will warn us not to expect immediate entry into the presence of God, and on the other, an appreciation that in all probability, a great number of souls languish in Purgatory for a very long time with very few Catholics to help them. In doing these two things, the

---

33. Ibid., 110–111.

plight of the holy souls will be forever embedded in the hearts of the faithful and the communion between the two states of the one Mystical Body will grow stronger.

St. Mary Magdalene de Pazzi was also granted visions of certain deceased nuns in the Carmel, and knowledge as to why purgation had been necessary. In one case, a nun had spent sixteen days in Purgatory for three specific reasons: first, she had done unnecessary work on a feast day; secondly, because, as a senior mother of the religious family, she had failed once to notify the superiors of something which she felt she ought to make known for the welfare of the monastery; and thirdly, because she was too attached to her relatives. It was also revealed however, that her sufferings had been shortened because of the great care she had taken in maintaining a pure and simple faith, the great charity she had endeavored to show, and the general good will of her soul. The nuns who were present during this ecstasy described the Saint's joy upon receiving the vision of her liberation:

> Therefore our Saint saw, afterwards, that this happy soul, purified from all stains, and rich in merits, was going to enjoy the Sovereign Good, accompanied by her Guardian Angel and St. Miniato, Martyr, who, according to the custom of the monastery, had been appointed her protector for that year.[34]

On another occasion in 1589, while St. Mary Magdalene was in the choir praying, the soul of a deceased nun of the Carmel appeared to her, covered in flames, as if wrapped in a mantle under which a white habit was apparent. The dead nun was praying in adoration before the Eucharistic Lord. The Italian mystic asked God the meaning of this, and she was given to understand that the white habit had been given to the sister for having preserved her virginity inviolate until death, and the mantle of fire was purification for some faults. She was specifically before the Blessed Sacrament covered with that mantle, in punishment for having several times during life omitted Holy Communion; and that for this neglect, she had to stay every day for one hour in adoration until she had wholly

34. Ibid., 109.

atoned for the fault. Again, as with the previous vision, St. Mary Magdalene saw the soul ascend towards heaven soon after.

These accounts of undoubtedly holy persons suffering temporal punishment beg the question: Do we have to resign ourselves to a sojourn in Purgatory? St. Mary Magdalene's own opinion was that souls could avoid Purgatory altogether "if one performed all his actions with the pure intention of giving glory to God";[35] even the least actions could become meritorious in the eyes of God if done in this way. But in terms of aiding those already imprisoned there; acts of charity, fasts, recitation of psalms, and the offering of the merits of Christ's Passion would all be most beneficial.

As with all the great mystics, the Florentine saint embraced harsh penances in order to subdue the flesh and allow her spirit to rise ever closer to Jesus. Everything was done for love of others; for God in the first instance, but then as a direct consequence of that love, for sinners in danger of damnation and the suffering in Purgatory. St. Mary Magdalene had a tremendous zeal to win souls for Christ at any cost; that explains why her mortifications were so severe: austere fasts on bread and water, walking bare foot in winter even in the snow, sleeping on the floor, and using a variety of instruments to chastise her body including a belt of nails. Of course to the "rational" mind of the twenty-first century, these penances may seem extreme and even pointless, but they offer a mystical insight into the gravity of sin, the severity of offending God and the proliferation of evil. In the heart of the saints, they are doing no less than imitating Jesus in his cruel sufferings. Reparation is accepted in love, to extend the communion of saints and thus offer greater glory to the Holy Trinity.

Pope Benedict XVI elucidated perfectly the life of self-sacrifice that consumed the great mystic of Florence in a Letter marking the fourth centenary of her death:

> The purified love that pulsated in her heart opened her to desire full conformity with Christ, her Spouse, even to sharing with him the "naked suffering" of the Cross. Her last three years of life were

---

35. Ibid., 202.

a true Calvary of suffering for her.... As, while she was alive, grasping the bells she urged her Sisters with the cry: "Come and love Love!," may the great Mystic, from Florence, from her Seminary, from the Carmelite monasteries that draw their inspiration from her, still make her voice heard in all the Church, spreading to every human creature the proclamation to love God.[36]

If we reflect briefly on the era that was graced by the presence of these two great Carmelite mystics, we see that it was one of religious turmoil caused by the Protestant Reformation; and as we have already seen, the Council of Trent had restated the dogma of Purgatory in the face of its rejection by the Lutherans. But looking back now, with the benefit of hindsight, we can also perceive the intervention of God in this period by enriching the mystical tradition that put flesh, not only on the teachings concerning Purgatory, but the entire doctrine of the communion of saints. If the protestant leaders had led the way in rejecting much of Catholicism as superstition and idolatry (with its veneration of saints), then these luminous figures along with many others reinvigorated the Mystical Body by ensuring that the Church was understood and acknowledged in its entirety: that is as a communion of love that transcends time and earthly reality. They bore powerful witness to the reality that the holy souls and the saints in heaven are not merely "at rest" but are active members of the one Church that seeks to ensure the Church Militant overcomes, through God's grace, the age old battle against the forces of evil.

St. Pio of Pietrelcina

The two remaining Saints that we will study in this chapter are both immense figures central to the Church of the twentieth century; and in a sense, were placed in a similar situation to the mystics of the Counter Reformation. Except it was the onslaught of Modernism, rather than a schism, that posed the greatest threat to the Church Militant in their time. Both St. Pio and St. Faustina Kowal-

---

36. Pope Benedict XVI, "Letter to the Archbishop of Florence on the Occasion of the Fourth Centenary of the Death of St. Mary Magdalen de Pazzi," April 29, 2007.

ska were granted extraordinary gifts that lifted the veil to a certain extent on the mysteries of eternal life, and at the same time encouraged the faithful to make greater efforts to assist their brothers and sisters in the communion of saints.

St. Pio (1887–1968)—or, to give him the name familiar to millions around the world, Padre Pio—exemplified the mystical tradition of the Church to an almost perfect degree. By that, I mean his imitation of Christ: his holiness, his sufferings, his total love for the sick, both spiritually and bodily. Everything about this Saint speaks of total giving. Nothing was held back in his quest to love God and man. Perhaps the reason he is possibly the most revered priest of recent times is because his likeness to Jesus was remarkable—and people saw it in life, and still sense it today.

Like his Divine Master, the humble Capuchin Friar offered his life as a sacrifice in atonement for sin; he felt very deeply the need to appease the just anger of God, and thus placed himself between divine judgment and humanity. In this way, St. Pio worked tirelessly for the salvation of souls, to keep them out of hell and to spread God's dominion over them. But his concern for them didn't end there. He desired to spare them as much temporal punishment as possible, as we see in a letter addressed to his spiritual director, Padre Benedetto of San Marco in Lamis:

> Now, my dear Father, I want to ask your permission for something. For some time past I have felt the need to offer myself to the Lord as a victim for poor sinners and for the souls in Purgatory. This desire has been growing continually in my heart so that it has now become what I would call a strong passion. I have in fact made this offering to the Lord several times, beseeching him to pour out upon me the punishments prepared for sinners and for the souls in a state of purgation, even increasing them a hundredfold for me, as long as he converts sinners and quickly admits to Paradise the souls in Purgatory. . . . It seems to me that Jesus really wants this.[37]

---

37. Padre Pio of Pietrelcina, *Letters*, vol. 1 (Foggia: Editions Padre Pio Da Pietrelcina, Our Lady of Grace Capuchin Friary, 1984), 234.

As in the case of St. Mary Magdalen de Pazzi, Padre Pio did not "advertise" his remarkable gifts; the stigmata he bore for fifty years, for instance, was a source of constant "embarrassment and unbearable humiliation."[38] He desired the suffering to continue, for the sake of others, but no doubt he was aware of the danger of a cult of personality that could detract from the Lord, therefore he wanted the mystical aspect of his life hidden wherever Jesus would allow it. Because of this, many of his encounters with the dead were related by the other friars at San Giovanni Rotondo where he lived so much of his life.[39]

Padre Alessio Parente, who helped St. Pio in the latter years of his life, recalled the great mystic once say: "more souls of the dead than the living climb this mountain to attend my Masses and seek my prayers."[40] Padre Alberto D'Apolito, at one time a seminarian in San Giovanni Rotondo, quoted the Saint affirming: "I see so many souls from Purgatory that they don't frighten me anymore."[41] In fact, after Padre Benedetto had given permission for St. Pio to make his offering as a victim for sinners, the visitors from Purgatory became ever more frequent in requesting his powerful intercession.

Padre D'Apolito relates in his book *Padre Pio of Pietrelcina, Memories, Experiences, Testimonials* a very interesting story told by the Saint himself involving one of the earliest apparitions of a soul in the friary. The background to the episode concerns a visit made by the Italian Bishop, Alberto Costa, to see Padre Pio. While in conversation, the Bishop asked him if he had ever seen a soul from Purgatory. St. Pio then related what had transpired in the guest room of the Friary one day during World War One:

---

38. Ibid., 1218.

39. There are however many instances in his Letters where visions and interior locutions are recorded; the Lord Jesus, the Blessed Virgin, St. Pio's Guardian Angel and Satan were frequently present in his monastic cell. The latter inflicted vicious beatings on many occasions out of pure hatred for the souls that were being snatched away from him.

40. Fr. Alessio Parente O.F.M. Cap., *The Holy Souls, "Viva Padre Pio"* (Foggia: Editions Padre Pio da Pietrelcina, 1998), 25.

41. Fr. Alberto D'Apolito, *Padre Pio of Pietrelcina: Memories, Experiences, Testimonials* (Foggia: Editions Padre Pio da Pietrelcina, 1986), 84.

> They went out of the guest room [Padre Paolino and his Sister] and pulled the door after them, and I was left alone near the fireplace. I was absorbed in prayer, when the door opened and an old man came in, dressed in the traditional mantle commonly worn by the elderly people of San Giovanni Rotondo, and he sat beside me. I looked at him but never thought of how he had managed to get into the friary at that hour. I asked him: "Who are you? What do you want?" The man answered: "Padre Pio, I am Pietro di Mauro, nicknamed Precoco. I died in this friary on 18 September 1908 in room number 4, when this friary was still a home for the elderly. When in bed one night, I fell asleep with my cigar burning. My bed caught fire and I died. I suffocated and burned alive. I am still in Purgatory, and I need a Mass to free my soul from it. God has given me permission to come to you and ask for your prayers." After I had listened to his story I said: "You can rest assured that I will celebrate Mass tomorrow for your liberation."[42]

Padre Pio concluded the story by telling Bishop Costa that Pietro di Mauro entered the glory of heaven the following day.

As we have already seen with the two beloved Carmelite mystics, it was not uncommon for the Lord to allow deceased fellow religious from their Orders to visit them imploring prayer and help; and with St. Pio it was no different. In 1937, Padre Bernardo D'Alpicella, the former Provincial, died, and as was the custom, all the priests of the Province offered three Masses for the repose of his soul. One night soon after, Padre Pio was about to leave the choir loft, but before doing so, he approached the railing and looked down towards the tabernacle in order to express his love for the Lord before retiring to bed. Immediately, he saw very clearly Padre D'Alpicella walking from the altar of the Blessed Virgin towards the sacristy. For three consecutive nights, Padre Pio witnessed an apparition of this priest, a fact confirmed by many friars whom he had told.[43]

Another similar event occurred on December 30, 1936, which was recorded by the friary's chronicler, Padre Ferdinando of San Marco

---

42. Ibid., 84–87.
43. *The Voice of Padre Pio*, vol. 12, no. 5 (1982), 7.

in Lamis.[44] Padre Pio had been informed of the grave illness of a very close friend, Padre Giuseppantonio, who before being transferred to a friary in Foggia, had spent five years with the Saint in San Giovanni Rotondo. In the early hours of the morning, Padre Pio was prostrated in prayer imploring God's help for his friend when suddenly he heard a knocking on the door. After instructing the person to come in, Padre Pio, to his surprise, was confronted by Padre Giuseppantonio. Not knowing that he had actually died, St. Pio said: "How are you? I was told you are gravely ill and in a lot of pain, but now you are here?" "I am well" was the reply. "All my pains have vanished and I have come to thank you for your prayers." After saying this, he vanished. As an aside, it is worth mentioning that the friary's chronicler recorded this apparition as occurring at 2:00 a.m., the exact time as the Padre's death (as recorded in the register at Foggia).[45]

There were many other instances of holy souls visiting St. Pio to thank him for his intercession. In one famous case, while eating the evening meal in the refectory with the other friars, Padre Pio abruptly got up and walked to the entrance where he struck up a lively conversation with an invisible presence. When he returned to his place, the bemused friars asked whom he had been talking to. He replied: "Oh don't worry. I was talking to some souls who were on their way from Purgatory to Heaven. They stopped here to thank me because I remembered them in my Mass this morning."[46] On another occasion, one evening during World War II, after the doors had been locked, the friars heard a crowd inside the entrance hallway shouting: "Viva Padre Pio!" The Superior at the time, Padre Raffaele, asked the brother porter to investigate and ensure that the people making the din were ejected from the Friary. Upon arriving in the hallway, he found it in darkness with the door properly bolted. The following day, Padre Raffaele asked St. Pio for a possible

---

44. Interestingly, Padre Ferdinando was told this by none other than Padre D'Alpicella, the Provincial who within a year would be appearing to Padre Pio in his own deceased purgatorial state.

45. *Voce di Padre Pio, anno IX,* no. 11 (1978), 16.

46. *The Voice of Padre Pio,* vol. 11, no. 6 (1981), 7.

explanation. He replied that they were deceased soldiers who had come to thank him for his prayers.[47]

The mystical gifts of St. Pio were not confined merely to conversing with the holy souls; in many cases he had more specific knowledge concerning the duration and type of sufferings endured. The late Italian politician Gerardo de Caro, a close friend of the Padre's, kept notes of his conversations with the Capuchin mystic. On one such occasion de Caro recommended the soul of an author whose books he had enjoyed reading in his youth. He continued the conversation:

> I said no more. I didn't even mention his name. The Padre, however, understood perfectly to whom I was referring. He went red in the face as if distressed, sorry for the sufferings of others. Then he said: "He loved creatures too much!" I asked him how long that soul would stay in Purgatory, and he replied: "At least one hundred years. We must pray for the souls in Purgatory. It is unbelievable what they can do for our spiritual good, out of the gratitude they have towards those on earth who remember to pray for them."[48]

On another occasion, while conversing about the disposition of the soul nearing death and the necessity for repentance as a final opportunity to turn away from impending damnation, St. Pio remarked: "You would be amazed to find souls in Paradise whom you would never have expected to find there."[49]

The doctrine of the communion of saints lies at the heart of the sanctity of St. Pio of Pietrelcina, and is a perfect illustration of why the dogma must be rekindled in the hearts of all. Simply put, love and compassion consumed his time on earth; whether it was refusing absolution in confession for souls who were not truly repentant (with the intention of piercing their conscience), or building the *Home for the Relief of Suffering* for the sick. Padre Pio loved every soul as a true brother and sister because he saw Christ in them. He loved sinners especially, and desired their salvation with an immense

---

47. Ibid.
48. Gerardo de Caro, *Manuscript*, cited in: Fr. Alessio Parente O.F.M. Cap., *The Holy Souls, Viva Padre Pio* (Foggia: Editions Padre Pio da Pietrelcina, 1998), 155–156.
49. Ibid.

passion. His Letters reveal the inner workings of divine grace deep within his soul, and present us with a love that should inspire us to live the *sanctorum communio* with a zeal that surpasses those zealous for death and destruction. The Padre's heart was large enough to accommodate all without fail, a modern icon of the Sacred Heart of Jesus:

> I am consumed by love for God and neighbor. God is continually fixed in my mind and imprinted in my heart. I never lose sight of him. I have to admire his beauty, his benevolence, the agitation he causes, his mercies, his vengeance, or rather the severity of his justice. . . . How is it possible to see God saddened by evil and not be saddened likewise? To see God on the point of letting fly his thunderbolts? To parry them there is no other remedy than to raise one hand to restrain his arm and with the other hand beckon urgently to one's brothers for a twofold reason: that they may cast evil aside and move away at once from where they stand, since the Judge's hand is about to come down on them. . . . For my brothers? Alas! How often, not to say always, I have to say to God the Judge, with Moses: *either forgive them their sin or else blot me out of the book of life.* . . . Pray dear Father, that a torrent of water may descend on me to cool me a little from these devouring flames which are burning in my heart without the slightest respite.[50]

St. Faustina Kowalska

To conclude this chapter, we turn towards the extraordinary life and experiences of the Polish mystic and messenger of Divine Mercy, St. Maria Faustina Kowalska (1905–1938). This daughter of the Congregation of the Sisters of Our Lady of Mercy has left the Church a magnificent compendium detailing the richness of her mystical life in the form of a Spiritual Diary: *Divine Mercy in my Soul.* Written in obedience to her spiritual director, this work has become a spiritual classic of twentieth-century mysticism and rightly takes its place among the great spiritual volumes of the Christian era.

---

50. Padre Pio of Pietrelcina, *Letters,* vol. 1 (Foggia: Editions Padre Pio Da Pietrelcina, Our Lady of Grace Capuchin Friary, 1984), 1393–1394.

Although the theology of mercy is at the heart of the charism and writings of St. Faustina, the communion of saints is the framework in which mercy flowers. Why? Because mercy exists to bring salvation to the world through the Church and therefore increase the number of the elect destined for salvation. If mercy first and foremost emanates from the Heart of Jesus, it then must emanate from the hearts of the baptized; spreading out in a ripple effect encompassing all humanity: to those outside God's friendship, and to those in need within the Church Militant and Church Suffering. This element of Christian duty is emphasized time and again in the Diary of St. Faustina. The flame of divine love is to be passed on through acts of charity and mercy, with a marked intensity directed towards the dying and the deceased.

In order to best appreciate the mercy of God in relation to these souls, a reading of the entire text of the *Diary* is recommended; nevertheless, we will endeavor to accentuate this particular aspect though the mysticism of this great Apostle of Divine Mercy.

Before we look at the visions of St. Faustina concerning Purgatory, it is worth recalling an episode which certainly taught her the seriousness of sin, and perhaps increased her love for the holy souls. In the first notebook of her *Diary*, the Saint recounted an experience where she suddenly appeared before the judgment seat of God and beheld the Lord as he was during his Passion. Then, his wounds disappeared except for the five in his hands, feet and side. St. Faustina explained:

> Suddenly I saw the complete condition of my soul as God sees it. I could clearly see all that is displeasing to God. I did not know that even the smallest transgressions will have to be accounted for. What a moment! Who can describe it? To stand before the Thrice-Holy God! Jesus asked me, who are you? I answered, "I am Your servant, Lord." You are guilty of one day of fire in Purgatory. I wanted to throw myself immediately into the flames of Purgatory, but Jesus stopped me and said, Which do you prefer, suffer now for one day in Purgatory or for a short while on earth? I replied, "Jesus, I want to suffer in Purgatory, and I want to suffer also the greatest pains on earth, even if it were until the end of the world."

Jesus said, one [of the two] is enough; you will go back to earth, and there you will suffer much, but not for long.[51]

We may ponder the question as to whether the period of suffering for one day in Purgatory corresponded exactly to her sufferings on earth from that moment (which would affirm various saints opinions that the pain of Purgatory is much greater than anything on earth); however, suffice to say that St. Faustina embraced the totality of suffering not primarily for her own benefit, but for the sake of poor souls whose spiritual care she had been entrusted with.[52] In one prayer of the Polish mystic we have ample evidence of this fact:

> O Jesus, I understand that Your mercy is beyond all imagining, and therefore I ask You to make my heart so big that there will be room in it for the needs of all the souls living on the face of the earth. O Jesus, my love extends beyond the world, to the souls suffering in Purgatory, and I want to exercise mercy toward them by means of indulgenced prayers.[53]

As we can see from this prayer, St. Faustina, like all mystics, allowed herself to become a true reflection of God's undying love. She desired to place her life within the salvific action of the Lord and therefore experienced a burning love for all; and not only that. By God's grace she understood some of the pain and anguish of the holy souls which undoubtedly increased her desire to help them. In one instance on July 9, 1937, the Saint was visited by one of the deceased sisters from her convent who asked her for one day of fasting and all the spiritual exercises from that day. St. Faustina agreed and the following day set about complying with these wishes. During Mass, St. Faustina had a brief experience of her torment: "I experienced such intense hunger for God that I seemed to be dying

51. St. Maria Faustina Kowalska, *Divine Mercy In My Soul* (Stockbridge: Marian Press, 2005), n. 36.

52. Confirmation of this is found in the Diary. In one passage the crucified Christ spoke these words to the Saint: "Consider well, My daughter, what you are doing for their salvation. . . . Know, My daughter, that your silent day-to-day martyrdom in complete submission to My will ushers many souls into heaven." Ibid., 269.

53. Ibid., 185.

of the desire to become united with Him. This lasted only a short time, but I understood what the longing of the souls in Purgatory was like."[54] Of course, St. Faustina always sought to live God's Will, and in interceding for purgatorial souls she was fulfilling it to the letter; for on various occasions the Lord had revealed to her his wishes: to "enter Purgatory often,"[55] and to offer them indulgenced prayers.

The most explicit plea from Jesus in this direction is found on the eighth day of a Novena in honor of his divine mercy. St. Faustina related how the Lord had dictated to her each of the intentions for the nine days, beginning on Good Friday and ending on the vigil of the Feast of Divine Mercy. It is worth recalling the exact words of the Lord as they provide a perfect summons for living the communion of saints in the most generous way possible:

> Today bring to Me the souls who are in the prison of Purgatory, and immerse them in the abyss of My mercy. Let the torrents of My Blood cool down their scorching flames. All these souls are greatly loved by Me. They are making retribution to My justice. It is in your power to bring them relief. Draw all the indulgences from the treasury of My Church and offer them on their behalf. Oh, if you only knew the torments they suffer, you would continually offer for them the alms of the spirit and pay off their debt to My justice.[56]

St. Faustina, like St. Pio, seemed to live in a state almost between two worlds where the dead mingled with the living in eager expectation of help. The many visions recounted in the Diary offer fascinating insights into the reality of the communion of saints, that rather than presenting a sort of "fairy tale" element of mystery, instead offer us a chance to glimpse the truth which remains hidden from most of us. These souls are real people with real lives behind them, and they are still remarkably close to the day-to-day travails of life; which for the mourner should be a source of great comfort

---

54. Ibid., 269.
55. Ibid., 378.
56. Ibid., 276.

and joy. A perusal of these mystical encounters will help to illustrate this vital point.

One of the most important experiences of St. Faustina concerning Purgatory is related near the beginning of her *Diary*, in which she described being taken to visit the Church Suffering accompanied by her Guardian Angel:

> [The next night] I saw my Guardian Angel, who ordered me to follow him. In a moment I was in a misty place full of fire in which there was a great crowd of suffering souls. They were praying fervently, but to no avail, for themselves; only we can come to their aid. The flames which were burning them did not touch me at all. My Guardian Angel did not leave me for an instant. I asked these souls what their greatest suffering was. They answered me in one voice that their greatest torment was longing for God. I saw Our Lady visiting the souls in Purgatory. The souls call her "The Star of the Sea." She brings them refreshment. I wanted to talk with them some more, but my Guardian Angel beckoned me to leave. We went out of that prison of suffering. [I head an interior voice] which said, *My mercy does not want this, but justice demands it.* Since that time, I am in closer communion with the suffering souls.[57]

Immediately after recounting this episode, St. Faustina related another rather disconcerting one, in which she had been visited by a recently deceased nun, Sister Henry Losinska, who asked the Saint to arrange for a Mass to be offered for the release of her soul.[58] St. Faustina agreed, but later the following day decided not to go and asked the Mother Directress of Novices to arrange this because she doubted if this had really happened. The next night Sr. Henry appeared again, and St. Faustina had no more doubt, but again in the morning decided she would not go unless the nun appeared in the daytime. The Saint then described how she immediately "ran into" Sr. Henry in the corridor who "reproached" her for not speak-

---

57. Ibid., 29.
58. Sister Henry Losinska died on January 23, 1926, in Cracow, the same day Helen Kowalska (St. Faustina) arrived at the convent to finish her postulancy. Ibid., 404.

ing to the Mother Directress. Happily, Sr. Henry returned on the third day and said to the Polish mystic: "may God repay you."[59]

Even if this occurrence shows St. Faustina doubting in a similar way to St. Thomas in the Gospel, nevertheless it does also show a healthy attitude to supernatural manifestations. The true mystic does not seek the extraordinary, but instead remains steadfast in pursuing union with God; and in this sense their lives illuminate more profoundly the life of God. It is this closeness to the divine that allows them to "touch" the mystical dimension of life. On the other hand, the story also shows clearly a beautiful human dimension. The mystic is still human with human weakness, not some kind of demigod, and in running into the deceased Sr. Henry, the two states of the Church meet in a symbolic and quite corporeal way.

Among other visions concerning Purgatory and the holy souls, the messenger of Divine Mercy experienced being woken by a soul tapping her night table asking for prayers; the gradual purifying ascent of a religious sister, including a physical embrace after her entrance into Heaven[60], and even the sight of suffering souls among demons. In one particular vision, a nun who had died two months previously came to her in flames; her face terribly distorted, so much so that the saint wasn't sure if she was in Purgatory or Hell. Nevertheless, St. Faustina offered prayers for her. The following night the nun appeared again this time in even greater torments. The perplexed mystic revealed their conversation:

> "Haven't my prayers helped you?" She answered that my prayers had not helped her and that nothing would help her. I said to her, "And the prayers which the whole community has offered for you, have they not been any help to you?" She said no, that these prayers had helped some other souls. I replied, "If my prayers are not helping you, Sister, please stop coming to me."[61]

---

59. Ibid., 29.

60. Of this experience, St. Faustina wrote: "I understood how closely the three stages of a soul's life are bound together; that is to say, life on earth, in Purgatory and in heaven [the Communion of Saints]." Ibid., n. 594.

61. Ibid., 39.

The Sister then disappeared and St. Faustina continued to pray for her. Later that same night the Sister returned, this time without the flames, her face beaming with joy. She told the Saint that her prayers had helped greatly; that soon she would leave Purgatory. After praising St. Faustina for her love of neighbor, she encouraged the mystic to continue her great work of charity for the holy souls.

Returning briefly to the plight of this nun, two aspects stand out. Firstly, we could ask why she stated that prayers had not helped and nothing further would. There appears to be two possible answers for this: on the one hand, until that point, God had directed all the prayers offered to her both from St. Faustina and the community to others; possibly because divine justice demanded that she suffer for a certain period (which would explain why she only appeared to the mystic two months after death). Or on the other hand, she was suffering as part of her purification a type of dark night of the soul in which she couldn't see a way out—which is why she stated nothing could help her—even though she was allowed by God to visit the saint. Perhaps it was a mixture of both. The second aspect relates to the problem of why her sufferings were worse the second time she appeared, even though she had benefitted from a very powerful intercessor. The answer to this would appear to be that the duration of suffering was greatly reduced at the price of a more intense purification.

St. Faustina's revelations also reveal other interesting elements that apply particularly well to this discussion. In one enlightening passage, she describes how the Lord had led her to understand that among his chosen ones, he would often call certain souls to a higher form of holiness—seraphic souls—who would enjoy an exceptional union with him. The soul would be aware of this demand for immense love through a special interior grace, but would be free to accept or reject this invitation. However, if the soul resisted this, it would suffer greatly in Purgatory because it would have certain knowledge of God's desires that it had ignored. St. Faustina explained:

> I have learned that there is a place in Purgatory where souls will pay their debt to God for such transgressions; this kind of torment

is the most difficult of all. The soul which is especially marked by God will be distinguished everywhere, whether in heaven or in Purgatory or in hell. In heaven, it will be distinguished from other souls by greater glory and radiance and deeper knowledge of God. In Purgatory, by greater pain, because it knows God more profoundly and desires Him more vehemently. In hell, it will suffer more profoundly than other souls, because it knows more fully whom it has lost. This indelible mark of God's exclusive love, in the [soul], will not be obliterated.[62]

St. Faustina's interaction with the holy souls was not just confined to visitations within the convent; she also recorded several fascinating manifestations at the cemetery in which the dead revealed something of their inner disposition. On one occasion while she was praying, and having reached the cemetery gate, the saint asked the souls interiorly: "You are very happy are you not?" And they answered: "We are happy in the measure that we have fulfilled God's will."[63] On another occasion at dusk, just prior to All Souls Day, St. Faustina returned there and said to them: "If you need something, my dear little souls, I will be glad to help you to the extent that the rule permits me." Again they responded in similar fashion, but with a little spiritual advice of their own: "Do the will of God; we are happy in the measure that we have fulfilled God's will."[64] And on All Souls Day, 1936, after Vespers, the Polish mystic experienced a vision of one of the deceased sisters while visiting the same cemetery in Cracow:

> I had been praying for a while when I saw one of our sisters, who said to me: "We are in the chapel." I understood that I was to go to the chapel and there pray and gain the indulgences. The next day, during Holy Mass, I saw three white doves soaring from the altar toward heaven. I understood that not only the three souls that I saw had gone to heaven, but also many others who had died beyond the confines of our institute. Oh, how good and merciful is the Lord![65]

62. Ibid., 342.
63. Ibid., 147.
64. Ibid., 148.
65. Ibid., 195.

In conclusion, we can see how the mystics stand at the center of the mystery of the *sanctorum communio*. Their lives point in several directions: the vertical and horizontal of the Cross. By that I mean *up* towards union with God, *down* towards the purgatorial suffering of the underworld, and *across*, to the plight of their pilgrim brothers and sisters on earth. The engine of their compassion is love and mercy, virtues that are ignited by Love himself—the Holy Spirit. Even if to us these sublime figures of sanctity may seem out of reach, they and their experiences should inspire us to seek a similar path where we place ourselves wholeheartedly at the service of God and neighbor. That way we can be sure that a continuous and steady stream of souls can make their way to the Father with gratitude in their hearts for the charity they received from us. St. Faustina explains perfectly this objective in a Letter to a fellow Sister, Ludwina Gadzina, which serves as a fitting coda to this chapter:

> And if only we are faithful to this mission, then surely many souls will owe us heaven. But we must remember that our mission is sublime, resembling the mission of Jesus. We must fully possess the spirit and features of Jesus, that is, complete self-emptying out of love for God for the sake of immortal souls, and in particular [we must take care of] those souls whom Jesus has entrusted to us. Sister dear, let us not fear a sacrifice similar to that of Jesus on the cross. Let us not fear at all, because love will give us the strength and courage to offer it. What a joy it is to empty ourselves for our immortal King and Spouse. What a joy it is to be like a wild flower under the feet of Jesus, wilting slowly and delighting His divine Heart with our fragrance.[66]

---

66. Saint Faustina Kowalska, *The Letters of Saint Faustina* (Cracow: Misericordia Publications, 2007), 154.

❧ 8 ❧

Spiritual Purgation:
From Self Love to Pure Love

That our life in the world should be like his, means that his love has had its way with us to the full, so that we can meet the day of judgement with confidence. Love has no room for fear; and indeed, love drives out fear when it is perfect love, since fear only serves for correction. The man who is still afraid has not yet reached the full measure of love. (1 Jn. 4:17–18)

IN A SENSE, this chapter is a continuation of the previous one, in that we will remain within the realm of the mystic while searching for deeper theological roots to the question of Purgatory. If chapter seven provided us with a broad range of supernatural experiences that remove the veil of mystery surrounding the *ecclesia patiens*, in this chapter I hope to center more on the actual spiritual state of the soul; and how purgation must be embraced either in this life or the next in order to counter the influence of self-love, thus dressing oneself in the garment of perfect charity. In order to do this, we will study the teachings of two masters of the spiritual life: St. Catherine of Genoa (1447–1510), and St. Therese of Lisieux, Doctor of the Church (1873–1897).

St. Catherine of Genoa

St. Catherine was born into the aristocratic Genoese Fieschi family that had produced two popes (Innocent IV and Adrian V), and many cardinals. She was the youngest of five children from the marriage of Giacomo Fieschi, the former Viceroy of Naples, and his wife Francesca di Negro. St. Catherine benefitted from the sound Chris-

211

tian education given by her mother, and desired to enter the Augustinian convent of Santa Maria Delle Grazie, and thus follow the path of her elder sister, who was a contemplative nun. Unfortunately, being the tender age of thirteen, her request was refused; her sadness was soon compounded by the death of her Father in 1461. At the age of sixteen, Catherine was given in marriage to Giuliano Adorno for seemingly political and financial motives (at the behest of her eldest brother, Giacomo). The couple were married in the Cathedral of San Lorenzo by her uncle, Bishop Napoleone Fieschi. The first ten years of this marriage brought great hardship; Giuliano was a gambler, bad tempered and an adulterer. His mistress bore him a child. For Catherine, these were years of loneliness, even bitterness; she withdrew from the social life that would have been central to her aristocratic background. However, at the prompting of family members, after five years she began to embrace this worldly culture as a means to escape from the melancholy of soul that she was experiencing. It didn't work. Catherine became ever more depressed; psychologically she was a broken woman. Her early spiritual vitality seemed a distant past. At this point on March 22, 1473, the Lord intervened to spark a profound conversion that changed her life forever.

It was on this day that Catherine had gone to visit her sister, Limbania, at her convent. Feeling indisposed to receive the sacrament of confession, Limbania instead suggested Catherine seek out the saintly chaplain for a blessing. This she did, and immediately experienced the astonishing yet wondrous love of God, while at the same time receiving the grace of an acute sense of contrition for her sins. As a result of this remarkable revelation, Catherine spontaneously exclaimed within her soul: "No more world; no more sins!"[1] She returned home and remained in a recollected state for several days, immersing herself in God's mercy and contemplating, tearfully, the state of her soul.

At this time Catherine also experienced a vision of Jesus, bent beneath the weight of his Cross. While in this short period of self-

---

1. Friedrich Hügel, *The Mystical Element of Religion as Studied in Saint Catherine of Genoa and Her Friends*, vol. 1 (London: J.M. Dent & Co., 1909), 105.

imposed isolation, Catherine was given instruction on prayer and uttered in profound adoration these words: "oh Love! can it be that you have called me with so much love, and revealed to me at one view, what no tongue can describe?"[2] As a consequence of these extraordinary days, Catherine made a general confession and began to live a new life, one of intense purification and renewal. For years to come, Catherine would perform great fasts and penances while feeling constant sorrow for her sins. Her charity was legendary, especially for the sick in the Pammatone Hospital in Genoa where for a time she served as Director.

Perhaps as a result of her miraculous conversion, Catherine's husband Giuliano also experienced the love of God, and began to serve the poor and the sick, something he would do for the rest of his life. Leaving behind his empty life of dissipation, he became a Third Order Franciscan and the couple lived out their marriage in perpetual continence.[3] They moved into a small house among the poor and close to the hospital where Catherine's influence spread to the extent that a group of disciples formed around her, no doubt inspired by her love and compassion for the impoverished and suffering of Genoa. Catherine continued this work of mercy until her death on September 15, 1510.

Noteworthy in this second period of her life is the duality of interior and exterior spiritual growth which never became a source of conflict, but rather exemplified her desire to live the seemingly contradictory charisms of contemplative and worker; in essence St. Catherine of Genoa was Martha and Mary rolled into one. She could remain hours in ecstatic prayer, immersed in a spousal union with the Lord and yet make a seamless transition to serve the sick and dying. Of course what we are really describing is the marvel of the communion of saints at work; the source of her dedication to the least of society flowed from the intimacy she had with God, and

2. St. Catherine of Genoa, *The Life and Doctrine of Saint Catherine of Genoa* (Grand Rapids: Christian Classics Ethereal Library, 2009), 10.

3. Friedrich Hügel suggests that Giuliano informed Catherine soon after his conversion of a daughter, Thobia, born to his mistress. Records of St. Catherine's will show the constant love and care she had for this child and her mother. Von Hugel, *The Mystical Element*, vol. 1, 129.

therefore she desired to transmit that pure love to those around her. In that sense St. Catherine shares a great similarity of charism to Blessed Teresa of Calcutta.

Now that we have looked briefly at the life of this beautiful Saint, we can turn to her teachings that concern us most, namely her doctrine on Purgatory. Within the context of spiritual purgation, St. Catherine centers on the ever-present conflict between *self-love* and *pure love*—a conflict which may not be resolved until a certain period after death. Her theology revolves around the notion that God, as pure love, continually seeks to bind man to himself by imparting supernatural grace, which in turn makes the possibility of defeating self-love a reality. In this way, grace allied to spiritual purification leads to ultimate fulfilment and the eternal union of man and God in the beatific vision. Earthly life therefore is to be understood as a perennial conflict zone between the higher calling of holiness and the lower temptation of worldliness.

St. Catherine's teachings are found in three sources: the *Vita*, *Trattato* (better known as *Purgation and Purgatory*, and the *Dialogo tra l'anima e il corpo* (Dialogues on the Soul and the Body). It should be noted at this juncture that these writings were not written by the Saint herself; rather, they contain her words and spiritual reflections that were recorded by her spiritual director, Don Cattaneo Marabotto, and her spiritual son, Ettore Vernazza.[4]

Before we venture into the specific text concerning Purgatory, let us begin by briefly exploring some important passages from the *Vita* that will serve to enhance our understanding of St. Catherine's theology.

The basis for any sustained encounter with God consists in dying to oneself and embracing the divine will; it is the central key element that allows the Christian to remain resolutely by God's side even in this life. As we know from Sacred Scripture, the rejection of God's will led to banishment from the Garden of Eden, and it was

---

4. The *Libro de la Vita mirabile et dottrina santa, de la beata Caterinetta da Genoa. Nel quale si contiene una utile et catholica dimostratione et dechiaratione del purgatorio* was published in Genoa in 1551 and approved by Pope Innocent XI in 1683.

only through the Son's obedience to the Father's will that friendship was restored. If the divine will could be lived, then pure love would issue forth as a result. St. Catherine was given instruction in this by the Lord, in precious words that apply to all seeking pure love:

> My daughter, observe these three rules, namely: never say I will or I will not. Never say mine, but always ours. Never excuse yourself, but always accuse yourself.... When you repeat the Our Father take always for your maxim, *Fiat voluntas tua*, that is, may his will be done in everything that may happen to you, whether good or ill; from the Hail Mary take the word *Jesus*, and may it be implanted in your heart, and it will be a sweet guide and shield to you in all the necessities of life. And from the rest of Scripture take always for your support this word, *Love*, with which you will go on your way . . . this love will consume all the inclinations of the soul, and the desires of the body, for the things of this life.[5]

St. Catherine was convinced that the quest for divine perfection lay in recognizing that good can only come directly from God's blessing; that he alone can instigate a sanctifying ascent that would erase the imperfections afflicting all humanity. At the same time, she was equally convinced that evil could be blamed on nobody but oneself; not even Satan:

> if, on the other hand, I do anything evil, it is I alone who do it, nor can I charge the blame of it upon the devil or upon any other creature; it is purely the work of my own will, inclination, pride, selfishness, sensuality, and other evil dispositions, without the help of God I should never do any good thing.[6]

In the *Vita*, we discover an explanation of how the Genoese saint understood God's work of transformation in the soul: In the first instance, God grants the instinct to practice virtue, and then he implants a desire for perfection which is followed by "true annihilation" through infused grace, which leads to spiritual transformation. The soul is then directed by the Lord himself without the need for any other recourse. The consequence of this divine intervention

---

5. St. Catherine of Genoa, *The Life and Doctrine of Saint Catherine of Genoa* (Grand Rapids: Christian Classics Ethereal Library, 2009), 18.

6. Ibid., 22.

is that the soul feels total peace, immovable and imperturbable. It is liberated from worldliness and rests in the arms of the Father, feeding off divine love in a process that continues daily until God calls it to its heavenly reward.

On one occasion, seeking to understand how this state of transformed love could still leave room for others, St. Catherine asked the Lord to explain, and he replied: "He who loves me loves also all whom I love. It suffices that for the welfare of the neighbor thou shouldst do all that is necessary for his soul and body. Such a love as this is sure to be without passion; because it is not in himself but in God that the neighbor should be loved."[7]

In this answer of the Lord, we have an explanation of pure love. Charity is accomplished with an intention that seeks no gain for oneself, but instead for the good of others: the conditions for a better life, and ultimately salvation. The lover of purity sees Christ in everyone; he turns no one away but embraces all, desiring to transmit the warmth that radiates from the Heart of Jesus. Pure love has no other aim than to continue dousing the flames of evil, of unfurling the banner of God's victory and instilling Christian hope in those who live under the yoke of slavery. It is the power of God himself in which every act of love affirms that humanity can be raised to new life, that the life of sin and corruption will not have the last word.

A major part of St. Catherine's theological deliberations contrast the two types of love: pure love and self-love. As we have already looked at the former, it is beneficial in the light of her theology of Purgatory to grasp the meaning of the latter.

If pure love has a divine origin, then it stands to reason that self-love must have a different origin. In the teaching of St. Catherine, self-love could just as easily be called self-hate; such is its destructive quality. It has no master except Satan, who tempts the soul to turn in on itself, enticing it with a false freedom that entertains every sort of immorality. The Mystic of Genoa described is thus:

7. Ibid., 49.

The true self-love has these properties: first, it cares not whether it injures either its own soul and body or those of its neighbor, nor does it value the goods and reputation of either itself or others; for the sake of accomplishing its ends it is as rigorous with itself as with others, and will submit to no possible contradiction. When it has resolved upon any action, it remains unmoved by either promises or threats, how great so ever they may be, but perseveres in its course, caring neither for slavery nor poverty, for infamy nor weakness, for Purgatory, death, nor hell, for it is so blind that it cannot see these things or recognize their importance. . . . Self-love is so subtle a robber that it commits its thefts, even upon God himself, without fear or shame, employing his goods as if they were its own, and assigning as a reason that it cannot live without them.[8]

St. Catherine also explains how a spiritual form of self-love is even more dangerous than a corporeal one, a diagnosis that reinforces the timely interventions of Pope Benedict XVI and Pope Francis, who, as we have already seen, have pointed out in a variety of ways this most serious malady that gravely wounds the beauty of the Mystical Body:

But the spiritual self-love is much more perilous than the corporal, for it is bitter poison whose antidote is hard to find. It is yet more artfully veiled, and passes sometimes as sanctity or necessity, or again, as charity or pity, hiding itself beneath almost infinite disguises, the sight of which causes my heart almost to faint within me. Behold also what blindness self-love occasions between God and man, and know that no evil can be so great as this; yet man does not perceive it, but seems to hold it as salutary, and to rejoice over what ought rather to make him weep.[9]

For the soul drowning in this sea of evil, there is only one escape route: that of sincere repentance and purgation; and in the doctrine of St. Catherine we discover a quite novel approach to this subject. The Mystic of Genoa does not see Purgatory in a restrictive sense that is related only to a specific time and place in the next life. Instead, she understands it as a purifying process that begins in this

8. Ibid., 52.
9. Ibid., 53.

world, an interior fire setting in motion the gravitational pull towards God. If the process is not complete on earth, then it may continue in the world to come.

The originality of this theology is rather impressive, given that during the medieval period, and even to a certain extent up to the present day, Purgatory was seen as an exterior punishment confined to a place of unknown location. It is most probable that this teaching was born out of St. Catherine's own life; that through contemplation of her years of early marriage, conversion and purification, she came to realize that the Lord invites the soul to undergo spiritual purgation even before it arrives at the judgment seat. In this way, we see how St. Catherine of Genoa's life mirrors perfectly the doctrine she taught. With this in mind, let us delve into the second part of the *Libro* to ascertain what *Purgation and Purgatory* tell us about this vital element of Christian life.

The text introduces us immediately to the concept of purgatorial suffering within the context of St. Catherine's life: "While still in the flesh this blessed soul experienced the fiery love of God, a love that consumed her, cleansing and purifying all, so that once quitted this life she could appear forthwith in God's presence."[10] The saint begins by unveiling the disposition of the souls detained in Purgatory; noteworthy in that they do not analyze the reasons for their detention, or express regret for actions which led to them being there. They instead live only for God's will:

> These souls cannot think, "I am here, and justly so because of my sins," or "I wish I had never committed such sins for now I would be in paradise," or "that person there is leaving before me...." They cannot remember the good and evil in their past nor that of others. Such is their joy in God's will, in his pleasure, that they have no concern for themselves but dwell only on their joy in God's ordinance, in having Him do what he will.[11]

St. Catherine also reveals another dispositional aspect which binds together both the love and will of God. She states that souls only see

10. Catherine of Genoa, *Purgation and Purgatory: The Spiritual Dialogue* (Mahwah: Paulist Press, 1979), 71.
11. Ibid., 71.

the goodness and mercy of God; they are not aware of the sins of others because perfect charity does not allow it, and to deviate from that would be to deviate from God's will. A more startling result of this union of wills is that the souls no longer associate their sufferings with the sins they committed on earth; rather they solely relate to the hindering of what St. Catherine calls the "instinct for beatitude."[12] This instinct, given by God, but weakened by the stain of original sin, can either grow or diminish through life, depending on the response to divine love's beckoning. When the soul keeps alive the first instinct of creation, "the instinct for beatitude asserts itself with such impetus and fiery charity that any impediment becomes unbearable. The more the soul is aware of that impediment, the greater it's suffering."[13] St. Catherine teaches that the only time the holy souls know of the reason for their Purgatory is at the moment of death, when the actions of self-love are weighed against the demands of pure love. Thereupon however, that knowledge evaporates in the desire to live perfect charity in the divine will.

It is often thought (reading Catholic devotional material) that the sufferings of these poor souls are so intense that in reality Purgatory is little less than hell; but truth be told, that is far from the case. If we remove the speculation concerning bodily punishments (insofar as that is possible),[14] there is a great chasm between the two states, and this chasm is first and foremost at an interior level. Hate consumes the damned. They are devoid of any goodness whatsoever; they possess an evil will which loathes everything. Their greatest torment is to know what they have voluntarily lost forever; and yet their malice does not allow even the tiniest hint of remorse and repentance.[15]

---

12. Ibid., 73.

13. Ibid.

14. It seems entirely possible that God allows the "sensation" of possessing a physical form even though the body lies in the tomb. We may recall St. Faustina running into the deceased Sr. Henry, or the soul who woke her by tapping on the table.

15. St. Catherine of Genoa suggests that God's mercy even reaches the damned: "He who dies in mortal sin deserves an infinity of suffering in a time without end; God's mercy, however, brings it about that only the time has no limit but not the intensity of the suffering." *Purgatory and Purgation*, 75.

Purgatory is fundamentally different. By leaving this world in a state of grace, the holy souls have desired to love God and seek his friendship. As St. Catherine explains: "they grieved for their sins and were determined to sin no more. It is this sorrow over their sins that makes God forgive them, so that the only thing remaining in them is the rust and deformity of sin which fire then purifies."[16]

As a consequence of reaching salvation, even in the intermediate state of the *Ecclesia Patiens*, these souls experience a joy that is not comparable to anything on earth. Only the happiness of heaven supersedes it. This joy increases daily as the soul's instinct for beatitude grows, allowing divine love to flood it in ever greater measure. Of course, just as in earthly life joy and suffering are not mutually exclusive, so it is in Purgatory. The saved suffer greatly because they have a hunger for God which cannot yet be satisfied, but at the same time, their joy is unbounded because they see their lives becoming ever more conformed to the life of the Lord. St. Catherine understands the greatest suffering in Purgatory within this context:

> I also see, however, that the divine essence is so pure and light-filled—much more than we can imagine—that the soul that has but the slightest imperfection would rather throw itself into a thousand hells than appear thus before the divine presence. Tongue cannot express nor heart understand the full meaning of Purgatory, which the soul willingly accepts as a mercy, the realization that the suffering is of no importance compared to the removal of the impediment of sin. The greatest suffering of the souls in Purgatory, it seems to me, is their awareness that something in them displeases God, that they have deliberately gone against His great goodness.[17]

The souls are so immersed in their longing for God that they do not concern themselves with the level of suffering, rather they dwell on their inability to reciprocate that pure love offered to them. They know and accept fully the divine sentence, and their torture lies in not being able to ascend any quicker than the Lord decrees. St. Catherine stresses that God does not forgive "one spark" of the debt

16. Ibid., 75–76.
17. Ibid., 78.

due, and therefore the souls can do nothing but proceed along the path of purification in the manner set by the divine Judge. Their only hope is in the full manifestation of the communion of saints whereby indulgences and prayers are offered for their speedy entrance into the beatific vision.

The mystical insight of spiritual purgation led St. Catherine to place great emphasis on avoiding Purgatory if at all possible. This attitude explains why she cultivated a theology of love which exposed the evils of self-love and urged the pursuit of pure love. She hoped to influence the lives of those around her so that a clear path could emerge towards living the divine will. In *Purgation and Purgatory*, we have a vivid illustration of this point:

> Having seen all this in the divine light, I would want to frighten people, to cry out to each and every one, "O wretches who let yourselves be blinded by this world and make no provision for this one most important need, even when you are aware of it! You seek refuge under the mercy of God, which you claim to be great—but do you not see that the great goodness of God will judge you for having gone against His will?"... Do not rely on yourself and say, "I will confess myself, receive a plenary indulgence, and with that be cleansed from my sins." The confession and contrition that is required for the plenary indulgence is such, and so demanding, that were you to realize it you would tremble in terror.[18]

If we try to discern what the teachings of St. Catherine of Genoa mean for us today, they remind us in the first place, that the great commandments to love God and neighbor require a pureness of intention that leaves no room for selfish motives; that there is no alternative to embracing perfect charity. One way or another, the soul must be refashioned through an interior fire in order to walk through the narrow gate (cf. Matt. 7:13), and in the humble opinion of the Mystic of Genoa it is less painful to welcome it in this life than the next. The two keys to unlock the door to immaculate purity consist of surrendering one's life to the divine will, and a constant desire for pure love—two marvels of God that if nurtured, will be made manifest in a life of supreme sanctity.

18. Ibid., 84.

St. Catherine teaches us that rather than worrying ourselves about Purgatory's sufferings, we should instead see it as nothing more than a continuation of purification that is the lot of all. Purgatory can only be understood as an experience of love and mercy, not a medieval chamber of horrors. However, as this humble witness to God's love reveals, no suffering outside of hell compares with the pain of the holy souls as they thirst for the presence of God that they cannot have. And yet, St. Catherine tells us that if a soul were admitted into Heaven with one hour of purgation still to undergo, it would suffer more than ten purgatories, for it could not endure circumventing divine justice even if only briefly.

Perhaps a final point for our consideration should be the necessity of regularly examining our conscience, and more specifically, our attitude to our brothers and sisters, not only within the Church but without. In the immediate aftermath of death, we carry the baggage of life with us; if we have been selfish, that miserly nature goes with us. Have we been arrogant? We should not expect to suddenly embrace the humility of saints. Only the intense flames of purification can dissolve these horrible vices, and as we know from the revelations of the mystics, this can take many years to accomplish. Like all the saints, St. Catherine of Genoa is a prophet of divine love, a witness to the awe-inspiring love and mercy of God. Her life speaks of the divinization of humanity to which we are all called, and Purgatory is but one part of that process.

St. Therese of Lisieux, Doctor of the Church

In the figure of St. Therese of Lisieux (1873–1897), we return swiftly to the outstanding mystical tradition of the Carmelite Order. Born in Alençon, France, on January 2, 1873, to her holy parents Blessed Louis and Zelie Martin, this beautiful soul, Doctor of the Church and Patroness of Missions, has become one of the most beloved saints of all time, a veritable icon of the *Sanctorum Communio*. The main reason for her popularity stems from the publication of her autobiography, *The Story of a Soul*[19] which has been translated into

---

19. This principle work is made up of three autobiographical manuscripts, A, B and C. Manuscript A describes the stages of her religious experience from child-

numerous languages in the years since her death. Pope Benedict XVI, while giving a discourse on her life, was keen to encourage the reading of this spiritual classic:

> I would like to invite you to rediscover this small-great treasure, this luminous comment on the Gospel lived to the full! *The Story of a Soul*, in fact, is a marvellous story of Love, told with such authenticity, simplicity and freshness that the reader cannot but be fascinated by it! But what was this Love that filled Thérèse's whole life, from childhood to death? Dear friends, this Love has a Face, it has a Name, it is Jesus! The Saint speaks continuously of Jesus.[20]

St. Therese shares several things in common with St. Catherine of Genoa: her desire to enter consecrated life at an early age, a profound conversion experience, and finally, the primacy of divine charity in her writings. This last characteristic, so prophetic and revelatory, contemplates not the fear of punishment, but rather the love of God, manifested in the Holy Face of Jesus, and in this vision, Therese and Catherine stand out as superlative witnesses to an authentic reading of the Gospel.

Before we venture into St. Therese's specific and quite unique doctrine on Purgatory, we would do well to look deeper into her sanctity, to grasp the depth of love that consumed her soul, for in that way we will perceive a mystic in love with God and humanity. It is a love that far from being sentimental, drank the dregs of suffering in imitation of the Lord Jesus.

Therese's life was marked on several momentous occasions by divine interventions which instilled in her an ever increasing conformity to the crucified Christ. On Pentecost Sunday, 1883, she was miraculously cured of a serious nervous disorder through the intercession of the Blessed Virgin. She experienced a "complete conversion" on Christmas Day, 1886, which led to her being able to "run as

---

hood, including her First Communion and Confirmation, until her entrance into the Carmel and her first profession. Manuscript B, written during her retreat in 1896, reveals St. Therese's vocation in the Church, and offers some of the most beautiful passages of all, while Manuscript C, composed in June and the first days of July 1897, completes the recollections found in Manuscript A on life in the Carmel.

20. Pope Benedict XVI, "General Audience," April 6, 2011, www.vatican.va.

a giant."[21] Finally, on the night of Holy Thursday, 1896, she began to live her own passion which would lead eventually to her death from tuberculosis on September 30, 1897.

Throughout these years, Therese gained a deeper intuition of her divine calling. At the age of fourteen, she took to heart the fate of Henri Pranzini, a notorious murderer who was destined for the guillotine. Her burning desire was to bring about his conversion and thus spare him hell for all eternity. With St. Therese's humble intercession and trust in the mercy of God, he repented at the last moment before execution, kissing a Crucifix three times.

On June 6, 1895, the Feast of the Holy Trinity, Therese made an *offering to merciful love* which was soon followed by a mystical wound which she received as she prayed the Stations of the Cross. The text of this offering opens a window into the soul of this remarkable saint; it reveals not only an immense love already present, but a desire to increase that love in the measure that God wills. Therese begins by expressing a desire to live most passionately the two greatest commandments, the heart and soul of the communion of saints:

> O My God! Most Blessed Trinity, I desire to Love You and make you Loved, to work for the glory of Holy Church by saving souls on earth and liberating those suffering in Purgatory. I desire to accomplish Your will perfectly and to reach the degree of glory You have prepared for me in Your Kingdom. I desire, in a word, to be a saint, but I feel my helplessness and I beg You, O my God! to be Yourself my Sanctity! . . . I offer You, too, all the merits of the saints (in heaven and on earth), their acts of Love, and those of the holy angels. Finally, I offer You, O Blessed Trinity! The Love and merits of the Blessed Virgin, my dear Mother. It is to her I abandon my offering, begging her to present it to You.[22]

One of the most outstanding passages found in St. Therese's writings comes towards the end of this offering when she states:

21. St. Therese of Lisieux, *Manuscript A*, 44v, 45r, www.archives-carmel-lisieux. fr.

22. St. Therese of Lisieux, *Story of a Soul* (Washington, DC: ICS Publications, 1976), 276.

After earth's Exile, I hope to go and enjoy You in the Fatherland, but I do not want to lay up merits for heaven. I want to work for Your Love Alone with the one purpose of pleasing You, consoling Your Sacred Heart, and saving souls who will love You eternally. In the evening of this life, I shall appear before You with empty hands, for I do not ask You, Lord, to count my works.[23]

In this text we discover perhaps the deepest level of holiness; one that has not the slightest interest in gaining merits or praise for working in the Lord's vineyard, because in a sense, that is still a worldly desire. St. Therese's sanctity consisted entirely in pleasing the Lord, of replacing the pain he suffers over humanity's coldness with her own love. Of course this is not possible without the total self-surrender to God's will, and the Mystic of Lisieux found her happiness in embracing it wholeheartedly.

There is no doubt that a certain suspicion of "sugary piety" has at times been levelled against St. Therese, but that is to misunderstand the nature of her relationship with the Lord. Her love on earth was childlike and pure, allied to a humble simplicity where she trusted that God would draw her into his divine life. However, that did not mean that Therese was living a form of quietism; on the contrary, God's love directed her to work for the salvation of others, and to bring relief to the suffering souls in Purgatory. She could not contemplate a Christianity where the love of God is not translated into corporal and spiritual works of mercy. One of her poems, *Living on Love* captures this attitude perfectly: "Living on Love is wiping your Face, It's obtaining the pardon of sinners. O God of Love! may they return to your grace, And may they forever bless your Name."[24] If for most of us meeting Jesus at the individual judgment with empty hands would be a frightening consideration, for Therese it took on a new meaning; it was not the emptiness found in the parable of the talents (cf. Matt. 25:14–30) but an emptiness instigated by divine charity. The saint would have nothing to show because she had

---

23. Ibid.
24. St. Therese of Lisieux, *Living on Love*, Poem 17, www.archives-carmel-lisi eux.fr.

given it all away: graces, indulgences and merits of sacrifices. That is the proof of *agape* at work in her soul.

As we have seen from the *offering to merciful* love, the doctrine of the communion of saints was at the heart of St. Therese's spirituality. She desired to increase the Kingdom of God on earth through offering her sufferings for the salvation of souls, while aiding the purgatorial souls in their journey to God. She also had devotion to many saints including some from the Old Testament such as David and Moses, and she invoked the intercession of the Archangels Gabriel and Michael.

Her writings and letters also reveal a rich knowledge of hagiography, which enabled her to point out certain virtues and traits found in the lives of the saints. Suffice it to say, St. Therese also had an exceptional devotion to the Blessed Virgin, which is evident in a poem from May, 1897 entitled *Why I Love You, O Mary!*:

> Oh! I would like to sing, Mary, why I love you,
> Why your sweet name thrills my heart,
> And why the thought of your supreme greatness
> Could not bring fear to my soul.
> If I gazed on you in your sublime glory,
> Surpassing the splendor of all the blessed,
> I could not believe that I am your child.
> O Mary, before you I would lower my eyes!
>
> Soon I'll hear that sweet harmony.
> Soon I'll go to beautiful Heaven to see you.
> You who came to smile at me in the morning of my life,
> Come smile at me again . . . Mother. . . . It's evening now!
> I no longer fear the splendor of your supreme glory.
> With you I've suffered, and now I want
> To sing on your lap, Mary, why I love you,
> And to go on saying that I am your child![25]

St. Therese's concept of the *sanctorum communio* was not just restricted to canonized saints or angels; she also had a prophetic

---

25. St. Therese of Lisieux, *Why I Love You, O Mary,* Poem 54, v. 1, 25, www.archives-carmel-lisieux.fr.

sense of the heavenly influence of her own deceased parents. In a letter to one of her sisters, she stated:

> I am thinking more than ever about you ever since our dear Father has gone up to heaven; I believe you are experiencing the same feelings as ourselves. Papa's death does not give me the impression of a death but of a real life. I am finding him once more after an absence of six years, I feel him around me, looking at me and protecting me. . . . Dear little Sister, are we not more united now that we gaze on the heavens to find there a Father and a Mother who offered us to Jesus?[26]

On several occasions St. Therese also expressed a spiritual closeness to her mother whose power of intercession from heaven was invoked by an expectant daughter. Her first Holy Communion was received with the perception that her mother was also present, filling the young Therese with great happiness.

St. Therese was not shy in revealing her great joy at the communion of love present within the Mystical Body of Christ. In one letter[27] sent to another sister, Celine, who was about to make her profession, she described in a most imaginative way how the entire heavenly court would partake in the joy of Celine's vows to the Lord: St. Peter opening the portals of heaven, the angels and saints forming the court ready for the Lord and his bride, the Blessed Virgin descending to Purgatory to release many souls, the apostles gathering all those saved through Celine's faith, and her entire family on earth and in heaven reunited to share in this joyous occasion. The text is like an ornate tapestry, vivid in its elucidation of how the Mystical Body is bound together by divine love.

One of the most fascinating aspects of this Doctor of the Church was her cherished desire to continue the Lord's work of love and mercy in the glory of heaven. Therese's writings reveal a strong conviction of an imminent entry into eternal bliss, one that can only

---

26. St. Therese of Lisieux, "Letter to Sister Therese Dosithee," August 20, 1894, www.archives-carmel-lisieux.fr.

27. St. Therese of Lisieux, "Letter to Sister Genevieve," February 23, 1896, www. archives-carmel-lisieux.fr.

come from an exceptional holiness. They remind us of St. John the Apostle's words: "Love has no room for fear; and indeed, love drives out fear when it is perfect love, since fear only serves for correction. The man who is still afraid has not yet reached the full measure of love"(1 Jn. 4:18). St. Therese makes reference to this future vocation in one of the most famous passages from her works:

> I feel that I'm about to enter into my rest. But I feel especially that my mission is about to begin, my mission of making God loved as I love Him, of giving my little way to souls. If God answers my desires, my heaven will be spent on earth until the end of the world. Yes, I want to spend my heaven in doing good on earth. . . . I can't make heaven a feast of rejoicing; I can't rest as long as there are souls to be saved. But when the angel will have said: "Time is no more!" then I will take my rest; I'll be able to rejoice, because the number of the elect will be complete and because all will have entered into joy and repose. My heart beats with joy at this thought.[28]

This vision of continual and expanded work within the communion of saints was at the forefront of the mystic's charism in the years leading up to her death. In a letter to her missionary brother, Father Roulland, St. Therese explained in detail her innermost thoughts concerning the advent of a new and more influential role:

> When you receive this letter, no doubt I shall have left this earth. The Lord in His infinite mercy will have opened His kingdom to me, and I shall be able to draw from His treasures in order to grant them liberally to the souls who are dear to me. Believe, Brother, that your little sister will hold to her promises, and, her soul, freed from the weight of the mortal envelope, will joyfully fly toward the distant regions that you are evangelizing. Ah! Brother, I feel it, I shall be more useful to you in heaven than on earth, and it is with joy that I come to announce to you my coming entrance into that blessed city. . . . I really count on not remaining inactive in heaven. My desire is to work still for the Church and for souls. I am asking God for this and I am certain He will answer me. Are not the

---

28. St. Therese of Lisieux, *The Last conversations from the Yellow Notebook*, July 17, 1897, www.archives-carmel-lisieux.fr.

angels continually occupied with us without their ever ceasing to see the divine Face and to lose themselves in the Ocean of Love without shores? Why would Jesus not allow me to imitate them?[29]

From our reflections thus far, we have discovered how St. Therese embraced fully the doctrine of the communion of saints. She bore the hallmarks of that pure love of which St. Catherine of Genoa spoke, and thus purified in the crucible of suffering, she scaled the heights of holiness. The result of this sanctity was an outpouring of charity and mercy, and an illumination of the highest ideals of the Gospel at a time when the world was about to enter a century of great evil, and the Church suffer the scourge of modernism; as St. John Paul II wrote on the occasion declaring St. Therese of the Child Jesus and the Holy Face a Doctor of the Church:

> Through spiritual childhood one experiences that everything comes from God, returns to him and abides in him, for the salvation of all, in a mystery of merciful love. Such is the doctrinal message taught and lived by this Saint.... She sang of all the expressions of Christ's divine charity, as they are presented in the Gospel.[30]

As we have already seen, St. Therese had a great concern for the souls in Purgatory; her *offering to merciful love* provides evidence of that. But what interests us at this point, is her theology of Purgatory, a theology that shares similarities with St. Catherine of Genoa as well as differences. In the first place, St. Therese shares a belief in a purifying fire that begins in this life, a process that transforms a weak *philo*[31] into *agape*. She espouses the notion that the life of faith

29. St. Therese of Lisieux, "Letter to Father Roulland," July 14, 1897, www.archives-carmel-lisieux.fr.

30. Pope John Paul II, Apostolic Letter, "Divini Amoris Scientia," October 19, 1997, www.vatican.va.

31. In the Greek translation of St. John's Gospel, when the Lord questions Peter by the shore after the Resurrection and asks: "do you love me" three times, the first two times Jesus says: *Simon iona agapas me?* (*agapas* the divine sacrificial love). Peter cannot respond with the use of *agapas*; he can only muster *philo*, that is: "you know Lord I am *fond* of you." The third time Jesus asks the question, he no longer uses agapas and replaces it with *phileis*, as if sadly accepting Peter's lesser form of love.

is a precious opportunity to embrace the way of purification; that we should not "expect" to have to enter Purgatory because we think we cannot avoid it. On the contrary, for St. Therese, Purgatory should be superfluous, *if* the human heart allows itself to be captured by the heart of God. In Manuscript A, she describes this conviction with typical ardor:

> I need have no fear of Purgatory. I know that of myself I would not merit even to enter that place of expiation since only holy souls can have entrance there, but I also know that the Fire of Love is more sanctifying than is the fire of Purgatory. I know that Jesus cannot desire useless sufferings for us, and that He would not inspire the longings I feel unless He wanted to grant them. Oh! how sweet is the way of Love![32]

The Saint of Lisieux also used her poetry to reinforce the point that cathartic spiritual transformation is not a form of punishment per se, but a reinvigoration of the soul whereby divine love becomes a taste of eternity in time. In the beautiful poem *Living on Love*, we sense the joy of one who trusts Jesus's capacity to prepare his beloved for heaven:

> Living on Love is banishing every fear,
> every memory of past faults.
> I see no imprint of my sins.
> In a moment love has burned everything
> Divine Flame, O very sweet Blaze!
> I make my home in your hearth.
> In your fire I gladly sing:
> "I live on Love"![33]

A poem written to the Sacred Heart of Jesus in the same year as the *Offering* (1895), also expresses similar sentiments:

> To be able to gaze on your glory,
> I know we have to pass through fire.
> So I, for my Purgatory,

---

32. St. Therese of Lisieux, *Manuscript A*, 84v, www.archives-carmel-lisieux.fr.
33. St. Therese of Lisieux, *Living on Love*, Poem 17, www.archives-carmel-lisieux.fr.

Choose your burning love, O heart of my God!
On leaving this life, my exiled soul
Would like to make an act of pure love,
And then, flying away to Heaven, its Homeland,
Enter straightaway into your Heart.[34]

St. Therese was not afraid to share her wisdom concerning the subject of Purgatory with her fellow sisters and novices, even if it appeared somewhat revolutionary and out of step with the prevailing opinion at the time. In a Letter from Sister Marie of the Eucharist (the cousin of St. Therese) to her Father, Isidore Guerin in July, 1897 we read:

> Loving God the way she does, she'll receive such a warm welcome Up Above; she'll certainly go straight to heaven. When we talked to her about us going to Purgatory, she said: "Oh! how you grieve me! You do a great injury to God in believing you will go to Purgatory. When we love, we can't go there."[35]

Even years before, while a novice, Therese had displayed an exceptional understanding of what God requires from the soul that seeks to avoid the necessity of future purgation. She links two virtues that disarm the justice of God: *trust* and *conformity to the divine will.* Evidence of this comes from a conversation between the Saint and a fellow novice, Sr. Marie Philomena. The Sister had suggested the common assumption that Purgatory was virtually unavoidable, to which Therese responded:

> You do not have enough trust. You have too much fear before the good God. I can assure you that He is grieved over this. You should not fear Purgatory because of the suffering there, but should instead ask that you not deserve to go there in order to please God, Who so reluctantly imposes this punishment. As soon as you try to please Him in everything and have an unshakable trust He purifies you every moment in His love and He lets no sin remain.

34. St. Therese of Lisieux, *To the Sacred Heart of Jesus*, Poem 23, www.archives-carmel-lisieux.fr.

35. Sr. Marie of the Eucharist, "Letter to Isidore Guerin," July 8, 1897, www.arc hives-carmel-lisieux.fr.

And then you can be sure that you will not have to go to Purgatory.[36]

These observations should cause us to meditate a little on what they tell us concerning God's grace and mercy. Firstly, St. Therese tells us that God "grieves" over the soul who does not trust in his goodness, who does not see divine help as capable of uprooting sin. Essentially, the soul with this disposition brings God down to a poor human level that doesn't recognize either the power to make the impossible possible, or even the real desire to do it. And from this error we discover a second which is equally wrong. St. Therese says that God "reluctantly" imposes punishment (which of course stems from his justice), but for the soul who has only met God in the form of a caricature, punishment is gratuitous, serving only as an outlet for his terrible anger. Therefore Purgatory becomes unavoidable because on the one hand trust in the Lord's power to heal is missing, and on the other, we believe he wants us there anyway.

St. Therese's message is the antithesis of this; it is radical and filled with hope. For her, God has no desire for Purgatory because he wants to recreate us in *this* life through Baptism, a sacramental life, and the indwelling influence of the Holy Spirit. If we add the sincere acceptance of suffering for love of God and neighbor, and all in conformity with his will, then Purgatory will be accomplished on earth.[37] Of course, we must bear in mind that, sadly for many, the reality is that neither trust in God nor conformity to His will form the central pillars of day to day living; we would much rather go it alone, trusting our own instincts and deciding ourselves what is best for us. The consequences of that temptation mean neglecting the true path to happiness mapped out for us by the Lord.

Continuing our deliberations as to the uniqueness of St. Therese's theology of Purgatory—that is, the twofold issue of whether God wants us there at all, and whether we should trust enough to be able to avoid it—we have an interesting, if little known, mystical experience of the "Little Flower of Lisieux" that amply demonstrates the correctness of her doctrine.

---

36. *Annales de Sainte Therese, Lisieux*, nr. 610, Feb. 1982. Cited from the German publication, *Der Fels*, December 2001 Ed., 344.

The episode relates to her relationship with another Carmelite, Sister Febronie of the Holy Infancy, who was the subprioress when the fifteen-year-old Therese entered the Carmel of Lisieux. Sister Febronie would at times discuss theological matters with the saint, and on one occasion took issue with the notion that God's justice could be lessened through his divine mercy. St. Therese responded thus: "You want God's justice? You will get God's justice. The soul receives exactly what it expects from God. . . . This justice which has terrified so many souls, is the reason for my joy and my confidence."[38] Sr. Febronie died in a flu epidemic on January 4, 1892, and several months later St. Therese informed Mother Marie de Ganzague of a dream in which she had encountered Sr. Febronie:

> O my Mother, my Sister Febronie came this night to ask that we pray for her. She is in Purgatory without doubt, for she did not count enough on the mercy of the good God. By her suppliant and profound look, she seemed to tell me: "You had reason, all justice is accomplished in me, but it was my fault; if I had believed you, I would have gone straight to heaven."[39]

37. Confirmation of St. Therese's trust in God's love and mercy for sinners came in the beatification testimony of Sr. Marie of the Trinity and of the Holy Face, the favorite novice of the Saint. Sr. Marie's testimony included part of a text she wrote in 1899 entitled *Conseils et souvenirs*: "I asked her one day whether Our Lord was not displeased at the sight of my many failings. This was her answer: 'Be comforted, for He Whom you have chosen as your spouse has every imaginable perfection; but—dare I say it?—He has one infirmity too—He is blind! And there is a science about which he knows nothing—adding up! . . . Were it necessary that He should be clear-sighted, and familiar with the science of figures, do you not think that, confronted with our many sins, He would send us back into nothingness? But His Love for us makes Him positively blind. If the greatest sinner on earth should repent at the moment of his death, and draw his last breath in an act of love, neither the many graces he had abused, nor the numerous crimes he had committed, would stand in his way. Our Lord would see nothing, count nothing, but the sinner's last prayer, and without delay He would receive him into the arms of His Mercy.'" www.archives-carmel-lisieux.fr.

38. Guy Gaucher, *The Passion of Therese of Lisieux* (New York: Crossroads Publishing Company, 1990), 141.

39. Quoted by Sister Marie of the Angels, from the *Annales de Sainte Therese de Lisieux*, February, 1983.

The lesson to be learned from this account is that no matter in what spiritual state we find ourselves, regardless of the merits accrued or sins committed, ultimately we have no choice but to invoke the divine mercy and repeat often "Jesus I trust in you!" In this way we can begin to change our perception of Purgatory and work towards ensuring that our purgation occurs in this life, not the next, where merits can no longer be gained and sufferings are more intense.

St. Therese promotes an understanding of God as a loving and merciful Father, and in a certain way, anticipates the divine mercy message of St. Faustina in which trusting God is a central component of the devotion. Her theology of Purgatory along with her "little way" of spiritual ascent, encourages a humble and simple acceptance of God's dominion over souls. It impels us to work at our sanctification, not through our own efforts but through the grace of God, so that the flame of His love burns away our sins. Not only that; it breeds confidence that divine mercy is greater than divine justice, fostering the very attitude that St. Therese advocated so much. To present oneself before the throne of God with empty hands and no desire for reward is to present Jesus with a manifestation of pure love that surely delights his Sacred Heart. In the profound wisdom of St. Therese of Lisieux we encounter the sublime truth that our reliance should be on the merciful love of God, not on the fear of Purgatory. The Christian life on earth should have the sole focus of loving God and working to increase the communion of saints. If we accomplish that we will have the joy to say in union with this illustrious model of pure love: "I'll not regret having done nothing to avoid it [Purgatory]. I shall not feel sorry for having worked solely for the salvation of souls."[40]

---

40. St. Therese of Lisieux, *Last Conversations, Yellow Notebook*, June 4, 1897, www.archives-carmel-lisieux.fr.

☙ 9 ❧

Eliminating the Debt:
The Treasury of Divine Mercy

Beloved, thou art playing a faithful man's part in shewing such kind-
ness to the brethren, even when they are strangers to thee. They have
borne public witness before the church of thy charity, and thou wilt
do well to set them forward on their journey in such a manner as
befits God's service.   (3 Jn: 5–7)

IN THE FINAL chapter concerning the Church Suffering, we will
endeavor to grasp how the practical application of the communion
of saints affects the Church Militant, configuring it ever more
closely to the merciful heart of its Lord and Master. The exploration
of Purgatory that we have undertaken has hopefully given us a new
appreciation of the plight of these poor souls; of their intense sufferings, and thirst for God that cannot be quenched until divine justice has been administered appropriately. They are not alone
however. They belong to the Mystical Body in which the precious
Blood of Christ courses incessantly, purifying and sanctifying all
those destined to have their names written in the Book of Life (cf.
Rev. 20:12). As such, they are still beneficiaries of the divine charity
of God, able to gain the necessary graces offered on their behalf in
expiation for their sins. From this standpoint, we will seek to discern how we can come to their aid, seeing how we can live the communion of saints in the most generous way possible. And as a
humble suggestion, perhaps St. Francis de Sales' famous phrase "*cor*
cordi loquitur" (heart speaks to heart)[1] could serve as a useful refer-

---

1. This phrase originated in an essay: *On the Preacher and Preaching* given by St.
Francis to the new Archbishop of Bourges, Andre Fremont. *Oeuvres completes de St.*

ence for us throughout this chapter. Even if in the first instance it refers to our relationship with God, nevertheless it succinctly describes the love that should exist on a personal level between us and the holy souls.

The Application of Merit

At this juncture, I would like to return to one significant aspect of the Catholic faith that I touched upon in the introduction, namely the concept of the spiritual Treasury of the Church. In the Catechism of the Catholic Church we read that:

> In the communion of saints, a perennial link of charity exists between the faithful who have already reached their heavenly home, those who are expiating their sins in Purgatory and those who are still pilgrims on earth. Between them there is, too, an abundant exchange of all good things. In this wonderful exchange, the holiness of one profits others, well beyond the harm that the sin of one could cause others. Thus recourse to the communion of saints lets the contrite sinner be more promptly and efficaciously purified of the punishments for sin.[2]

It is this profitability of holiness that concerns us here, and specifically how it can be applied to someone else in the *sanctorum communio;* as the Catechism explains:

> We also call these spiritual goods of the communion of saints the Church's treasury, which is not the sum total of the material goods which have accumulated during the course of the centuries. On the contrary the "treasury of the Church" is the infinite value, which can never be exhausted, which Christ's merits have before God. They were offered so that the whole of mankind could be set free from sin and attain communion with the Father. In Christ, the Redeemer himself, the satisfactions and merits of his Redemption exist and find their efficacy. . . . This treasury includes as well the prayers and good works of the Blessed Virgin Mary. They are truly immense, unfathomable, and even pristine in their value

---

François de Sales, Tome Premier (Paris: Berche et Tralin, 1898), XL. Blessed John Henry Newman also took the phrase for his motto.

2. *Catechism of the Catholic Church,* no. 1475, www.vatican.va.

before God. In the treasury, too, are the prayers and good works of all the saints, all those who have followed in the footsteps of Christ the Lord and by his grace have made their lives holy and carried out the mission in the unity of the Mystical Body.[3]

The doctrine concerning the treasury of the Church's merits is intimately linked to the entire question of justification that we examined earlier. For the protestant reformers, the good works of the saints have no intrinsic value in terms of salvation history, as there is no temporal punishment and consequently no satisfaction to be made. Any meritorious work is worthless, with the exception of bearing witness to a Christian life. Fundamentally though, any particular act of love adds nothing to salvation or sanctification.

In the doctrine of Christ's Church, however, that is not the case. The constant teaching from the earliest centuries is that the Lord has willed to include His adopted children in the work of salvation, thereby strengthening the bonds of love that unite them as a family. St. Paul assures us of this fact in his Letter to the Colossians: "I am glad of my sufferings on your behalf, as, in this mortal frame of mine, I help to pay off the debt which the afflictions of Christ still leave to be paid, for the sake of his body, the Church" (Col. 1:24). It is particularly noticeable in this text that the holy Apostle senses a joy in suffering for others, as he knows his sufferings have merit in the eyes of God. Conspicuously, he also places the teaching within the context of Christ's Mystical Body, the Church. That is, he understands that the debt his sufferings cancel is applied to its members, and is distributed as the Lord sees fit.

In the Book of Revelation, we also have corroboration of this marvellous truth: "His bride has clothed herself in readiness for it [the wedding feast of the Lamb]; hers it is to wear linen of shining white; the merits of the saints are her linen" (Rev. 19:7–8). The linen represents the purity of those who have overcome the onslaught of the devil; therefore if the good works are that fabric, then they are salvific in nature and certainly precious in the eyes of the Lord.

---

3. Ibid., 1476–1477.

The notion of a "treasury" needs to be understood within a biblical concept of rewards. In the New Testament for instance, we discover various references that assure us of this fact: "Yes, for ever henceforward, the Spirit says; they [the saints] are to have rest from their labours; but the deeds they did in life go with them now" (Rev. 14:13). In St. Matthew's Gospel we read of the promise of a prophet's reward for those who welcome a prophet (cf. Matt. 10:41), rewards for secret almsgiving and private prayer (cf. Matt. 6:4, 6), and rewards for bearing persecutions for the sake of the Gospel (cf. Matt. 5:12). Jesus also warns us to store up treasure in heaven rather than on earth (Matt. 6:19–20). And in the following verse we get to the crux of the matter: "Where your treasure-house is, there your heart is too" (Matt. 6:21).

Now of course, as we have seen in the case of true holiness, there is no other reward than loving God and seeing him loved; the reward in a temporal sense is still too earthly. But for the Lord, there is great value in what his disciples have done for him, and his mercy desires that the rewards for these actions be bestowed on others. St. Thomas Aquinas addressed this particular issue in his *Summa Theologica*, where he states that the merits of the saints greatly surpass the entire debt of punishment due at a given time, and because of that, may be applied to the entire Body of the Church for all time.[4]

This Spiritual treasury therefore testifies to God's predilection towards all requiring his mercy. In a certain way, it is the continuation of the fruits of redemption, because just as his Passion and Death did not bring to an end suffering and sin, so his salvific action did not end on Calvary. If we still have the chance to fall, we also have the chance to rise. And even if one single drop of Christ's Blood were enough to surpass all the debt for ever, the Lord has decreed that the communion of saints exist to partly fund this expiatory action. In this way, we can perceive the treasury as a furnace of love in which all the merits are intertwined with those of the Savior: "Where your treasure-house is, there your heart is too" (Matt. 6:21).

---

4. St. Thomas Aquinas, *Summa Theologica* (Supplementum Tertiæ Partis) Q.25. 1, www.newadvent.org.

The heart of the saint resides in the heart of Jesus, and his merits too. For us sinners, we can be thankful that we have a God who is not wasteful, who does not disregard excess merit as worthless, but instead offers it to us out of divine charity.

A natural progression of this discussion takes us to the vitally important yet controversial subject of indulgences. But what do we mean by this term? The Catechism tells us:

> An indulgence is a remission before God of the temporal punishment due to sins whose guilt has already been forgiven, which the faithful Christian who is duly disposed gains under certain prescribed conditions through the action of the Church which, as the minister of redemption, dispenses and applies with authority the treasury of the satisfactions of Christ and the saints.[5]

There are two types of indulgence: *partial* and *plenary*. A partial indulgence removes only a certain amount of temporal punishment, while a plenary indulgence eradicates the debt entirely. These indulgences are taken from the treasury of merit in a way similar to a common fund that is used for charitable purposes.

But where is the authority for the Church Militant to grant such spiritual treasures? We find our answer in the words Jesus addressed to Peter: "I will give to thee the keys of the kingdom of heaven; and whatever thou shalt bind on earth shall be bound in heaven; and whatever thou shalt loose on earth shall be loosed in heaven" (Matt. 16:19). Undoubtedly, this power invested in the first pope and each of his successors relates to the absolving of sins—mortal and venial—and the cancelling of debt after forgiveness has taken place. But how do we know this? The answer comes in the first part of Jesus's words: He gives Peter the "keys" to the Kingdom. The image of keys tells us that Peter is the guardian of the door. It is within his God-given power to open the door to those under his jurisdiction. Now we have to ask ourselves: if the Lord required no intermediary between himself and the soul as Luther would have it, why was Peter commissioned in this way? Why specifically was he given keys that in the Protestant doctrine were not his by right? Furthermore, Jesus

---

5. *Catechism of the Catholic Church*, no. 1471, www.vatican.va.

confirms Peter's position of authority by confirming his power to bind and loose—a power that is ratified in heaven. The metaphor of keys is simple yet effective. Anyone who has ever locked themselves out of the house will appreciate the holder of a spare key; but of course we know the Lord gave a spare key to no one!

So the granting of indulgences falls within the authority of the pope as an act of mercy for the repentant sinner; in essence, an extension of the Sacrament of Confession. But knowing that the Holy Father is the Vicar of Christ on earth, we have the assurance that in utilizing this treasury of merits, he is carrying out the divine will.[6] These indulgences may be applied to the individual himself, or if he so wishes, in a generic way to the holy souls in Purgatory. In the former case, we know that the individual will definitely gain, but we cannot say for certain if God applies the principle of vicarious atonement when offering an indulgence for a *particular* deceased soul. The main reason for this assumption is that the Pope's judicial powers do not extend into eternal life; they remain solely within the realm of the *ecclesia militans*. Another factor would be the possibility that the soul in question is not even in Purgatory at all. There is good reason to believe, however, that God would impart at least a measure of satisfaction for a specific soul, (even if divine justice did not allow the benefit of a plenary indulgence for instance), simply on the basis that the penitent on earth had shown such love and mercy towards that person, and thus imitated the charity and mercy of God himself.

The gaining of indulgences is one of the most precious ways in which we can bring relief to the souls in Purgatory, but how do we gain them? For a complete answer to this question, including the many ways in which individual indulgences are granted, I recommend reading the *Enchiridion of Indulgences*[7] issued by the Sacred Apostolic Penitentiary, but for the sake of brevity, I will outline the essentials.

---

6. We may recall here the Lord's words to St. Faustina: "Draw all the indulgences from the treasury of My Church." *Divine Mercy In My Soul*, n. 1226.

7. For an English translation *see*, http://www.2heartsnetwork.org/The.Enchiridion.of.Indulgences.pdf.

Eliminating the Debt: The Treasury of Divine Mercy

In order to gain a plenary indulgence, certain conditions must be met: absolution in the Sacrament of Confession (although one visit is enough for several plenary indulgences), reception of Holy Communion and prayers for the Pope's intentions. It is further required that all attachment to sin, even venial sin, be absent; meaning in effect that we must have absolutely no desire to commit even the tiniest sin: "But you are to be perfect, as your heavenly Father is perfect" (Matt. 5:48). If this latter disposition is not perfectly present, or the other conditions are not fully met, the indulgence becomes partial.[8] Only one plenary indulgence can be granted per day, with the exception of the moment of death.[9] All indulgences are attached to specific pious works carried out by the penitent,[10] and even if the works are related to objects or places, i.e. churches or relics, nevertheless it is the action that is meritorious. One further condition must be met: in order to gain any indulgence, a person must have: "a least a general intention to gain them."[11]

For example, in gaining a plenary indulgence as prescribed by Holy Mother Church, as well as fulfilling the conditions described above, the pious work could be one of: adoration of the Blessed Sacrament for at least half an hour; devout reading of Sacred Scripture for half an hour; the recitation of the Rosary (five complete decades) in a family group; the reception of the *Urbi et Orbi* papal blessing (even if only received through radio or television) or a pious walking of the Way of the Cross (all fourteen stations, and legitimately erected, in a Catholic Church or chapel for example). There are also many other works attached to feast days, for example: visits to the parochial church on its titular feast, partaking in devotions on Divine Mercy Sunday, or alternatively if that is not possible on the same day, reciting the Our Father, Creed and the pious invo-

---

8. There are exceptions to this rule in the case where the conditions cannot be met either through impediments of health, or the impossibility of receiving the sacraments due to remoteness of location, etc.

9. Partial indulgences may be gained more than once a day.

10. The three conditions of Confession, Holy Communion and prayers for the pope's intentions may be fulfilled several days before or after the work, although it is recommended that the latter two coincide with the day of the holy work itself.

11. *Enchiridion*, 22.2.

cation: "Merciful Jesus, I trust in you!" before the Tabernacle.[12] A plenary indulgence is also granted when one renews their baptismal vows either during the Easter Vigil, or on the anniversary of their baptism. This list is not exhaustive, but it gives an idea of how it is possible to gain these great graces regularly, as long as our disposition is oriented towards love of God and acceptance of His mercy.

In the case of partial indulgences, there are many opportunities to gain them each day. A partial indulgence is attached to the devout use of a crucifix, rosary or scapular (as long as they have been properly blessed by a priest), and the recitation of various prayers and hymns. These include: *Adore te devote*, the "Angel of God, our Guardian" prayer, the *Angelus, Anima Christi, De profundis*, and the *Memorare*. Making a spiritual communion, by which we invite the Lord to enter our soul when we cannot receive Holy Communion, also has a partial indulgence attached to it. There are many other pious works for each type of indulgence described in the *Enchiridion* that have the ability to greatly affect our spiritual lives and those of the holy souls.

Our consideration of the treasury of the Church and its fruitfulness in the form of indulgences takes us to the very heart of the communion of saints. Of course, with the free will we have, we could utilize these spiritual gifts for our own benefit, lessening the temporal punishment applicable to us and hastening our own entrance into the Kingdom of God. But is it not the case that a greater intensity of love awaits us if we leave our own concerns to the side (even if we have to suffer the consequences in Purgatory) so that we may help our beloved brothers and sisters enter eternal glory? That is the type of vulnerability that surely brings joy to the heart of Jesus, when charity overrides every other concern. In relinquishing these indulgences we are in fact placing ourselves even more at the feet of his mercy.

---

12. This plenary indulgence is not to be confused with the promise Jesus gave to Saint Faustina that the soul who would go to confession and receive Holy Communion on Divine Mercy Sunday would be freed from all temporal punishment. This wonderful grace is different in that it does not require the conditions set out for a plenary indulgence—notably the freeing of all attachment to sin—and it cannot be transferred to the Holy Souls (cf. *Divine Mercy in My Soul*, n.699, 1109).

There exists a further measure by which we can be of service to the holy souls; namely, the selfless *Heroic Act of Charity* in which we offer to God, for the souls in Purgatory, all the satisfactory works which we will perform during our lifetime, and also all the suffrages which we may accrue after death. Tradition also recommends that they be placed into the hands of the Blessed Virgin for her to distribute in conformity with the divine will.[13] As the title of this Act suggests, it should not be entered into lightly, but with a certain amount of prayer and reflection considering the seriousness of what it involves. However, the wonderful testament of St. Therese of Lisieux should give us confidence that, under the correct disposition, we could still appear before the Just Judge *with* empty hands.

Without doubt, the most powerful form of prayer beneficial to the Church Suffering is the Holy Sacrifice of the Mass, which may be offered for an individual deceased soul. And as we have already seen, a tradition originating with Pope St. Gregory the Great of offering thirty Masses has remained a formidable treasure to this day. The recitation of the Rosary and devotions directed towards the holy souls are also powerful means by which we can bring solace to those suffering in the flames of purification; while the sacrifices borne from fasting and almsgiving are also opportunities to manifest the communion of saints. Holy Water is a sacramental that may also be used; perhaps while blessing oneself with it, we could ask the Lord to wash away their remaining stains, transforming their attire into the brilliant white linen garment of the saints (cf. Rev. 19:8).

There is a further possible benefit to our own spiritual lives when focusing our attention on these poor souls which perhaps is often somewhat overlooked. It concerns the temptation to be judgmental towards those who live among us, those whose lives are seen to be contradictory to the demands of the Gospel. But why do I say this? It is due to the tendency to see the souls in Purgatory only from the standpoint of their mystical presence, removed from their past existence. The reality is of course quite different. Purgatory will be a kaleidoscopic view of humanity in its wounded sinful state, ranging

---

13. *See, Acta Sanctae Sedis*, 1885, 337, www.vatican.va.

from those repentant of all sorts of depravity, to those bearing only a tiny spec of dirt on their wedding garment. As the Lord tells us to judge no one, but to love all, isn't it the case that we need to start looking at those we judge in the light of the purgatorial souls? So that instead of waiting until these individuals perhaps become part of the Church Suffering, we learn to love them this side of eternity, embracing the charity and mercy that is required of us. It is far easier to say we love the holy souls in a collective sense, rather than to say we love a person who bears us ill will here and now.

A Communion of Love: The Importance of Witness

From the perspective we have taken thus far, the communion of saints at its deepest level may seem to be confined to the great mystics; a little too abstract for those living in the commotion of the twenty-first century. But I would like to share two personal examples that I hope will show how this most beautiful and dynamic reality concerns all the members of the Mystical Body.

The first instance occurred in March 2001. One night, I was suddenly awoken to find my mind alert to the name of the famous American author, Robert Ludlum. I didn't know why, as I had no interest in his life, and I didn't sense anything of the mystical. However, I simply couldn't stop thinking about him until I fell asleep again sometime later. The following day, I was having lunch watching the news when it was announced that the author Robert Ludlum had died. Like anyone who has been taught from their earliest years to pray for the deceased, that is exactly what I did, and of course the circumstances of the previous night suddenly became more understandable. But there is a little more to the story than that. When I was ten or eleven years old, I had discovered one of Robert Ludlum's books on a shelf in my home. Before long, I was reading an explicit description of the sexual antics of one of his main characters. In truth, I returned to that passage on several occasions. Was it the case that the two of us had some connection that had begun under sinful circumstances—his writing of graphic impurity and my "interest" in it—which then became something else upon his death? Did the Lord allow me to feel his need for prayer in order to repair what had happened many years before? Of course only God knows the truth, but for me, it was a very real sense of the communion of saints at work in a special way.

The second incident happened in 2007. One day, I was praying before a Crucifix in my local Catholic Church when suddenly I sensed a very powerful interior inspiration which in effect told me to immediately start praying the chaplet of Divine Mercy for a specific lady whom I had never met or whose name I didn't know. The person in question was the mother of someone my wife knew at the time. I was aware that she had led a somewhat promiscuous lifestyle. I obeyed what I believed was the Lord's will and began praying the Chaplet. When I returned home, I said nothing about what had happened. Exactly one week later my wife received the news that this lady had died on that very day the previous week, and I thought about how Jesus had told St. Faustina that through reciting the Chaplet: "unfathomable mercy envelops the [dying] soul."[14]

Hopefully, these examples will serve to show that even in the ordinary circumstances of life, far away from the silence of the cloister, God can make use of us to draw other souls into his Kingdom of holiness and love. On our part, we need to broaden our horizons so that in imitation of Jesus we place no restrictions on where our love and compassion is focused. Even if the specific doctrine applies internally to the Mystical Body—that is, to members of the Church —the reality is that we must venture out to the existential peripheries in search of the lost sheep so they too can become part of the communion of love. In that sense, communion and evangelization are not mutually exclusive. Souls need to be saved and Purgatory needs to be emptied; that is the kernel of our mission in the Church Militant.

The Church Suffering is much neglected in our days. Perhaps this neglect is a consequence of a questionable post-Vatican II atmosphere in which popular piety was rather frowned upon. Or perhaps the blame can be placed at the feet of a theological community which to a certain extent drifted away from the mysteries of the faith as taught and upheld by the Magisterium. Whatever the reason, as part of the Mystical Body of Christ, these children of God

---

14. *Divine Mercy in My Soul*, n. 811.

are our concern and must not be forgotten. We can be sure that in coming to their aid, we are building unique friendships which will endure forever, and it is not beyond the realm of possibility that an entourage of grateful souls will be waiting to greet us at the gates of heaven.

In utilizing the treasury of the Church, we should be greedy. Greedy in the only way God approves: *for charity*, as St. Augustine tells us: "If you see charity, you see the Trinity."[15] The souls in Purgatory are relying on our hunger, on our eagerness to shun indifference and apathy. For us to be of real use to them, we need to experience the communion of saints, living the mystery of divine love each day through prayer and good works. In that way we will draw close to them, seeing them not as a faceless crowd, but as individual guests being readied for the wedding feast. Their purifying sufferings should touch our hearts greatly, enabling love and mercy to flow out from us to them, and in doing so, we will activate our own purification, ensuring that our souls journey together along the same road of sanctification.

A Final Gift of Merciful Love

Before leaving this chapter, I wish to briefly return to the subject of indulgences. Until now, we have focused our attention on how we can help the holy souls either lessen, or eradicate completely, their temporal punishment in readiness for heaven. But it is also important to explain how it is possible to avoid it altogether for oneself. In the *Enchiridion* of Indulgences, Holy Mother Church, in her wonderful benevolence, has left a precious gift for the dying; one which is very rarely mentioned or promoted among the faithful. We read:

> To the faithful in danger of death, who cannot be assisted by a priest to bring them the sacraments and impart the Apostolic Blessing with its plenary indulgence .... Holy Mother Church nevertheless grants a plenary indulgence to be acquired at the point of death, provided they are properly disposed and have been in the habit of reciting some prayers during their lifetime. The use

---

15. St. Augustine, *De Trinitate*, bk VIII, 8. 12 CCSL v. 50, 287.

of a crucifix or a cross to gain this indulgence is praiseworthy. The condition: provided they have been in the habit of reciting some prayers during their lifetime supplies in such cases for the three usual conditions required for the gaining of a plenary indulgence. The plenary indulgence at the point of death can be acquired by the faithful, even if they have already obtained another plenary indulgence on the same day.[16]

The condition of no attachment to sin remains, but one would hope that in the moments before death—as long as one is conscious—there would be only thoughts of repentance, and a sincere desire to live the will of God fully. We must presume (as the Church has not told us any different) that even this plenary indulgence could be offered for the poor souls, but nevertheless the choice is there for the individual to make. As God loves a grateful soul, and knowing the future benefit of this great indulgence, perhaps we should pray regularly through life in anticipation of this grace, asking the Lord to prepare our souls for it in a way pleasing to him and thanking him in advance, as a sign of our trust in his infinite mercy.

Now that we have concluded our reflections on the Church Suffering and the path of purification from self-love to pure love, we can turn our attentions to the Triumphant Church of the saints—the divinization of man in the glory of God.

16. *Enchiridion,* 28.

PART III

The Church Triumphant

～ 10 ～

Company of the Blessed:
The Testament of Divine Victory

And then I saw a great multitude, past all counting, taken from all nations and tribes and peoples and languages. These stood before the throne in the Lamb's presence, clothed in white robes, with palm-branches in their hands, and cried with a loud voice, To our God, who sits on the throne, and to the Lamb, all saving power belongs. And all the angels that were standing round the throne, round the elders and the living figures, fell prostrate before the throne and paid God worship; Amen, they cried, blessing and glory and wisdom and thanksgiving and honour and power and strength belong to our God through endless ages, Amen. (Rev. 7:9–12)

IN THE CONCLUDING part of this triptych concerning Christ's Mystical Body, we will meditate on a variety of aspects that will hopefully turn our gaze ever more to the nature of heaven and its glorious company. We will encounter the Blessed Virgin, the perfect icon of communion with God and the "singular custodian of the bond between the universal Church and Christ."[1] We will study the joys of the saints: in the beatific vision and in relation to one another, and the tangible and contemporary influence of the Church Triumphant upon the Church Militant. Finally, we will seek to examine the eschatological corporeality of the new heaven and earth, where the consummation of the world will give way to the flowering of a transfigured universe of which there will be no end. But before we enter those discussions, I would like to begin with a

---

1. Pope Francis, "Angelus Address," November 1, 2014, www.vatican.va.

study of the saints themselves, encompassing their lives as revealed in Sacred Scripture, Tradition and the Magisterium. In this way, we will discover how they are prophetic witnesses to Christ's final victory over evil, and powerful intercessors within the communion of saints.

The Heavenly Cohort

The Feast of All Saints, celebrated on November 1 each year, is a festival purposely celebrated for all the baptized that throughout history have "fought the good fight [of faith]" (2 Tim. 4:7), seeking to live the divine will as faithfully as possible while cultivating the virtues that lead to true holiness. As opposed to the canonized saints, these men, women and children are the vast majority: hidden gems who silently ploughed the fields of salvation in this life, and who now form a multitude of saints together with their more famous counterparts. However, we should not perceive two "divisions" of saints in which one has a kind of "celebrity status"; rather together, they form only one body of holiness: the Church Triumphant. Their holiness is not comparable to the imperfect holiness we understand on earth; as the Lord himself explained: "I tell you, there is no greater than John the Baptist among all the sons of women; and yet to be least in the kingdom of heaven is to be greater than he" (Lk. 7:28). Also included in this array of shining stars are the saints of the Old Testament such as Abraham, Moses and David; the company of prophets, and all who were "watered by the same prophetic rock which bore them company, the rock that was Christ" (1 Cor. 10:4).

From a Scriptural point of view, the Book of Revelation is the most fitting place for us to begin this reflection; for within its pages, we are drawn into the vision of the final eschatological battle that began with the overthrowing of Satan's power through the sacrificial victory of Jesus, the Lamb of God. With the opening of the gates of heaven, there now exist a company of saints that gradually grows through time, a triumphant procession of those who clung to the Cross, nailing the lures of the world to it. The Book of Revelation, rich in symbolism both apocalyptic and liturgical, reveals many different aspects of the epoch of the Church; but it must be considered in the context of when it was written and for what reason. Although there are many exegetical works that treat these issues in detail, suffice it to say that as a book of consolation and hope, it was in the first instance beneficial for the early Church undergoing savage persecution under various Roman emperors. The mystical visions of St. John would have helped the faithful to see suffering and martyrdom in the context of the life of Jesus. That is, they would be following the same path, embracing the same pattern of death, and inheriting the same triumph of resurrection. In short, they would recognize the visions as prophesying their own glorious future as saints in the Kingdom of God.

One of the most striking aspects of the saints in the Book of Revelation is their fervent activeness. The text completely dismisses any idea that heaven is a place where we live in some kind of eternal retirement (albeit with joys unimaginable) where spiritual action is a thing of the past. Various passages present the image of a community gathered together in solemn liturgies, singing canticles in praise and thanksgiving to the Most Holy Trinity; and if we work chronologically through the chapters, we sense this still further.

Chapter four presents us with this captivating vision:

> And all at once I was in a trance, and saw where a throne stood in heaven, and one sat there enthroned. He who sat there bore the semblance of a jewel, jasper or sardius, and there was a rainbow about the throne, like a vision of emerald. Round it were twenty-four seats, and on these sat twenty-four elders, clothed in white garments, with crowns of gold on their heads.... And in the midst, where the throne was, round the throne itself, were four living figures, that had eyes everywhere to see before them and behind them.... And as often as these figures gave glory and honour and blessing to him who sat on the throne, who lives for ever and ever, the twenty-four elders fell down in worship before him who sat on the throne, who lives for ever and ever, and threw down their crowns before the throne, crying out, Thou, our Lord God, claimest as thy due glory and honour and power; by thee all things were created; nothing ever was, nothing was ever created, but in obedience to thy will. (Rev. 4:2–4, 6, 9–11)

St. John, in relaying this magnificent scene, cannot even begin to describe the God who sits on the throne; it is not possible for the poor human mind to articulate accurately; therefore he speaks of a precious jewel instead. Around the throne sit the twenty-four elders who symbolize the twelve tribes of Israel and the twelve Apostles of the New Covenant; by extension, they also symbolize all the holy people of both the old law and the new. The rainbow about God's Throne recalls the immensity of divine love directed towards these chosen ones. The four living figures seem to be Angels with their six wings and eyes back and front.[2]

In the following chapter a new figure appears amid this exalted company: a Lamb who stands upright, yet slain (v.6) (he stands because he has overcome death). He moves forward to take the scroll from God's right hand, as only he, the Lord of history, can open its seals, revealing the mysteries hidden in God. At this point the elders prostrate themselves in the Lamb's presence, recognizing the saving figure of Jesus the Christ:

> Each bore a harp, and they had golden bowls full of incense, the prayers of the saints. And now it was a new hymn they sang, Thou, Lord, art worthy to take up the book and break the seals that are on it. Thou wast slain in sacrifice; out of every tribe, every language, every people, every nation thou hast ransomed us with thy blood and given us to God. Thou hast made us a royal race of priests, to serve God; we shall reign as kings over the earth. (Rev. 5:8–10)

Of significance here is that the twenty-four elders have the prayers of the saints rising up to God through the bowls of incense. This suggests the "official" nature of the sacred liturgy, in that the prayers come through the ministers of God, the primary channels of the Church. The "new" hymn they sing signals the definitive turning point of history; they acclaim Jesus as the One who will direct events towards the completion of his divine plan to "make all things new" (Rev. 21:5), and they proclaim their own royal nobility in a reign which will never end. This "royal race" brings to fulfilment the prophecy of the Lord from Exodus: "You shall serve me as

---

2. St. John Paul II suggests they symbolize God's divine presence at the four cardinal points of the universe. See "General Audience," March 31, 2004, www.vatican.va.

a royal priesthood, as a consecrated nation" (Ex. 19:6). St. John also describes a huge company of angels crying aloud in unison: "Power and Godhead, wisdom and strength, honour and glory and blessing are his by right, the Lamb that was slain" (Rev. 5:12). It is a recognition by the entire heavenly court of the majesty of the Lord who lowered himself in order to raise us.

The vision of the *ecclesia triumphans* in chapter seven suddenly takes on much greater dimensions, revealing the full extent of the Kingship of Christ over his saints:

> Then I heard the count of those who were sealed, a hundred and forty-four thousand of them, taken from every tribe of the sons of Israel.... And then I saw a great multitude, past all counting, taken from all nations and tribes and peoples and languages. These stood before the throne in the Lamb's presence, clothed in white robes, with palm-branches in their hands, and cried with a loud voice, to our God, who sits on the throne, and to the Lamb, all saving power belongs. (Rev. 7:4, 9–10)

The great multitude described here from all nations and all languages brings to mind the command of the Lord to evangelize the world (cf. Mk. 16:15), spreading his Kingdom to the remotest regions; and in its mystical dimension, reveals to us the vision of its fulfilment. One of the elders also provides the understanding for how these saints came to be in the presence of the Almighty:

> These, he said, have come here out of the great affliction; they have washed their robes white in the blood of the Lamb. And now they stand before God's throne, serving him day and night in his temple; the presence of him who sits on the throne shall overshadow them. (Rev. 7:14–15)

If we take this passage and view it through the prism of those early Christian communities undergoing hardship and persecution, we can see that they were not being promised a miraculous, "millenarian" escape from the evil that was being thrown at them. On the contrary, the full ferocity of the enemy's onslaught meant they were being promised a life of struggle and violent conflict. But one that in time—in eternity—would end in the triumph of sanctity. That was where they could nurture the theological virtue of hope; in seeing earthly time as one where Jesus gradually breaks open the seven seals that lead to the ultimate defeat of evil.

This particular passage would also have shown these disciples that the fruits of their labors would continue into eternity, in serving the Lord before his throne "day and night." In this way, a primitive understanding of the communion of saints between heaven and earth would have taken root. The saints in heaven would not be mere bystanders in the comfort of God's presence but active co-workers still immersed in the fight for God's Kingdom, knowledge that would be a source of joy and encouragement for those still in the midst of tribulation.

This influence of the saints in the Church Triumphant is also evident in chapter eight:

> There was another angel that came and took his stand at the altar, with a censer of gold; and incense was given him in plenty, so that he could make an offering on the golden altar before the throne, out of the prayers said by all the saints. So, from the angel's hand, the smoke of the incense went up in God's presence, kindled by the saints' prayer. Then the angel took his censer, filled it up with fire-brands from the altar, and threw it down on to the earth; thunder followed, and mutterings, and lightning, and a great earthquake. (Rev. 8:3–5)

Several elements of this passage are particularly noteworthy. The censer and altar are both made of gold, suggesting great value (from a spiritual point of view) in its liturgical use. The angel is given plenty of incense, which implies a great amount of prayer from the saints is to be offered,[3] and perhaps most importantly of all, the angel does not set to work chastising the world until the prayers have risen as smoke before the throne of God. The sacred celestial liturgy, bearing a striking resemblance to the solemn supplications offered at Holy Mass,[4] tells us that the prayers of the saints have

---

3. Pope Benedict XVI also sees the prayers of the Church Militant within this golden censer. See, "General Audience," September 12, 2012, www.vatican.va.

4. The Vatican II Constitution on the Sacred Liturgy, *Sacrosanctum Concilium*, sees a similarity and even a unity of liturgical action between the *ecclesia militans* and the *ecclesia triumphans*: "In the earthly liturgy we take part in a foretaste of that

great intercessory power, which influences events on earth. It is noticeable throughout the visions of Revelation that God does not speak; yet the angelic host and the victorious saints are always in close proximity to his Throne. Therefore the Eternal Father does not resemble a ruler who throws orders about; rather He allows the pleas of the Church to reach His ears, and then allows His divine will to proceed. This divine will is expressed above all in the actions of His Son rather than Himself; for as head of the Mystical Body, it is to the Lamb that all authority in heaven and on earth has been given (cf. Matt. 28:18). Therefore, the entire vision of the Apocalypse portrays Jesus as the One who acts to bring about the recapitulation of creation until the time comes when: "he places his kingship in the hands of God, his Father, having first dispossessed every other sort of rule, authority, and power; his reign, as we know, must continue until he has put all his enemies under his feet, and the last of those enemies to be dispossessed is death" (1 Cor. 15:24–26).

Chapters twelve and thirteen present us with the full manifestation of Satan's fury against the saints of the Church Militant. As he cannot devour the child (cf. Rev. 12:5) or destroy the woman, his mother (Rev. 12:14–16), he makes war on her children through the persecution of the "Beast" who comes "out of the sea" (Rev. 13:1)[5]; that is the Antichrist, who will reign for forty-two months in a frenzy of absolute cruelty against God's chosen ones. Chapter fourteen presents a vision of the symbolic one hundred and forty-four thousand with the Lamb upon Mount Sion. These are the ones who endured not only the tortuous reign of the Son of Perdition, but all the persecutions of those who prefigured him. They refused to carry the mark of the Beast; instead they bore the Lamb's name and the

heavenly liturgy which is celebrated in the holy city of Jerusalem toward which we journey as pilgrims, where Christ is sitting at the right hand of God, a minister of the holies and of the true tabernacle; we sing a hymn to the Lord's glory with all the warriors of the heavenly army; venerating the memory of the saints, we hope for some part and fellowship with them; we eagerly await the Savior, Our Lord Jesus Christ, until He, our life, shall appear and we too will appear with Him in glory." *Sacrosanctum Concilium*, no. 8, www.vatican.va.

5. The sea possibly symbolizes the destructive power of sin; therefore in a sense, the Antichrist is born out of evil when it reaches its high point in history.

Father's name on their foreheads (Rev. 14:1). St. John also describes hearing an immense sound from heaven:

> This sound which I heard seemed to come from harpers, playing on their harps, as they sang a new song, there before the throne, and the living figures, and the elders. It was a song none else might learn to sing but the hundred and forty-four thousand that were ransomed from the earth. (Rev. 14:2–3)

This "new song" is that which is first encountered in chapter five. It recalls Psalm 144 (143) in which the psalmist sings:

> With heavenly aid, from yonder flood deliver me; rescue me from the power of alien foes, who make treacherous promises, and lift their hands in perjury. Then, O my God, I will sing thee a new song, on a ten-stringed harp I will sound thy praise; the God to whom kings must look for victory, the God who has brought his servant David rescue. Save me from the cruel sword, deliver me from the power of alien foes, who make treacherous promises, and lift their hands in perjury. (Ps. 144:7–11)

This psalm has an eschatological dimension in that it expresses the hope of definitive triumph over the forces of evil. Hence it can only be sung by those who have transcended the shallowness of sin, first through the waters of baptism, and then by ensuring the name of God is never erased from their forehead by imitating the Lamb's sacrificial love. These victors, having now departed the Church on earth for the Church in heaven, continue their rejoicing with harps in hand singing a paschal song; that of Moses and the Lamb. In the case of Moses, they are recalling Israel's Passover from Egypt, the foreshadowing of their own now accomplished:

> Lord God almighty, they cry, the deeds thou doest are great and wonderful; King of all the ages, thy ways are just and true. Lord, who alone art holy, who shall refuse reverence and glory to thy name? All the nations shall come and fall down before thee, now that thy just retribution has been made known. (Rev. 15:3–4)[6]

---

6. In the Book of Exodus we read: "What power is there, Lord, that can match thee? Who, as thou art, is august in holiness, who so worthy of fear and of praise, who so wonderful in his doings?" (Ex. 15:11)

This canticle expresses the truth that God's justice shall one day be fully manifested; that his glorious deeds shall prevail over the machinations of the evil doers. It ties in closely with the promise found in chapters sixteen and seventeen that the persecutors—those drunk with the blood of saints—will face the full force of divine wrath: "Then I heard the angel of the waters cry out, Holy thou art, O Lord, and wast ever holy, and this is a just award of thine, blood to drink for those who have shed the blood of thy saints and prophets; it is their due" (Rev. 16:5–6). Once God's justice is accomplished, the cry of victory will be acclaimed: "Triumph, heaven, over her fall, triumph, you saints in heaven, apostles and prophets; God has avenged you on her" (Rev. 18:20).

Chapter nineteen contains a canticle of praise for the overthrowing of the harlot who poisoned the earth. It is a scene that encapsulates the joy of salvation—thanksgiving that everything promised by the Lord has been fulfilled. The multitudes are crying out "Alleluia," praising the power and glory of God. The twenty-four elders and the four living creatures worship before the throne of God crying: "Amen, Alleluia" (Rev. 19:4). Now, the Church Triumphant has reached its zenith. The days of suffering and tears are over and now the saints can rest from their labors. A mighty roar of elation fills the heavens, proclaiming the final establishment of this Kingdom of divine love and unity:

> Alleluia, the Lord our God, the Almighty, has claimed his kingdom; let us rejoice and triumph and give him the praise; the time has come for the wedding-feast of the Lamb. His bride has clothed herself in readiness for it; hers it is to wear linen of shining white; the merits of the saints are her linen. (Rev. 19:6–8)

From this image of festive joy, we are presented with what can only be described as a vision of warrior-like magnificence. We appear to encounter a description of the Lord's second coming in which The King of glory rides out of heaven with his army of saints, ready to welcome the *ecclesia militans* and *ecclesia triumphans*[7] in one eternal Kingdom:

---

7. The *ecclesia patiens* will cease to exist at this moment when the final judgment takes place.

Then, in my vision, heaven opened, and I saw a white horse appear. Its rider bore for his title, the Faithful, the True; he judges and goes to battle in the cause of right. His eyes were like flaming fire, and on his brow were many royal diadems; the name written there is one that only he knows. He went clad in a garment deep dyed with blood, and the name by which he is called is the Word of God; the armies of heaven followed him, mounted on white horses, and clad in linen, white and clean. (Rev. 19:11–14)

The Apocalypse of St. John is without doubt a complex array of visions which cannot be deciphered properly unless it is understood within the entire context of salvation history; that is the struggle to lift the fog that clouds the vision of humanity. Sometimes the fog is more dense, sometimes less so. But what is does show vividly is the continual life of prayer of the entire heavenly host that penetrates the heart of God. The saints now live the fullness of that which the mystics lived partially on earth. It is adoration in its most perfect form, the spiritual perfection of the Church in impeccable communion with the Trinity. This worship is active on several levels: thanksgiving for the sacrifice of redemption, for the invitation to share the divine life; praise for the goodness of God in creation and His just judgments; and entreaty for the faithful who still suffer below. Individually, they are like holy "Thomas Cromwells"—they have the King's ear; they are influential in the Royal Court, able to impact events on the ground—but if their activity is now solely one of prayer, this is not the case with the angels.

Turning our attention to the angels, we know from the Catechism of the Council of Trent that they too form part of the *ecclesia triumphans*: "The Church triumphant is that most glorious and happy assemblage of blessed spirits, and of those souls who have triumphed over the world, the flesh, and the devil."[8] The Apocalypse described by the Seer of Patmos illuminates the mission of these emissaries of God; they are in the vanguard of the holy army, waging war against the spirits of evil. Famously, there is the battle between St. Michael and the angels who throw Satan and his legion

---

8. *Catechism of the Council of Trent* (Baltimore: James Myres, 1833), 93.

out of heaven (Rev. 12:7–9), and then the mighty angel who chains up Satan for a thousand years (Rev. 20:1–2). But their activities do not stop there. They are central figures in the drama of human history, especially in this last phase from the Incarnation to the day of final judgment, and in a very real sense they are the executioners of divine justice. We hear of the four angels who stand at the four corners of the world, holding back the wind (Rev. 7:1), the four who are given permission to lay waste land or sea (Rev. 7:3), the seven angels with seven trumpets who initiate a series of terrible chastisements, and finally the seven angels who administer seven plagues from seven golden cups. Seven, incidentally, in biblical language, represents fullness and maturity.[9]

But they also have a prophetic role, as we see in chapter fourteen, where an angel carries a "final gospel" to all those on the earth: "Fear the Lord, he cried aloud, and give him the praise; the hour of his judgement has come. Fall down before him who made heaven and earth, and the sea, and the springs of water" (Rev. 14:7). Another two angels follow, proclaiming the collapse of Babylon, and warning those marked with the sign of the Beast that eternal punishments will be their lot. It is a role strikingly similar to the fire and brimstone of the Old Testament prophets, but with an intensity that comes from knowledge that the sands of time are about to run their course.

St. John does not hide the fact that he is overcome with the luminosity of God's glory that radiates from these angels. At one point he falls down before the feet of one of the angels, ready to worship, until he is reminded by the blessed spirit that he too is a servant of God (cf. Rev. 19:10); such is the holiness that God instills in them. Towards the end of the Apocalypse, an angel holding a golden measuring rule takes him up a high mountain to view the stunning descent of the New Jerusalem as it comes out of heaven. He then

---

9. In the opening chapter of the Apocalypse, we encounter the "seven stars," that is, seven angels who are held in the hand of the risen Jesus. They seem to be the guardians of the "seven candlesticks" (the seven churches described in Rev. 2 and 3). It is probable that they actually refer to bishops rather than angels, as St. Augustine taught (cf. Letter 43), www.newadvent.org.

proceeds to measure the holy city in a symbolic manner which reveals its perfect proportions. Then finally, the angel announces sacred words addressed to all: "These words are sure and true. The Lord God who inspires his prophets has sent his angel to tell his servants what must soon find its due accomplishment" (Rev. 22:6).

So we see from the rich symbolism present in these visions a Church that is still utterly focused on ensuring that God's eternal plan to unite all things in heaven and earth (cf. Eph. 1:10) is accomplished in conformity with the divine will. The Church Triumphant cannot rest until everything is as it should be. That is the situation now, and has been for the past two millennia. The smoke of incense rises continuously through the liturgical action of the angels and saints who minister at the golden altar, acclaiming the victory of the Lamb; and in this cosmic liturgy, there is a solemnity that we in our parish communities would do well to imitate, when striving to make the Mass an experience worthy of the presence of God.

Above all, the adoration of the blessed spirits and souls in this service of worship is oriented towards the Lamb of Sacrifice—the very same Lamb whom Catholics behold and then receive in the celebration of the Eucharist—and in one sense there is a perfect theology at work in both liturgies. This revolves around the expectation of the second coming of Jesus, otherwise known as the *parousia*. For the Church on earth, hope and consummation are at the heart of the Mass. Jesus truly comes here and now, veiled under the appearances of bread and wine. And yet he is *still* to come. In the heavenly liturgy there is a similarity. True, the Lord is no longer veiled, but communion with him is still *partly* expectation because the resurrection of the body still lies in the future. Until that occurs, all liturgical activity within both states of the Mystical Body will be concerned with invoking the great prayer that is found in the penultimate verse not only of the Book of Revelation, but the Bible itself: *Maranatha!* Come Lord Jesus!

Scott Hahn, the well-known Catholic biblical scholar and convert from Presbyterianism, recounts how his understanding of the heavenly liturgy as described in the Apocalypse was suddenly illuminated upon encountering the Catholic liturgy:

It was only when I began attending Mass that the many parts of this puzzling book suddenly began to fall into place. Before long, I could see the sense in Revelation's altar (Rev. 8:3), its robed clergymen (4:4), candles (1:12), incense (5:8), manna (2:17), chalices (ch. 16), Sunday worship (1:10), the prominence it gives to the Blessed Virgin Mary (12:1–6), the "Holy, Holy, Holy" (4:8), the Gloria (15:3–4), the Sign of the Cross (14:1), the Alleluia (19:1, 3, 6), the readings from Scripture (ch. 2–3), and the "Lamb of God" (many, many times). These are not interruptions in the narrative or incidental details; they are the very stuff of the Apocalypse.[10]

The Book of Revelation leaves us with a wonderfully visual appreciation of the workings of the Church Triumphant in heaven, one that should serve us well as we move forward in our undertaking to discern the communion of saints from this glorious perspective.

The Book of Revelation was written towards the end of the first century AD, toward the closing of the apostolic age (the apostolic age ends with the death of St. John, author of the Apocalypse and the last surviving apostle). This meant that in the dawning post-apostolic age, the Church Fathers had a text upon which to found an apocalyptic theology. This refers to a theology that is a "revealing" of the eschatological nature of the Church. Notable among these patristic figures were: Hippolytus, Origen, Irenaeus of Lyons, Victorinus of Poetovio, Andrew of Caesarea, Jerome, Caesarius of Arles, Bede the Venerable and Ambrose Autpert. For many Fathers though, the Book of Revelation was integrated into their writings alongside various other passages from Sacred Scripture. Among these are included: Justin, Dionysius of Alexandria, Tertullian, Lactantius, Cyprian of Carthage, Hilary of Poitiers and Augustine of Hippo.

The Principle of Veneration

One of the main tasks of these early Christian writers was to formulate an understanding of the Mystical Body in its unity between heaven and earth. For, as the martyrs and other faithful departed this life, the Church of heaven began to swell, thus influencing the

---

10. Scott Hahn, *The Lamb's Supper: The Mass as Heaven on Earth* (New York: Doubleday, 1999), 66–67.

life of the Church on earth. Christians therefore needed the doctrine in place by which they could perceive the state of the angels and saints and understand their own relationship with them. St. Cyprian of Carthage was one such figure who nurtured this concept in his writings. In his *Letter to Cornelius* he writes:

> Let us remember one another in concord and unanimity. Let us on both sides always pray for one another. Let us relieve burdens and afflictions by mutual love, that if any one of us, by the swiftness of divine condescension, shall go hence the first, our love may continue in the presence of the Lord, and our prayers for our brethren and sisters not cease in the presence of the Father's mercy.[11]

St. Cyprian also placed his teachings within the context of vicious persecution (that of the emperors Decius and Valerian) and, by way of preparation and solicitude for those entrusted to his care, he evoked a powerful image of the victorious saints that recalls the multitude spoken of in the Apocalypse of St. John:

> If to soldiers of this world it is glorious to return in triumph to their country when the foe is vanquished, how much more excellent and greater is the glory, when the devil is overcome, to return in triumph to paradise, and to bring back victorious trophies to that place whence Adam was ejected as a sinner . . . to be made equal to the angels; with the patriarchs, with the apostles. With the prophets, to rejoice in the possession of the heavenly kingdom![12]

The martyrs of the early Church seem to have been the catalyst for the veneration of saints that eventually blossomed into the form it has today. Not surprisingly, they were seen to be faithful imitators of the true Lamb and thus bore holiness to a heroic degree. In Stephen Benko's *The Meaning of Sanctorum Communio*, he explains from a historical perspective this novel situation for these primitive Christian communities:

> Martyrs were regarded as God's especial elect, and because of this they came to be looked upon as intermediaries. For this reason many made arrangements to be buried near the grave of a martyr,

11. St. Cyprian of Carthage, *Letter* 56, www.newadvent.org.
12. St. Cyprian of Carthage, *Treatise* 11, 13, www.newadvent.org.

hoping to share in the martyr's superfluous merits on the day of resurrection. From this came the expression *sepultura ad sanctos*, by which is meant not the saints in heaven, but the mortal remains or relics of the martyrs. Evidence of this is discernible in various grave inscriptions such as *Irene tibi cum sanctis, Meruit sanctorum sociari sepulchre* and *Meruit sanctorum esse consortem.*[13]

Origen of Alexandria, writing at the same time as Cyprian and in the midst of the same persecution of Decius, utilized his brilliance as a theologian and exegete to grasp the truth contained in Sacred Scripture concerning the prayerful unity of the Mystical Body. In his *libellus de oratione* he writes: "Also it may well be that the assemblies of believers also are attended by angelic powers, by the powers of our Lord and Savior himself, and indeed by the spirits of saints, including those already fallen asleep."[14] And in his *Commentary on the Song of Songs* which explores the concept of the Church as *Bride*, Origen advances the notion that the saints in heaven, as part of the Church, are active members with the ability to invoke God's help: "Neither will it be unsuitable if we should say that all the saints who have departed this life, still having charity towards those who are in this world, are concerned for their salvation and help them with their prayers and intercessions with God."[15]

In the following century, the organic development of the doctrine on the Church Triumphant became more engrained in the teachings of the Fathers. St. Cyril of Jerusalem's "mystagogical catecheses" reveals for instance that during the Eucharistic Liturgy, the prayers of the faithful were in part directed to the saints: "Then we commemorate also those who have fallen asleep before us, first, Patriarchs, Prophets, Apostles, Martyrs, that at their prayers and intervention God would receive our petition."[16]

We also discover devotion to particular individuals of known sanctity. For example, at the end of St. Gregory of Nyssa's *Vita atque*

---

13. Benko, op. cit., 71.

14. Origen, *De Oratione*, P.G., XI, 554.

15. Origen, *The Song of Songs: Commentary and Homilies* (New York: The Newman Press, 1957), 194.

16. St. Cyril of Jerusalem, *The Catechetical Lectures of St Cyril Archbishop of Jerusalem* (Oxford: John Henry Parker, 1839) 275.

encomium sancti patris nostri Ephraem Syri, he invokes the protection of the great Eastern Father: "Do thou, [Ephraem] that art standing at the Divine altar, and art ministering with angels to the life-giving and most Holy Trinity, bear us all in remembrance, petitioning for us the remission of sins, and the fruition of an everlasting kingdom."[17] St. Gregory Nazianzus likewise honors and prays to St. Cyprian in a similar way: "May you watch over us from above in your mercy and give direction to our lives and words; and may you shepherd this holy flock, or help its shepherd, by warding off from it the ravening wolves . . . and by granting to us in greater fullness and clarity the radiance of the Holy Trinity, at whose side you now stand."[18]

St. John Chrysostom, another of the great Eastern Fathers, offers us a marvellous glimpse into the way these heroic figures were venerated during the first few centuries of Christianity, and how that veneration allowed a theological maturing in which the Church Triumphant could be properly understood. The homily he delivered for the feast of Saint Philogonius[19] is a prime example of this. To begin, he paraphrases a quote from the Book of Proverbs which states: "the just are remembered still" (Pv. 10:7). He then explains that it is not the deceased that are benefitted by this remembrance; rather it is us on earth who stand to gain by association with the blessed. St. John then proceeds to describe for his listeners the image of the Church Triumphant of which Philogonius is now a blessed member:

> But he mounted up to another city, the city of God. He left this Church here but he is a citizen in the Church of the firstborn who are enrolled in heaven. He left these festivals here on earth but he entered into the festal gathering of the angels. For up in heaven there is a city, there is a Church, there is a festival. . . . In heaven the throngs which come together are much larger, holier and more

---

17. St. Gregory of Nyssa, *Vita atque encomium sancti patris nostri Ephraem Syri*, P.G., XLVI, 850.

18. St. Gregory of Nazianzus, *Select Orations*, trans. Martha Vinson (Washington, DC: The Catholic University of America Press, 2003), 156.

19. The homily was given on December 20, AD 386, sixty-two years after the death of Philogonius, Bishop of Antioch in 324.

august. Nor are the crowds made up of city dwellers or country folk. Instead, in one place in heaven, we find myriads of angels, in another place, thousands of archangels, elsewhere, companies of prophets, in another place, choirs of martyrs, battalions of just men, and many various groups of people in whom the Lord has been well pleased.[20]

The Doctor of the Church then compares the festivals on earth and in heaven, by asking the question: Whoever saw a King coming to a festival? He answers his own question by stating no one has seen it. But in heaven, the true King is ever present in the eternal festival: "They can see him in their midst, and they can also see how he sheds on all who are gathered there the brightness of his own glory."[21] Continuing the comparison between the earthly and the heavenly, St. John recalls how on earth there is tumult and disturbance; but not in heaven: "There everything is in proper order and well arranged. There, voices raise in rhythmic harmony, as if blending with the lyre in the sweetest music, to praise the master who created heaven and earth."[22]

Moving from the Eastern Church to the Western, we come to St. Augustine of Hippo. A contemporary of St. John Chrysostom, St. Augustine addresses an issue that lies at the heart of devotion to the saints, and one that is of vital importance to the communion of saints: the question of a saint's power to change the course of events in the lives of individuals on earth. We need to bear in mind that a correct form of devotion needed to be affirmed, ensuring that exaggerated forms didn't arise leading to the saints becoming demigods in the minds of the faithful. The focus of all devotion would have to have a Christological center; that is, all intercessory activity would ultimately flow from the wellspring of Jesus, crucified and risen. The saints couldn't act alone nor would they want to. The great Bishop of Hippo writes:

20. St. John Chrysostom, *Fathers of the Church: On the Incomprehensible Nature of God* (Washington, DC: The Catholic University of America Press, 1984), 166–167.
21. Ibid., 167.
22. Ibid., 168.

To what do these miracles witness, but to this faith which preaches Christ risen in the flesh, and ascended with the same into heaven? For the martyrs themselves were martyrs, that is to say, witnesses of this faith, drawing upon themselves by their testimony the hatred of the world, and conquering the world not by resisting it, but by dying. For this faith they died, and can now ask these benefits from the Lord in whose name they were slain. For this faith their marvellous constancy was exercised, so that in these miracles great power was manifested as the result. For if the resurrection of the flesh to eternal life had not taken place in Christ, and were not to be accomplished in His people, as predicted by Christ, or by the prophets who foretold that Christ was to come, why do the martyrs who were slain for this faith which proclaims the resurrection possess such power? For whether God Himself wrought these miracles by that wonderful manner of working by which, though Himself eternal, He produces effects in time; or whether He wrought them by servants, and if so, whether He made use of the spirits of martyrs as He uses men who are still in the body, or effects all these marvels by means of angels, over whom He exerts an invisible, immutable, incorporeal sway, so that what is said to be done by the martyrs is done not by their operation, but only by their prayer and request; or whether, finally, some things are done in one way, others in another, and so that man cannot at all comprehend them—nevertheless these miracles attest this faith which preaches the resurrection of the flesh to eternal life.[23]

Similarly, in his Exposition on Psalm 86, St. Augustine stresses the point that intercession from the saints will continue until the earthly city is replaced at the end of the world with the heavenly:

> For our Lord Jesus Christ still intercedeth for us: all the Martyrs who are with Him intercede for us. Their intercessions pass not away, except when our mourning is passed away: but when our mourning shall have passed away, we all with one voice, in one people, in one country, shall receive comfort, thousands of thousands joined with Angels playing upon harps, with choirs of heavenly powers living in one city.[24]

23. St. Augustine of Hippo, *Civitate Dei*, bk. XXII, 9, www.newadvent.org.
24. St. Augustine of Hippo, *Nicene and Post-Nicene Fathers: First Series, Volume VIII* (New York: Cosimo, 2007), 418–419.

From the early days of Christianity, history shows that the Church was plagued with various heresies, such as Arianism, Donatism, Montanism and Gnosticism. Sadly, there was not universal support for everything the Church taught. An example of this came from the Gallic priest Vigilantius of Calagurris, an acquaintance of both St. Paulinus of Nola and the great biblical scholar, St. Jerome. Vigilantius argued against devotion to the martyrs, the intercessory power attributed to them, and the veneration of relics. In essence, he was almost a proto-Protestant. When these views came to the attention of St. Jerome, Vigilantius faced a stinging rebuke. Jerome's response was contained in the treatise *Contra Vigilantium*, in which the saint refutes these heretical opinions:

> You say, in your pamphlet, that so long as we are alive we can pray for one another; but once we die, the prayer of no person for another can be heard, and all the more because the martyrs, though they cry for the avenging of their blood (Rev. 6:10), have never been able to obtain their request. If Apostles and martyrs while still in the body can pray for others, when they ought still to be anxious for themselves, how much more must they do so when once they have won their crowns, overcome, and triumphed?[25]

The specific question of the intercessory power of saints cannot be separated from the more expansive question regarding the supernatural activity of the Church Triumphant. As the Apocalypse has shown us, the blessed spirits and blessed souls adore together (we may recall that beautiful image of the angel's censer filled with the prayers of the saints). They work in harmony, bound by a common goal to see God glorified in his creatures. The Book of Revelation would not have revealed the image of prayer rising like smoke if there was no merit in it. Otherwise, prayer in heaven would become obsolete, a manifestation of quietism. But if we see prayer as a *way of life* that permeates all activity, then it makes perfect sense that in heaven not only does it continue, but it takes on far greater depth. The scope to be a co-worker in God's cause reaches a new

---

25. St. Jerome, *Against Vigilantius*, 6, www.newadvent.org.

dimension with the increased holiness. St. Therese of Lisieux fully understood this when she said: "I want to spend my heaven in doing good on earth." The activity of the angels from a biblical perspective amply demonstrates this truth.

The Angelic Marvel

In the Old Testament, we see various instances where the angels are active in carrying out God's will. Among others: the Cherubim who guarded Eden after Adam's exile (cf. Gen. 3:24), the angel who instructed Agar from heaven, thus saving her son Ishmael (cf. Gen. 21:17), the angel who stayed the hand of Abraham as he was about to sacrifice Isaac (cf. Gen. 22:11), and the angel who drove the flames away from Azarias and his companions in the furnace (cf. Dan. 3:49–50).

Perhaps the most conclusive proof, though, of prayer as "activity" *and* "intercession" comes from the Book of Tobit. The Book tells the story of Tobias, a devout Israelite who suffers various misfortunes, culminating in his being blinded by bird droppings. Because of this he begs the Lord to let him die. However, remembering the large sum of money he has deposited in Media, he asks his son to travel the long distance to retrieve it. In Media, at the same time, a young woman called Sara is also praying for death because of the loss of her seven husbands who have been killed on each wedding night by the evil spirit, Asmodaeus. In answer to the prayers of Tobias the elder and Sara, the Lord sends the Archangel Raphael to earth disguised as a man named Azarias. Raphael accompanies the younger Tobias to Media, and while on the way, when Tobias is attacked by a "monstrous" fish as he washes in the River Tigris, Raphael tells him to seize it, and to remove its heart, gall, and liver because of their medicinal properties. Later, Tobias marries Sara upon the recommendation of Raphael, and upon entering the bridal chamber, burns a piece of the fish's liver on live coals which expels Asmodaeus, just as the Archangel had predicted. When Tobias returns home with Raphael (with Sara returning later), he takes the fish's gall and rubs it on the eyes of his Father, and soon after, his sight is restored. After prayerful thanksgiving, Raphael reveals something extraordinary:

When thou, Tobias, wert praying, and with tears, when thou wert burying the dead, leaving thy dinner untasted, so as to hide them all day in thy house, and at night give them funeral, *I, all the while, was offering that prayer of thine to the Lord.*... And now, for thy healing, for the deliverance of thy son's wife Sara from the fiend's attack, he has chosen me for his messenger. Who am I? I am the angel Raphael, and my place is among those seven who stand in the presence of the Lord. (Tob. 12:12, 14–15)

Raphael makes clear to Tobias the elder and his son, that it was God's will rather than his own that enabled him to come to them (Tob. 12:18). However, it shouldn't go unnoticed that this holy Archangel was silently interceding before the Throne of God on behalf of Tobias in an act of great individual charity. It is also important to note that Raphael's intervention was not restricted to just that of a messenger; it was far greater than that. His mission prefigured that of Jesus and the ministerial priesthood of the Church: healing, exorcism, teaching the sanctity of marriage, prayer, spiritual direction and a witness to the love and mercy of God. The significance for us is that God *willed* Raphael to act in this intercessory way, and therefore we can conclude that the company of heaven has the knowledge and power to embrace the suffering and needy, coming to their aid when required.

In the New Testament, we also see a substantial presence of these blessed members of the *Ecclesia triumphans*: the visitations of the Archangel Gabriel to Zachary (cf. Lk. 1:11–20) and then the Blessed Virgin (cf. Lk. 1:26–38), the appearance of the angel to Joseph in two dreams (cf. Matt. 1:20–23, 2:13), the angelic presence at the empty tomb (cf. Lk. 24:4–7), immediately after the Ascension (cf. Acts: 1:10–11), and in rescuing Peter from prison (cf. Acts. 12:7–10). The letter of St. Jude also makes reference to the "dispute" between St. Michael the Archangel and Satan over the body of Moses (cf. Jude. v.9).

Within the life of Jesus, we also sense the importance of the angels in the unfolding of the divine plan. Two decisive events demonstrate this. The first occurred after the temptations of the devil in the desert when the angels ministered to him (cf. Matt. 4:11). Although it is not stated, we may assume that they were in some way helping Jesus prepare for the road of suffering that lay ahead, perhaps by way of comfort and encouragement in light of the temptations he had just endured. For us, we can also see the powerful imagery of these spiritual beings to right and left of Jesus. The devil was literally hell bent on disrupting the Lord's mission to end his murderous reign. But once Jesus had overcome the temptations, heralding the Kingdom of light, the angels appeared ready to serve. In that way, the scene could be indicative of the Church in heaven anticipating its intercessory role for the Church on earth. St. Augustine in his Exposition on Psalm 138 seems to perceive something along these lines:

> There is a Church below, there is a Church above also; the Church below, in all the faithful; the Church above, in all the Angels. But the God of Angels came down to the Church below, and Angels ministered to Him on earth, (Matt. 4:11) while He ministered to us; for, "I came not," saith He, to be ministered unto, but to minister (Matt. 20:28).[26]

The ministering of the angels therefore seems to imitate the ministering of Jesus for the Church Militant; essentially, it is of a spiritual, salvific nature.

The second instance is that of the angel comforting Jesus in the Garden of Gethsemane (cf. Lk. 22:43). This intervention can be seen in a similar light. Luke records in his Gospel that the devil would return to tempt Jesus at the appointed time (cf. Lk. 4:13), and that time certainly came in the bitter agony on the evening of Holy Thursday.[27] What was the temptation exactly? Presumably it took on various forms: the futile sufferings for those who would despise him through the centuries; a cruel twist on the abandonment of his Father—that perhaps these sufferings would have no effect at all—

---

26. St. Augustine of Hippo, *Nicene and Post-Nicene Fathers: First Series,* vol. VIII (New York: Cosimo, 2007), 633.

27. Pope Benedict XVI states: "Every day, but particularly in Lent, Christians must face a struggle, like the one that Christ underwent in the desert of Judea, where for 40 days he was tempted by the devil, and then in Gethsemane, when he rejected the most severe temptation, accepting the Father's will to the very end." Pope Benedict XVI, "Homily for Ash Wednesday," March 1, 2006, www.vatican.va.

because the Father really had rejected him forever (inducing despair); the torments he was putting his Mother through, and the enticement of abandoning the divine will in order to escape the terrible sufferings that were beginning to engulf him. Now if the angel came to bring encouragement and strength, we can assume that he in some way helped the Lord fight these temptations, possibly through negating the devil's suggestions by recounting to Jesus the souls who would be saved by his redemption. However, what is unquestionable is that this member of the Church in glory appeared because he had the *ability* in some way to positively affect the human nature of the Lord in this most critical of hours.

What this also reveals is something wonderful concerning the angel's relationship with his Master. It could be tempting to view the angels as quasi-robotic emissaries who are merely "employed" by God; but what this passage of Scripture unveils is a most tender love between Creator and creature. At that moment, Jesus *needs* the Angel; that much is clear. If he didn't, there would have been no point in the angel being there. But in the silence and loneliness of his unimaginable anguish, with the apostles sleeping and Jesus wanting company (cf. Matt. 26:40), the angel intervenes to bring consolation and love. It tells us that the Heart of God is movable, capable of being touched by the love of all his creatures. This is an astounding truth when we consider it in all its implications. The Almighty is in a sense "vulnerable!" And that is why the angels and saints have the power of intercession because the Heart of Jesus is open and responsive to them; there is no pretence, only the joy of acceding to their humble requests for intervention.

In the Lord's teaching on the Kingdom of God, the presence of the angels is never far away. We are told that the angels rejoice over the repentance of sinners (cf. Lk. 15:10); that the angels of the "little ones" are continually in the presence of the Eternal Father (cf. Matt. 18:10) (which seems to relate to the ministry/intercession of guardian angels for every individual). In the questioning of the Sadducees concerning the issue of marriage in heaven, the Lord replied by saying that children of the resurrection will be like the angels because they cannot die any longer (cf. Lk. 20:27–40). And in the Gospel of St. John, when Jesus met Nathanael, he told him: "Believe me when

I tell you this; you will see heaven opening, and the angels of God going up and coming down upon the Son of Man" (Jn. 1:51). St. Augustine saw in this prophecy a primitive teaching concerning Jesus's divinity *and* his presence within the Mystical body. By saying the angels descend and ascend to him, the Lord has to be both above and below. Therefore, applying Jesus's words to the persecuting Saul "why dost thou persecute me?" (Acts. 9:4), (meaning the Church), Augustine sees the angels descending to him in a different but very real way.[28] Although the Bishop of Hippo doesn't say it, by extension, the descending of the angels to the Church implies a ministering of intercession: invisible for the most part, but similar to the way prefigured by Raphael in his intervention with Tobias.

Finally, there is the eschatological dimension of the angels. Jesus tells us that at the end of the world "the Son of Man will give charge to his angels, and they will gather up all that gives offence in his kingdom, all those who do wickedly in it, and will cast them into the furnace of fire, where there will be weeping, and gnashing of teeth" (Matt. 13:41–42). In a similar passage, the Lord also reveals how the angels will be with him as he descends on the clouds of heaven to pronounce the Last Judgment: "When the Son of Man comes in his glory, and all the angels with him, he will sit down upon the throne of his glory, and all nations will be gathered in his presence, where he will divide men one from the other, as the shepherd divides the sheep from the goats" (Matt. 25:31–32). This apocalyptic scenario corresponds to that which we saw in the Book of Revelation; that part of the angelic mission is to rid the world of impurity by executing God's justice and thus cleansing humanity and creation in readiness for his glorious return.

As in the case of the saints, the patristic era also saw an interest in developing a theology of the angels. St. Gregory the Great for instance, presented a rich exposition on these blessed spirits in his *Homily* 34 *on the Gospels* in which he posits various teachings concerning their nature and ministry. Taking as his starting point Luke chapter fifteen, which concerns the parables of the lost sheep and

---

28. Cf. St. Augustine, Sermo 72, *Sermons on Selected Lessons of the New Testament*, vol. II (Oxford: John Henry Parker, 1845), 520.

the woman who loses one of her ten silver coins, and concludes with the Lord's words that there will be rejoicing among the angels over one repentant sinner (cf. Lk. 15:10), the Pope expounds upon the integration between humanity and the angels as part of the Church in glory.

Concerning the parable of the Lost Sheep, St. Gregory notes that there were 100, which is, symbolically, a perfect number. But one sheep was lost when the human (Adam) left the pasture of God by sinning; therefore 99 were left in the desert. These 99 constitute the majestic choirs of angels in heaven, and in order to restore the amount to the perfect sum, Jesus goes in search of the lost sheep. Upon finding the lost sheep, the Lord places it on his shoulders and carries it back to his Kingdom; meanwhile the angels rejoice at this restoration and unification of the blessed. Similarly, in the parable of the lost coin, when it is found, the friends and neighbors are invited to rejoice by the woman, which symbolizes the heavenly powers: "They are close to the highest Wisdom when they draw near to him through the grace of their continuous vision."[29] St. Gregory also sees symbolism in the amount of coins: nine in reference to the choirs of angels, and the tenth (lost and found) referring to humanity:

> There are nine orders of angels, and humanity was created as the tenth; thus the number of the elect has been made perfect. . . . We spoke of the nine orders of angels because we know that sacred scripture clearly bears witness to Angels, Archangels, Virtues, Powers, Principalities, Dominations, Thrones, Cherubim, and Seraphim. . . . The books of the prophets, as is known, often speak of the Cherubim and Seraphim. And the apostle Paul enumerated the names of four orders when he said to the Ephesians: *Above every principality and power and virtue and domination.* Again writing to the Colossians he said, *whether thrones or powers or principalities or dominations. . . .* Thus when the Thrones are joined to those four orders he had spoken of in Ephesians, that is, Principalities, Powers, Virtues and Dominations, there are five

29. Stephen Chase, *Angelic Spirituality: Medieval Perspectives on the Ways of Angels* (Mahwah: Paulist Press, 2002), 97.

orders that are mentioned. When Angels, Archangels, Cherubim and Seraphim are added, nine orders of angels are found to exist.[30]

St. Gregory also makes an interesting distinction between the name "angel" (which in Greek means "messenger") and the actual spirit. He says that the name signifies their ministry rather than their essential nature:

> For the holy spirits of the heavenly homeland are indeed always spirits, but they are by no means always able to be called angels, since they are only "angels" when some message is announced through them. Thus the psalmist says, he makes his spirits angels.[31]

In this hierarchy, it is archangels who are given the most important tasks, and consequently, they are given names to emphasize this. In the case of St. Michael, which means "who is like God," the name signifies the Archangel's interventions through which evils are overcome by good; and as Pope Gregory points out, it is the power of God manifest through him. Fitting it is then, that as the Apocalypse shows, St. Michael battles and defeats him who would be like God. For St. Gabriel, which means "the strength of God," we encounter the Archangel who announces the coming of the Son who will destroy with his strength even death itself. Finally, as we have already seen, St. Raphael is the beholder of "the healing of God."

The great Pontiff also takes it upon himself to describe how titles indicate specific duties assigned to each group of angels: *Virtues* are spirits through whom signs and wonders are most frequently accomplished. *Powers,* who comprehend greatly the nature of potency, work to halt the evil influence of opposing spirits. *Principalities* preside over the spirits of good angels, ensuring their divine ministries are carried out. *Dominations* transcend the power of Principalities and arrange whatever must be accomplished by angels under their authority. *Thrones* are filled with such divine grace that God manifests his justice through them, while *Cherubim* are so filled with perfect knowledge "that they contemplate the glory of

---

30. Ibid., 97.
31. Ibid., 98.

God from the vantage point of immediate proximity."[32] The *Seraphim* burn with such an intense love for the Creator that no other angel may intervene between themselves and God; nothing is able to break this fiery intimacy that consumes them constantly.

St. Gregory then asks the question: what profit is there for us to contemplate these angelic spirits? His answer begins by suggesting that the Church Triumphant will be populated by as many humans as there are angels who did not rebel, and because the humans are ascending through purification, they should aspire to imitate the angels:

> Clearly, there are ways of human life that coincide with single orders of angelic bands. By means of a correspondence in virtue, these people are counted worthy of the heavenly city by sharing in the angelic nature.... For instance there are many people who comprehend little but who do not desist from making the little they do know piously available to their brothers and sisters. These people dwell among the angels. And there are other brothers and sisters who have been revived by the gifts of divine bounty and who succeed in receiving and announcing the highest secrets of heaven. Where can we include these men and women except among the Archangels?[33]

The Saint continues along this train of thought by comparing those on earth who perform miracles with the *Virtues* and those involved in the deliverance ministry, exorcists etc. with the *Powers*.

What therefore do we come away with from this great exposition on the heavenly realm? Without doubt, Pope Gregory desires that we see the Mystical Body in its great unity; that there is a certain parallelism between humanity in its ascendance and the angelic choirs in their blessedness. The astounding knowledge and love of the Cherubim and Seraphim for instance, speak of the saints similarly endowed with great wisdom and love; while the integration of activity and contemplation affecting both demonstrates that virtuous works and prayer are not opposed, as we saw clearly in the ministry of Raphael. As God is not circumscribed, the blessed spirits

32. Ibid., 100.
33. Ibid., 101.

and the Christian faithful are able to minister in practical ways without ever leaving the divine presence. For the Angels it is the glorious vision of God; and for the devout on earth, contemplation deriving from the indwelling of the Holy Spirit.

St. Thomas Aquinas in his *Summa Theologica* also dealt at length with questions relating to angels and their activity, and although it would need a book on its own to do it justice, for our purposes it will suffice to offer a few insights from this *Doctor Angelicus*.

To begin with, St. Thomas places the existence of angels within the context of a perfect universe in which God wills that He be known and understood entirely by his creatures. For this to happen there is the requirement of intellectual beings whose intelligence derives from God himself: "And the perfect assimilation of an effect to a cause is accomplished when the effect imitates the cause according to that whereby the cause produces the effect; as heat makes heat. Now, God produces the creature by His intellect and will. Hence the perfection of the universe requires that there should be intellectual creatures."[34] St. Thomas argues that as intelligence cannot come from any corporeal faculty which suffers from the restriction imposed by the limits of "here" and "now," a perfected universe requires pure spirits: "Movement [of the angels] is there taken in the sense in which it is applied to intelligence and will. Therefore an angel is called an ever mobile substance, because he is ever actually intelligent, and not as if he were sometimes actually and sometimes potentially, as we are."[35]

A question that naturally occurs in the wake of this discussion is whether angels have a will, and if it is free will. St. Thomas responds positively to both. He affirms that as angelic intellect derives from the divine will, it must be inclined to that which is good; therefore it seeks it with both understanding and will. Taking this logic a step further, he states that where there is intellect, there has to be free will because knowledge allows the spirit to make a judgment ascer-

34. St. Thomas Aquinas, *Summa Theologica*, Prima Pars, 50, 1, www.newadvent. org.

35. St. Thomas Aquinas, *Summa Theologica*, Prima Pars, 50, 1. 2, www.newavent .org.

taining whether something is good or not, and in that judgment, free will is available to pursue the good. Conversely, irrational creatures who act on natural instinct alone cannot possess free will because their intelligence is not sufficient to override the instinct.

One of the most fascinating aspects of angelic theology found in the *Summa* concerns the perfection of the angels in the holy city: were they created in beatitude or grace? Did they undergo an ontological change after admittance to the beatific vision? Can they still sin? Is there the possibility of advancement in their spiritual state? In answer to the first question, the great Dominican excludes the possibility of the immediate beatific vision because biblical revelation reveals that Lucifer and his legion fell, and in the beatific vision it is not possible to sin, as we read:

> The beatified angels cannot sin . . . their beatitude consists in seeing God through His essence. Now, God's essence is the very essence of goodness . . . it is impossible for any man either to will or to do anything except aiming at what is good; or for him to wish to turn away from good precisely as such. Therefore the beatified angel can neither will nor act, except as aiming towards God. Now whoever wills or acts in this manner cannot sin. Consequently the beatified angel cannot sin.[36]

St. Thomas states that their angelic dignity meant that these blessed spirits were created with a natural perfection which came from their innocence. However, in order to receive the ultimate beatitude—the vision of God's essence—grace would be required, due to the fact that created intellect was not sufficient on its own to direct the will towards something higher than its nature. Nonetheless, once this grace was bestowed upon them, coupled with their inclination to natural perfection, only one act of charity was necessary for reception of the beatific vision. And as we have seen, the absence of an inclination to sin after beholding the divine vision proves an ontological change took place. But the Angelic Doctor also suggests that natural knowledge and love, which they were originally endowed with, remains as well: "Now it is manifest that nature is to beatitude

36. Ibid., 62, 8.

as first to second; because beatitude is superadded to nature. But the first must ever be preserved in the second. Consequently nature must be preserved in beatitude: and in like manner the act of nature must be preserved in the act of beatitude."[37] This means that the natural forms were not replaced but *perfected* by the new higher form of holiness.

The final question addressed by St. Thomas in this particular section of the *Summa* asks if angels can advance in beatitude once the beatific vision is beheld. He answers negatively for the simple reason that merit only applies to a subject (man or angel) that is moving towards its end; working actively towards the summit of God's presence. Perfect charity unlike imperfect has no quality of merit; instead it basks in the enjoyment of the reward. In a sense as St. Paul says: "I have finished the race" (2 Tim. 4:7). Once the race is over there is no more to be gained by running; the position is fixed, and in that sense, St. Thomas concludes that according to divine predestination, the angels are in their highest degree possible. He does however state that the angels can gain an increase in *joy* from the salvation of those on earth to whom they minister; but this comes not from merit, but rather from the "virtue of their beatitude."[38]

The reflections we have made thus far in this chapter have allowed us to grasp the full scope of the heavenly Church in its glorious state. We realize that in the marvellous plan of God, the saints and angels are still close to us, closer than we could dare to hope. The graves of our loved ones may tell the story of the scourge of sin and its awful consequence; but our faith—the faith of our Mother the Church—tells a different story. It narrates the truth of a future blossoming from the winter of death to the advent of eternal spring. And in this spring we move from the Church to the Church; by which I mean we remain within the same Mystical Body, in the same communion of love in which we participated on earth. Pope Benedict XVI describes it with beautiful imagery:

37. Ibid., 62, 7.
38. Ibid., 62, 9.3.

Visiting a botanical nursery garden, one is amazed by the variety of plants and flowers, and often one is drawn to think of the imagination of the Creator who has given the earth a wonderful garden. A similar feeling of wonder strikes us when we consider the spectacle of sainthood: the world appears to us as a "garden," where the Spirit of God has given life with admirable imagination to a multitude of men and women Saints.... All of them, however, were impressed with the 'seal' of Jesus (cf. Rv. 7:3) or the imprint of his love witnessed through the Cross. They are all in joy, in a festival without end, but, like Jesus, they achieved this goal passing through difficulties and trials (cf. Rv. 7:14).... On this day we revive within us our attraction to Heaven, which impels us to quicken the steps of our earthly pilgrimage. We feel enkindled in our hearts the desire to unite ourselves forever to the family of Saints, in which already now we have the grace to partake.[39]

Within this one family of saints, the Apocalypse allows us to peer behind the curtain of our uncertainty to see how similar the Church Triumphant is to the Church Militant. The difference is in the degree of holiness and charity that pervades the company of the blessed. Liturgically speaking, at the heart of both is the one desire to worship the God of creation, who wills to extend the communion of love within his three divine Persons to those created in his image. But It would be wrong to think that in the exalted company of heaven, and the glory of the beatific vision, those blessed members have no thought or memory of us; for if the Lord never forgets us, how could they, who follow him wherever he goes? (cf. Rev. 14:4). The basis for our gladness lies in the truth that they are the Church, and as such they act like the Church, through prayer and concern for those fellow pilgrims in the communion of saints. In our favor, they offer intercession from one essential vantage point: that of breathing sanctity from within the divine will; and consequently, prayer is always channelled in a way that God desires. That is the fruit of spiritual perfection.

To conclude this discussion, I would like to recall the title of this chapter: *Company of the Blessed: The Testament of Divine Victory.*

---

39. Pope Benedict XVI, "Angelus Address," November 1, 2008, www.vatican.va.

The saints in particular offer an eloquent prophetic witness to the triumph of God's love over the evil aspirations of the hellish cohort. In them, we see the possibility to say "no" to the voices that suggest we gently lay down the Cross without the Lord hearing; "no" to those who urge us to embrace a conformist spiritual worldliness. Instead, we have the joy of knowing a multitude that have already trampled on the Evil One through living the beatitudes in exemplary fashion. They must be our inspiration and guides in the violent struggle that seems to increase with each passing year. But like Jesus, who held out his hand to Peter (cf. Matt. 14:31), the saints too hold out their hands encouraging us to trust in the Lord's words proclaiming final victory: "take courage, I have overcome the world" (Jn. 16:33).

✺ 11 ✺

The Golden Censer:
Incense and Intercession

There was another angel that came and took his stand at the altar, with a censer of gold; and incense was given him in plenty, so that he could make an offering on the golden altar before the throne, out of the prayers said by all the saints. So, from the angel's hand, the smoke of the incense went up in God's presence, kindled by the saints' prayer. (Rev. 8:3–4)

IN PART TWO, we reflected upon the issue of intercession directed from the Church Militant to the Church Suffering. We discovered the possibilities that come with a loving concern for these poor souls; opportunities to put faith into practise on behalf of the helpless. In this chapter, the tables are turned somewhat. We will, in a sense, look down from the Church above to the Church below, trying to discern how the saints involve themselves in the lives of those in need on earth. There are also several offshoots from this doctrine: the veneration of saints, the use of statues and sacred images, pilgrimages to shrines and the reverence given to holy relics. All these spiritual elements combine to strengthen the bonds that exist within the communion of saints and all need to be addressed somewhat in order to appreciate the blessings that come from living the doctrine to the full.

In the previous chapter, we examined the theology behind the angels' and saints' ability to intercede for the *Ecclesia Militans*. We saw that Sacred Scripture clearly demonstrates a heavenly liturgy in which the blessed are offering prayers before God's throne. With that in mind, we can ask the question: what evidence is there that this intercessory power produces tangible results? It is a vitally important question from a contemporary viewpoint, considering the quite devastating way rationalism has weakened the sense of the supernatural, leading to a descent into neo-paganism, and it must be said apostasy, especially in the West. For many Catholics though, this intercession from the blessed is a treasure greater than any jewel. It is a channel of grace from which many jobs have been found, health restored, babies conceived, vocations discovered, and lost items recovered. Of course, the sceptics will dismiss such interventions as pure coincidence or a sort of placebo effect; but for the faithful who at times have found themselves in desperate situations, there is nothing more consoling than knowing the perfect charity of these friends in heaven.

Looking at this beautiful reality objectively, the process of beatification and canonization is a good point of reference for this discussion, as this is where we find some of the most astonishing interventions from the Church Triumphant.

The Divine Seal of Approval

After the death of a member of the Mystical Body, one renowned for holiness, a process may begin (normally five years later), in which a diocesan investigation is opened by the bishop (with the approval of the Vatican). The investigation determines whether the candidate lived the virtues to a heroic degree. At this point they are referred to as "servant of God." If a diocesan tribunal and then the bishop conclude with a positive answer, the *Acta* (documentation of the case) is sent to the Congregation for the Causes of Saints in Rome where a Relator compiles the *positio*—a volume detailing the formal argument for the approval of canonization. Once this is complete, a theological commission votes on the cause, and their recommendation is then passed to the Cardinal Prefect of the Congregation along with the other bishops of the dicastery, who in turn vote. If approval is given, the recommendation of a *Decree of Heroic Virtues* is sent to the Holy Father, whose judgment is final. If the Pope says yes, the candidate is then known as "venerable." At this point the venerable are one step away from beatification. Beatification means official papal approval for public veneration of the individual at a local level, or within religious institutes associated with the candidate. The beati are known as "blessed."

It is between the stages of venerable and blessed that the *sanctorum communio* comes to the fore. In order for the beatification ceremony to proceed, the candidate must have a miracle attributed to their intercession, thus showing their influence before the throne of God. The miracle is then investigated in the diocese where the miracle occurred by scientific and theological commissions. The criteria confirming a miracle is that it must have no natural explanation and must have permanence in regard to any healing. The theological commission decides whether the event can be attributed to the intercession of the person in question. So, for instance, was the beneficiary of the miracle either praying to this person specifically, or were others doing so on their behalf? The preference in both commissions is for instantaneous cures where doctors had given up any hope; although as we shall see, this is not the only type of miraculous intervention attributable to the saints. If the diocesan commission approves the miracle, the judgement and documentation is forwarded to Rome to be studied again by two more commissions who then vote along with the Cardinal and bishops of the Congregation for the Causes of Saints. The last hurdle is for the Supreme Pontiff to approve the reality of this miracle. The same process occurs in the final step from beatification to canonization; although the second miracle needed at this point must have occurred after the beatification ceremony.[1]

Perhaps one of the most intriguing aspects of this subject is that in an age when the focus has somewhat shifted away from the mystical element of the Church, and with it, a sense of the totality of union with the Church Suffering and Triumphant, the Lord has granted more saints and blessed than ever before. In effect, this has meant that there has been a more or less continuous stream of inexplicable interventions that have illuminated the workings of the heavenly citizens, and yet, disconcertingly, at times it seems as if we have become almost embarrassed to speak of it. In fact, St. John

---

1. The Pope has the authority to waive the necessity of a miracle. Pope Francis did just that in canonizing Pope John XXIII on April 27, 2014.

Paul II faced much criticism from some quarters for "making" so many saints, when in fact it was the Lord's will to grant miracles in response to the prayers of these blessed souls. We should not be afraid to raise our voices in joyful thanksgiving to God for allowing His generosity to become manifest in such an extraordinary way. By neglecting to proclaim these wonders we only serve to diminish the remembrance that makes the saints present to us, and thus we become more detached from the vitality of the communion of love that binds us together.

I believe it is useful at this juncture to look briefly at several of the many miracles that have been approved by the Popes in the canonization process, as this will illustrate perfectly the quality of intercessory prayer lining the golden censer held by the angel ministering at the altar of heaven (cf. Rev. 8:3).

The first relates to the canonization of the Maltese priest, St. George Preca. In July 2001 a newborn named Eric Catania had developed severe liver problems and was sent to a local hospital in Malta. His condition worsened and so he was transferred to King's College Hospital in London. On July 14, doctors concluded he would die if he didn't have a liver transplant. Faced with this devastating news, Eric's Catholic parents prayed for the miraculous intercession of Blessed George Preca; they placed a glove on his body that had touched the body of Blessed George during his exhumation. On July 20, his liver began to function normally and four days later, doctors decided that surgery was no longer required because Eric's liver had recovered completely. Anil Dhawan, a professor of paediatric hepatology at King's College Hospital, who testified before the canonization medical Commission in Rome stated: "There was a 90 percent plus chance that he wasn't going to survive without a liver transplant. But he survived. Furthermore, he improved on his own. Acute liver failure in children is quite a devastating illness. The majority of them die. Scientifically I do not have an explanation for this child's recovery."[2]

---

2. http://www.telegraph.co.uk/news/worldnews/1552423/Babys-miracle-recovery-in-British-hospital-to-give-Malta-its-first-saint.html.

St. Louis de Montfort, the great teacher of authentic Marian spirituality, will be a name familiar to many Catholics who love the Rosary, but the miracle attributed to his intercession and approved as part of his canonization process is not well known. I have been in the most fortunate situation to live just a few miles from where this wonderful event took place; therefore I am familiar with the episode. On September 11, 1924, Sister Gerard of Calvary, a religious of the Congregation of the Daughters of Wisdom (founded by St. Louis de Montfort) arrived at the Convent in Romsey, England. Since 1922 she had begun to suffer from intense abdominal pain and subsequently a sever cough. For many months after arriving at Romsey, she had been unable to perform any duties due to this terrible suffering. On February 5th, 1925, she was operated on at Romsey Nursing Home by Dr. Cowan, chief surgeon of the South Hampshire Hospital at Southampton, assisted by Dr. Van Someren. The operation involved removing a tumor. Following this, Dr. Van Someren told the Reverend Mother that within two or three years, the disease would spread. Unfortunately his diagnosis was correct, and Sister Gerard continued to suffer abdominal pain with frequent discharges of pus from the operation wound. Things deteriorated so much that by December 1926 she was fainting regularly. Dr. Van Someren, declared that he could do nothing for her. Tubercular peritonitis was general and the intestines had been affected. By March 1927, she was struggling with terrible convulsions and on April 3 she was given the Last Sacraments. On April 8, it was obvious to the other sisters that she was dying; her pulse was imperceptible, her breathing was "Cheyne-Stokes";[3] her feet and hands were cold and discoloured and her eyes were sunken. Her abdomen was greatly swollen and her body gave off an overpowering odor.

On this same day, the sisters completed a novena to the then Blessed Louis de Montfort, and the Mother Provincial of the Daughters of Wisdom, who had come to visit Sister Gerard, pre-

---

3. Cheyne–Stokes respiration is an abnormal pattern of breathing characterized by progressively deeper and sometimes faster breathing, followed by a gradual decrease that results in a temporary stop in breathing called an apnea.

pared her to make her perpetual vows. Before the ceremony she had a relic of Blessed Louis brought into the room and gave it to the dying Sister to kiss, afterwards putting it under her pillow. Sister Gerard then uttered her vows in a voice that was scarcely audible. The Mother Provincial then said in a loud voice: "Blessed Father, this is the last appeal that we address to you on behalf of one of your daughters. From your place in heaven deign to look down on her and cure her." Then three Hail Marys and three invocations to Blessed Louis were said. At this point the community of nuns left the room and the Mother Provincial left for a few moments to assist at Benediction.

While Sister Gerard was alone, her pains grew more violent, so she prayed to her founding Father and took hold of his relic from under her pillow, murmuring: "If the others must suffer from my death, I am ready to stay on earth, if it be God's will." All at once, Sister Gerard, being in full possession of her senses, saw a cloud of incense at the foot of her bed, and in this cloud she perceived very clearly the figure of the Blessed Virgin, all radiant with light. She could not make out clearly the expression on Our Lady's face, but she distinctly heard a voice say: "Child, what has it to be?" Unable to speak, Sister Gerard replied by a murmur, and immediately, turning her head to the right, saw Blessed Louis de Montfort near her bed and outside of the cloud. His figure was quite clear, and she recognized him at once by the habit of the Montfort Missionaries that he was wearing, and by his long hair, like that seen in portraits of him. He smiled at her with a heavenly countenance. As soon as she saw him, she said: "Father, give me your blessing." Thereupon, she closed her eyes, made the sign of the cross with the relic and applied it to the spot where the pain was most severe. On opening her eyes, Sister Gerard felt that the pain had gone and saw that she was alone. At the spot where she had seen the Blessed Virgin, there remained only a light cloud which vanished about a minute afterwards. The Mother Provincial returned within ten minutes to discover Sister Gerard sitting up and crying out: "I am cured! I am cured!" From that moment on, Sister Gerard was completely cured, and by April 11, she was polishing the entire corridor and two classrooms, while making a swift return to study. The wound from the operation was no longer visible, and she took no further medication. St. Louis de Montfort was canonized by Pope Pius XII on July 20, 1947.[4]

As I mentioned earlier, cures of terminal health conditions are not the only type of miracles granted by the Lord through his saints. One of the most breathtaking occurred on a Peruvian submarine, the *BAP Pacocha*. On the evening of August 26, 1988, the *Pacocha* collided with the 412-ton Japanese fishing trawler *Kiowa Maru*. Four men, including the captain died immediately and the submarine sank to a depth of fifteen meters. Inside the vessel, with water flooding the compartment where the survivors were, Lieutenant Roger Cotrina Alvarado realized that the pressure from the water was going to make closing an internal hatch impossible. He recounts: "I couldn't breathe and so I began to think as hard as I could about Sister Maria Petkovic (foundress of the Congregation of the Daughters of Mercy). I closed my eyes and I prayed. I repeated the prayer that I had heard, I thought of her and suddenly I saw a brilliant light."[5] Immediately, he was given strength to close the hatch, despite later calculations from a commission of scientific experts who concluded the water pressure was 3.8 tons.[6] Two commissions, one military and one from the Vatican, considered it humanly impossible for Lieutenant Cotrina to do what he did in those few seconds. Twenty-two survived the disaster. But why was a Peruvian submariner invoking the intercession of a Croatian nun who died in 1966? Alvarado explained: "When I was little, I heard the story of Maria Petkovic because my mother had a book on her, and every night she read a few pages to me before I went to bed.... For me, Maria Petkovic was an extraordinary woman, she helped the poor of the whole world, in particular those of South America."[7] Maria

4. The description of the miraculous cure of Sister Gerard of Calvary can be found here: www.montfort.org.uk/Documents/St Louis Marie de Montfort (Canonization book).pdf.

5. *See*, http://www.catholicnewsagency.com/news/documentary_on_miracle_o f_pacocha_submarine_debuts_in_peru/.

6. *See*, http://www.30giorni.it/articoli_id_3664_l3.htm?id=3664.

7. *See*, http://www.zenit.org/en/articles/submarine-crew-owed-survival-to-croati an-s-intercession.

Petkovic, who was beatified by St. John Paul II on June 6, 2003, had founded orphanages and charitable centers in Latin America.[8]

One of the interesting ways God allows this flow of intercessory prayer to work is that the choices of positive intervention are never arbitrary. There is always a specific reason that illuminates not only the mercy of the Lord, but also the close ties that exist between the suffering and the blessed soul; as we saw in the case of Roger Alvarado and Blessed Maria Petkovic, the seeds were sown years before. Famously, the miracle used for the beatification of Pope John Paul II was the curing of Parkinson's disease from the ravaged body of a French nun, Sister Marie Simon Pierre; the Pope had suffered for years with the same ailment. In the case of St. Luigi Orione, it was the disappearance of a lung tumor from the 78-year-old Pierino Penacca, who had known Don Orione in his youth. And for the canonization of the Italian physician and mother of four, Gianna Beretta Molla, it was the miraculous saving of an unborn Brazilian baby who had no chance to survive considering the total absence of amniotic fluid and other complications from very early in the pregnancy. It was Elisabete Comparini Arcolino's fourth baby. This case was doubly significant because St. Gianna had sacrificed her own life in order that *her* fourth baby could survive, and also because in her youth she had wanted to go to Brazil as a volunteer doctor. The rich symbolism is intensified when we consider that the miracle required for her beatification also involved a Brazilian baby.

The Glory of Unity and Love in the Mystical Body

The conviction that the Lord entrusts our spiritual wellbeing at least in part to the saints, leads us to consider the essential aspect of our veneration of them. It has been a major stumbling block in ecu-

---

8. Another miracle not related to cures, occurred through the intercession of the Spanish Friar, St. Juan Macias, canonized in 1975 by Blessed Paul VI. This was the multiplication of rice in Olivenza, near the Saint's home town of Rivera del Fresno. The cook of a canteen for the impoverished was running short of rice (she only had one and a half pounds worth) and so prayed to the Friar. The multiplication allowed 150 hungry people to eat. *See*, the *Observer Reporter*, Washington, PA, September 29, 1975 edition, Section B.

menical dialogue ever since the Reformation, because for Protestants Jesus's one mediation with the Eternal Father has meant all avenues have been closed to any form of advocacy emanating from the Blessed Virgin or anyone else within the company of the blessed. Unfortunately, that view, while perhaps well-meaning in terms of ensuring the unique redemptive act of Jesus is not downplayed, has also necessarily meant a certain refashioning of the figure of the Lord so that he appears almost in isolation from his own Church. This view is contrary to the clear biblical evidence that the Lord wills a communion of love where people work for each other from within him, so to speak, in order to benefit from the fruits of his redemption. The veneration of the saints, far from being a threat to the worship due to God alone, actually reinforces it because the devotee sees the results of divine activity in the sanctified soul, and therefore recognizes the power behind it—thus spurring an increased effort to draw closer to the Lord.

Authentic veneration is also nothing more than affirming the holiness that vivifies the entire Mystical Body; on the one hand drawing the two states of the Church closer together in the form of the two souls (the saint of fulfilment and the saint of the novitiate), and on the other hand inspiring the devotee to imitate the same virtues that led the saint to stand in the presence of the Lamb. St. Bernard of Clairvaux, in a homily for the Feast of All Saints, places the concept of veneration firmly within the context of the One Church in which humility allows us to reverence those whom we have seen clothe themselves with Christ (cf. Gal. 3:27):

> The saints have no need of honor from us; neither does our devotion add the slightest thing to what is already theirs. Clearly, when we venerate their memory, it is serving us, not them. But I tell you, when I think of them, I feel myself inflamed by a tremendous longing to be with them. Calling the saints to mind inspires, or rather arouses in us, above all else, a longing to enjoy their company which is desirable in itself. We long to share in the citizenship of heaven, to dwell with the spirits of the blessed, to join the assembly of patriarchs, the ranks of the prophets, the council of apostles, the great host of martyrs, the noble company of confessors and the choir of virgins. In short, we long to be united in hap-

piness with all the saints.... Come, let us at length spur ourselves on. We must rise again with Christ, we must seek the world which is above and set our mind on the things of heaven. Let us long for those who are longing for us, hasten to those who are waiting for us, and ask those who look for our coming to intercede for us. We should not only want to be with the saints, we should also hope to possess their happiness.[9]

The veneration of saints has developed throughout the centuries in various forms and for a variety of reasons; we can think of the great devotion to St. Thomas the Apostle in India because of his evangelization there at the dawn of Christianity, or similarly to Saints Cyril and Methodius who brought the Gospel to the Slavic peoples of Eastern Europe in the ninth century. At times, the Lord also encourages specific devotion through the extraordinary out-pouring of grace that is evident in places where the saints lived and worked. Often these places become pilgrimage destinations where souls are refreshed through sacramental confession and penance, and in many cases catalysts for complete conversions of heart.[10] One such destination, perhaps little known outside the British Isles, is St. Winefride's Well in Flintshire, Wales.

The story relates to Winefride, a beautiful and saintly seventh-century girl. She was proposed marriage by Caradog, the son of a chieftain, but because she desired perpetual virginity, she rejected his request. Caradog became enraged and beheaded her. Winefride's head rolled down the hill and when it stopped, a powerful spring instantly burst forth. Over time, the Well became a pilgrimage destination, which today still attracts many pilgrims. Fr. John Gerard, a Jesuit priest during the Reformation, has left us a wonderful historic record of the miraculous nature of the place and of his pilgrimage there. Although Fr. Gerard only gave the date of November 3 for his visit, it probably occurred in the early 1590s:

---

9. Robert Atwell, *Celebrating the Saints* (Norwich: Canterbury Press, 2004), 643–644.

10. The pilgrimage on foot to the Shrine of St. James at Santiago de Compostela, Spain is one which is often taken up by the young; as is the Shrine of St. Francis at Assisi, Italy.

Once I was there on the 3rd of November, St, Winefride's feast, and saw the change that takes place in the Well that day. (The water rises a good foot above its ordinary level, and turns red[11] as it rises, but the next day it is clearer than ever.) I myself watched the water moving and turning a reddish color, water (mind you) that on any other day is so remarkably clear that you can pick out a pin lying on the bottom.[12]

Fr. Gerard also recounts some other supernatural events at this holy place in his autobiography *The Hunted Priest*:

There is the story of the Protestant visitor who was watching some Catholics bathe and stood mocking their devotion. "What are they up to washing here in the water? I'll show them. I'll clean my boots in it." So in he jumped, boots, sword and all. Scarcely had he touched the water than he felt its supernatural powers which he had refused to believe in. There and then he was struck with paralysis: he lost the use of his limbs; his sword could hardly be pulled out of his grip. For several years afterwards he was wheeled around in a push-cart like a cripple. . . . I have myself spoken to a number of people who saw the crippled man and heard the story both from his own lips and from men who knew him. It was they who told me the sequel: how the man repented and recovered the use of his limbs in the very well where he had been struck down.[13]

The Well is most famous for the amount of cures of people with various ailments, much like the Marian Shrine of Lourdes, France. Today, there remains a collection of crutches dating back several centuries from people who no longer needed them after bathing in the hallowed water.

Fr. Gerard recounts the story of his friend, Blessed Edward Old-corne, one of the glorious martyrs of Elizabethan England. Fr. Old-corne was suffering from a form of mouth cancer which he thought would stop him preaching, so he decided to go on pilgrimage to St. Winefride's. On his way, he stopped at the house of two sisters who

---

11. This relates to the blood of the saint. The rocks within the well are also the color of fresh blood, and Fr. Gerard recounts how pilgrims would chip off bits, and at the place where they were chipped, it would then turn from white to red.

12. Fr. John Gerard, *The Hunted Priest* (London: Collins, 1951), 62.

13. Ibid., 62–63.

had a priest staying with them secretly. This priest had already been to the Well and taken a stone covered in the blood of the Saint. During Mass, the stone used to be placed on the altar with other relics. When Fr. Oldcorne noticed this he "took it in his hands and kissed it reverently. Then, going aside by himself, he went down on his knees and began to lick the stone and hold part of it to his mouth. He prayed silently all the time. After half an hour he got up: all the pain was gone and the cancer cured."[14] Fr. Oldcorne then carried on to the Shrine in thanksgiving rather than supplication.

Fr. Gerard was fond of recounting heavenly interventions during these dark days, probably because they illuminated the doctrine of the merits of the saints at a time when they were greatly under threat from the Lutheran influence. He recounts several other striking manifestations of God's blessing on the saintly witnesses, which give us good reason to acknowledge that veneration of these faithful heroes is a vital component of the communion of saints.

One instance concerns St. John Rigby, who appeared before the courts on behalf of the daughter of Sir Edmund Huddlestone, his employer. She was sick and had asked him to testify to this. While doing so, under questioning, he admitted that he had been reconciled with Rome. Later at his trial: "He heard the [death] sentence with great joy, and while it was being pronounced, the chains in which he stood bound before the court, came loose and fell from his legs. The gaoler replaced them, but (I think I am right) they fell a second time."[15]

Two further instances relate to the capture and martyrdom of Blessed Edward Oldcorne. In the first, Fr. Gerard reveals that in the courtyard of the house where he had been arrested, an "imperial crown" had formed in the grass, grass that was completely different in shade and texture to the grass surrounding it. It was also taller than the other grass. After the arrest, the house was abandoned and animals found their way into the courtyard through the broken gate. For several months they grazed there, but not one ate or trod on the crown. It was viewed as an indication of Blessed Edward

14. Ibid., 63.
15. Ibid., 92.

Oldcorne's eternal reward.[16] The second instance concerns the fact that at his execution, his intestines, when thrown on the fire, burned continuously for sixteen days which corresponded to the sixteen years he had preached in England. It was also noted that during torrential rain, the flames grew higher.[17]

One of the ways in which the communion of the *ecclesia militans* and *ecclesia triumphans* becomes palpable is through the veneration of holy relics. These relics can be classed in three categories: first class, which are part of the saint, (for example, bones or hair); second class, items of clothing worn by the saint or items belonging to them, and third class, items which have touched a first or second class relic. But is this reverence not rather ghoulish and superstitious? The answer, as in all answers concerning the saints and their heavenly enterprise has a Christological center. In the case of relics, we are drawn back to the primary event of fundamental importance to salvation history: the Incarnation. Why? Because in taking on human flesh, the Son of the Eternal Father has sanctified the corporeal nature of man; in fact in Jesus it is more than that. Divine, no less. Furthermore, in the glory of his Resurrection, flesh and bone are made new, raised from a natural to a supernatural state in perfect holiness. Therefore, in the veneration of saints' relics, we are affirming the truth that Jesus has sanctified these bones; that the body as well as the soul have fought together to conquer Satan.

As an example of this, we could consider the missionary who has walked mile upon mile in the service of God to bring his saving message to the ignorant. Perhaps at the end of life those feet are battered and bruised. Do those bones not bear an eloquent witness to the holiness which the Lord imparts? St. Paulinus of Nola (354–431 AD) tells us concerning St. Felix:

> But the divinely implanted grace in the Saint's limbs could not die and be buried with the flesh ... Felix lives on after his body's span, a saint presiding over his own bones; and those bones of the saint's body are not choked with the dust of death, but endowed with a hidden seed of eternal life, so that from the tomb they breathe out

16. Ibid., 204.
17. Ibid., 203.

the life-giving fragrance of his triumphant soul, by which efficacious healing is granted to the sick who pray for it.[18]

St. Paulinus, in another poem, adds that the bones of the saints:
"never lose the presence of the Holy Spirit, whence a living grace
comes to the sacred tombs."[19] This theology of the body ensures
that veneration of relics is not separated from the whole truth concerning man and his final destiny. The act of devotion toward them
invigorates faith in life everlasting, and instills an eagerness to join
the Church in glory. This idea finds its greatest expression in the
miraculous preservation of certain saints, because in them, we have
a visual miracle that in a sense prefigures the resurrection on the
last day. By halting the natural process of decay, the Lord teaches us
that nothing is impossible to him and therefore encourages the virtue of hope to grow within; while for the spiritually blind, lost in the
rationalism of modern life, a reason to reach out for the hand of
Christ Jesus.

The great Lebanese Maronite priest St. Charbel Maklouf is a
wonderful contemporary example of this theological proposition.
After his death on December 24, 1898 he was buried in the vicinity of
St Maroun's Monastery—Annaya. Soon after, supernatural lights
were seen emanating from his grave, and his body was perspiring
sweat and blood. With permission, his body was moved to a new
tomb and crowds began to flock asking for his intercession. Many
cures were credited to his intercession, and in 1950 his tomb was
opened revealing a medically certified incorrupt body. After that, the
healings multiplied even beyond the borders of Lebanon to the furthest ends of the earth. Yet most important of all were the plethora of
spiritual healings, which must be considered the real fruits of the
communion of saints.[20] These spiritual conversions testify to the

---

18. St. Paulinus of Nola, *The Poems of Saint Paulinus of Nola* (New York: Newman Press, 1975) 119–20.

19. St. Paulines of Nola, *Carmen XXI*, 632–633, 596, http://www.documenta-
catholicaomnia.eu/02m/0353-0431,_Paulinus_Nolanus_Episcopus,_Poemata,_MLT
pdf.

20. One of the most astonishing miracles associated with St. Charbel concerns
Nohad El Chamy, who in 1993 was suffering from a left hemiplegia which meant

yearning for something greater than the corruption the world offers. Sadly, in recent decades, the all too pagan "new age" movement has filled the mystical void for many people, but there is little doubt that the grace God bestows upon his children through these precious relics acts like an arrow heading towards an eschatological target, one that awakens the soul to eternal realities. It recalls the scales that fell from Saul's eyes on the Road to Damascus (cf. Acts. 9:18).

The veneration of saintly men and women takes on several forms, relics perhaps being the most misunderstood and controversial; but another of great importance concern sacred images and statues. St. John Damascene (676–749 AD), Doctor of the Church and figure of great stature in Byzantine theology, was one of the first to incorporate a conception of veneration towards sacred images within acceptable spiritual practice. His *Apologia against those who decry*

---

obstruction of 80% of the left-brain arteries and 70% of the right ones. There was no cure, and at home she was bed ridden and had to take food and water through a straw. On the night of January 22, while suffering intense pain, she started asking the Blessed Virgin and St. Charbel: "Why have you done this to me? What sin have I committed to deserve all this?" At about 11 PM Nohad fell asleep and had a dream in which two monks approached her bed. One of them placed his hand on her neck and said, "I am here to operate on you." She turned around but couldn't see his face due to a blinding light that was coming out of his body and eyes. He then revealed he was Fr. Charbel. As he began rubbing her neck, she felt acute pain. Once the "operation" was over, the other monk came forward with a pillow and helped her sit up; he then gave her a cup of water to drink. At that moment, Nohad woke up and realized she actually was drinking this water, and sitting in the position the monk in the dream had left her in. She was able to move her legs, and so she got out of bed, knelt to thank the Blessed Virgin and St. Charbel and then walked to the bathroom. Upon looking in the mirror, she noticed two large incisions in her neck. A week later, she saw St. Charbel in a dream, who said: "Don't leave the people. Keep on your faith. I incised you through divine intervention so that people can see you. A lot of them have strayed from the Church. They are neglecting both to pray and respect the saints. You can't do anything for the people. Those who want anything from me, I am Father Charbel, and I am always at the hermitage. I want you to visit the hermitage every 22nd day of the month, and attend the mass for the rest of your life." On August 15, 1993, St. Charbel came in a dream once again and asked for the Rosary to be recited on the first Saturday of each month. From that day a portrait of the Saint began exuding oil in Nohad's home; and on September 2, 1993, she experienced another dream in which St. Rita revealed that the monk who had given her the drink was St. Maroun, a fourth century Syriac and the spiritual father of the Maronite Church. *See,* http://www.saintcharbel-annaya.com/.

Holy Images is perhaps his best known work and one that expounds clearly the reasons why the use of such images is legitimate.

The initial problem that confronted Christians in their new liturgical practices was that in Jewish tradition, any such idea was banned, as we read in Exodus: "Thou shalt not carve images, or fashion the likeness of anything in heaven above, or on earth beneath, or in the waters under the earth, to bow down and worship it" (Ex. 20:4–5).[21] St. John Damascene carefully formulated a theological principle that made a distinction between *latreia* (worship) and *proskynesis* (veneration). The first could only apply directly to God, whereas the second could apply to an image that is *representative* of God. Taking the Incarnation as a starting point much in the same way we did with relics, St. John saw that now that God had taken on human form, he could therefore be recognized—unlike the situation in the Old Testament in which he was invisible:

> Then the Invisible One becomes visible to flesh, you may then draw a likeness of His form. . . . Depict His ineffable condescension, His virginal birth, His baptism in the Jordan, His transfiguration on Thabor, His all-powerful sufferings, His death and miracles, the proofs of His Godhead, the deeds which He worked in the flesh through divine power, His saving Cross, His Sepulchre, and resurrection, and ascent into heaven. Give to it all the endurance of engraving and color. Have no fear or anxiety; worship is not all of the same kind.[22]

Going on to explain the difference between worship and veneration, the great Eastern Saint writes:

> Of old, God the incorporeal and uncircumscribed was never depicted. Now, however, when God is seen clothed in flesh, and conversing with men, I make an image of the God whom I see. I do not worship matter, I worship the God of matter, who became

---

21. God did however command the making of two golden cherubs (Ex. 25:18), carved cherubs on doors (1 Kings. 6:32) and the bronze serpent for Moses to cure those bitten by fiery serpents (Num. 21:8). The commandment was that they were not to be worshiped. In the case of the bronze serpent, that is what the Israelites did, and so it was broken into pieces (cf. 2 Kings. 18:4).

22. St. John Damascene, *On Holy Images* (London: Thomas Baker, 1898), 8–9.

matter for my sake, and deigned to inhabit matter, who worked out my salvation through matter. I will not cease from honouring that matter which works my salvation. I venerate it, though not as God.[23]

Enlarging the concept a little, St. John Damascene teaches that all matter has been sanctified and bears witness to the presence of God, and because of this, veneration of matter is praising God for his creativity: "Do not despise matter, for it is not despicable. Nothing is, which God has made."[24] Concerning the veneration of saints' images, he has strong words for those who would argue against venerating them:

> But the adversary says: "Make an image of Christ or of His mother who bore Him (της θεοτοκου) and let that be sufficient." O what folly this is! On your own showing, you are absolutely against the saints. For if you make an image of Christ and not of the saints, it is evident that you do not disown images, but the honour of the saints. You make statues indeed of Christ as of one glorified, whilst you reject the saints as unworthy of honour, and call truth a falsehood.[25]

But what is his reason for allowing veneration of holy images that are not depicting the Blessed Trinity? His answer lies in the holy union that exists between Christ and his chosen ones, that is those grafted onto the true Vine. St. John reiterates the truth that the children of God are no longer servants, but sons; and if sons, then heirs also to a divine inheritance (cf. Gal. 4:7). St. John the Apostle, following the same line of thought, is equally candid in the dignity bestowed on the baptized: "But we know that when he comes we shall be like him" (1 Jn. 3:2). So the truth concerning the saints is that by participating in the Death and Resurrection of Jesus, they become gods—not by nature—but through the flow of divine grace. St. John Damascene uses the analogy of a man who comes into contact with fire. He is not fire by nature, but becomes fire

---

23. Ibid., 15–16.
24. Ibid., 17.
25. Ibid., 20–21.

through participation; therefore when man becomes one with the fire of divine love, he partakes in "the divine glory of sovereignty."[26]

In part three of the *Apologia*, we see a description of "image" as a concept, which reminds us how photographs are used to venerate the memory of loved ones: "The image is a canticle and manifestation and monument to the memory of those who have fought bravely and won the victory to the shame and confusion of the vanquished."[27] Theologically speaking then, the veneration of saintly images (and statues) has several elements which form a well-rounded approach to utilizing them in the spiritual life. On the one hand, our perception passes *through* the saint's image to the instigator behind it; therefore in a real sense we are admiring the One who *really* sketched the portrait before us rather than the painter himself. By this I mean "sketched" in the sense of creating the holiness of the saint to which the portrait bears testimony. On the other hand, we are venerating the saint who testifies to that sanctifying work of the Creator. The image helps us to reflect in a more tangible way to the creative, redemptive and sanctifying power that God's selfless love manifests in those created in his image.[28]

Veneration and Intercession in the Divine Will

The final issue I would like to address in this chapter is a rather simple one, and yet extremely important, especially to those who are as yet not part of the Catholic Church. Do we actually need to pray to the saints or could we just bypass them and go at once to God? The simple answer is no we don't need to. We could petition the Lord directly. But perhaps a more pertinent question would be: Is it God's will that we *should* pray to the saints? The simple answer to

---

26. Ibid., 23.

27. Ibid., 87.

28. St. Paulinus of Nola, several centuries before St. John Damascene, had sensed the value in sacred images. He decorated his Basilica with paintings that served as a visual catechesis. As he explained to St. Nicetas of Remesiana while giving him the guided tour: "In this way, as the paintings beguile their [spiritual] hunger, their astonishment may allow better behaviour to develop in them." *Carmen XXVII*, 583, St. Paulinus of Nola, *The Poems of St. Paulinus of Nola* (New York: Newman Press, 1975), 291.

that question would be a resounding yes. Let us therefore look at the reasons why this would be the case.

The reasoning behind this affirmation lies in the way the Lord has decreed his Church to act. Throughout this book so far, we have seen one central feature: that of *communio*. Communion between the three persons of the Most Holy Trinity, between God and his people Israel, between Jesus and the angels, between Jesus and his Church, and then between the faithful and elect of the Mystical Body. This truth reveals much about the manner in which the Lord wishes to carry out his salvific plan.

Consider the stupendous mystery of the Annunciation of the Archangel Gabriel to Mary where heaven awaited the "yes" of human cooperation to bring the Divine Child into the world or the unfathomable humility of Jesus in allowing the priest to invoke his coming at every Eucharistic Sacrifice. God has never in salvation history acted unilaterally; he has always willed that humanity contribute to its own redemption, and in the Church—whether the saints on earth or in heaven—he has expected much interest on his capital. In essence, this means that he has placed an expectation on those who have been blessed with an abundance of grace. The holiness of these saints cannot be left to dwell within, but must fan into a flame the fire of the Holy Spirit. For the saints of the novitiate, that means prayer, sacrifice, looking after the poor and the widow, etc. For those in heaven, it means being attentive to the supplications of those on earth. Now it is certain, as evidenced by the visions of the Apocalypse, that the Lord does not want saints who are for all intents and purposes holy statues who bask in the glory of final triumph. If the world continues to exist, then humanity in general, and the Church Militant in particular, have need of heavenly assistance, and as God desires not to act alone, he wills that the saints respond to the pleas expressed by their brothers and sisters below.

By praying for the intercession of the saints, we are allowing God the opportunity to manifest his great benevolence upon us in the way he has always acted; that is by rewarding the loyalty of his most faithful by consenting to their requests. It would seem a very strange situation that the Lord could accept petitions on earth, for instance the mediation of Mary at Cana (cf. Jn. 2:3), or even the

Roman Centurion's plea for his servant's cure (cf. Lk 7:2–10) and yet not have a similar receptivity to those who now share in his divinity. It makes no sense considering the immutability of God. If God's love is responsive to those he loves on earth, then the same must be true in heaven where the incense of prayer rises before the throne of the Almighty (cf. Rev 8:4). Perhaps the main stumbling block to accepting this premise is the way in which we see the company of heaven. Do we see a multitude of "individuals" who have been saved, or do we see a "community," a "holy communion"? The crux of the matter is that the blessed souls are still part of the Mystical Body of Christ, a Body that is alive and active; and as such they have the same relationship to the Lord as we do on earth, with the exception that sin can no longer interfere in their longings for God's glory. We should also take into account the knowledge the Lord has concerning at what cost these souls entered eternal repose. Surely it is not unreasonable to think he takes great joy in responding to those who fought and overcame the Dragon? The miraculous interventions we have discussed in this chapter certainly confirm this conviction.

A Church in heaven that is dormant is in reality no Church at all. It is only when we see the Church as a communion of saints in its totality, that is in its three states, that we are truly able to appreciate the active participation that dwells within each member. Because of this, we should embrace the opportunity to grasp the friendship of these illustrious victors as that is what God wills. We should not be afraid to humbly petition them, knowing that the Lord loves nothing more than to share his divine life with them.

As a final thought to reflect on, let us recall the fact that the saints will be granted the God-given task of judging at the end of the world, as we read: "Jesus said to them, I promise you, in the new birth, when the Son of Man sits on the throne of his glory, you also shall sit there on twelve thrones, you who have followed me, and shall be judges over the twelve tribes of Israel" (Matt. 19:28). And St. Paul, teaching along the same lines writes:

> You know well enough that it is the saints who will pass judgement on the world; and if a world is to abide your judgement, are you

unfit to take cognizance of trifling matters? You have been told that we shall sit in judgement on angels; how much more, then, over the things of common life? (1 Cor. 6:2–3)

Now we must ask ourselves that if God has commissioned this most august task to the saints at the end of time, would he not also task them with ensuring the spiritual and physical well-being of their brethren in the age preceding that Judgment? If the answer is no, then we are affirming a Church Triumphant that is asleep until the last day; but if the answer is yes, then we know that the incense of intercession is rising continually for us and even more so when we personally implore the help of the saints.

≈ 12 ≈

Mary: Apex of
Communion with God

The Holy Spirit will come upon thee, and the power of the most High will overshadow thee. Thus this holy offspring of thine shall be known for the Son of God. . . . And Mary said, Behold the handmaid of the Lord; let it be unto me according to thy word. (Lk. 1:35, 38)

ONE OF THE MOST compelling cases for venerating the saints is the inspiration they can give for our own spiritual development. We can see from their lives how the Lord traced a path that led them to abandon their own will in order to embrace wholeheartedly the divine will; and seeing the beautiful fruits of that conformity and communion with God can help us to navigate our own journey towards ultimate union with the Eternal Father. If there is one figure of supreme holiness who testifies to this communion between God and humanity in its most perfect form, it is Mary: Daughter of the Father, Mother of the Son, and Spouse of the Holy Spirit. In this chapter, we will contemplate why Mary *is* the apex of communion why she is the Queen of the *sanctorum communio* and the perfect image of the eschatological Church in its transfigured state.

The mystery of Mary, sublime and unparalleled among the mysteries of creation, is one that has enchanted the Church ever since its birth. Why? Because in Mary's own life is reflected the entire journey of the Church from beginning to end and thus the Church recognizes its own passage to full communion with God through this exalted Woman. Before ascending the Throne of Peter as Pope Benedict XVI, Joseph Ratzinger had meditated on the profound link between ecclesiology and Mariology: "Mariology can never be purely Mariological. Rather, it stands within the totality of the basic Christ-Church structure and is the most concrete expression of its inner coherence."[1] This means that there exists a hermeneutic which places the Marian dimension firmly within the theology of Christ and his Church; therefore Mary is not reduced to a purely biological role, but truly Mother of her Son's Mystical Body also. Not only that. The mysteries of the Church are the mysteries of Mary herself:

> The patristic period foreshadowed the whole of Mariology in the guise of ecclesiology, albeit without any mention of the name of the Mother of the Lord: The *virgo ecclesia* [virgin Church], the *mater ecclesia* [mother Church], the *ecclesia immaculate* [immaculate Church], the *ecclesia assumpta* [assumed Church]—the whole content of what would later become Mariology was first conceived as ecclesiology.[2]

Lost Communion Restored: Mary's Predestination

Our first priority in this discussion is to examine in what way the Blessed Virgin's interior life from the moment of conception was marked by the most intimate union with God; and from there, we will seek to appreciate how it blossomed into the fullness of communion that is exemplified by her Assumption and subsequent coronation as Queen of heaven.

To begin with, we should place this meditation within the context of the original communion God had desired to share with his children, that which had been wrecked by Adam and Eve's sin. From that moment of rupture, God had set in motion His plan of redemption, which of course was designed solely to restore that lost communion. Yet, even before that, in eternity, the *predestination* of Mary had been determined—intimately linked to the *predestination* of the Word—that would bring about a recapitulation of communion even greater than before, because the *Logos* would raise the dignity of man to an exalted state higher than the angels. Mary, the

---

1. Joseph Ratzinger, "Thoughts on the Place of Marian Doctrine and Piety in Faith and Theology as a whole," *Communio International Catholic Review*, Spring 2003, 156.

2. Ibid., 154.

chosen Vessel of God, would be the only possible destination for the "new communion" to be established because only she possessed the spiritual faculties that would not reject the overtures of the Holy Spirit. So what was it that was so exceptional in the soul of Mary? The answer seems two-fold. On the one hand, an absolute adherence to the divine will that emanated entirely from her own free will—the thought of which perhaps captivated the heart of God in eternity—and on the other hand, a singular privilege in which she was conceived without the stain of original sin, thus becoming the Immaculate Conception.

Although we have already considered one aspect of this dogma,[3] namely the action of the Holy Spirit in the soul of the Blessed Virgin, we need to address the critical point concerning how this stupendous grace was bestowed before the act of redemption had been carried out. It could appear that Mary was somehow exempt from needing redemption, rendering the sacrifice of Jesus superfluous. But undoubtedly, that view would be heretical. Mary needed redeeming; that is unquestionable. The exceptional Franciscan theologian Blessed John Duns Scotus (c.1266–1308) was the first to carefully formulate a convincing argument in favor of the truth contained in the eventual dogma. Known as the *Doctor subtilis* (Subtle Doctor) and *Doctor Marianus* (Marian Doctor), he was a great speculator who worked tirelessly to unlock the door of these sacred mysteries in order that they could be appreciated ever more.[4] He lived at a time when the prevailing theological opinion was that Mary had been sanctified in the soul *after* conception in a way similar to John the Baptist; St. Bernard of Clairvaux, St. Bonaventure

3. Blessed Pius IX defined the dogma of Mary's preservation from original sin on December 8, 1854.

4. Apart from his contribution to Mariology, it was his study of the Incarnation which offered profound insights. He held the view that even if humanity had not sinned, the Word would still have become incarnate: "To think that God would have given up such a task had Adam not sinned would be quite unreasonable! I say, therefore, that the fall was not the cause of Christ's predestination and that if no one had fallen, neither the angel nor man in this hypothesis Christ would still have been predestined in the same way" (*Reportatio Parisiensis* III Sent., d. 7, 4). *See*, Pope Benedict XVI, "General Audience," July 7, 2010, www.vatican.va.

and St. Thomas Aquinas were all notable adherents to this view. For Blessed Scotus, Mary was still totally dependable on the sacrifice of her Son; the question was rather one of timing. He believed that God could preserve her soul at the moment of conception in anticipation of the fruits of the redemption, and this because Christ's Passion had always been predestined in the depths of eternity. If God could bestow sanctifying grace at the moment of baptism, he could do the same for Mary at the moment of her soul's creation.

His case rests on the idea that if Christ is the perfect Redeemer, then he had to redeem his Mother in the most perfect manner; and to redeem in the most perfect manner is to preserve one from original sin altogether. But why was it necessary for Mary to be perfect in holiness? The answer to that question lies in the will of God that Mary should become the New Eve; not through following the original natural order, but in the order of grace.[5] Mary was going to carry the glory of heaven within her womb; she was destined to not only untie Eve's knot, but ensure the knot was never tied again by taking on a unique salvific role as the co-redemptrix of humanity, as Simeon had announced to her (Lk. 2:35). In that sense, Mary was

---

5. St. Bernard of Clairvaux and St. Bonaventure both wrote extensively on the subject of Mary as the New Eve; they took the Annunciation as the central praiseworthy event in Mary's life from a salvific point of view. St. Bernard tells us: "It pleased him [God] to reconcile man to himself in the same way and by the same means that had caused him to fall.... Just as the devil deceived the woman first and then overcome man through the woman, so now he was going to be lead astray by a virgin woman and later be vanquished openly by the man Christ." St. Bernard of Clairvaux, *Homilies in Praise of the Blessed Virgin Mary*, trans. Marie-Bernard Saïd with an introduction by Chrysogonus Waddell (Kalamazoo, MI: Cistercian, 1993), 25. St. Bonaventure continuing along the same lines writes: "The human race had fallen through the suggestion of the devil, through the consent of a deceived woman, and through a begetting become lustful that handed down original sin to the offspring. Conversely, and most fittingly, there was here [at the Annunciation] a good angel persuading to what was good, a Virgin believing him and consenting to the proposed good, and the love of the Holy Spirit making her both holy and fruitful for a virginal conception. Thus, 'evils were healed by their opposites.'" St. Bonaventure, *Breviloquium*, 4.3.3, taken from: *The Works of Bonaventure*, trans. José de Vinck (Paterson, NJ: St. Anthony's Guild Press, 1963), 151. The quote St. Bonaventure used was from St. Gregory, *Homiliae in Evangeliae*, II, from Homily 32:1.

going to share in the most profound and holy work of her Divine Son (as the New Adam) and therefore her supreme sanctity enabled her to conform exactly to the task entrusted to her. As this plan of salvation was not temporal but eschatological, it required both the New Adam and New Eve to be free from original and actual sin, thus paving the way for the Ascension of Jesus and Assumption of Mary. Blessed Duns Scotus argues that because Mary was the beneficiary of so great a grace, she was actually *more* reliant on Jesus and obligated to him than the rest of the redeemed:

> Therefore, She is under a greater obligation, because the sin and offense were remitted Her in a more noble way than the others, in whom the sin was present, since it is more noble to remit a sin by preserving from the presence of the sin ... than it is to permit that the sin be present and then remit it afterwards.[6]

In this way of thinking, a clear distinction between Mary and the saints becomes visible. For the Mother of God, it is a matter of "preservation" that comes from the merits of Christ's future Passion, while for her spiritual children the merits have a liberating effect from sins already committed.[7]

So we see that through predestination, Mary was willed to be in the closest type of union with the Most Holy Trinity—that of spiritual perfection. The wonderful grace granted to her illuminates the magnificence of the redemptive act itself because divine power, love and mercy combined to ensure that its fruits were anticipated and fulfilled in the one person who could bring about the conditions (through her *fiat*) in which the actual redemption could take place.

6. Blessed John Duns Scotus, *Lectura* III, d. 3, q.1, no. 22. See, *Blessed John Duns Scotus and His Mariology* (New Bedford: Franciscans of the Immaculate, 2009), 56.

7. The great theologian also addresses the question as to the immediate destination of Mary had she died before her Son's crucifixion. He states that just as the ancient Fathers who had expiated their sins still had to wait until Jesus descended into the underworld, so too would Mary have had to wait. His reasoning was that more merit was needed to go through the "door" as opposed to the amount needed to open it, and as such, the foreseen merits applied to Mary's preservation would not have been sufficient to allow the immediate vision of God.

Mary in the Fullness of Time

If the Immaculate Conception of Mary was the foundational grace upon which her extraordinary communion with the Lord was built, then the Annunciation and Incarnation were the sealing of it. At the point of giving her assent to the Father's Will, the Word became Jesus, the God who saves, and heaven descended into the one place on earth which resembled it. This pivotal divine action brought about a bond of love in which both the Mother and Son reciprocated essential gifts necessary for the completion of their redemptive work. For Mary, it was the active giving of her human nature, and for Jesus the active giving of divine grace. As a consequence, this mutual giving enabled the hypostatic union of two natures (divine and human) in the person of Jesus Christ to become a reality, while his mother was now nothing less than *Theotokos*, the Mother of God. For Mary, communion was pure contemplation of the Divine Word silently imparting love, peace and wisdom deep within her soul, nine months of rapturous joy as the Heart of Jesus began to beat in unison with her own. The intensity of love Mary must have experienced during this period of waiting surely left her soul already at the gates of heaven as it were; and yet, she had to be in communion not only with the love of her Son, but also with his sufferings. In this way, Mary became the resplendent image of Jesus in joy and sorrow, molded and prepared for the salvific communion for which she had been chosen.

In chapter three, we looked in detail at the spousal relationship between Mary and the Holy Spirit, but at this point I would like to explore the seldom discussed communion between Mary and Almighty God; a relationship existing on the level of Father and Daughter. But how does this come about?

In order to answer this question we need to go back to the idea of Mary's predestination. In the eternal contemplation of God, Mary was to be the pinnacle of all creation, subordinate in holiness to nobody except the Most Holy Trinity, and from the moment of the incarnation, an impeccable reflection of Jesus in every way. Because of that, we must see God's great affection for his daughter through the prism of the affection He has for His Son. If Jesus is the first born of the Father, then Mary is in a sense the second; not through divine substance, but by unique association with her Son and his redemptive work. God sees His work of creation come to fruition in the Immaculate Heart, and in the Incarnation, a communion spanning heaven and earth.

If we look at Sacred Scripture, we see a sort of parallel affirmation of God's blessing on His Son and adopted daughter. At the Baptism of Jesus in the Jordan, we read: "And even as he came up out of the water he saw the heavens opened, and the Spirit, like a dove, coming down and resting upon him. There was a voice, too, out of heaven, Thou art my beloved Son; in thee I am well pleased" (Mk. 1:10–11). In St. Luke's Gospel we find something similar concerning Mary: "Then the angel said to her, Mary, do not be afraid; thou hast found favour in the sight of God. . . . The Holy Spirit will come upon thee, and the power of the most High will overshadow thee" (Lk. 1:30, 35). Two things immediately stand out here: on the one hand, the divine proclamation concerning the Father's predilection towards Mary; He is pleased with her as He is with his Son; and on the other hand, the descent of the Holy Spirit upon both as a divinely sealed commission to unchain creation from the fetters of the devil.

The responses from God's Son and daughter are equally significant. The Letter to the Hebrews tells us that on coming into the world, Jesus said: "I am coming to fulfil what is written of me, where the book lies unrolled; to do thy will, O my God" (Heb. 10:7); while Mary replied to the Archangel Gabriel: "Behold the handmaid of the Lord; let it be unto me according to thy word" (Lk. 1:38). In the eyes of the Father, Mary is the wonder of creation. He can look at her virtues and conformity to His will and see Jesus, and because of that she is His daughter in a unique way, set apart from His other adopted daughters who will inherit eternal life.

The divine reflection present in Mary that so captivates the Eternal Father is conspicuous in various ways as revealed by the teaching of the Church. She mirrors Jesus's love, his self-sacrifice, his wisdom, his mediation, his conformity to the divine will, his love for the Church and even his resurrection, as we shall see later. Yes, in all these things she is second, but in terms of a creature, she is the summit, the fullness of what is possible for humanity. The following words of St. Irenaeus of Lyons could undoubtedly be applied to Mary more than anyone else:

> For the glory of God is a living man; and the life of man consists in beholding God. For if the manifestation of God which is made by means of the creation, affords life to all living in the earth, much more does that revelation of the Father which comes through the Word, give life to those who see God.[8]

This takes us towards another perspective concerning this beautiful relationship. God sees His daughter primarily through the image of His Son, but He also sees her through the image of His original design for creation. We know that God's love, being creative, was not closed in on itself, but rather outreaching, calling into existence creatures who would be formed in His own image, and who would live in perfect communion, reflecting the communion of the three divine persons. In Mary He saw past the betrayals, the rebellions, and the disobedience. Is it too far to suggest that in Mary, God saw a reason to continue with humanity after the fall? Probably not, if we look at papal teachings of a mariological nature. Blessed Pius IX in his Apostolic Constitution *Ineffabilis Deus* states:

> Above all creatures did God so love her that truly in her was the Father well pleased with singular delight. Therefore, far above all the angels and all the saints so wondrously did God endow her with the abundance of all heavenly gifts poured from the treasury of his divinity.[9]

Pope Pius XII, renowned for his devotion to the Blessed Virgin, similarly extols her greatness before the sight of God:

> Hence it cannot be doubted that Mary most Holy is far above all other creatures in dignity, and after her Son possesses primacy over all. "You have surpassed every creature," sings St. Sophronius. "What can be more sublime than your joy, O Virgin Mother? What more noble than this grace, which you alone have received

---

8. St. Irenaeus of Lyons, *Adversus Haereses*, bk IV, ch. 20, 7, www.newadvent.org.

9. Blessed Pius IX, Apostolic Constitution, *Ineffabilis Deus*, December 8, 1854, www.ewtn.com.

from God?" To this St. Germanus adds: "Your honor and dignity surpass the whole of creation; your greatness places you above the angels." And St. John Damascene goes so far as to say: "Limitless is the difference between God's servants and His Mother."[10]

If God's just judgment spared those faithful who lived in times of great evil, then the logical conclusion is that for Mary alone was creation justified even if for no other. When God created man and woman he saw that it was "very good" (cf. Gen. 1:31), and even when he "repented" for having made man (cf. Gen. 6:6), that could never be the case for Mary, since she was always "very good." As God never repents of his gifts or his calls (cf. Rom. 11:29) we can see his daughter as the one example of perfection who fulfilled everything he desired from his creation.

This is evident most strikingly in the comparison between Eve and Mary. Even though Eve was created "very good," she followed an antithetical path to that of the Blessed Virgin. She welcomed through pride the suggestions of Satan that she could become like a god (cf. Gen. 3:5), which in effect meant being master of her own destiny, and craving the power to do it. Because of the conversation she engaged in with the devil, and her subsequent sin, she in fact allowed the evil one to enter into her, soiling her soul. She was now living under the seductive power that would always tantalize with illusory pleasures. Therefore, disobedience, pride, sensuality and even similarity to Satan were now the defining factors in Eve's life. For Mary, the new Eve, Satan would have no influence. Disobedience became obedience at the Annunciation; pride became humility: "because he has looked graciously upon the lowliness of his handmaid" (Lk. 1:48). Original sin became full of grace; sensuality became chastity and perpetual virginity. For the Eternal Father, Mary was superseding the image of Eve because through the presence of the Holy Spirit and the Incarnate Word (which were both lovingly embraced and actively willed to be there by Mary) she was working in the redemptive field to raise humanity to the heavenly state. If Eve was from the rib of Adam, Mary was from the divine grace of Jesus and thus a daughter

10. Pope Pius XII, Encyclical Letter, *Ad Caeli Reginam*, October 11, 1954, www. vatican.va.

alongside the Son in the most sublime sense.

The communion between Mary and Jesus at the Incarnation presents us with several interesting and prophetic elements that deserve our attention. The first concerns the fact that Jesus, hidden in the Womb of Mary, was foreshadowing his Eucharistic presence in the souls of his faithful. Mary became the prototype of the Church in its adoration of Jesus, truly present under the appearances of bread and wine. She was the *Tabernacle* because Jesus was enclosed within her; the *Ciborium* because from her Jesus was given to us, and the *Monstrance* because the Eternal Word was made visible through Mary's flesh. St. John Paul II intuited this mariological/ecclesiological link in his Encyclical *Ecclesia de Eucharistia*:

> In a certain sense Mary lived her Eucharistic faith even before the institution of the Eucharist, by the very fact that she offered her virginal womb for the Incarnation of God's Word. The Eucharist, while commemorating the passion and resurrection, is also in continuity with the incarnation ... there is a profound analogy between the *Fiat* which Mary said in reply to the angel, and the Amen which every believer says when receiving the body of the Lord. Mary was asked to believe that the One whom she conceived "through the Holy Spirit" was "the Son of God" (Lk. 1:30–35). . . . In continuity with the Virgin's faith, in the Eucharistic mystery we are asked to believe that the same Jesus Christ, Son of God and Son of Mary, becomes present in his full humanity and divinity under the signs of bread and wine.[11]

The great Polish Pope also perceived Mary's journey towards the consummation of her Son's Passion through the sacrificial dimension of the Eucharist in which she was being prepared daily through an intense spiritual union that bound her in a salvific way to the Redeemer:

> In her daily preparation for Calvary, Mary experienced a kind of "anticipated Eucharist"—one might say a "spiritual communion"—of desire and of oblation, which would culminate in her union with her Son in his passion, and then find expression after

11. St. John Paul II, Encyclical Letter, *Ecclesia de Eucharistia*, April 17, 2003, www.vatican.va.

Easter by her partaking in the Eucharist which the Apostles celebrated as the memorial of that passion.[12]

If Mary was the "Woman of the Eucharist"[13] who foreshadowed
the mystery of communion between Jesus and his Church on earth,
then a second prophetic element of the Incarnation reveals that she
was also the Woman who foreshadowed the communion between
God and His saints at the end of the world. This idea stems from the
comparison between the first and second coming of the Lord. At the
first, the Word descended from heaven into the sanctified Womb of
Mary, the saint of all saints. He made his home with her and thus
she was part of the new creation, their union anticipating the fully
realized "new heaven and new earth." At the Lord's return in glory,
he will once again descend from heaven to establish his perfect
communion with all the saints. They will be ready to receive him, as
was Mary, through the sanctification wrought by the Holy Spirit,
and then the divine intimacy which was once confined to Mother
and Son will blossom for the entire communion of saints.

The Magnificat: A Canticle of Praise

Although we have to a certain extent already looked at Mary's communion with her Divine Son from the point of view of her divine
maternity and salvific mission, we can also uncover the richness of
spiritual union from her Canticle of praise: the *Magnificat*. If we
recall, this joyful proclamation of Mary was a response to the threefold blessing of her cousin Elizabeth: "Blessed art thou among
women, and blessed is the fruit of thy womb. . . . Blessed art thou for
thy believing; the message that was brought to thee from the Lord
shall have fulfilment" (Lk. 1:42, 45). Essentially, Elizabeth was greeting Mary by affirming her exalted status that pertained to her singular union with God;[14] and in a prophetic sense she was speaking on

12. Ibid.
13. Ibid.
14. Elizabeth, in that final blessing, also had the added significance of her husband Zachary's refusal to believe the Archangel Gabriel's message concerning the
conception of St. John the Baptist; which contrasted sharply with Mary's humble
acceptance.

behalf of the Israel of the Old Covenant and the New. Before we briefly analyze Mary's response, let us read the text in its entirety:

> My soul magnifies the Lord; my spirit has found joy in God, who is my Savior, because he has looked graciously upon the lowliness of his handmaid. Behold, from this day forward all generations will count me blessed; because he who is mighty, he whose name is holy, has wrought for me his wonders. He has mercy upon those who fear him, from generation to generation; he has done valiantly with the strength of his arm, driving the proud astray in the conceit of their hearts; he has put down the mighty from their seat, and exalted the lowly; he has filled the hungry with good things, and sent the rich away empty-handed. He has protected his servant Israel, keeping his merciful design in remembrance, according to the promise which he made to our forefathers, Abraham and his posterity for evermore. (Lk. 1:46–55)

To begin with, it is particularly noticeable that Mary does not shy away from the praise being bestowed upon her; rather she expresses her marvel at the work the Lord has done within her. *My soul magnifies the Lord.* With these words the Blessed Virgin proclaims the truth that her soul radiates the majesty and goodness of God, that her life is a living gospel that continually bears witness to that unique communion she enjoys with each of the three divine persons. In her soul there is the complete eschewing of any sense of self-importance; in fact she recognizes that it is her humility that has won God's favor, in contrast to those who clothe themselves in vainglory and pride: *in the conceit of their hearts; he has put down the mighty from their seat, and exalted the lowly.* Mary's joy comes from the presence of the God who saves; for even though she is full of grace, the Mother knows she still has need of her divine child to consummate on the Cross what was predestined in eternity.

Behold, from this day forward all generations will count me blessed. This remarkable prophecy inspired by the Holy Spirit reveals to us that Mary was very much aware of the far reaching consequences of the mission entrusted to her; not only in the immediate sense of giving birth to the Savior and guiding his human nature in its infancy, but more profoundly in the context of her spiritual maternity. We could see in this prophecy a two way process of fulfilment.

On the one hand, Mary sees the future in which she will be called *blessed* because the faithful will recognize in her the dawn of salvation through her Immaculate Conception and consent at the Annunciation; and on the other hand, *blessed* because she will always be the *Hodegetria* who guides the way towards communion with her Son. In this second element the Church will always honor its Mother because of her maternal assistance that never fails. She is the "neck" of the Mystical Body who dispenses the graces from the Son to her children, and thus she has the sphere of influence that her devotees will always seek to utilize through prayer and blessing.[15] If we view this from yet another angle, Mary is also blessed because she is the perfect model to emulate, as St. Ambrose suggests: "But let everyone have the spirit of Mary, so that he may rejoice in the Lord. If according to the flesh there is one mother of Christ, yet, according to faith, Christ is the fruit of all."[16]

There is one further point connected to this prophecy which we should address: the words, being divinely inspired, confirm the truth that devotion to Mary is something willed by God and should always be encouraged, even within the confines of protestant ecclesial communities. If Mary is relegated to the "loft" and only appears at the Nativity once a year, then it is rather too close to saying: "no we will not call you blessed." In recognizing Mary's holiness and union with God, we are in fact praising the work of the Lord in giving us a second chance through this new Eve. The greatest misconception concerning devotion to Mary is that it takes us away from the focus on Jesus; and yet without Mary's astounding virtues there

15. Pope Pius XII writes: "Besides, the Blessed Virgin possessed, after Christ, not only the highest degree of excellence and perfection, but also a share in that influence by which He, her Son and our Redeemer, is rightly said to reign over the minds and wills of men. For if through His Humanity the divine Word performs miracles and gives graces, if He uses His Sacraments and Saints as instruments for the salvation of men, why should He not make use of the role and work of His most holy Mother in imparting to us the fruits of redemption?" Encyclical Letter, *Ad Caeli Reginam*, October 11, 1954, www.vatican.va.

16. St. Ambrose, *Expositio evangelii secundum Lucam*, 2:26, cited in St. Thomas Aquinas, *Catena Aurea*: vol. 3, *St. Luke* (Southampton: The Saint Austin Press, 1997), 43.

would be no God-Man to worship. The Eternal Word would still be inaccessible to us. On the contrary, Mary always has and always will lead us by the hand to Jesus. That is confirmed by the Lord himself when he said from the Cross: "*eis tà ìdia*" take Mary into your "inner life" (Jn. 19:27). Jesus knows first-hand the benefit of communion with Mary. Why? Because the Father willed that his human nature grow under her loving influence, and therefore, if that is good enough for the Almighty, then it is good enough for us. If we truly want to imitate the Son, then Mary's blessedness should never be far from our lips.

It is also significant in this hymn of praise that Mary "implies" the privileges granted to her by God *because he who is mighty, he whose name is holy, has wrought for me his wonders*. This begs the question: in what sense did Mary understand her role in salvation history? Did it for instance extend beyond the simple fact that she would give birth to the Savior? In the first instance, we can affirm that the "wonders" Mary refers to are those of which she had explicit knowledge at that point: her freedom from all sin and by extension, immunity from concupiscence; her royal status as Mother of God; her perpetual virginity and her unique relationship as spouse of the Holy Spirit. The key to answering the question rests on the belief that Mary had knowledge of the Scriptures, especially the passage from Genesis concerning the *protoevangelium* and those from Isaiah concerning the Suffering Servant. These texts would have left Mary with the awareness that on the one hand she would be personally involved in the overthrowing of Satan, and on the other, that great suffering would be hers. If we add in the decisive factors that she was the *Seat of Wisdom* (Jesus being Eternal Wisdom) and the recipient of the specific *gift* of wisdom, then we can assume that the Holy Spirit had already enlightened Mary at least to some extent on the nature of her life and sufferings. Certainly the prophecy that all generations would call her blessed signifies Mary's discernment that God intended to exalt her for her contribution to our salvation.

In the second half of the *Magnificat*, Mary moves away from the very intimate portrait of her own communion with God and instead expresses her joy at the communion God offers to those who love and serve him. We hear of the mercy bestowed on those who fear him, the exaltation of the lowly, and the hungry who are filled with good things. But perhaps most importantly of all, Mary speaks of the promise kept to Israel; that God never abandoned them as his chosen people, and in this aspect the Canticle comes full circle. In Mary, this promise is now about to find complete fulfilment. The fullness of time has arrived (cf. Gal. 4:4) and God intends to bring about the total liberation of which the first Passover was only the herald. The *Magnificat* therefore is a privileged access into the depth of Mary's love for God and God's love for her. It is an invitation to discover the joy of communion with Divine Love, and a summons to reject everything that stand in its way.

The entire span of the Blessed Virgin's earthly life can be summed up as a total immersion in the life of God. Her Seven Sorrows[17] reveal a union of suffering with Jesus that corresponds to the nature of her mission (God's will being that Mary always remain within the enclosure of the Son, and thus experience the full weight of sin). But the one factor above all others that ensured Mary could accept the bitter chalice was her capacity to love. It meant she never recoiled at the thought of pain and grief, instead offering everything to the Father with the same generous spirit as her Son. This is the fundamental truth about Mary's relationship with the Most Holy Trinity: that her love is *their* love. She brings to perfection the words of St. John: "That our life in the world should be like his, means that his love has had its way with us to the full" (1 Jn. 4:17).

If we reflect on the moment when Jesus departed home to begin his public ministry, we can to some extent imagine the pain that flooded Mary's soul: the gut-wrenching truth that she could no longer offer him maternal protection and an atmosphere of love, joy and peace. Mary had to "release" her Son from the warmth of her loving embrace and allow the divine plan to unfold in the manner God had decreed. But her communion with the Lord transcended this temporal separation because over and above the physical reality

---

17. These are: the prophecy of Simeon, the flight into Egypt, the loss of the Child Jesus, the meeting of Jesus and Mary on the way to Calvary, the Crucifixion, the piercing of Jesus's side and taking down of his Body, and the burial of the Lord.

was the spiritual union, woven together by the Holy Spirit in a way not dissimilar to that of the Father and Son. Love ruled Mary's heart in such a way that exclusion from communion with God was all but impossible; her Immaculate Heart acted like a magnet for the Holy Spirit and thus every action, every prayer was inspired by his blazing love. Mary was the blank canvas on which the Holy Spirit created his greatest masterpiece; blank because she held nothing back from what was her own (love and free will), and with that freedom to work, the Lord of life was able to conform this marvel of creation to the divine image.

In terms of salvific activity, Mary's communion with God reached its apex at the foot of the Cross. She was united with the Father above all because she had helped ensure that His will could be carried out perfectly in reaching this point, and as the flesh of the new Adam being immolated was taken from her flesh, she could legitimately offer back to God the necessary sacrifice; as Pius XI teaches: "she brought forth for us Jesus our Redeemer, and nourished Him, and offered Him as a victim by the Cross, by her mystic union with Christ and His very special grace she likewise became and is piously called a reparatress."[18]

Mary's union with the Holy Spirit must have been especially intense in those terrible hours in order for her to be able to endure the Passion of her Son and her own spiritual martyrdom. Through him, she was able to reaffirm her *Fiat* in that hour swamped by evil; through him, she was able to say with Jesus "Father, forgive them; they do not know what it is they are doing" (Lk. 23:34), and through him, she alone was able to keep the lamp of faith lit awaiting the glory of Jesus's Resurrection.

But of course ultimately it was the union of Mary and her Divine Son that figured most decisively at Golgotha. Where Adam and Eve were once united in sin around the tree, now the New Adam and New Eve had come to take their place, sanctifying the wood with blood, tears and obedience. For this redemptive union, the words found in St. Paul's Letter to the Romans seem particularly apt: "but,

18. Pope Pius XI, Encyclical Letter, *Miserentissimus Redemptor*, May 8, 1928, www.vatican.va.

as our fault was amplified, grace has been more amply bestowed than ever" (Rom. 5:20). Through Mary, not only was Eve's sin cancelled, but God exalted humanity by sending his Son to become a true Brother, providing a superabundance of grace for the divinization of man and the world. In God's overflowing generosity, it was not enough to just restore the original equilibrium; no, for the true routing of the devil, Heaven was to come down to Earth and instigate a transfiguration surpassing the beauty of the former type in Eden. Adam's nakedness was replaced by the new Adam's eschatological robe of glory, and the seed of the new earth was sown in the soil of Calvary.

If the mystery of Mary's communion with God was in the first place related to the events of salvation history—the Annunciation and Passion of Jesus—we would be mistaken to think that her subsequent life was anything less. We have already seen how Mary's spiritual maternity, born when the Church came into existence, enabled the embryonic Christian community to witness first-hand the beauty of total, mystical union with God. But what was to happen when the time came for Mary to depart this life? Did the privileges granted to her continue into eternity, or was her role as the New Eve somehow temporary?

Mary: Transcendence and Transfiguration

The question needs to be raised for several reasons. First, the Blessed Virgin had been conceived as the Immaculate Conception; therefore the stain of sin that meant death *and* decay for the rest of humanity was not present on her soul, and as such, this meant she *could* be exempt from that penalty. When we also consider that Christ's sacrifice had now been accomplished, resulting in the freedom to enter heaven, the possibility arises that Mary could follow Jesus into the glory of the Resurrection at the end of her earthly life. A second reason stems from the eschatological nature of Mary as the New Eve. We discovered earlier that the plan of salvation was not temporal but eternal; meaning that it was directed towards recreating man in a divinized form, as St. Paul teaches: "he will form this humbled body of ours anew, moulding it into the image of his glorified body" (Phil. 3:21). This essentially meant that through the

Resurrection, not only was a new spiritual state being prepared, but a physical one as well, bearing the divine seal of immortality. So the New Eve's mission was profoundly related to the *novissimis*; that is, the last things, in which are incorporated the making new of all creation in the new heaven and new earth. With this theological backdrop, it makes perfect sense that Mary should share in the immediate glory of the Resurrection, sitting enthroned at the right hand of the New Adam, for she had played a unique human role in bringing this recapitulation about.

St. John Damascene argues that Mary's body could not possibly be allowed to decay because of her cooperation in the work of redemption. In fact he places the Assumption as the culmination of Mary's various privileges, privileges which she had utilized completely for the good of the human race rather than herself:

> And just as the all holy body of God's Son, which was taken from her, rose from the dead on the third day, it followed that she should be snatched from the tomb, that the mother should be united to her Son; and as He had come down to her, so she should be raised up to Him, into the more perfect dwelling-place, heaven itself. . . . It was fitting that the body of her, who preserved her virginity unsullied in her motherhood, should be kept from corruption even after death. She who nursed her Creator as an infant at her breast, had a right to be in the divine tabernacles. The place of the bride whom the Father had espoused, was in the heavenly courts. It was fitting that she who saw her Son die on the cross, and received in her heart the sword of pain which she had not felt in childbirth, should gaze upon Him seated next to the Father.[19]

St. Modestus of Jerusalem (d. 634) also shares the same belief that the unique redemptive communion between Mother and Son led to Mary's Assumption:

> As the most glorious Mother of Christ, our Savior and our God and the giver of life and immortality, has been endowed with life by him, she has received an eternal incorruptibility of the body

---

19. St. John Damascene, *On Holy Images Followed By Three Sermons on the Assumption* (London: Thomas Baker, 1898), 191–192.

together with him who has raised her up from the tomb and has taken her up to himself in a way known only to him.[20]

For St. Germanus of Constantinople (d. 740), the focus was on the perfect holiness of Mary's body:

> Your virginal body is entirely holy, entirely chaste, entirely the dwelling place of God so that, even for this reason, it is absolutely incorruptible. It is unchangeable since what was human in it has been taken up in incorruptibility, remaining alive and absolutely glorious, undamaged, and sharing in perfect life. Indeed, it was impossible that the one who had become the vase of God and the living temple of the most holy divinity of the Only Begotten One be enclosed in the sepulchre of the dead.[21]

St. Robert Bellarmine strikes a similar tone, one that perhaps could serve as a good point of reflection for those who would deny this privilege of the Blessed Virgin:

> And who, I ask, could believe that the ark of holiness, the dwelling place of the Word of God, the temple of the Holy Spirit, could be reduced to ruin? My soul is filled with horror at the thought that this virginal flesh which had begotten God, had brought him into the world, had nourished and carried him, could have been turned into ashes or given over to be food for worms.[22]

Apart from the theological reasoning of Mary's Assumption, there is also the very simple question of whether her Son would have wanted this privilege to be granted before the end of time. Even in the most natural sense, it would seem absurd that the one who holds in his hands the keys of death (cf. Rev. 1:18) would not cherish the opportunity to unbind his own Mother from its decaying clutches; but how much more so when we consider that Mary gave her life to the Lord in order that his burning desire could be fulfilled in setting humanity free. If the Eternal Word willed to enter

---

20. St. Modestus of Jerusalem, *Encomium in dormitionem Sanctissimae Dominae nostrae Deiparae semperque Virginis Mariae*, 14, P.G. 86–II, 3311.

21. St. Germanus of Constantinople, *In Sanctae Dei Genetricis Dormitionem, Sermo I.*, P.G. 98, 344–346.

22. St. Robert Bellarmine, *Conciones Habitae Lovanii, De Assumption B. Mariae Virginis* (Coloniae Agrippinae: apud Ioannem Crithium, 1615), n.40.

into the physical body of Mary in its unique "heavenly" state, then surely he willed that this same Body should experience his own heavenly state in order to fully appreciate the divine triumph. It also seems likely that a secondary reason would have related to the Mystical Body. For the blessed souls of the Church Triumphant, contemplating the New Eve in the transfiguration of a glorified body would be the anticipatory joy of their own future destiny, and for the Church Militant, hope that in the midst of battle, a Mother watches over them from Heaven—one who has reached in a tangible way the new heaven and new earth.

In the plans of divine providence, it fell to the great Marian Pope, Pius XII, to finally put the seal of papal infallibility on the constant teaching of the Church that Mary had been assumed body and soul[23] into heaven, as he stated in the Apostolic Constitution *Munificentissimus Deus*:

> By the authority of our Lord Jesus Christ, of the Blessed Apostles Peter and Paul, and by our own authority, we pronounce, declare, and define it to be a divinely revealed dogma: that the Immaculate Mother of God, the ever Virgin Mary, having completed the course

---

23. Pope Pius XII left open the question of whether the Blessed Virgin actually experienced death, although this was not for the reason of denying death had taken place; rather he didn't see it as opportune to define it as revealed truth. In the patristic era it was accepted that Mary had followed her Son into the tomb. St. Jacob of Serug tells us: "Unto the Mother of this Jesus Christ, Son of God, death came that she might taste his cup.... The heavens and the mountains and all the plains which were adorned, broke forth in praise when the virginal body was being laid in the grave." See *Jacob of Serug: On the Mother of God* (New York: St. Vladimir's Seminary Press, 1998), 89–100. In recent centuries, a belief has grown that Mary did not actually die, but St. John Paul II in his ordinary magisterium, has refuted that suggestion: "It is true that in Revelation death is presented as a punishment for sin. However, the fact that the Church proclaims Mary free from original sin by a unique divine privilege does not lead to the conclusion that she also received physical immortality. The Mother is not superior to the Son who underwent death, giving it a new meaning and changing it into a means of salvation.... To share in Christ's Resurrection, Mary had first to share in his death." *See* General Audience of June 25, 1997. www.vatican.va. Sometimes it is said that people die of a broken heart, but in the case of Mary perhaps we should say she died because love could *no longer be contained* in her Immaculate Heart. Understood that way, her death was as much a mystical transition as a natural death.

of her earthly life, was assumed body and soul into heavenly glory. Hence if anyone, which God forbid, should dare willfully to deny or to call into doubt that which we have defined, let him know that he has fallen away completely from the divine and Catholic Faith.[24]

In trying to visualize the glorious scene of the Assumption, we can imagine the gradual ascent of the Mother, perhaps surrounded by angels in festive song, while the Lord Jesus anticipates her arrival by stepping out of heaven. Then, taken by the hand of the Lord (and how wonderful that must have felt), being greeted at the gates of the Holy City by a multitude of angels and saints. If we dare to put it in an earthly context, it must have been the joy of the greatest wedding procession, albeit with an unsurpassable supernatural joy. The procession then leads to the Throne of the Eternal Father where a coronation takes place; it recalls the words found in the Psalm: "at thy right hand stands the queen, in Ophir gold arrayed . . . thy beauty, now, is all for the king's delight; he is thy Lord, and worship belongs to him" (Ps. 45:10, 12). With this royal act, Mary's salvific role is honored in the most solemn way: she is crowned Queen of heaven and earth. Thus she rules as a maternal monarch in the fullness of communion with her divine King, overflowing with love and the majesty of humility. St. Andrew of Crete describes the enthronement thus:

> For look, all of you who hear my words, look at what is now before our eyes: the Queen of the nations—I mean the Church of the faithful—today leads the solemn procession for the Queen of our race, who today is received royally into the Kingdom of heaven by God, the King who rules over all. The Church brings in tribute today her most beautiful and festive processions. She who turned dust into heaven today strips the dust away, lays aside the veil of this world of change and gives back to the earth what belongs to it.[25]

24. Pope Pius XII, Apostolic Constitution, *Munificentissimus Deus*, November 1, 1950, www.vatican.va.

25. St. Andrew of Crete, *Oratio 2, in Beatae Mariae Virginis Dormitionem*, P.G. 97, 1079.

The Crowning of Mary is, as the Glorious Mysteries of the Holy Rosary tell us, the glory of all the saints. It is the exaltation of her communion with Jesus, and as such, the manifestation of her primacy within the communion of saints. The Book of Revelation clearly reveals this in the vision of Mary wearing a crown of twelve stars and the sun for a mantle (Rev. 12:1); she is Queen of the saints from both Covenants and her attire is the regal brightness of her Son. Because of this, she radiates his light and grace, directing both towards her loving subjects. The crowning is also recognition that every hope, every merit, every prayer and every sacrifice from time immemorial is found perfectly realized in her inherent holiness; and because she consented to be the Mother of God she brought forth that perfection into the royal court of the Most Holy Trinity.

So as we conclude this chapter on the most wonderful mystery of love that is Mary, how does her peerless union with God affect us within the *sanctorum communio*? What can we learn that will influence our lives for the better? In the first instance we must strive to imitate her sacrificial love, the love that rose splendidly to the challenges posed by the Divine Will. We must imitate her heroism, so that in these days of gradual persecution and ridicule, we do not run away from the Cross, but remain faithful to the truth that sets us free (cf. Jn. 8:32). And in her exceptional relationship with the Holy Spirit, we can learn the art of silent listening, so that we become aware of his inspirations, and thus gradually become ever more conformed to the will of God. In Mary, we see humility as the key to communion with God because undoubtedly, that is what He found in her so attractive; and humility is the gateway for love to blossom. Mary is also the perfect icon of the Church, therefore she exemplifies everything that the Mystical Body stands for; she is the mother, the evangelizer, the co-redeemer, the worker, the contemplative, and the guardian of the poor. If certain saints illuminate specific virtues, then Mary illuminates them all, and that is why she is the greatest template for aspiring saints.

But of course, as well as imitating Mary, we should entrust ourselves to her; perhaps by consecrating ourselves and our families to her Immaculate Heart. If we accept her as our Queen *and* Mother, then we are placing in her hands the right to intervene in our journey towards full communion with the Lord. That intervention will ensure us a share in her spiritual riches, which within the communion of saints stand alone, pristine in holiness and merit. Like her Jesus, she will not rest until this unification between God and man is achieved with the last of the chosen incorporated into the Mystical Body. Until that day comes, the Mother must work as the Mediatrix of Mercy, a supreme witness to the wellspring of happiness that comes from participation in the life of God.

Let us conclude by meditating on some beautiful words of Pope Pius XII, whose own love for Mary is something we can all aspire to imitate:

> Let all, therefore, try to approach with greater trust the throne of grace and mercy of our Queen and Mother, and beg for strength in adversity, light in darkness, consolation in sorrow; above all let them strive to free themselves from the slavery of sin and offer an unceasing homage, filled with filial loyalty, to their Queenly Mother. Let her churches be thronged by the faithful, her feast-days honored; may the beads of the Rosary be in the hands of all; may Christians gather, in small numbers and large, to sing her praises in churches, in homes, in hospitals, in prisons. May Mary's name be held in highest reverence, a name sweeter than honey and more precious than jewels; may none utter blasphemous words, the sign of a defiled soul, against that name graced with such dignity and revered for its motherly goodness; let no one be so bold as to speak a syllable which lacks the respect due to her name.[26]

---

26. Pope Pius XII, Encyclical Letter, *Ad Caeli Reginam*, October 11, 1954, www.vatican.va.

☙ 13 ❧

Sanctorum Communio:
Unity of Divine Love in the
New Heaven and New Earth

Then I saw a new heaven, and a new earth. The old heaven, the old earth had vanished, and there was no more sea. And I, John, saw in my vision that holy city which is the new Jerusalem, being sent down by God from heaven, all clothed in readiness, like a bride who has adorned herself to meet her husband. I heard, too, a voice which cried aloud from the throne, Here is God's tabernacle pitched among men; he will dwell with them, and they will be his own people, and he will be among them, their own God. (Rev. 21:1–3)

EVERYTHING we have discussed until now has in some way pointed towards the eschatological future of the Church, in which the waters of salvation history will finally cascade into eternity. The old world will pass away, death will be consigned to the past, and the universe will be reborn in a transfigured state. Biblically speaking, everything spoken of from the beginning of time seeks to enlighten and prepare for this new time in which the citizens of Christ's Kingdom will sing of a glorious peace without end. The Resurrection will become reality for all the redeemed, and the communion of saints will find in this a new and everlasting expression of holiness. This ultimate state of being raises several questions which we will seek to analyze in this final chapter: What is the nature of the new heaven and new earth? What is the nature of the glorified body? What are the joys experienced by the saints? How will the redeemed relate to one another? These are all issues that need to be addressed in order for us to contemplate the future that God desires to give us.[1] But before we venture into these discussions, it is beneficial if we briefly explore how this final state of salvation will be reached.

The Birth of a New Creation

Before the second coming of Jesus at the end of the world, certain biblical prophecies must be fulfilled: (1) the Gospel must be spread to all creation (cf. Matt. 24:14); (2) a great apostasy will lead many to reject the Christian Faith (cf. 2 Thess. 2:3); (3) a final, universal persecution under the tyrannical reign of the Antichrist will take place (cf. 2 Thess. 2:4); (4) the Jews will convert as a people to the true faith (cf. Rom. 11:15). Until these events have happened, the Church will remain in a period of vigilance, seeking to discern the signs of the times. When Jesus does return to judge the living and the dead, he will descend on the clouds in a theophany of absolute glory and power, in complete contrast to his first coming in humility and poverty. This final coming will manifest before the whole of humanity the true identity of the Lord of history. It will bring to fulfilment the words recounted in the Apocalypse: "Behold, he comes with clouds about him, seen by every eye, seen by those who wounded him" (Rev. 1:7).

St. Paul adds an interesting detail. He tells us that Jesus will not come alone, but with all his saints (cf. 1 Thess. 3:13); which essentially means that a victorious procession of the Church Triumphant will follow him. Why do they come "visibly" in that way? It is because they are part of his Body, and thus are about to share in the judgement (cf. Matt. 19:28, 1 Cor. 6:2–3). Not only that. They come as one "holy communion" because they are about to be united with their brothers and sisters of the Church Militant (those still alive at

---

1. As strange as it may seem considering the Resurrection is the nexus of our Faith, the concept of the new world seems to have been lost somewhat; perhaps as a consequence of the lack of teaching on the *novissimis* in recent times. Pope Benedict XVI lamented this situation in these terms: "Our preaching, our proclamation, really is one-sided, in that it is largely directed toward the creation of a better world, while hardly anyone talks anymore about the other, truly better world. We need to examine our consciences on this point." Pope Benedict XVI, *Light of the World* (London: CTS, 2010), 179.

the Lord's arrival) and the Church Suffering. With the promise of the Lord to make all things new about to be realized (cf. Rev. 21:5), the eschatological Church gathers to inherit the earth, as foretold in the Beatitudes (cf. Matt. 5:4).

But before that can happen, the Last Judgment must be proclaimed before the assembled masses: those damned and those saved. At the sound of God's trumpet and the command of the Archangel (cf. 1 Thess. 4:15), those who had died in Christ will rise first (which obviously applies to those seen coming out of heaven with Jesus), and then the damned. No matter where death struck—land, sea or sky—the result will be the same: body and soul will be reunited. Humanity will face the just sentence with the totality of its being. For the hell bound, a disfigured monstrosity that symbolizes its wickedness and subjection to Satan; while for the redeemed, a glorious body fashioned in the image of the Incarnate God.

Once Jesus has delivered his judgment, there is, as St. Matthew tells us, a quite disconcerting development that for all intents and purposes serves as the very end of history: "And these shall pass on to eternal punishment, and the just to eternal life" (Matt. 25:46). It is very difficult to think of this final parting of the two branches of humanity that will never meet again. Dare we hope like Hans Urs von Balthasar that maybe, just maybe, there is a way out for those who appear to march inexorably towards eternal death? The Scriptures would suggest not;[2] however, who can place limits on the mercy of God? Certainly if there are souls in hell, it is because they firmly rejected any desire to be in communion with the Lord; and it is to be hoped that those who *truly* realize the gravity of their choice and still proceed are indeed a rarity.

We are now left with the image of the Bridegroom and his Bride, the Church, united together for the first time in the glory of eternal

---

2. In St. Matthew's Gospel, Jesus warns the inhabitants of those cities where he had worked miracles that hell would be their destination unless they repented (cf. Matt. 11:20–24). St. Paul also speaks in the most severe terms to those who lead evil lives: "Make no mistake about it; it is not the debauched, the idolaters, the adulterous, it is not the effeminate, the sinners against nature, the dishonest, the misers, the drunkards, the bitter of speech, the extortioners that will inherit the kingdom of God" (1 Cor. 6:9–10).

life; the saints now possessing what they have always longed for: a body that is totally at the disposal of a soul full of grace. This resurrection of the body presupposes the existence of a physical world in which the new material nature can be utilized; and in St. Peter's Second Letter, we discover the process that leads to the new world rising from the ashes of the old:

> The heavens will vanish in a whirlwind, the elements will be scorched up and dissolve, earth, and all earth's achievements, will burn away.... And meanwhile, we have new heavens and a new earth to look forward to, the dwelling-place of holiness; that is what he has promised. (2 Pet. 3:10, 13)

This apocalyptic action seems to be the work of the Holy Spirit who, as the Psalmist tells us, will renew the face of the earth (cf. Ps. 104:30). He will do for creation precisely what he did through history for man: purify and sanctify. The reason for this is that creation, in the former heaven and earth, was also subject to the devastating effects of sin, as Pope Benedict XVI teaches:

> After the fall and the divine curse it was to produce only "thorns and thistles," and only in exchange for the "toil" and the "sweat of your face" would it bear fruit (cf. Gen. 3:17–19). The dust of the earth no longer recalls the creative hand of God, one that is open to life, but becomes a sign of an inexorable destiny of death: "You are dust, and to dust you shall return" (Gen. 3:19). It is clear in this Biblical text that the earth participates in man's destiny.[3]

St. Paul understood very well how creation was bound by the sin of Adam, and yet could look forward to a similar redemption:

> Created nature has been condemned to frustration; not for some deliberate fault of its own, but for the sake of him who so con-

---

3. Pope Benedict XVI, "Homily for Ash Wednesday Mass," February 22, 2012, www.vatican.va. The patristic era also saw a theology develop in which the earth "suffered" from the wounds of original sin: "Adam was created pure by God to serve him. All creatures were created for the service of man. He was destined to be lord and king over all creatures. But when he embraced evil he did so by listening to something outside himself. This penetrated his heart and took over his whole being. Thus ensnared by evil, Creation, which had assisted and served him, was ensnared together with him." (Pseudo-Macarius, *Homily* 11, 5: P.G. 34, 547)

demned it, with a hope to look forward to; namely, that nature in its turn will be set free from the tyranny of corruption, to share in the glorious freedom of God's sons. The whole of nature, as we know, groans in a common travail all the while. (Rom. 8:20–22)

As with the sanctification of man, the universe can only be divinized by the presence of God; and in the final chapter of the Apocalypse, we see this marvelously described:

> Here is God's tabernacle pitched among men; he will dwell with them, and they will be his own people, and he will be among them, their own God. He will wipe away every tear from their eyes, and there will be no more death, or mourning, or cries of distress, no more sorrow; those old things have passed away. And he who sat on the throne said, Behold, I make all things new. (These words I was bidden write down, words most sure and true). (Rev. 21:3–5)

St. Irenaeus of Lyons, seeking to develop an ever deepening Christology, drew up a *theology of recapitulation* that was rooted in St. Paul's teaching that Christ would give history its fulfilment: "by resuming everything in him, all that is in heaven, all that is on earth, summed up in him" (Eph. 1:10). This meant that in Jesus, creation itself would not only attain its original objective which had been frustrated by original sin, but actually surpass it: "God recapitulated in Himself the ancient formation of man, that He might kill sin, deprive death of its power, and vivify man."[4] In this concept, God takes the place of Adam who was earthly by nature, and instigates a new beginning which will be divine by nature: *earth will become heaven*. This recapitulation involves the making new of creation itself: "For God is rich in all things, and all things are His. It is fitting, therefore, that the creation itself, being restored to its primeval condition, should without restraint be under the dominion of the righteous."[5]

At this point, it is worth pausing a moment to contemplate this magnificent vision of the future, because it certainly appears that for many Christians, the full grandeur and mystery of heaven is not fully appreciated. It seems strange, for instance, that preaching often

---

4. St. Irenaeus of Lyons, *Adversus Haereses*, bk III, ch. 18.7, www.newadvent.org.
5. St. Irenaeus of Lyons, *Adversus Haereses*, bk V, ch. 32.1, www.newadvent.org.

does not include the wonderful truth that those saved will live again on the *renewed earth*; that we are not destined to live in a vague afterlife somewhere above the clouds, but truly here below with a resurrected body in a new creation. For the bereaved, this certainty tells them that the physical loss is only temporary, that at some future date they will embrace their loved ones again, safe in the knowledge that thereafter, they will never be parted. The image of Jesus embracing Mary at her Assumption should be for all in sorrow an invitation to hope, hope that the original family life on earth will be recapitulated in a far greater and more joyful way; for the resurrection can only be truly understood in the wider context of a new physical universe that will serve the saints for all eternity.

If we now have before us the knowledge of this new earthly paradise, it does raise questions concerning its nature. We have to be honest at this point and say that to a large extent, it is a mystery that has not been revealed, even in mystical literature. It would seem that the Lord has decided that this will remain a surprise of great wonder, as St. Paul tells us: "no eye has seen, no ear has heard, no human heart conceived, the welcome God has prepared for those who love him" (1 Cor. 2:9). We do however have certain glimpses that are revealed through Sacred Scripture and interestingly, it is the Old Testament that provides us with the greatest clues.

Although we are somewhat familiar with the phrase "new heaven and new earth" from Revelation 21, it first appears in the Book of Isaiah, written over seven centuries before:

> See where I create new heavens and a new earth; old things shall be remembered no longer, have no place in men's thoughts. Joy of yours, pride of yours, this new creation shall be; joy of mine, pride of mine, Jerusalem and her folk, created anew. I will rejoice in Jerusalem, take pride in my people, and the sound of weeping and lament shall be heard among them no more. (Is. 65:17–19)

Perhaps the most important aspect that Isaiah articulates concerning this new world is the sense of universal reconciliation and peace that reigns throughout all creation. Gone is the natural fight for survival and conflict between different species; now all live under the loving dominion of God, a true communion of living beings in harmony with one another:

332

Wolf shall live at peace with lamb, leopard take its ease with kid; calf and lion and sheep in one dwelling-place, with a little child to herd them! Cattle and bears all at pasture, their young ones lying down together, lion eating straw like ox; child new-weaned, fresh from its mother's arms, playing by asp's hole, putting hand in viper's den! All over this mountain, my sanctuary, no hurt shall be done, no life taken. (Is. 11:6–9)

Hostilities between nations and peoples that so disfigured the first heaven and earth are also annihilated in the Kingdom of divine love; for the Prince of Peace rules with justice and a tender love (cf. Is. 9:7): "They will melt down their swords into plough-shares, their spears into pruning-hooks, nation levying war against nation and training itself for battle no longer" (Is. 2:4). Isaiah's focus on the fate of the individually wicked is also evident: "Vanished, the triumphant foe, scornful incredulity is silenced; where are they now, that spent themselves on wrongdoing, watching a man's words to convict him of guilt, defrauding him of justice at the city gate, setting aside, with a quibble, the plea of the innocent?" (Is. 29:20–21)

As we saw with the theology of St. Irenaeus, it is the holiness of the Lord Jesus that permeates the new creation. He rules in the very midst of his saints: "Soon as he hears thee crying out to him, the answer will come" (Is. 30:19). Because of this newly established closeness between Creator and creature, there is no need to think that the Lord will reside in separate surroundings with a secretary to act as an intermediary; on the contrary, he will be in some certain sense with one and all in an eternal present. In fact, we can see Jesus's true presence in Holy Communion (and our communal reception of him) as prefiguring this future reality in a most beautiful way:

This, too, he promises: Enduring your race and name shall be as the new heavens, the new earth I fashion, to stand continually in my presence. Month after month, sabbath after sabbath shall go by, and still all mankind shall come to bow down before me, the Lord says. (Is. 66:22–23)

The Book of Isaiah also conjures up the delightful image of a new vitality rising from the hallowed soil, one which stands in stark contrast to the "dust" that was the price of Adam's sin. We read how the

Lebanon forest shall be as fruitful as Carmel, and the present fruitful land become like a forest (cf. Is. 29:17); how the new fine wines will be used in the banquet prepared by the Lord (cf. Is. 25:6),[6] and how the barren desert will become the flower bed of the new earth; nothing less than the recapitulation of Eden:

> Thrills the barren desert with rejoicing; the wilderness takes heart, and blossoms, fair as the lily. Blossom on blossom, it will rejoice and sing for joy; all the majesty of Lebanon is bestowed on it, all the grace of Carmel and of Saron. . . . Springs will gush out in the wilderness, streams flow through the desert; ground that was dried up will give place to pools, barren land to wells of clear water; where the serpent had its lair once, reed and bulrush will show their green. (Is. 35:1–2, 6–7)

Similar words found later in the book confirm the Prophet's message:

> And has the Lord no pity for Sion, left desolate, no pity on her ruined state? Doubt not he will turn that wilderness into a garden of delight, that loneliness into a paradise; in her, too, mirth and gladness shall be found, there shall be thanksgiving and songs of praise. (Is. 51:3)

It should be stressed that in the rebirth of creation, it is not only the world we inhabit that will be made new; the entire universe will share in the glorification of the risen Christ, and this raises intriguing possibilities of accessing these other areas of creation which will pose no problem for the glorified body. Of course it is pure speculation, but we know God creates everything for a reason, and perhaps the deepest recesses of space will manifest some other wonderful secrets of divine activity at the time when the Universal Restoration comes (cf. Acts. 3:21). At any rate, Sacred Scripture does reveal certain details concerning heavenly objects in the new age. Isaiah tells us for instance that the moon's light will be as bright as the sun, while the sun will shine seven times brighter than now, as if the

---

6. The Apocalypse also makes reference to this fruitfulness: "On either side of the river, mid-way along the city street, grows the tree that gives life, bearing its fruit twelvefold, one yield for each month. And the leaves of this tree bring health to all the nations" (Rev. 22:2).

light of seven days were joined in one (cf. Is. 30:26). However, the symbolism of this is understood later when Isaiah writes:

> No longer wilt thou have the sun to shine by day, or the moon's beam to enlighten thee; the Lord shall be thy everlasting light, thy God shall be all thy splendour. No more, for thee, the setting of suns, the waning of moons, now that the Lord is thy everlasting light. (Is. 60:19–20)

As was mentioned earlier, the number seven denotes completeness, therefore the "seven times brighter" refers to the fullness of divine light which brings about the full realization of Jesus's words: "I am the light of the world" (Jn. 8:12). The Apocalypse also reiterates this truth: "There will be no more night, no more need of light from lamp or sun; the Lord God will shed his light on them, and they will reign for ever and ever" (Rev. 22:5). In the light of these texts, do we therefore conclude that the sun will in reality cease to exist? An explanation is given in St. Hildegard of Bingen's *Scivias* revelations, which perfectly marries the two seemingly contradictory texts of Isaiah. The voice from heaven (God the Father) says:

> And the sun and moon and stars will sparkle in the firmament like precious stones set in gold, with great glory and brilliance; and they will no longer restlessly revolve in orbit so as to distinguish day from night. For the world will have ended and they will have become immutable; and from that time on there will be no darkness, and day will be perpetual... for the ruler of all, in the immutable glory of His Divinity, will illuminate those who in the world have by His grace escaped the darkness.[7]

The sun therefore remains, but "rests" from its previous duty to light the world; instead it reflects the sevenfold brightness of the Lord.

Without doubt, we must remember that there is an intense symbolism to what we read concerning the various elements that will make up the new world; how much of that will actually be literal is a question that cannot be answered this side of eternity. But it does seem safe to say, that as Jesus told us he would make *all* things new, we are not just in the realm of the allegorical. It would seem that

---

7. St. Hildegard of Bingen, *Scivias* (Mahwah: Paulist Press, 1990), 520–521.

animals, for instance, will form part of the new creation. Can God restore those that have already existed, even if they do not presently possess an immortal soul? Let's leave the question totally open and affirm with Jesus: "to God all things are possible" (Matt. 19:26).[8] If we consider the world we inhabit now with its many wonders—exotic creatures, beautiful flowers, stunning waterfalls, majestic mountains—then perhaps we can see in it a foretaste and "prototype" creation that will give way to something even more wondrous, yet still modelled on the original. In that sense, the rest of creation would mirror the natural life of man where the first Adam was raised in supernatural dignity and sublimity by the second Adam.[9] With this backdrop therefore, of a dazzling, divinized world fit for the household of God and his community of saints, we can begin to explore the life of the resurrected elect and seek to discern at least a glimmer of the glory of life everlasting that awaits.

The Glory of God: Man Fully Alive

Our first priority in this task is to understand the nature of a glorified body, and the Gospel accounts of the Resurrection of Jesus are

---

8. The Prophet Hosea seems to allude, like Isaiah, to the presence of animals on a renewed earth: "Beast and bird and creeping thing to peace pledge I; bow and sword and war's alarms break I; all shall sleep safe abed, the folk that dwell in her" (Hos. 2:18). From a theological viewpoint, animals were created good, and shared in God's Covenant: "Here is a covenant I will observe with you and with your children after you, and with all living creatures, your companions, the birds and the beasts of burden and the cattle that came out of the Ark with you, and the wild beasts besides" (Gen. 9:9–10). St. Paul clearly teaches that they share in the sufferings caused by sin: "that nature in its turn will be set free from the tyranny of corruption, to share in the glorious freedom of God's sons" (Rom. 8:21). Thus in God's plan they deserve, as "good" creations, to share in the same liberty as a redeemed humanity. We know that the original plan for them was to be, like humanity, quite different to what they have experienced since the Fall: they were not to eat each other, but instead feed on seeds and herbs (cf. Gen 1:29). So it seems a sort of "justice" will be applicable to them because, through no fault of their own, they have suffered; hence their restoration in the new earth will give them the capacity to glorify God in the way he always intended for them.

9. Pope Francis explains: "All of nature that surrounds us is created like us, created together with us, and in a *common destiny it tends to find its fulfillment and ultimate end in God himself*—the Bible says 'new heavens and a new earth' (cf. Is

the most fitting place to start, primarily because the testimonies bear witness to some remarkable facets that are entirely "new." In St. John's Gospel, it is Mary Magdalen who first sets eyes on the Lord and yet she doesn't recognize him; it is only when he calls her "Mary" (cf. Jn. 20:16) that she knows his identity. Similarly, on the road to Emmaus, the two disciples did not recognize the traveller who had joined them, and it was only when he broke the bread that their eyes were opened (cf. Lk. 24:35). Evidently then, the holder of a glorified body has the ability to hide or alter their appearance. Along the same lines, it is noticeable that Jesus was also able to vanish in the presence of those around him (cf. Lk. 24:31). St. Thomas Aquinas explains that because the body is now *spiritual*, it is totally subject to the spirit, and therefore to the will: "Consequently, whoever has a glorified body has it in his power to be seen when he so wishes, and not to be seen when he does not wish it."[10] This quality, known as *subtility*, is one of four traditional qualities associated with a resurrected body. Subtility also allows the movement of the body to pass through material objects, as was seen by the Apostles when Jesus suddenly appeared in the room where the doors had been locked (cf. Jn. 20:19). The ability to suddenly appear in one place and then another, at will, also presupposes the capability of covering vast distances in an instant, a quality known as *agility*.

65:17, 2 Pet 3:13; Rev 21:1). This doctrine of our faith is an even stronger stimulus for us to have a responsible and respectful relationship with Creation: in inanimate nature, in plants and in animals, we recognize the imprint of the Creator, and in our fellow kind, His very image." Pope Francis, "Address to the Italian Catholic Scout Movement for Adults," November 8, 2014, www.vatican.va. In his recent Encyclical *Laudato si,* Pope Francis returned to the theme: "At the end, we will find ourselves face to face with the infinite beauty of God (cf. 1 Cor 13:12), and be able to read with admiration and happiness the mystery of the universe, which with us will share in unending plenitude. Even now we are journeying towards the sabbath of eternity, the new Jerusalem, towards our common home in heaven. Jesus says: 'I make all things new' (Rev 21:5). *Eternal life will be a shared experience of awe, in which each creature, resplendently transfigured, will take its rightful place* and have something to give those poor men and women who will have been liberated once and for all." Pope Francis, *Laudato si,* May 24, 2015, www.vatican.va.

10. St. Thomas Aquinas, *Summa Theologica,* Tertia Pars, 54, 1. 2, www.newadvent.org.

Another of the qualities is that of *impassibility*, in which the glorified flesh is eternally free from any pain, suffering or discomfort of any kind. In St. John's Gospel, Jesus invites Thomas to place his hand into the holes made by the nails, and also into his Side pierced by the lance: there is no pain or "infected" open wound (Jn. 20:27). St. Paul explains thus: "What is sown corruptible, rises incorruptible; what is sown unhonored, rises in glory; what is sown in weakness, is raised in power" (1 Cor. 15:42–43), and again: "the principle of corruption cannot share a life which is incorruptible" (1 Cor. 15:50). The Apocalypse also describes this new state of being: "and there will be no more death, or mourning, or cries of distress, no more sorrow; those old things have passed away" (Rev. 21:4).

The fourth fundamental quality known as *clarity* brings to the resurrected body a certain luminosity which stems from the glory it has obtained through imitation of the Lord: "Then, at last, the just will shine out, clear as the sun, in their Father's kingdom." (Matt. 13:43) This attribute had already been revealed during the Lord's Transfiguration on Mount Tabor when his face shone like the sun and his clothes became dazzlingly white (cf. Matt. 17:2); it was a foretaste of his own approaching glorification. Although this quality will be present in all the redeemed, it will not be to the same intensity of brightness. That will be solely dependent on the degree of holiness present within each person, as St. Paul teaches: "The sun has its own beauty, the moon has hers, the stars have theirs, one star even differs from another in its beauty. So it is with the resurrection of the dead" (1 Cor. 15:41-42).

The Gospel writers were very clear in showing how the body of Jesus after his resurrection was still able to work the same way as before even if it didn't need to. For instance, the Lord ate in front of them (cf. Lk. 24:43), he cooked fish on the shore by the Sea of Tiberias (cf. Jn. 21:9), he conversed with them in the same way as he had before (cf. Jn. 21:15–22, cf. Lk. 24:36–49), and he gave them his blessing (cf. Lk. 24:50). The point being stressed is that while the body has undergone an anthropological change, it nevertheless retains the original distinguishing features that made the unity of body and soul a human person; therefore we are far removed from a purely spiritual being like the angels. The resurrection will erase the defects and bring to perfection the physicality of the body, allowing human nature to express itself in full, divinized freedom, as St. Irenaeus tells us: "that He [Jesus Christ] might bring us to be even what He is Himself."[11]

If we are to become what "He is himself" then we must look towards how that is accomplished in the final consummation. In one way, we have already seen that the resurrection itself is part of that finality; our human nature is exalted in the manner decreed by the Lord. But that still leaves us with a missing piece in this mysterious mosaic: how does the *soul* experience God in such a way as to raise it to full communion with him? In order to answer that question, we need to try and understand as best we can the nature of the beatific vision and the beatitude that comes from that.[12]

Sacred Scripture assures us that at the end of our individual purification—whether on earth or in Purgatory—we will encounter God face to face, without any intermediary. Jesus, for instance said: "Blessed are the clean of heart; they shall see God" (Matt. 5:8), while St. Paul utilized imagery to express the same thought: "At present, we are looking at a confused reflection in a mirror; then, we shall see face to face; now, I have only glimpses of knowledge; then, I shall recognize God as he has recognized me" (1 Cor. 13:12). St. John too expressed similar sentiments: "But we know that when he comes we shall be like him; we shall see him, then, as he is" (1 Jn. 3:2). Pope Benedict XII, in his Constitution *Benedictus Deus* of 1336 defined this teaching as a dogma of the faith, stating that the souls of the saints:

> have seen and see the divine essence by intuitive vision, and even face to face, with no mediating creature, serving in the capacity of an object seen, but divine essence immediately revealing itself plainly, clearly, and openly, to them, and seeing thus they enjoy the

---

11. St. Irenaeus of Lyons, *Adversus Haereses*, Bk V, Preface, www.newadvent.org.

12. Although we are discussing this from the standpoint of the new heaven and new earth, we should also clarify that the beatific vision is possessed even now by the saints in heaven.

same divine essence, and also that from such vision and enjoyment their souls, which now have departed, are truly blessed and they have eternal life and rest.[13]

The beatific vision will consist of the soul sharing in the very life of God: his joys, his love, his will, and to a new extent, his knowledge.[14] This supernatural beatitude will be elevated by a singular divine grace: the *light of glory* which will make possible this vision of God. For, as St. Paul says: "his dwelling is in unapproachable light; no human eye has seen or can ever see him" (1 Tim. 6:16), and therefore it will only be through God, rather than through our own intellect, that this comes about. Coupled with this eternal grace, the Lord will bestow the redeemed with a new divine charity which will bring the soul into a complete unity with God—who is Love itself.

So what do we mean by seeing God face to face? Undoubtedly, this goes far beyond the physical element of seeing as we do on earth, because seeing with the eye does not allow one to penetrate into a person's inner life. With the beatific vision, God reveals Himself with the most startling clarity so that our intellect now comprehends divine wisdom, justice, mercy, truth and creativity in a way that was not possible before. The divine mysteries can finally be comprehended: the Communion of the three divine persons, the mystery of the Incarnation of the Eternal Word, the question of suffering and evil, the mystical power of the Sacraments, the mysterious unity of the communion of saints and the mysteries of the Universe. What we strived to understand formerly through faith will now be perceived through God himself; the saints will contemplate these sacred truths through His "eyes" as it were, marvelling at His inexhaustible inventiveness, and with a joy that is unimaginable to us here below.

---

13. Pope Benedict XII, Constitution, *Benedictus Deus*, January 29, 1336, cited in: Heinrich Joseph Dominicus Denzinger, *Enchiridion symbolorum, definitionum et declarationum de rebus fidei et morum*, 1000, www.patristica.net.

14. Knowledge, it would seem, would not be complete as even within this beatified state, the soul would still remain a creature and thus not possess the infinite capacity of God.

Of course, as the intellect and will are caught up in the beatific vision, so too is love. But the focus is not primarily our love for God, but God's love for us (cf. 1 Jn. 4:10). It is the very same divine love from which the Holy Spirit proceeds as the uncreated Immaculate Conception. However, the Eternal Father and Son will take our *own* poor love and bring it to perfection in a celestial beatitude, binding (through the Holy Spirit) the sanctified soul to them in a rapture of immense proportions. For even if the saints are unable to offer God the infinite love He offers them, nevertheless they will offer a love that is the maximum they are capable of.

In terms of the Mystical Body, the beatific vision must also have a Christological dimension because it is through Jesus that we will see the Father: "I am the way; I am truth and life; nobody can come to the Father, except through me" (Jn. 14:6). Perhaps at times the traditional understanding of the beatific vision has neglected the entire Trinitarian aspect that would place Christ and the Holy Spirit within the same divine experience as the Father. If Jesus, though the Holy Spirit, has raised humanity to the capacity of being able to behold the divine person of the Father, then we must perceive the centrality of being part of his Body within this context. The Father will look upon us as part of the Body of his Son—made possible through the sanctification of the Holy Spirit—and therefore we will enter fully into the Trinitarian life. In Jesus, the Son, we will share a filial vision of the Father in the communion of the same Divine Spirit.

If we are considering the ultimate things, we shouldn't forget that life on earth contains elements that are a foretaste of the life to come. The joys we experience in this life, for instance, are like tiny precursors of the joys to be experienced in the divine life, and they do serve to direct our restless hearts to the eschatological realities. In the temporal happiness they bring, they remind us of the instinct that dwells deep within our souls; that God-given longing for something so much greater, as St. Augustine famously wrote: "For Thou hast made us for Thyself and our hearts are restless till they rest in Thee."[15] The living of a constant, authentic Catholic life is oriented

---

15. St. Augustine, *Confessions* (London: Sheed & Ward, 1948), 1.

precisely toward this vision of glory, and as we saw in chapter four, the beatitudes are the template that prepares the soul in the most fitting way possible.

The beatific vision will also bring a new intensity to the communion begun through baptism. The saints will now have been transformed comprehensively through the action of the Holy Spirit and thus will fly to the Lord with a perfect act of charity. The soul will finally be able to say without hesitation: "Abba, Father" (Rom. 8:15); not that it cannot now on earth, but in heaven the words will resound with a new vitality that stems from the knowledge that it can never betray its Father through sin again. From this moment on, communion will exist in an eternal present in which love will flow continually. It will be forever the first instant, because if it were not, it could be envisaged that a lessening of that initial intensity were possible, thus bringing God's beatitude into the finite. The truth however is that God is eternally immutable; He lives as absolute Love, not in the past or future, but in the immediate moment, and when He beckons us with these rousing words: "come and share the joy of thy Lord" (Matt. 25:21), He will invite us to be consumed by his divine nature. Nothing will ever make us want to escape it for even the briefest second; in reality, we will be "gluttons" for God, seduced by his infinite goodness, charity, joy and holiness.

Finally, the saints will live in the divine will in such a perfect way that the two wills will correspond exactly. No longer will the souls of the just seek to *conform* their will while fighting against the rebellious poison of concupiscence, but in true freedom the beatific vision will enable them to act *identically* with the will of God. In terms of the era *within* salvation history, this will manifest itself most profoundly in their pleas on behalf of those still journeying towards the heavenly homeland. The saints, possessors of a perfect charity, will see the necessities of the Church Militant and Suffering from the divine volition, meaning that every prayer will be channelled in such a way as to aid the salvific plan as intended by God. In this way, the company of the blessed will live as one united force for good, operating with absolute precision in the work of the Lord.

Now that we have set in place the framework for our communion with God, we can look at the definitive communion that will prevail among the saints on the renewed earth, seeking to understand the pure bliss of loving interaction that will ensue. Before we do that however, something needs to be said concerning the nature of prayer among the community of the redeemed. As we have already seen, prayer takes on various forms while the first heaven and earth exist. But in the new time of eternity, the entire nature of worship will move in one direction: adoration. There will be no further need for intercession because the former things will have passed away, and because of the beatific vision, adoration will be continual; as St. Augustine says: "there perpetual praising, there Alleluia always without fail."[16] The new earth will become the setting for one continuous liturgy of the most solemn and perfect kind, a festival of rejoicing and thanksgiving that will never end!

The New Life: A Communion of Peace

If we turn to the relationships between the glorified children of God, the Gospels reveal some very informative words of Jesus on the subject. Matthew, Mark and Luke all relate the question of the Sadducees concerning marriage in the afterlife; because for them, there was to be no resurrection. They proposed a scenario where seven brothers were successively married to the same woman. Eventually she also died. They asked the Lord to whom would she be married in the resurrection? (cf. Lk. 20:27–33).[17] Jesus replied:

> The children of this world marry and are given in marriage; but those who are found worthy to attain that other world, and resurrection from the dead, take neither wife nor husband; mortal no longer, they will be as the angels in heaven are, children of God, now that the resurrection has given them birth. But as for the dead rising again, Moses himself has told you of it in the passage about the burning bush, where he calls the Lord the God of Abraham and the God of Isaac and the God of Jacob. It is of living men, not of dead men, that he is the God; for him, all men are alive. (Lk. 20:34–38)

16. St. Augustine, "Homily 10 on the First Epistle of St. John," 6, www.newadvent.org.

17. The discussion is also related in Matt. 22:23–33, and Mk. 12:18–27.

Leaving aside the issue of why the Sadducees were utterly wrong—they neither really knew the Scriptures nor truly believed in the power of God—Jesus clearly distinguishes between the life of the first heaven and earth and the second. He places earthly marriage in the context of being fruitful to increase the human race (cf. Gen. 1:28), while after the Fall there is the added complication of mortality. Marriage therefore has a precise role to play in ensuring the number of the elect is as God wills. In the new heaven and earth however, preparation will have given way to fulfilment and the earthly nature will have been superseded by a spiritual nature. That is why the Lord compares the resurrected saints to the angels—not that they will be of the same substance, but of the same disposition. It is also clear that in the resurrection, masculinity and femininity will remain, each still clearly distinct from one another.

If we go a little deeper into the question of the intensity of relationships—especially between man and woman—in this eschatological state, we can surmise that there will still be bonds that are special and have a uniqueness about them. And remaining within the context of marriage, since marriage, through its principle of procreative and unitive love resembles the love of the Most Holy Trinity, it is possible to see how the former expression of sexuality will be transformed into something new.

Our starting point for this discussion revolves around the gift of sexuality itself. It is without doubt the highest form of a purely earthly love, and when utilized in the way God intended, it brings together man and woman into a unity so great that it becomes creative. In that way it is communion *par excellence*. And when we consider that it comes from God's will and design, then we know that it is a most wonderful gift that is truly good and blessed. However, in a sense, sexuality is not too dissimilar to fire. As well as providing warmth it can burn; so much so that it can utterly destroy. We must be honest and confess that because of the weight of our sinful nature, very few will ever leave this life without having been scolded by it in some way great or small. Like life itself and free will, sexuality can be abused, with quite devastating consequences. This explains why the Church is so protective of this precious gift in its teachings. But in its most positive element, it perhaps comes

344

closest to imitating the intensity of love that will exist in the new earth.

So we should ask ourselves this question: does anything of marriage remain in the age to come? The answer must be a qualified yes, because God never takes away the good that has endured; he only ever strips away evil. So even if—as in the case of the seven brothers—each of them were married to one woman, in the Holy City of God there will still be a particular bond of love between each of them. Of course marriage itself will no longer be available, but the fruits of it most certainly will; the point of departure being that sexuality in its present form will give way to a higher, divine love in which the *spiritual* will reign supreme over the *physical*. Perhaps it doesn't seem possible that people (legitimately) married to more than one person on earth could tolerate this new situation; but there is one form of relationship that exists even now that goes some way to illuminating this concept: the one between the devoted son and the Blessed Virgin. It seems that those who possess a great love for Mary already experience even now a grace that is akin to the one to be bestowed on those who were married on earth. Why do I say this? It is because there is an especially deep affection for this beautiful icon of true femininity which would seem in some way to transcend purely earthly love. The holiness of Mary is like a perfume that enchants her devoted, and thus they can only *ever* see her femininity in the light of her transfigured glory. Could anyone ever contemplate anything other than a divine love towards her? Even for St. Joseph her spouse, we can imagine this being the case. Notwithstanding his own exceptional sanctity which could have desired virginity for the sake of the Kingdom, he must have loved Mary in such a way that he totally bypassed the desire for normal marital relations. In this way, Joseph and Mary were already living in the most sublime way that which those who were once married will live in eternity.

Understood in this way, relationships between man and woman in eternity will exhibit a new found liberty, free from tensions and earthly expectation. Each will recognize the other's physical perfection but crucially it will be appreciated in precisely the same way the Lord appreciates it: "And God saw all that he had made, and found

it very good" (Gen. 1:31). Earthly virginity for the sake of the Kingdom (cf. Matt. 19:12), to which Catholic priests and religious are
called, testifies to this new and definitive form of relationship in a
most remarkable and prophetic way; it anticipates through self-
renunciation a transcendent and spotless *divine* love. St. John Paul
II spoke of it in a series of general audiences in 1982:

> Such a human being, man and woman, indicates the eschatologi-
> cal virginity of the risen man. In him there will be revealed, I
> would say, the absolute and eternal nuptial meaning of the glori-
> fied body in union with God himself through the "face to face"
> vision of him, and glorified also through the union of a perfect
> intersubjectivity. This will unite all who participate in the other
> world, men and women, in the mystery of the communion of
> saints.[18]

Even if we accept that certain relationships will hold some special
significance in the New Jerusalem (cf. Rev. 21:2)—those familial or
those bound by a salvific significance[19]—we shouldn't insinuate that
communion between the glorified in a more general sense will be
any less committed or loving. Each and every one will rejoice in seeing the glory present in another; every friendship will have at its core
the presences of the Most Holy Trinity and thus a supreme charity
will reign. As a consequence of this, each person will delight in seeing a divine reflection manifest in another. The peace of the Lord
will rest upon all, instilling tranquillity and harmony far greater
than anything experienced in this life, and because of the primacy of
the beatific vision, all the joys experienced by the company of saints
will be realized through this prism of beatitude. Nothing will be
lacking; there will be no fear, doubt or envy, even when the holiness
of those closer to God is revealed. Quite the opposite will happen.
Those who experience the beatific vision to a lesser degree (it will be
proportionate to their level of holiness) will marvel at their fellow
saints who manifest a likeness to God closer than their own. In a

18. St. John Paul II, "General Audience," March 24, 1982, *L'Osservatore Romano*, Weekly Edition in English, March 29, 1982, 3.

19. Perhaps in the case where the prayers and sacrifices of one had contributed
to the salvation of another.

symbolic way, the doors of each house will be open at all times; neighbors will now be family, the gardens of the new earth, settings for the most serene and joyful encounters. "Acquaintance" will be a word no longer necessary since the new heart will beat in love for the least in the Kingdom to the greatest, and divine grace will flow continuously like a river coursing through the entire community.

The new life of the saints will bring to fruition everything willed by the Father for his Son Jesus because as St. John tells us: "It was through him that all things came into being, and without him came nothing that has come to be" (Jn. 1:3). Through the Son's recapitulation of creation therefore, humanity will achieve its purpose in sharing the divine life offered to it as a free gift from the depths of the Father's mercy. The Lord will garb his people with resplendent garments that reflect their dignity as citizens of the new earth, and from His throne of glory He will look with pleasure at His chosen ones as they form one united chorus in praise and thanksgiving. His delight will also be in the spiritual image of His Son, visible in the glorified bodies of the saints,[20] and thus all creation will sing of the vindicating triumph of the Lamb who was slain yet lives forever.

As we conclude this chapter, let us take stock of the marvellous recreation that awaits us, and let us reflect on it so that faith, hope and charity are energized within us, and within the communion of saints as a whole. We must look to the future with confidence knowing that time is moving ever closer to its consummation when Jesus will finally bring to completion the work entrusted to him by the Father. He will see to it that every enemy of his is defeated, that everything that hinders the path for his subjects on the road to true freedom is banished forever. Then, as St. Paul tells us, salvation history will be complete and the Son will present to his Father the fruits of his redemptive work:

---

20. If there is to be a visible similarity between the saints and their Savior, it may be that this includes a representation of age also. As tradition tells us that Jesus died and rose again at the age of 33, it must be a possibility that the resurrected body will look (in a transfigured way) to be that age. St. Augustine held this view (cf. *Civitate Dei*, bk. XXII, ch. 15), as did St. Thomas Aquinas (*Summa Theologica*, Supl. 81.1).

God has put all things in subjection under his feet; that is, all things have been made subject to him, except indeed that power which made them his subjects. And when that subjection is complete, then the Son himself will become subject to the power which made all things his subjects, so that God may be all in all. (1 Cor. 15:26–28)

In the new heaven and new earth, the mourning veil will finally be lifted and the redeemed will be presented with the full revelation of the mystery of the Most Holy Trinity. Creation, redemption and sanctification will be understood as never before in the light of the work of the three divine persons, and unspeakable joy will come from their divine presence dwelling forever with the company of the blessed. The vision of the interaction between Father, Son and Holy Spirit will finally reveal the full, beautiful truth concerning communion, and thus the saints will perfectly imitate it. In this way, the new world will be the exultation of unity: unity between all the varied forms of creation from the pinnacle of humanity, to angels, animal and then plant life.

This is the future that the Lord has mapped out for us. As a tender, loving Father He desires our complete happiness and thus he wills to transform and divinize us. In spite of the fracture caused by Adam and Eve's sin, he has rewritten the story with an epilogue of extraordinary glory; and it is ours if we so wish. The Lord in his mercy has made this possible by forming part of this communion within history—the Catholic Church—which is the seed and initial stage of the Kingdom to be manifested on the renewed earth. And as part of his Mystical Body, the members of this Church experience a tangible and loving communion with Jesus even now; most profoundly through his sacramental presence in the Holy Eucharist. To be a Catholic and live it to the full is to be part of the great tapestry of salvation history that cuts through time and finds its way into eternity, and it is my hope that these pages have shown that within this Church—the Church founded by Jesus for precisely this reason—the deepest longings of the human heart can be realized. The need to love and be loved which eludes no one, is a central pillar of Christianity and therefore within the Church, those suffering from the loneliness and emptiness of life can find a home where Jesus welcomes them with open arms. The eternal life of which we speak can begin the moment we embrace this invitation of the Lord and thus we can enter into the communion of love that has captivated countless souls throughout the ages. Jesus alone *is* the answer to the mystery of human existence that plagues mankind; he alone holds the keys of life and death, and he alone has the ability to raise us to new life one day. He promises us an eternal summer of the most glorious kind in the new time to come, and his Church on earth is the door that leads to it. For this reason, I encourage those who presently do not belong to the Catholic Church to see it as their true home from which they can participate fully in the communion of saints. There is no greater grace or joy in life than this.

Let us therefore rise and be on our way (cf. Jn. 14:31), ready to greet the Lord when he comes in glory with his saints. May the invocation *Maranatha*, Come Lord Jesus!, resound in our hearts as a prayer of hope and expectation until the Sun of Justice illuminates the new Universe, and finally, may we make this prayer of Pope Benedict XVI our own:

> Lord, make your promise come fully true. Break the rods of the oppressors. Burn the tramping boots. Let the time of the garments rolled in blood come to an end. Fulfil the prophecy that "of peace there will be no end" (Is. 9:7). We thank you for your goodness, but we also ask you to show forth your power. Establish the dominion of your truth and your love in the world—the "kingdom of righteousness, love and peace."[21]

---

21. Pope Benedict XVI, "Homily for Midnight Mass," December 24, 2010, www.vatican.va.

ༀ Epilogue ༀ

The Thousand Year
Kingdom of Christ and His Saints

These were endowed with life, and reigned as kings with Christ for a thousand years; but the rest of the dead remained lifeless while the thousand years lasted. Such is the first resurrection. Blessed and holy is his lot who has a share in this first resurrection; over such the second death has no power, they will be priests of God, priests of Christ; all those thousand years they will reign with him. (Rev. 20:4–6)

IN RECENT YEARS, noticeably with the plethora of reported apparitions and mystical events, there has been a growing interest in matters of an eschatological nature; that is the *novissimis* which relate to the end times and the establishment of the Lord's Kingdom, which we have just analyzed. As a consequence of that, certain interpretations have arisen which contradict the clear teachings of the Church. In this way, a sort of parallel magisterium has taken over *in some quarters* on questions relating to the sequence of events leading to the end of the world. One such interpretation which has gained traction more than others concerns the thousand year reign of Christ and his saints mentioned in Revelation chapter 20; the main exponent being Father Joseph Iannuzzi, OSJ. His thesis, while rejecting *one* classic form of the heretical concept of millenarianism (that Jesus will *physically* return to earth for a literal thousand years before the end of the world), still seeks to present a temporal Kingdom which is characterized by similar millenarian tendencies found in the former.

In Fr. Iannuzzi's interpretation, based in part on certain teachings from the Patristic era, he foresees a "spiritual millennium" which contains several elements before and during it. To begin with, he explains the meaning of the "Day of the Lord" as consisting of two tribulations and two triumphs separated by the millennium in between.[1] The first tribulation will consist of the persecution of the Antichrist, while the second will be by Satan himself. After the Antichrist's defeat, a first instance of the Last Judgement will take place and the "abolishment of all the earth's evildoers."[2] Christ will then "descend from heaven in his glorified spirit."[3] Fr. Iannuzzi explains that this descent of Jesus is not in the flesh, and that he will reign "over" the earth. With this new spiritual manifestation of Jesus, the world will be transformed and become the setting for a temporal kingdom in which Christianity will rule. Satan will be chained[4] and unable to have any power over the saints. In fact, Fr. Iannuzzi on the one hand says original sin will remain, but on the other, that the three forces that entice us to sin—the world, the flesh, and the devil—will lose their power. With the world transformed, its enticements will be "extinguished."[5] In this interpretation of Rev. 20, the resurrection of the saints at the beginning of this temporal kingdom is still taken literally, therefore the world will be inhabited by a remnant who have not yet tasted death, and a company of saints living an ontologically different existence altogether: glorified and non-glorified living side by side.

The world will also share in this new state of holiness: total peace and harmony among creatures, no sorrow or mourning and no illness. Not only that. The people of the earth will live the divine will perfectly, giving fulfilment to the petition prayed in the *Our Father*. Essentially then, we have before us an era of peace and holiness that

---

1. Joseph Iannuzzi, *The Triumph of God's Kingdom in the Millennium and End Times* (Havertown: St. John the Evangelist Press, 1999), 138. The case for belief in this millennial theory was also made in a second book, Joseph Iannuzzi, *The Splendor of Creation* (McKees Rocks: St. Andrew's Productions, 2004).

2. Ibid., 147.

3. Ibid., 164.

4. The chaining of Satan, within this interpretation, is a literal reading of Rev. 20:3, which is taken to mean he will be bound by the Angel immediately before the temporal era begins; an interpretation that, as we will discover, is at odds with Tradition.

5. Iannuzzi, 124.

is basically utopian and fully Christian in character.[6] It foresees an end to evil for a time with justice and divine love prevailing; a quite glorious scene. Of course this interpretation has not come out of thin air. It is based on some writings of early Church Fathers, and Fr. Iannuzzi quotes various passages from these figures to strengthen his argument.

The millennial theory was rooted in the concept of the seven days of creation; and as God rested on the seventh day, certain Fathers took that up and applied it also to a future time before the end of the world. Thus a seventh day seemed to fit well with the passage relating to a thousand year reign found in the Apocalypse. St. Justin, Tertullian, and even St. Augustine for a time held this view. For Fr. Iannuzzi however, it is Lactantius who wrote "perhaps the finest exposition on the millennium as developed in the Apostolic Tradition."[7] Let us read briefly from his *Divine Institutes* which are quoted in support of a spiritual millennium, as opposed to millenarianism:

> Therefore, since all the works of God were completed in six days, the world must continue in its present state through six ages, that is, six thousand years. For the great day of God is limited by a circle of a thousand years, as the prophet shows, who says "In Your sight, O Lord, a thousand years are as one day." And as God

---

6. In support of a theory that foresees a Christianization of the world, Fr. Iannuzzi, on page 75 of *The Triumph of God's Kingdom*, quotes from a 1952 "theological commission" which stated: "If before that final end there is to be a period, more or less prolonged, of triumphant sanctity, such a result will be brought about not by the apparition of the person of Christ in Majesty but by the operation of those powers of sanctification which are now at work, the Holy Ghost and the Sacraments of the Church." The reality is that this was written by Abbott Anscar Vonier (who died in 1938) as his singular contribution to a volume on Catholic doctrine. There was no theological commission. In any case, Abbott Vonier places this speculation not in reference to any spiritual millennium which he calls a form of "religious dreaming"—but in the hope of evangelization spreading throughout the world and being accepted. It cannot be used to imply a miraculous holiness that imbues all humanity within a temporal new heaven and new earth. See, *The Teaching of the Catholic Church: A Summary of Catholic Doctrine,* vol. II, edited and arranged by Canon George D. Smith (New York, The Macmillan Company, 1961), 1140.

7. Iannuzzi, 40.

laboured during those six days in creating such great works, so His religion and truth must labour during these six thousand years, while wickedness prevails and bears rule. And again, since God, having finished His works, rested the seventh day and blessed it, at the end of the six thousandth year all wickedness must be abolished from the earth, and righteousness reign for a thousand years; and there must be tranquillity and rest from the labours which the world now has long endured.[8]

Concerning Christ's "spiritual" coming we read:

Therefore the Son of the most high and mighty God shall come to judge the quick and the dead.... But He, when He shall have destroyed unrighteousness, and executed His great judgment, and shall have recalled to life the righteous, who have lived from the beginning, will be engaged among men a thousand years, and will rule them with most just command.[9]

Fr. Iannuzzi explains that the phrase "[Christ] will be engaged among men a thousand years" does not refer to a physical reign, but a reign in the Eucharist. However in chapter 19 of the *Divine Institutes*, it is clear that Lactantius foresees a physical presence of Jesus on earth at this time:

But other princes also and tyrants who have harassed the world, together with him [the Antichrist], *shall be led in chains to the king; and he shall rebuke them, and reprove them, and upbraid them with their crimes, and condemn them,* and consign them to deserved tortures. Thus, wickedness being extinguished and impiety suppressed, the world will be at rest.[10]

Lactantius makes no attempt anywhere in his eschatological writings to suggest Jesus will manifest his presence in the Eucharist. This text is clearly portraying Jesus sitting on a throne of judgment before his captives.[11]

---

8. Lactantius, *The Divine Institutes*, bk VII, 14, www.newadvent.org.

9. Ibid., bk VII, 24.

10. Ibid., bk VII, 19.

11. It should be noted that the early Church Fathers were not immune to errors in their writings, or even non-Christian influences. The great patristic scholar, Fr. Brian E. Daley S.J., in his eschatological work, *The Hope of the Early Church*, has

To complete this eschatological thesis, we are led to understand that at the end of the symbolic thousand years, Satan will be unchained and will set about seducing the nations and encircling the camp of the Saints. At that point the second instance of the Last Judgment will take place and Jesus will descend again, physically this time, to bring history to an end and send the devil and all evil-doers to their eternal fate.

Now that we have this theory in place, I would like to detail exactly why it is wrong, so that our hope is centered solely on the truth of Christ's second coming, which alone demands our eschatological attention through history.

In the first instance, we need to understand the concept of millenarianism. Fr. Iannuzzi is at pains to point out the various forms condemned by the Church in earlier centuries; they all one way or another are centered on several ideas: the physical presence of Jesus on earth for a thousand years with carnal feasting for the saints, or a mitigated version where the saints have spiritual blessings but with Jesus still physically present.

However, millenarianism is not just restricted to these ancient forms. Recent Popes have clarified that. Pope Benedict XVI referred to *liberation theology* as a "facile millenarianism" because it mistakenly "promised the full conditions for a just life immediately,"[12] while St. John Paul II placed millenarianism and various forms of

---

some damning words concerning Lactantius' millenarian writings: "Its contents, however, are a curious hybrid of Christian apocalypticism and the speculations of late pagan "propheti" literature—of works like the non-Christian Sibylline Oracles, the Hermetic tract Asclepius, and the Hellenized Zoroastrian work known as the Oracles of Hystaspes. This eclecticism is undoubtedly due in part to Lactantius' apologetic and popularizing intentions in writing the work, but it also represents the farthest development hitherto of what would become a much more widespread phenomenon: the blending of biblical eschatology with elements of folk religion, occult speculation and late antique literary traditions, in a vividly concrete picture of our individual and collective destinies. From now on, the apocalyptic myth Lactantius portrays, with both its Christian and its non-Christian elements, was to have a life of its own." Brian E. Daley, *The Hope of the Early Church* (Cambridge, Cambridge University Press, 1991), 66.

12. Pope Benedict XVI, "Interview During the Flight to Brazil," May 9, 2007, www.vatican.va.

messianism within the context of an illusory hope that is "restricted to this world and closed to transcendence."[13] Understood in this magisterial sense, millenarianism is the error that leads one to think that hope can be translated into fulfilment within an intra-historical setting—no matter what form it takes.

Without doubt, Nazism and Communism were political variants of the heresy. Concerning the specific idea as proposed by Fr. Iannuzzi of a temporal era of peace within history, the Congregation for the Doctrine of Faith had, in 1995, dealt with the issue when advising on negative aspects of the purported "messages" given to Mrs. Vassula Ryden. Referring to it as one of several "doctrinal errors," the notification stated:

> These alleged revelations predict an imminent period when the Antichrist will prevail in the Church. In *millenarian style*, it is prophesied that God is going to make a final, glorious intervention which will initiate on earth, even before Christ's definitive coming, an era of peace and universal prosperity.[14]

The Popes have at times stressed the truth that humanity and the Church will continue to battle the forces of evil constantly until the end of the world—which obviously leaves no room for a spiritual millennium. St. John Paul II stated: "As long as this world endures, history will always be the theatre of the clash between God and Satan, between good and evil, between grace and sin, between life and death."[15] How can this be possible if Satan is bound for a sym-

---

13. St. John Paul II, Apostolic Exhortation, *Ecclesia in Europa*, 10, June 28, 2003, www.vatican.va.

14. *Acta Apostolica Sedis*, 88 (1996), 956–957. It should be noted that Fr. Iannuzzi makes reference to a supposed answer Cardinal Ratzinger gave to Fr. Martino Penasa in 1990 relating in some way to a millennium stating: "The Holy See has not yet made any definitive pronouncement in this regard." Unfortunately we don't know the exact question that was asked, and, moreover, it was Cardinal Ratzinger who signed the above notification stating an era of peace within history was a doctrinal error; therefore the matter has now been dealt with by the Holy See. And as we shall see later, even long before 1990, Cardinal Ratzinger had dismissed this millennial idea.

15. St. John Paul II, "Homily at Mass for the Feast of the Assumption," August 15, 1998, www.vatican.va.

bolic thousand years? Pope Benedict XVI echoed his predecessor's words on route to Fatima in 2010: "The Lord told us that the Church would constantly be suffering, in different ways, until the end of the world."[16] The Holy Father touches on an important point here in that the Gospels are completely silent concerning any sense of millennial expectation on the part of Jesus. It is nowhere to be found in his teachings; on the contrary the Lord affirms in the parable of the wheat and the tares that good and evil will grow together in the field of the world until harvest time at the Last Judgment (cf. Matt. 13:24–30). The Vatican II Pastoral Constitution *Gaudium et Spes* is equally dismissive of any hope for a future golden age: "For a monumental struggle against the powers of darkness pervades the whole history of man. The battle was joined from the very origins of the world and will continue until the last day, as the Lord has attested."[17]

At this point, it would make sense to go back to the text of Revelation chapter 20 and seek answers to the true meaning of this seemingly perplexing text. Several important points stand out: Satan is chained by an Angel and imprisoned for a thousand years, after which he will be let out for a short time (v. 1–3). Those who were martyred for Christ are endowed with life and reign as kings with him for a thousand years in a first resurrection (v. 4–6). After the thousand years are over, Satan seduces the nations and then makes war on the camp of the saints until the Lord sends fire down to consume him. He is then thrown into the lake of fire where the beast and false prophet also reside (v. 7–10).

So how should we interpret the chaining of Satan if it cannot be placed immediately before a temporal kingdom? The answer lies in the words of Jesus recounted in St. Matthew's Gospel:

> But if, when I cast out devils, I do it through the Spirit of God, then it must be that the kingdom of God has already appeared among you. How is anyone to gain entrance into the house of a strong man and plunder his goods *without first making the strong*

16. Pope Benedict XVI, "Meeting with Journalists on the Flight to Portugal," May 11, 2010, www.vatican.va.

17. *Gaudium et Spes*, no. 37, www.vatican.va

man his prisoner? Then he can plunder his house at will. (Matt. 12:28–29)

In this text, Jesus makes clear that he has come down to earth (which through original sin had become the "house" of Satan), in order to plunder it, rooting out its evil "goods" and thus installing his own Kingdom within it. In order to do that, he says the strong man (Satan) must first be bound and made his prisoner. Understood in this way, the chaining of the devil occurred at the moment Jesus gave his life on the Cross to save humanity; it should also not escape our notice how the Lord relates this to his casting out of devils—exorcisms which manifest Jesus's power over evil spirits. St. Irenaeus writes:

> For as in the beginning he [Satan] enticed man to transgress his Maker's law, and thereby got him into his power; yet his power consists in transgression and apostasy, and with these he bound man (to himself); so again, on the other hand, it was necessary that through man himself he should, when conquered, be bound with the same chains with which he had bound man, in order that man, being set free, might return to his Lord, leaving to him (Satan) those bonds by which he himself had been fettered, that is, sin. For when Satan is bound, man is set free.[18]

St. Augustine also places these two passages of Scripture together:

> The Lord Jesus Christ Himself says, "No man can enter into a strong man's house, and spoil his goods, except he first bind the strong man"—meaning by the strong man the devil, because he had power to take captive the human race; and meaning by his goods which he was to take, those who had been held by the devil in various sins and iniquities, but were to become believers in Himself. It was then for the binding of this strong one that the apostle saw in the Apocalypse.[19]

---

18. St. Irenaeus, *Adversus Haereses*, Bk V, ch. 21. 3, www.newadvent.org.

19. St. Augustine of Hippo, *Civitate Dei*, bk XX, ch. 7, www.newadvent.org. St. John Paul II confirmed this exact interpretation in a general audience of August 20, 1986.

As I mentioned at the beginning of this epilogue, to a great extent these millennial ideas have arisen from the plethora of unapproved private revelations which have circulated, and without doubt, influenced many well-meaning Catholics. So is there any fully approved private revelation that can "confirm" the argument of which we are making? The answer is yes, and it comes in the form of the various visions granted to St. Hildegard of Bingen and affirmed by Pope Eugene III in 1147. Concerning the chaining of Satan we read:

> And around its neck a chain is riveted, which also binds its hands and feet; which is to say that the strength of the Devil was so broken and crushed by the power of Almighty God that he cannot freely work his evil and accost humans in the way. And this chain is firmly fastened to a rock in the abyss, confining it so that it cannot move about as its wicked will desires; for the power of God abides unfailingly and immovably for eternity, and by *saving souls oppresses the Devil so forcibly that he is not able by inner or outer means to take away redemption from the faithful.*[20]

As the devil is chained through the Divine Son's Sacrifice, we can place the beginning of the thousand years at the time when the Church was born; because as we saw in part one, the Church emanated from the pierced side of the Lord upon the Cross. It is also worth clarifying that the chaining, because it primarily relates to the act of redemption, does not take away Satan's influence on the world which will remain until the end of time; only that he can no longer stop salvation reaching individuals who respond to God's grace. With this in mind, let us consider the idea of the first resurrection. What can it mean? St. John describes his vision thus:

> I saw the souls of all those who went to execution for love of the truth concerning Jesus, and of God's word, and all who would not worship the beast, or its image, or bear its mark on their foreheads and their hands. These were endowed with life, and reigned as kings with Christ for a thousand years; but the rest of the dead remained lifeless while the thousand years lasted. Such is the first resurrection. Blessed and holy is his lot who has a share in this first

20. St. Hildegard of Bingen, *Scivias*, bk. II, vision 7.11 (Mahwah: Paulist Press, 1990), 297.

resurrection; over such the second death has no power, they will be priests of God, priests of Christ; all those thousand years they will reign with him. (Rev. 20:4–6)

Clearly then, we are talking about a Kingdom; but of what type? If we recall the Lord's words to Pontius Pilate: "My kingdom, said Jesus, does not belong to this world . . . my kingdom does not take its origin here" (Jn. 18:36). That is because it is a spiritual kingdom, not political or temporal. In fact with these words we could argue that Jesus condemns all Christian millenarian ideals because each of them will always be rooted within history, earthly in essence. The first resurrection therefore must be linked to the reception of baptism which allows one to enter into this spiritual kingdom, and by extension the entire communion of saints. In the Catechism of the Catholic Church, we read of the dignity bestowed through baptism:

> Christ, high priest and unique mediator, has made of the Church "a kingdom, priests for his God and Father." The whole community of believers is, as such, priestly. The faithful exercise their baptismal priesthood through their participation, each according to his own vocation, in Christ's mission as priest, prophet, and king. Through the sacraments of Baptism and Confirmation the faithful are "consecrated to be . . . a holy priesthood."[21]

In St. John's description of those who came to life during this thousand years he refers to them as "kings" (v. 4) and "priests" (v. 6) while confirming their role as prophets because they "went to execution for love of the truth concerning Jesus, and of God's word" (v. 4). If we understand the thousand years as pertaining to the entire duration of the Church Militant until the final coming of Jesus, then we see how this first resurrection makes possible the witness of martyrdom for the faith. By informing us that the rest of the dead remain lifeless until the thousand years are over, St. John alludes to the spiritual nature of the resurrection. Only those incorporated into Christ's Body can share in his new life of the spirit. There is another key indicator in the text which affirms a baptismal understanding of the first resurrection. The seer of Patmos writes:

---

21. *Catechism of the Catholic Church*, no. 1546, www.vatican.va.

"Blessed and holy is his lot who has a share in this first resurrection; over such the second death has no power" (Rev. 20:6). The second death is eternal damnation. Now if the first resurrection is bodily, then that sentence seems unnecessary because the body has already found salvation, but if it is spiritual, it is confirming baptism as the antidote to the second death.[22]

If we turn once more to St. Hildegard, we again have confirmation that there will be no saints walking the earth with resurrected bodies before the end of the world:

> But from those who burn in God's sight with his love they receive the answer that they will not be able to receive their bodies back before the last judgment or before the trembling of the elements when a tremendous fire will purge the elements while God reveals his great power. For God's voice will call all the dead to rise, whether they be damned or saved.[23]

As already stated, in the spiritual millennium hypothesis, the thousand year reign goes hand in hand with that of the seventh day of rest; the idea of seeing history through the lens of successive ages or millenniums, mirroring the seven days of creation, one that was loved by the Church Fathers. In the erroneous millennial understanding, we are in the sixth millennium moving ever closer to the seventh. Obviously, in the context of the thousand years relating to the era of the Church, we are already far advanced into the seventh day awaiting the eighth of eternity. In St. Hildegard's *Scivias*, there is incontrovertible evidence that the seventh day is with us now, as God the Father explains:

---

22. Pope Benedict XVI taught this interpretation of the "first resurrection" in a general audience for Ash Wednesday, 2007: "Dead in Christ to sin, the baptized person is reborn to new life, freely re-established with his dignity as a child of God. For this reason, in the primitive Christian community Baptism was considered as 'the first resurrection' (cf. Rev 20:5; Rom 6:1–11; Jn 5:25–28)." Pope Benedict XVI, "General Audience," February 21, 2007, www.vatican.va. With these words, the Holy Father corrects the false understanding of some early Fathers who believed in a literal resurrection of the body before the end of the world.

23. St. Hildegard of Bingen, *The Book of the Rewards of Life (Liber vitae meritorum)* (New York: Oxford University Press, 1994), 32.

For in six days God completed His works, and on the seventh day He rested. What does this mean? The six days are the six numbered epochs; and in the sixth epoch the latest miracles were brought forth in the world, as God finished his work on the sixth day. *But now the world is in the seventh epoch, approaching the end of time, as on the seventh day.*[24]

In a further revelation, the Lord explains things in more detail:

For, as was said, God completed His works in six days. Five days represent five numbered epochs; and in the sixth, new wonders were manifested on earth, as on the sixth day the first man was created. And now the sixth number is complete and *the seventh has come, and the course of the world is fixed in, as it were the seventh day of rest.* For now that work which the mighty doctors kept sealed in the holy Scriptures is revealed; it is openly expounded in gentle words, like the words of this book, as if on a Sabbath of rest. For there are six days of work and a seventh of rest; there is no other number of days. And what lies beyond cannot be known to you, O human, but is in the keeping of the Father. But you o humans, have a time to traverse from now on, until the coming of that murderer who will try to pervert the Catholic faith. But as to what may happen then, it is not for you to know the time of that moment, even as you cannot know what comes after the seven days of the week; for only the Father knows this, who has placed these things in his power. And about the days of the week and times of the ages, it is not for you, O human, to know more.[25]

It is interesting that in this second passage, the Father seems to link the seventh day rest with the completion of the salvific work of his Son, meaning that the rest applies to the accessible fruit of redemption. In Book III, Vision 11:24 the Almighty confirms this interpretation: "And so after five epochs of the world, My Son showed himself to the world as it began to move towards its end." This ties in beautifully with the theology of recapitulation that was espoused by St. Irenaeus; as God completed His work of creation on

---

24. St. Hildegard of Bingen, *Scivias*, bk III, vision 11.17 (Mahwah: Paulist Press, 1990), 498.

25. Ibid., bk III, vision 11.23, 500–501.

the sixth day, Jesus recapitulated creation in the sixth epoch. And as on the seventh day when communion existed fully between God and creation, so in the seventh epoch through the Son's sacrifice this communion was perfectly restored. This perhaps sheds light on the theology of "rest" found in the Letter to the Hebrews. The author of the Letter urges us to hold fast to the promise of this rest (which is eternal life): "this rest is only to be attained by those who, like ourselves, have learned to believe" (Heb. 4:3), and similarly: "We must strive eagerly, then, to attain that rest; none of you must fall away into the same kind of unbelief. God's word to us is something alive, full of energy; it can penetrate deeper than any two-edged sword, reaching the very division between soul and spirit" (Heb. 4:11–12).

This recalls the words from *Scivias* concerning the "gentle words" of Sacred Scripture that are revealed in the seventh day. As Pope Benedict XVI wrote: "the divine word, spoken in time, is bestowed and 'consigned' to the Church in a definitive way, so that the proclamation of salvation can be communicated effectively in every time and place."[26] The seventh day therefore corresponds to the time and mission of the Church in revealing the Word of God: "The Word goes forth from the Father, comes to dwell in our midst and then returns to the Father in order to bring with him the whole of creation which was made in him and for him. The Church now carries out her mission in eager expectation of the eschatological manifestation of the Bridegroom: the Spirit and the bride say: 'Come!'" (Rev. 22:17)[27]

At this point, let us return briefly to the concept of a temporal kingdom. It is at times claimed that St. Augustine allows the interpretation of a spiritual millennium,[28] because he says in the *City of God* that: "this opinion would not be objectionable, if it were believed that the joys of the saints in that Sabbath shall be spiritual [rather than carnal], and consequent on the presence of God; for I

---

26. Pope Benedict XVI, Apostolic Exhortation, *Verbum Domini*, September 30, 2010, www.vatican.va.

27. Ibid.

28. Fr. Iannuzzi states: "Conversely, it can be gleaned from his writings that his intention is explicit that all ways [different interpretations of the thousand years] are valid and equally worthy of respect." *The Triumph of the Kingdom*, 62.

myself, too, once held this opinion."[29] However something is quietly forgotten in this text. Augustine says it is "*consequent on the presence of God*," and this alone makes it objectionable. For God to be present would place it as pure millenarianism. If we look at another text of St. Augustine, his position is very clear. In his *Sermon on the Lord's Prayer*, he discusses the concept of God's Kingdom, completely eschewing any sense of temporality:

> Indeed, God has an eternal kingdom. For when did He not reign? When did He begin to reign? For His kingdom has no beginning, neither shall it have any end. . . . All the faithful, redeemed by the Blood of His Only Son, will be His kingdom. And this His kingdom will come, when the resurrection of the dead shall have taken place; for then He will come Himself.[30]

The Bishop of Hippo then addresses the notion of ages past and future:

> His kingdom will come to us, and will not tarry. For are there as many ages yet remaining, as have already passed away? The Apostle John has said, "My little children, it is the last hour." But it is a long hour proportioned to this long day; and see how many years this last hour lasts. But nevertheless, be ye as those who watch, and so sleep, and rise again, and reign. Let us watch now, let us sleep in death; at the end we shall rise again, and shall reign without end.[31]

It seems appropriate at this juncture to explore the theological problems associated with this millennial theory. First and foremost, it revolves around the question of free will: the choice between good and evil. If God has truly granted us the gift of freedom to seek His will or ignore it, it implies that it should be available to all humanity throughout history. A "golden age" within history would nullify that opportunity, bringing about conditions of human life resembling those to be found in eternity. Saint John XXIII referred to this in a radio address in 1962:

---

29. St. Augustine of Hippo, *Civitate Dei*, bk XX, 7, www.newadvent.org.
30. St. Augustine, *Sermon 7 on the New Testament*, www.newadvent.org.
31. Ibid.

Good and evil are with us still and will remain with us in the future. This is because the free will of man will always have the freedom to express itself and the possibility of going astray. But the final and eternal victory will be with Christ and His Church in every chosen soul and in the chosen souls of every people.[32]

Pope Benedict XVI, in his earlier years as Cardinal Ratzinger, wrote several times on this issue, dismissing any notion of a temporal era of peace:

The Christian hope knows no idea of an inner fulfilment of history. On the contrary, it affirms the impossibility of an inner fulfilment of the world. This is, indeed, the common consent shared by the various fragmentary pictures of the end of the world offered us by Scripture. The biblical representation of the End rejects the expectation of a definitive state of salvation within history. This position is also rationally correct, since the idea of a definitive intra-historical fulfilment fails to take into account the permanent openness of history and of human freedom, for which failure is always a possibility.[33]

In an earlier essay, he had warned of the confusion millenarianism would create in eschatological matters, and one which he probably didn't know at the time would turn out to be quite prophetic:

The term [chiliasm] refers to a conception which is indeed based in eschatology, that is, the expectation of a new world of God's making, but is not satisfied with the eschaton beyond the end of the world. *Instead it virtually duplicates eschatology by expecting God to achieve his purpose with man and history in this world as well as the next, so that even within history there must be an end time in which everything will be as it should have been all along.*[34]

Although this extract refers to *chiliasm*, one of the first forms of millenarianism, undoubtedly the principle applies to all theories where it is expected that God will "achieve his purpose with man

32. St. John XXIII, "Radio Address," September 11, 1962, *Acta Apostolicae Sedis*, 1962, 678–685.

33. Cardinal Joseph Ratzinger, *Eschatology: Death and Eternal Life* (Washington, DC: The Catholic University of America Press, 1988), 213.

34. Cardinal Joseph Ratzinger, *Joseph Ratzinger in Communio*: vol. 1: *The Unity of the Church* (Grand Rapids: Eerdmans Publishing Co., 2010), 13.

and history in this world." The reason I suggested these words were prophetic is because in much of Catholic mystical literature so prevalent today (from unapproved sources, and from those who claim to properly interpret them), there is talk of the "end times" but not possibly leading to the end of the world.[35] Countless websites and forums are full of those who believe the second coming of Jesus refers to some event in an age prior to the final judgment. The end times have been duplicated just as Cardinal Ratzinger warned. Even Fr. Joseph Iannuzzi in his book *Antichrist and the End Times* claims that references made in the fully approved *Diary* of Saint Faustina Kowalska concerning the approaching "final coming" of Jesus do not actually refer to the Last Judgment, but to "the beginning of a new era in the life of the Church." In fact he quotes the phrase "imminent return"—even though it is never used in any of St. Faustina's writings.[36]

Sadly, because certain commentators either place themselves as some sort of authority on eschatological matters, or are considered so by others, a situation has arisen in the past three decades in which certain elements within the Church openly ignore what the Magisterium has already declared, a prime example being the false notion that the Antichrist will *not* form the final assault against the Church. And yet the Catechism is clear:

> Before Christ's second coming the Church must pass through a *final* trial that will shake the faith of many believers. The persecution that accompanies her pilgrimage on earth will unveil the 'mystery of iniquity' in the form of a religious deception offering men an apparent solution to their problems at the price of apostasy from the truth. The supreme religious deception is that of the Antichrist, a pseudo-messianism by which man glorifies himself in place of God and of his Messiah come in the flesh.[37]

The *International Theological Commission* which works under the

---

35. It is important to note that the Apocalypse cannot be read with an exact timeline. For instance the end of the world is described in several places: Rev. 14:14–19, Rev. 19:7, 11–14, and Rev. 20:11.

36. *See* Joseph Iannuzzi, *Antichrist and the End Times* (McKees Rocks: St. Andrew's Publications, 2005).

37. *Catechism of the Catholic Church*, no. 675, www.vatican.va.

auspices of the Congregation for the Doctrine of the Faith, produced a document in 1992 entitled *Some Current Questions in Eschatology*, in which it perceived a lack of interest in the true coming of God's Kingdom at the end of the world because of a false belief in finding this first within history. It must be said that it is a statement that is pinpoint accurate:

> In this way a certain kind of "eschaton" is brought within historical time. This "eschaton" is not presented as the ultimate absolute, but as a relative absolute. *Nonetheless, Christian praxis is directed so exclusively to the establishment of this eschaton that the Gospel is read reductively, so that whatever pertains to the eschatological realities absolutely considered is in great part passed over in silence.* In this way, in a theological system of this sort, *"one places oneself within the perspective of a temporal messianism,* which is one of the most radical of the expressions of secularization of the Kingdom of God and of its absorption into the immanence of human history."[38]

Before we conclude this discussion, we need to briefly address issues relating to the end of the spiritual millennium. At the conclusion of the thousand year reign, we are told that Satan is let loose once more to deceive the nations and encircle the camp of the saints (cf. Rev. 20:7–8). There are several obvious issues here that cannot be easily overcome. Firstly, it hardly seems possible that in a world that has been Christianized for a thousand years (even if the thousand years is symbolic for a long time) and living the divine will with the fullness expressed in the Our Father, that these Christians could suddenly be swayed by the lures of Satan. In fact, it hasn't been explained why God would even allow Satan to once again begin to tempt them. Alongside that, there is the issue of what the devil could do to the encampment of the saints in any case. If we remember, these are the resurrected—and therefore are glorified and already saved.

It seems to me that something important has been missed in the entire debate about this chapter of the Apocalypse. It concerns the terminology used in reference to God's holy ones. If we recall, chapter 4 dealt with the notion of the "saints" on earth. Now it seems log-

---

38. International Theological Commission, *Some Current Questions in Eschatology* (1992), www.vatican.va.

ical that the saints being described in the "encampment" (Rev. 20:8) are not made up wholly or even partly of the resurrected (as has already been proven), but are those referred to as "saints" in other texts from the New Testament. This then allows us to see the thousand years in a different light. The "nations" which Satan seduces represent the worldly powers (which have existed throughout the millennium), while the encampment of the saints represents those within the Church Militant who have accepted the Gospel and are living it. Finally, the unchaining of Satan must correspond to a short period of time towards the end of the world in which the nations will welcome him through apostasy and immorality; while for the Church, it will result in a universal persecution which the Eternal Father will allow to make his final defeat all the greater. The Church will be crucified like its Master and then rise again to eternal glory.

From a slightly different angle, there is one interesting conundrum which should be addressed. It concerns the Jewish people. In the teachings of the Church, we are told that before Jesus's second coming, the Jews will convert to Christianity as a people. St. Paul tells us: "If the losing of them has meant a world reconciled to God, what can the winning of them mean, but life risen from the dead?" (Rom. 11:15). Tradition tells us that it will occur through the preaching of Enoch and Elijah. Now if a spiritual millennium were really to occur, with all its spiritual benefits and a Christianized world, that would mean the Jews had already converted; and if they didn't, it would suggest they would be rejecting what they knew to be the truth, i.e., that Jesus really was the Savior and God of Israel—and all this without the plea of invincible ignorance. Therefore, there is a puzzle with no answer: if the Jews convert at the start of the millennium then it has to be the end of the world from what the Church teaches;[39] and if they don't, it totally contradicts one of the key spiritual elements of the temporal Kingdom.

---

39. "The glorious Messiah's coming is suspended at every moment of history until his recognition by 'all Israel,' for 'a hardening has come upon part of Israel' in their 'unbelief' toward Jesus. . . . The 'full inclusion' of the Jews in the Messiah's salvation, in the wake of 'the full number of the Gentiles,' will enable the People of God to achieve 'the measure of the stature of the fullness of Christ,' in which 'God may be all in all.'" *Catechism of the Catholic Church*, no. 674, www.vatican.va.

A final word needs to be said about a famous phrase from the revelations of Our Lady of Fatima: "*In the end* my Immaculate Heart will triumph." This has often been cited as evidence for a temporal era of peace. But is that really the case? In his interview book *Light of the World*, Pope Benedict XVI was questioned by journalist Peter Seewald about the meaning of this phrase. He asked if the Mother of God could appear in a manner that would be tantamount to a triumph? Pope Benedict's response was most enlightening. To begin with, he corrects the idea by affirming that the triumph is the same event as the establishment of the Kingdom at the end of the world. Praying for the triumph he said: "is equivalent in meaning to our praying for the coming of God's Kingdom."[40] He then goes further and completely eschews the idea that a temporal and glorious era is what is about to arrive: "This statement [his prayer at Fatima imploring the coming of the triumph] was not intended—I may be too rationalistic for that—to express any expectation on my part that there is going to be a huge turnaround and that history will suddenly take a different course."[41] This explanation of the triumph concurs will similar statements made by Pope Pius XII, and St. John Paul II.[42]

To conclude, we must say that the idea of a temporal Kingdom does not find itself part of authentic Catholic eschatology, and if anything, it takes our focus away from the advent sense of watchfulness that should guide our daily lives. It may be that Pope Francis has this in mind when he refers to novelty seekers where apparitions are concerned. It has to be considered dangerous when clear doctrines like the second coming of Jesus are manipulated and twisted to fit a new interpretation. Is that any different from what the Protestant reformers once did? Our minds and hearts should remain firmly within the enclosure of St. Peter and thus we will avoid formulating and spreading our own opinions in matters already decided by the Magisterium. As Pope Benedict XVI said: "All our

---

40. Pope Benedict XVI, *Light of the World* (London: Catholic Truth Society, 2010), 166.

41. Ibid., 166.

42. *See* Stephen Walford, *Heralds of the Second Coming*, 184–185.

preaching must measure itself against the saying of Jesus Christ: 'My teaching is not mine.' (Jn. 7:16) We preach not private theories and opinions, but the faith of the Church, whose servants we are."[43] It is in that spirit that I offer these reflections.

43. Pope Benedict XVI, "Homily for Chrism Mass," April 5, 2012, www.vatican.va.

ᘐ Appendix ᘐ

Extra Ecclesiam Nulla Salus: Can Non-Catholics be Saved?

Master, we saw a man who does not follow in our company casting out devils in thy name, and we forbade him to do it. But Jesus said, Forbid him no more; no one who does a miracle in my name will lightly speak evil of me. The man who is not against you is on your side. Why, if anyone gives you a cup of water to drink in my name, because you are Christ's, I promise you, he shall not miss his reward.

(Mk. 9:37–40)

IN THIS short appendix, I would like to discuss an issue that must be considered in the light of Christ's Mystical Body and the communion of saints: can those Christians who are not formal members of the Catholic Church be saved? Can salvation extend to those of other faiths or no faith? These are questions that cause a certain amount of confusion and therefore some clarification is needed.

As a starting point, let us study the famous phrase *extra ecclesiam nulla salus*, which is translated as "outside the Church there is no salvation." The axiom occurs most prominently in the writings of St. Cyprian of Carthage (Letters 4 and 73) and thereafter in the decrees of the Fourth Lateran Council and the Council of Florence. Pope Boniface VIII also included it in his Bull *Unam Sanctam*;[1] it is

---

1. Pope Boniface VIII wrote: "We believe in her firmly and we confess with simplicity that outside of her there is neither salvation nor the remission of sins.... Furthermore, we declare, we proclaim, we define that it is absolutely necessary for salvation that every human creature be subject to the Roman Pontiff." Pope Boniface VIII, *Unam Sanctam*, November 18, 1302, www.newadvent.org. A succession of popes have taught this dogma; Blessed Pius IX wrote: "Also well known is the Catholic teaching that no one can be saved outside the Catholic Church. Eternal salvation cannot be obtained by those who oppose the authority and statements of the

thus part of Christian Tradition and cannot be denied as a truth of the faith. But is the phrase as blunt as it appears? Is there any room for maneuver, or is formal membership of the Catholic Church required for salvation?

To begin with we need to understand the historical context in which it was formulated. Fr. Francis Sullivan who has written extensively on the subject points out that in the case of St. Cyprian, he was writing to those already Catholic who were placing their souls in jeopardy through possible excommunication or schism. He was not preaching to those non-Christians who formed the majority of the population at that time.[2] Because St. Cyprian saw the Church as a unity of love, he saw betrayal from within as a sin of adultery that defiled that chaste love of Christ's bride. Consequently, the guilty would be placing themselves outside the salvific pact drawn up by Christ Jesus. But it wasn't only St. Cyprian who aimed this stern teaching at those already baptized: St. Ignatius, Origen and St. Irenaeus also sensed the necessity of firing a warning shot across the bows of those considering disembarking the Ark of salvation.

In the fourth and fifth centuries, as Christianity had become firmly rooted in the Roman Empire, the situation changed somewhat; the idea began to emerge that missionary activity had spread so far that those who were still not part of the Church had deliberately rejected the salvation offered, and thus were heading for eternal damnation. St. Ambrose, St. Gregory of Nyssa and especially St. John Chrysostom were all adherents of this view. In the case of St. John Chrysostom, not even ignorance of Christ could be excused.[3] Of course the doctrine that God's will desired to save all was kept fully in place, therefore the blame lay (in the eyes of these early Fathers) entirely with the individual. But what of those who lived before Christ? In St. Augustine's view, all who lived justly from the

same Church and are stubbornly separated from the unity of the Church and also from the successor of Peter, the Roman Pontiff, to whom 'the custody of the vineyard has been committed by the Savior.'" Blessed Pius IX, Encyclical *Quanto Conficiamur Moerore*, August 10, 1863, www.papalencyclicals.net.

2. Fr. Francis Sullivan S.J., *Salvation Outside the Church: Tracing the History of the Catholic Response* (Oregon: Wipf and Stock Publishers, 2002), 20.

3. *See* St. John Chrysostom, "Homily 26 on Romans," www.newadvent.org.

beginning of time were saved through Christ by means of some type of primitive faith, which would have been manifested through obedience to the natural law.

Without doubt, this seemingly harsh teaching was rooted in the truth that Jesus had founded the Catholic Church—and no other—in order to administer the sacraments of salvation; and because of this, the absolute uniqueness of what was being offered had to be protected: one was either in sanctifying grace through baptism, or one was not. And as we have seen from the magisterial quotes spanning centuries, this teaching seemed nothing short of disastrous for anyone not in communion with the Pope. However, with the arrival of the Second Vatican Council in 1962, something seemed to change. Suddenly a new openness to the possibility of salvation for non-Catholics arrived. In *Lumen Gentium* for instance we read:

> But the plan of salvation also includes those who acknowledge the Creator. In the first place amongst these there are the Muslims, who, professing to hold the faith of Abraham, along with us adore the one and merciful God, who on the last day will judge mankind. Nor is God far distant from those who in shadows and images seek the unknown God, for it is He who gives to all men life and breath and all things, and as Savior wills that all men be saved. Those also can attain to salvation who through no fault of their own do not know the Gospel of Christ or His Church, yet sincerely seek God and moved by grace strive by their deeds to do His will as it is known to them through the dictates of conscience. Nor does Divine Providence deny the helps necessary for salvation to those who, without blame on their part, have not yet arrived at an explicit knowledge of God and with His grace strive to live a good life. Whatever good or truth is found amongst them is looked upon by the Church as a preparation for the Gospel.[4]

Understandably, this startling language caused a seismic shock among traditionalist Catholics especially. For them it was a rupture, a novelty which could not be reconciled with the pronouncements of previous pontiffs. So how do we explain this? Is it a new doctrine?

4. Dogmatic Constitution, *Lumen Gentium*, November 21, 1964, www.vatican. va.

The answer to the second question is a definite no. Why? Because dogmas of the faith are infallible teachings and therefore cannot be altered; so the position remains the same today as two thousand years ago: outside the Catholic Church there is no salvation.

Now if that is the case, we are left with only one possible solution: that the understanding of the doctrine has developed through Tradition (which is always alive under the influence of the Holy Spirit) and thus new expressions of its truth have emerged. To understand how this can happen, we can turn to St. Vincent of Lerins who, writing in the fifth century foresaw that doctrine could and *should* be perfected through time. After explaining how the Christian soul is analogous to the growth and maturity of the body, he applies the very same logic to Catholic doctrine:

> In like manner, it behooves Christian doctrine to follow the same laws of progress, so as to be consolidated by years, *enlarged by time, refined by age*, and yet, withal, to continue uncorrupt and unadulterate, complete and perfect in all the measurement of its parts, and, so to speak, in all its proper members and senses, admitting no change, no waste of its distinctive property, no variation in its limits.... Therefore, whatever has been sown by the fidelity of the Fathers in this husbandry of God's Church, the same ought to be cultivated and taken care of by the industry of their children, the same ought to flourish and ripen, *the same ought to advance and go forward to perfection. For it is right that those ancient doctrines of heavenly philosophy should, as time goes on, be cared for, smoothed, polished; but not that they should be changed,* not that they should be maimed, not that they should be mutilated. They may receive proof, illustration, definiteness; but they must retain withal their completeness, their integrity, their characteristic properties.[5]

Unfortunately, in the polemical atmosphere of the post-Vatican II years, this essential understanding of doctrine has not been appreciated. It really should come as no surprise that the Holy Spirit is still speaking to the Church, revealing new insights into revealed truth; because as history continues, new circumstances emerge in which

---

5. St. Vincent of Lerins, *Commonitorium*, ch. 23, 56–57, www.newadvent.org.

certain truths can be better understood.[6] For instance, it seems not possible that members of other Christian communities who give their lives in martyrdom for love of Christ are not invited to the eschatological banquet; or those who tirelessly look after the poor and visit the sick. Somehow they *have* to be bound to Christ, even if formal membership or acceptance of all Catholic doctrine is lacking; and of course it would have to be acknowledged that there will be Christians of other denomination living far holier lives than some lukewarm souls within the Catholic Church. Significantly, on this point, St. Augustine tells us: "therefore, there is in the Catholic Church something which is not Catholic, so there may be something which is Catholic outside the Catholic Church."[7]

In the year 2000, the Congregation for the Doctrine of the Faith issued a document entitled *Dominus Iesus* on the unicity and salvific universality of Jesus Christ and the Church. The declaration reaffirmed that salvation can only be found in Jesus, and that he offers it through his Church—the Catholic Church—which alone holds the fullness of truth. But the document also affirms: "outside of her structure, many elements can be found of sanctification and truth, that is, in those Churches and ecclesial communities which are not yet in full communion with the Catholic Church."[8]

So how do we reconcile the seemingly contradictory statements from the past and the present? Formulated in a positive way, the axiom means that regardless of what Christian denomination or

---

6. A contemporary example of this concerns the fate of unbaptized babies. In the early Church, many thought they could not be saved because of the lack of baptism or baptism of desire. In recent years several developments have occurred. Magisterial teaching, while not definitely affirming their salvation, has gone a long way to invoking that hope through the mercy of God; the *sensus fidelium*—where the whole faithful *together* cannot err in matters of faith or morals (*Catechism of the Catholic Church* nos. 91, 92)—seems to be moving inexorably toward the same conclusion, and a fresh theological analysis of the question has been undertaken. See *The Hope of Salvation for Infants who Die without being Baptized*, International Theological Commission, 2007, www.vatican.va.

7. St. Augustine of Hippo, *On Baptism against the Donatists*, bk VII, ch. 39, www.newadvent.org.

8. *Dominus Iesus: On the Unicity and Salvific Universality of Jesus Christ and the Church*, June 16, 2000, www.vatican.va.

other religion someone belongs to (or not for that matter), salvation, if it comes, will come through the Catholic Church. So in some mysterious way, all those who are not formal members are bound by a unity (albeit imperfect) with the one Universal Church. For non-Catholic Christians, it will be through the one baptism, or baptism of desire, and for people of other faiths or no faith, the use of God's gift of conscience which when obeyed to the best of their ability, is in a sense reaching out to God by living the natural law inscribed upon their hearts. We can also affirm no contradiction with the words of Boniface VIII in *Unam Sanctam* concerning: "that it is absolutely necessary for salvation that every human creature be subject to the Roman Pontiff." This simply affirms the unique role of the Pope as guardian of the truth; his authority in binding and loosing (cf. Matt. 18:18) cannot be circumvented for two reasons: (1) he holds the keys to the Kingdom of heaven (Matt. 16:19), and (2) because he has a special charism of assistance for which Jesus prayed specifically: "but I have prayed for thee, that thy faith may not fail; when, after a while, thou hast come back to me, it is for thee to be the support of thy brethren" (Lk. 22:32).[9] In this context, the papal reference is a support in the understanding of "no salvation outside the Church."

At this point, let us look at several biblical passages that support the doctrinal development of this dogma and let us be guided by Pope Benedict XVI at the same time. In the Book of Genesis, we encounter the figure of Melchizedek who first appears in Genesis 14:18, after Abram had defeated Chodorlahomor and other kings allied with him: "Melchizedek, king of Salem, brought out bread and wine. He was a priest of God Most High. He blessed Abram with these words: 'On Abram be the blessing of the most high God, maker of heaven and earth, and blessed be that most high God, whose protection has brought thy enemies into thy power'" (Gen. 14:19–20). Pope Benedict tells us that Melchizedek was a pagan, and through him the pagan world entered into salvation history:

9. St. John Paul explained this charism in the General Audience of March 17, 1993, www.vatican.va.

In this figure can be seen the true veneration of the Most High God, of the Creator of the Heavens and of the earth. Thus the pagan world too experiences the expectation and profound prefiguration of Christ's mystery. In Christ himself everything is recapitulated, purified and led to its term, to its true essence.[10]

Benedict XVI goes on to explain more about this mysterious figure who we are told was without lineage (cf. Heb. 7:3):

After Abraham's victory over several kings, Melchizedek, King of Salem, of Jerusalem, appears and brings out bread and wine. This uncommented and somewhat incomprehensible event appears only in Psalm 110 [109] as has been said, but it is clear that Judaism, Gnosticism and Christianity then wished to reflect profoundly on these words and created their interpretations . . . he [Melchizedek] is a king of righteousness, he dwells in peace, he is king where peace reigns, he venerates and worships the Most High God, the Creator of Heaven and earth, and he brings out bread and wine (cf. Heb. 7:1–3; Gn. 14:18–20). . . . The Fathers stressed that he is one of the holy pagans of the Old Testament and this shows that even from paganism there is a path that leads to Christ. The criteria are: worshipping God Most High, the Creator, fostering righteousness and peace and venerating God in a pure way. Thus, with these fundamental elements, paganism too is on its way to Christ, and in a certain way, makes Christ's light present.[11]

So in Melchizedek we see the possibility that the soul can be drawn into a relationship with the Lord even while paganism is still evident. It recalls the teaching from *Lumen Gentium*: "Whatever good or truth is found amongst them is looked upon by the Church as a preparation for the Gospel."

The second text comes from the New Testament, and it confirms in the most satisfactory way possible the proposition argued here that no rupture of this dogma has been made. In St. Mark's Gospel, St. John tells the Lord that the apostles saw a man casting out devils in Jesus's name, and yet he was not part of their company, so they

---

10. Pope Benedict XVI, "Meeting with the Parish Priests of the Diocese of Rome," February 18, 2010, www.vatican.va.

11. Ibid.

"forbade him to do it." Jesus replied in the most serious and forthright way: "Forbid him no more; no one who does a miracle in my name will lightly speak evil of me. The man who is not against you is on your side. Why, if anyone gives you a cup of water to drink in my name, because you are Christ's, I promise you, he shall not miss his reward" (Mk. 9:38–40). "The man who is not against you is for you" said Jesus, and that suggests we must have the humility to accept that the Holy Spirit acts in others outside the visible bounds of the Catholic Church. In a sense, those Catholics who hold such a rigorist position that it is hardly possible for non-Catholic Christians to be saved because they see "invincible ignorance"[12] as more or less impossible in this day and age of knowledge, are mistaken for several reasons. Firstly, they fail to take into account that being told the Catholic Church is the one true Church can only be the starting point for many, rather than the destination; and secondly, that a variety of psychological or other factors may prevent them from drawing the conclusion one would hope for. The rigorist acts like St. John and the others who "forbade" the exorcism the man was doing. It was well intentioned, but wrong because it was trying to keep the Lord in a box, restricting his divine powers from flowing anywhere other than within the Church. In fact, the idea that the man was casting out devils implies he had great faith and a strong prayer life.[13] Pope Benedict XVI, preaching on this Gospel passage tells us:

> Therefore if a stranger to the community does good works in Christ's name, so long as he does so with upright intentions and with respect, members of the Church must not feel jealous but must rejoice. Even within the Church, people can find it difficult, in the spirit of deep communion, to value and appreciate good things achieved by the different ecclesial entities. Instead, we must all and always be able to appreciate one another, praising God for

12. Invincible ignorance is the principle that those who are unaware of the truth concerning the Catholic Church as the one sacrament of salvation bear no guilt whatsoever for not joining it, and thus can attain salvation.

13. The faith of the Centurion who asked Jesus to cure his servant (cf. Matt. 8:5–10) should also be considered in this context. The Lord, undoubtedly moved by this man's faith, announced to his followers: "Believe me, I have not found faith like this, even in Israel."

the infinite "creativity" with which he acts in the Church and in the world.[14]

These reflections now inevitably prompt the question: if it is possible to attain salvation without formal membership in the Catholic Church, why join it? It certainly isn't the case that one is free to ignore it if faith and conscience reveal it to be the Church of Christ. It should be noted that such is the importance of the Church to the spiritual life of the soul, that the Second Vatican Council still reiterated one essential feature of the *extra ecclesiam nulla salus* doctrine: "Whosoever, therefore, knowing that the Catholic Church was made necessary by Christ, would refuse to enter or to remain in it, could not be saved."[15]

It is my prayerful hope that this book has shown that the Catholic Church, understood as part of the Mystical Body of Christ, is so intimately bound to its founding Lord and Savior, that all who desire to grow closer to Jesus will see it as the *way initiated by the divine Son himself*, so that gathering a communion of saints around him, he can, at the end of time present it to his Eternal Father as a family of divine love. By living within his Church and striving to imitate him, Jesus has promised his faithful eternal life and the joy of union with God.

If we remember, after his Resurrection, he broke the bread for the disciples at Emmaus; he gave power to forgive sins in his name to the Apostles (cf. Jn. 20:23); he told Saul that persecuting the Church was persecuting him (cf. Acts. 9:5); and he told St. Peter, the first pope, to feed his lambs and feed his sheep (cf. Jn. 21:15–17). In essence he was setting in place the sacramental life of the Catholic Church in which Peter and his successors would ensure the lambs would be nourished with true spiritual food. The Catholic Church cannot and must not be seen as just one of many Christian communities to choose from; it stands alone because it was conceived in eternity to be the bride of the bridegroom, and it knows its Lord's heart because the Holy Spirit ensures that it is so. To be part of the Catholic Church is to believe and cherish the words of the One who said:

14. Pope Benedict XVI, "Angelus Address," September 30, 2012, www.vatican.va.
15. *Lumen Gentium*, 14, www.vatican.va.

It is I who am the bread of life. Your fathers, who ate manna in the desert, died none the less; the bread which comes down from heaven is such that he who eats of it never dies. I myself am the living bread that has come down from heaven. If anyone eats of this bread, he shall live for ever. And now, what is this bread which I am to give? It is my flesh, given for the life of the world. (Jn. 6:48–52)

In truth, salvation can only be found inside the Church, but many factors may legitimately stop one from knowing that. It is for those of us blessed to be within its family to witness to its beauty and truth, encouraging those outside to take that initial step of courage and enter into its sanctifying life. And ironic as it may seem, as we conclude this book, we should strive to make these words attributed to St. Francis of Assisi our own: "preach the Gospel and if necessary use words." May the Lord and his communion of saints help us all in this urgent, yet most gratifying task.

᪥ Select Bibliography ᪥

Adam, Karl. *The Spirit of Catholicism*. Tacoma: Angelico Press, 2012

Aquinas, St. Thomas. *Catena Aurea*, vol. 3, *St Luke*. Southampton: The Saint Austin Press, 1997

Arles, St. Caesarius of. *Sermons*, vol. 2. Washington, DC: The Catholic University of America Press, 1964

Atwell, Robert. *Celebrating the Saints*. Norwich: Canterbury Press, 2004

Avila, St. Teresa of. *Collected Works*, vol. 1: *The Book of Her Life, Spiritual Testimonies, Soliloquies*. Washington, DC: ICS Publications, 1976

————. *Collected Works*, vol. 2: *The Way of Perfection, Meditations on the Song of Songs, The Interior Castle*. Washington, DC: ICS Publications, 1980

————. *The Collected Works of St. Teresa of Avila*, vol. 3: *The Book of Her Foundations and Minor Works*. Washington, DC: ICS Publications, 1985

Balthasar, Hans Urs von. *Explorations in Theology*, vol. 3, *Creator Spirit*. San Francisco: Ignatius Press, 1993

Benedict XVI. *Jesus of Nazareth*. London: Bloomsbury, 2007

————. *Jesus of Nazareth, Holy Week: From the Entrance into Jerusalem to the Resurrection*. San Francisco: Ignatius Press, 2011

————. *Light of the World*. London: CTS, 2010

Benko, Stephen. *The Meaning of Sanctorum Communion*. Naperville: Alec R. Allenson, Inc., 1964

Biffi, Cardinal Giacomo. *Casta Maretrix: An Essay on the Ecclesiology of St. Ambrose*. London: The Saint Austin Press, 2000

Bingen, Hildegard of. *Hildergardis, Causae et curae*. Leipzig: In aedibus B.G. Teubneri, 1903

————. *Scivias*. Mahwah: Paulist Press, 1990

————. *The Book of Divine Works*. Santa Fe: Bear & Company, 1987

————. *The Book of the rewards of Life (Liber vitae meritorum)*. New York: Oxford University Press, 1994

————. *The Letters of Hildegard of Bingen: Vol. 1*, trans. Joseph L. Baird and Radd K. Ehrman. New York: Oxford University Press, 1994

————. *The Personal Correspondence of Hildegard of Bingen*, ed. Joseph L. Baird. New York: Oxford University

Bonaventure, St. *The Works of Bonaventure*, trans. José de Vinck. Paterson, NJ: St. Anthony's Guild Press, 1963

Catechism of the Council of Trent. Baltimore: James Myres, 1833

Chase, Stephen. *Angelic Spirituality: Medieval Perspectives on the Ways of Angels*. Mahwah: Paulist Press, 2002

Chrysostom, St. John. *Fathers of the Church: On the Incomprehensible Nature of God*. Washington, DC: The Catholic University of America Press, 1984

Clairvaux, St. Bernard of. *Homilies in Praise of the Blessed Virgin Mary*, trans. Marie-Bernard Saïd with an introduction by Chrysogonus Waddell. Kalamazoo, MI: Cistercian, 1993

———. *The Letters of Saint Bernard of Clairvaux*. Kalamazoo, MI: Cistercian Publications, 1998

Daley, Brian E. *The Hope of the Early Church*. Cambridge: Cambridge University Press, 1991

Damascene, St. John Damascene. *On Holy Images*. London: Thomas Baker, 1898

D'Apolito, Fr. Alberto. *Padre Pio of Pietrelcina, Memories, Experiences, Testimonials*. Foggia: Editions Padre Pio da Pietrelcina, 1986

Denzinger, Heinrich Joseph Dominicus. *Enchiridion symbolorum, definitionum et declarationum de rebus fidei et morum*. www.patristica.net

Duns Scotus, Blessed John. *Blessed John Duns Scotus And His Mariology*. New Bedford: Franciscans of the Immaculate, 2009

Garrigou-Lagrange, Fr. Reginald. *Everlasting Life and the Immensity of the Soul*. Rockford: Tan Books, 1952

———. *Providence*. Rockford: Tan Books, 1937

Gaucher, Guy. *The Passion of Therese of Lisieux*. New York: Crossroads Publishing Company, 1990

Genoa, Catherine of. *Purgation and Purgatory, The Spiritual Dialogue*. Mahwah, NJ: Paulist Press, 1979

———. *The Life and Doctrine of Saint Catherine of Genoa*. Grand Rapids, MI: Christian Classics Ethereal Library, 2009

Gerard, Fr. John. *The Hunted Priest*. London: Collins, 1951

Great, St. Gregory. *The Dialogues of Saint Gregory the Great*. Merchantville, New Jersey: Evolution Publishing, 2010

Guardini, Romano. *The Lord*. London: Longmans, 1956

Hahn, Scott. *The Lamb's Supper: The Mass as Heaven on Earth*. New York: Doubleday, 1999

Heine, Ronald E. *Origen Homilies On Genesis and Exodus*. Washington: Catholic University of America Press, 1982

Hippo, St. Augustine of. *City of God*. www.newadvent.org

————. *Confessions.* London: Sheed & Ward, 1948

————. *Nicene and Post-Nicene Fathers: First Series,* vol. VIII. New York: Cosimo, 2007

————. *Sermons on Selected Lessons of the New Testament* vol. II. Oxford: John Henry Parker, 1845

Hugel, Friedrich. *The Mystical Element of Religion as Studied in Saint Catherine of Genoa and Her Friends, Volume 1.* London: J.M. Dent & Co., 1909

Iannuzzi, Joseph. *The Triumph of God's Kingdom in the Millennium and End Times.* Havertown: St. John the Evangelist Press, 1994

Jerome, St. *Prologue to Isaiah, The Lives of the Holy Prophets.* Buena Vista: Holy Apostles Convent Publications, 1998

Jerusalem, St. Cyril of. *The Catechetical Lectures of St Cyril of Archbishop of Jerusalem.* Oxford: John Henry Parker, 1839

John Paul II, St., *Catechism of the Catholic Church,* www.vatican.va

Jurgens, William A. *The Faith of the Early Fathers,* vol. 2. Collegeville: Liturgical Press, 1979

Kalvelage, Bro. Francis M. *Kolbe, Saint of the Immaculata.* San Francisco: Ignatius Press, 2002

Kowalska, St. Maria Faustina. *Divine Mercy in My Soul.* Stockbridge, MA: Marian Press, 2005

————. *The Letters of Saint Faustina.* Cracow: Misericordia Publications, 2007

Lisieux, St. Therese of. *Story of a Soul.* Washington, DC: ICS Publications, 1976

Lubac, Henri de. *Catholicism.* London: Burns & Oates, 1962

McGinnis, Charles F. *The Communion of Saints.* St. Louis: B. Herder, 1912

Monteau-Bonamy, H.M., O.P. *Immaculate Conception and the Holy Spirit.* Kenosha, WI: Prow Books/Franciscan Marytown Press, 1977

Nazianzus, St. Gregory of. *Select Orations,* translated by Martha Vinson. Washington, DC: The Catholic University of America Press, 2003

Nola, St. Paulinus of. *The Poems of Saint Paulinus of Nola.* New York: Newman Press, 1975

O' Donnell, Christopher. *Love in the Heart of the Church.* Dublin: Veritas, 1997

Origen. *The Song of Songs, Commentary and Homilies.* New York: The Newman Press, 1957

Palardy, Peter William B. *St. Peter Chrysologus: Selected Sermons,* vol. 2. Washington, DC: The Catholic University of America Press, 2004

Parente, Fr. Alessio O.F.M. Cap. *The Holy Souls, "Viva Padre Pio."* Foggia:

Editions Padre Pio da Pietrelcina, 1998

Pazzi, Maria Maddalena de. *Selected Revelations*. Mahwah: Paulist Press, 2000

Pazzi, St. Mary Magdelen de. *The Life of St. Mary Magdelen de Pazzi*, Compiled by Rev Placido Fabrini. Philadelphia: Isoleri, 1900

Pietrelcina, Padre Pio of. *Letters*, vol. 1. Foggia: Editions Padre Pio Da Pietrelcina, Our Lady of Grace Capuchin Friary, 1984

Ratzinger, Cardinal Joseph. *Eschatology: Death and Eternal Life*. Washington, DC: The Catholic University of America Press, 1988

——————. *Communio*: vol. 1: *The Unity of the Church*. Grand Rapids: Eerdmans Publishing Co., 2010

Sales, St. Francis de. *The Catholic Controversy*. London: Burns & Oates, 1909

Schonborn, Christoph. *Loving the Church, Spiritual Exercises in the Presence of Pope John Paul II*. San Francisco: Ignatius Press, 1998

Sullivan, Fr. Francis S.J. *Salvation Outside the Church: Tracing the History of the Catholic Response*. Oregon: Wipf and Stock Publishers, 2002

The Genuine Epistles of the Apostolic Fathers. Hartford: Parsons And Hills, 1836

INDEX

Index

⚜ About the Author ⚜

STEPHEN WALFORD resides with his wife Paula and five children in Southampton, England. He is the author of *Heralds of the Second Coming*, a study of the papal prophetic charism. He has written for various print and online Catholic journals on eschatological and mariological themes. He is also a pianist and teacher.

9 781621 382171